Gods of this World

Gods of this World

A Philosophical Discussion and Defense of
Christian Demonology

Shandon L. Guthrie

☙PICKWICK *Publications* · Eugene, Oregon

GODS OF THIS WORLD
A Philosophical Discussion and Defense of Christian Demonology

Copyright © 2018 Shandon L. Guthrie. All rights reserved. Except for brief quotations in critical publications or reviews, no part of this book may be reproduced in any manner without prior written permission from the publisher. Write: Permissions, Wipf and Stock Publishers, 199 W. 8th Ave., Suite 3, Eugene, OR 97401.

Pickwick Publications
An Imprint of Wipf and Stock Publishers
199 W. 8th Ave., Suite 3
Eugene, OR 97401

www.wipfandstock.com

PAPERBACK ISBN: 978-1-5326-3304-1
HARDCOVER ISBN: 978-1-5326-3306-5
EBOOK ISBN: 978-1-5326-3305-8

Cataloguing-in-Publication data:

Names: Guthrie, Shandon L., author.

Title: Gods of this world : a philosophical discussion and defense of Christian demonology / Shandon L. Guthrie.

Description: Eugene, OR : Pickwick Publications, 2018 | Includes bibliographical references and index(es).

Identifiers: ISBN 978-1-5326-3304-1 (paperback) | ISBN 978-1-5326-3306-5 (hardcover) | ISBN 978-1-5326-3305-8 (ebook)

Subjects: LCSH: Demonology. | Angels—Christianity—History of doctrines. | Demonology—History of doctrines.

Classification: BL480 .G85 2018 (print) | BL480 .G85 (ebook)

Manufactured in the U.S.A. 10/26/18

Scripture quotations, unless otherwise noted, are from The ESV® Bible (The Holy Bible, English Standard Version®), copyright © 2001 by Crossway, a publishing ministry of Good News Publishers. Used by permission. All rights reserved.

Other Scripture quotations are from the Revised Standard Version of the Bible, copyright © 1946, 1952, and 1971 Division of Christian Education of the National Council of the Churches of Christ in the USA. Used by permission. All rights reserved.

To my wife, Shelli, whose love has possessed me
for over twenty wonderful years.

Contents

Acknowledgments | ix

1. Introduction | 1

I. BACKGROUND

2. Theological Foundations for a Christian Philosophy of Demonology | 13
3. Demonic Realism in the History of Christian Philosophy | 39

II. EXISTENTIAL MATTERS

4. Philosophical Arguments for Demonic Anti-Realism | 69
5. Philosophical Arguments for Demonic Realism (I) | 97
6. Philosophical Arguments for Demonic Realism (II) | 127

III. ONTOLOGICAL MATTERS

7. On the Spiritual Nature of Demons | 151
8. On the (Delimited) Powers of Demons (I): Cognitive Interaction and Psychokinesis | 182
9. On the (Delimited) Powers of Demons (II): The Exclusivity of Cognitive Interaction | 202

IV. OBJECTIONS

10. Objections Based on Passages in the Old Testament | 223
11. Objections Based on Passages in the New Testament | 238
12. Philosophical Objections | 254

V. CONCLUSION

13. Gods of this World | 273

    Bibliography | 287

    Author and Names Index | 307

    Subject Index | 311

Acknowledgments

A LEADING NOTE OF gratitude goes out to my former doctoral supervisor at Manchester Metropolitan University, Dr. Lloyd Strickland, for his guidance, challenging criticisms, and support of this project from its inception to its fruition. It was his scholarly interactions with my work that made much of it what it is today. Thanks also go to my former doctoral examiners, Dr. Charles Taliaferro and Dr. Christopher Partridge, for some helpful feedback and encouragement over the ramifications of this research. I would also like to thank Jordan Fishel and Jason Valentine for our many hours of stimulating conversation over the seminal ideas that ultimately gave impetus to the book now in your hands. Both of them encouraged me unequivocally to take on this research. I must also thank Dr. Alan Rhoda, a fine scholar, colleague, and friend, for some insightful challenges and thoughts he added to the subject.

The feedback that I received from papers delivered at meetings of the Society of Christian Philosophers in relation to some of the content of this book was invaluable as well as inspiring. Even in the hallways after my presentations, I was always moved by how many philosophers and theologians voiced an appreciation for the work this book embodies. I also benefited from conversations on the subject with a number of students from my philosophy of religion courses that I taught at Regis University. All of the sound reasoning and discussions in this book are surely the product of the refinements made by those with whom I have been acquainted over the years. But any poor reasoning and ineptly crafted ratiocinations that remain are surely my own, and I take full responsibility for any of this book's deficits.

From non-philosophical quarters, I have been encouraged by local college ministries that allowed me to share with them a more palatable and distilled version of some of the core arguments of this book. They received it well and, through various challenges and inquiries thrown at me, revealed the desperate need for someone to communicate on this topic from a philosophical point of view. Also, the engaging dialogues I had with sundry pastors, ministers, educators, and countless parishioners underscored the fact that this subject has been neglected and grossly misunderstood for far too long. It is due to the motivations derived from these numerous interactions that I can confidently say that the days of neglect are now over.

Acknowledgments

Perhaps no greater support has been offered to me than that of my wife, Shelli, who loved and supported me during the entire development of this book. She has been my conscience and my anchor during times when I did not believe in myself. She is indeed the love of my life and I am forever grateful for her. I have also benefited in unexpected ways from our children, Alexander, KatieAnn, and Rebekah. They made it possible for me to disengage from the stress of daily research in order to enjoy the moment.

"[T]he main part he will not understand,
another part he will not believe,
and the rest he will laugh at"

−Immanuel Kant (*Dreams of a Spirit-Seer*)

1

Introduction

Demonology: A Doctrine in Disarray

ANGELOLOGY AND ITS FILIAL by-product, *demonology*, have long been subjects on the fringe of serious intellectual investigation within, *inter alia*, the field of philosophy; and they have done so with very few historical exceptions. Perhaps this is due to the exotic, speculative, and unscientific nature of talk of spirit beings like those in the ideations of angels and demons. The notions themselves bear the unmistakable stench of mythology that further make them matters too obsolete for the scientist or historian and too archaic for the philosopher. Not surprisingly, these areas of inquest have been relegated to the specialized discipline of pneumatology in strictly theological quarters. With the advent of modernity and its contribution to metaphysics that the universe is but a world-machine, disenchanted members of the clergy were finding increasingly fewer places in our universe for the continued operations of angels and demons. At the later christening of psychology and psychiatry as sciences of the mind, talk of mental disorders and other psychodynamic factors finally buried the idea that one's conscience was in part guided or manipulated by external spiritual forces beyond the material realm.

The recycled tongue-in-cheek question, "How many angels can dance on the head of a pin?" is often a clichéd reminder that intellectual discussions about things like angels can never be, so we are told, resolved from the standpoint of discursive reasoning. There is no doubt that demonology, as more or less the delimited study of deviant angels (or their offspring), is unarguably a far more vilified discipline than its adjoining cousin. Yet many detractors in the contemporary world are ill-informed about what angels and demons are and on what grounds one has to think that they exist despite the funereal pronouncements of the intelligentsia. No doubt the cynic will find demonology to be inherently laughable such that the shock of merely uttering its tenets aloud becomes its own refutation. Yet the believer's response is often no better, for she simply retreats to the safe confines of her intimate cliques and fellowships wherein the mutual exchange of such ideas can be insulated from the scoffs of naysayers and critics. It's the academic equivalent of an unrelenting trench warfare. Accordingly, neither the skeptic nor the believer has the intellectual upper hand.

But it gets even worse for twenty-first-century adherents. A number of religious people who pontificate on the subject invariably derive their doctrinal material from less-refined, casual sources like sermons from one's local gathering, popular-level books on "spiritual warfare," and even from vehicles of entertainment including movies, television shows, and novels. In fact, talk of literal demons in the Western world today owes much of its conceptual grooming to literary classics such as Dante Alighieri's *Divine Comedy* (1320), Heinrich Kramer's *Malleus Maleficarum* (1487), the fanciful stories in the sixteenth century of the fictional Dr. Faustus, and the unparalleled epic of John Milton's *Paradise Lost* (1667). These works have led to the modern caricaturing of Satan and his demons as human gremlins dawning goatees, pitchforks, and red union suits who gleefully dish out hellfire judgment to society's most egregious offenders. It is doubtful whether the average person even knows where an official canonized demonology ends and a fictional depiction of demons begins.

Despite the relative silence on the part of believers within the academic community, demonology among the rank and file figures quite prominently in populations around the world. In fact, a number of Christians and non-Christians alike, including those in the United States and Great Britain, believe that Satan and his demons actually exist.[1] There is even evidence showing that the number of believers is steadily increasing.[2] For the believer, it evidences its credibility in the face of rampant opposition and academic virulence. But for the cynic, it only means that there remains a gullible subset of folks willing to believe anything indiscriminately. Is it not surprising, then, that believing academics have kept the doctrine at arm's length? Only those who wish to take the doctrine seriously as a body of knowledge—that is, one concerned about a literal race of superhuman spiritual beings—tend to confine their discussions to protected circles of theology or English literature within the halls of private universities. But despite having the appearance of being a superstition for the ignorant, it may shock the cynic to know that belief in demons is actually held by a number of academics.[3] Consequently, one should expect that there is a case to be made for their literal

---

1. YouGov, "Do You Personally Believe in the Existence of the Devil or Not?"; YouGov, "18% of Brits Believe in Possession by the Devil."

2. Christopher Partridge and Eric Christianson track the notable increase in such belief in America by pointing out that in 1968 "60 percent believed in the literal existence of Satan. In 1994 it had risen to 65.5 percent and in 2001 a Gallup poll found that it had again risen to 68 percent . . . During the last decade, it has grown from 65.5 percent in 1994 to 70 percent in 2004" ("Introduction," 11).

3. Alvin Plantinga, in commenting on academia, writes that "[t]here are large numbers of educated contemporaries (including even some with Ph.D's!) who believe . . . that there are both demons and spirits who are active in the contemporary world. As a matter of historical fact, there are any number of contemporaries, and contemporary intellectuals very well acquainted with science, who don't feel any problem at all in pursuing science and also believing in miracles, angels, Christ's resurrection, the lot" (*Warranted Christian Belief*, 405).

Introduction

existence that can repeal the cultural sentiment of demonology as a mere fascination for the uninformed and easily-entertained.

If that was not burden enough, believers–academic or otherwise–will also need to offer a coherent understanding of what demons are and what they can do. While positing their existence had been a congenial pursuit in Christian history, there has been, and remains, a substantial lack of clarity and coherence in the metaphysics of such beings. The third-century Christian philosopher Origen once made the following observation that applies equally to the modern situation as it did when he wrote these words:

> Regarding the devil and his angels, and the opposing influences, the teachings of the Church has laid down that these beings exist indeed; but what they are, or how they exist, it has not explained with sufficient clearness.[4]

Attempts to formulate such a philosophy of demonology have been confounded by the lack of any explicit biblical teachings that clarify such matters. But as with other doctrines with similar deficits of biblical material, Christian philosophers and theologians had gone to work in clarifying, and in some cases "creedalizing," their results. Alas! Christian philosophers are still far from reaching the diabolical Promised Land. Those who have meticulously written on the subject have only echoed the tenets of their Dominican forbearers and with that all of the shortcomings the church Fathers failed to rectify. These sins of the fathers have indeed become the sins of the sons. And the unwelcome consequence for realists is that demonology remains a doctrine in disarray. And, yet, if demonic realists are ever going to win over their skeptic interlocutors that evil spirits genuinely exist, they must declutter their metaphysical labyrinth and postulate a viable model worthy of sanction.

The Devil's Advocate

There is something unsettling about volunteering to defend the existence and nature of Satan, the putative Prince of Darkness, and his minions. But one must understand that a defense of Satan in this way is not meant to be taken as a defense in the sense of *sticking up* for the practices of the Dark One. The project of advocating for the devil is more of a defense of a particular kind of worldview as espoused by many predecessors in the philosophy of religion. It is an advocating of additional tenets of belief that co-constitute an unexpurgated, ramified natural theology. Put another way, one must appreciate the pursuit to identify their suspect before prosecuting the case against them. Accordingly, such an enterprise is essentially no different than a project devoted to the existence and coherence of God. And those projects are themselves no different than those endeavoring to defend the existence and nature of abstract objects. These issues have been fair game since the days of Plato. In fact, the same goes for talk of

---

4. Origen, preface to *De Principiis*, 240.

demons! For pre-Christian Greek philosophers have readily affirmed the existence of the *daimon* in one form or another.[5] Like talk of God and abstract objects, talk of *daimonion* is every bit a part of philosophy's ancestry as they.

The goal of this book, then, will be similar to other projects in the philosophy of religion: to offer up reasons to think that a particular set of ultramundane beings (Satan and the demons) exist and that a viable doctrine of demonology can be held in confidence despite impetuous resistance from those with little patience on such matters. Toward this goal, all thinkers–not just Christians–can consider this particular way of viewing the world as being, in some sense, genuinely inhabited by evil spirits. It is true that many crude demonologies have been advanced in the past. Some have given rise to the deleterious effects that have marred the church. And yet the same could be said about scientific knowledge and the abuses of medical experimentation, weapons of mass destruction, and government surveillance. In the hands of a madman *anything* can be used for ill. Instead, this book is designed to contribute to a field of knowledge left vacated by the majority of philosophers. That someone might consider it licensure for harmful social practices will not only be going beyond the discussions of this book, but they would be failing to apprehend its distinct conclusions. For one of the main arguments of this work verily *demythologizes the powers of demons*,[6] and so undermines the pockets of McCarthyism that ensued since the witch crazes of early modern Europe and colonial America to the "satanic panic" of the late twentieth century. This is to say that reasons will be offered to think that demons are likely *incapable* of the sorts of things alleged by those believing demons to have creative powers. That they cannot wield extravagant magic, adversely affect nature, or even appear as ominous extramental specters will be one of the unique conclusions setting this work apart from its predecessors. In fact, it is more accurate to say that these conclusions do not so much demythologize inasmuch as they "un-retrofit"[7] preexisting assumptions wrongly intimated into a biblical demonology.

While demonology is not the sort of thing that is exclusive to Christianity (indeed, it is not even exclusive to *religion* as evidenced in popular-level works of nonfiction such as Rosemary Guiley's *The Encyclopedia of Demons and Demonology*), it assumes the central tenets of its orthodoxy including, but not necessarily limited to, the existence of God and the life, ministry, death, and resurrection of Jesus of Nazareth. What is *not* stipulated is any tenet of demonology that is not arrived at by argument. Guiding readers toward a reasonable view worth committing to will be the burden of this book. It is a burden to be backed by rigorous philosophical assiduity informed by a biblical framework. But surely not all readers will agree with every conclusion drawn. Perhaps less so in the arguments that arrive at those conclusions. Even so, this

---

5. See chapter 3.

6. This is one of the conclusions I came to in conducting the research that culminated in my doctoral thesis. See Guthrie, "A New Metaphysics for Christian Demonology."

7. I am borrowing this word from Henry Ansgar Kelly. See his *Satan*, 318.

Introduction

work is designed to expose one to a thoughtfully argued demonic realism that emends both what the biblical canon leaves unaddressed and what the church has addressed. In the introduction to his classic novel, *The Screwtape Letters*, C. S. Lewis sums up the two kinds of polarizing extremities this book is pushing back against:

> There are two equal and opposite errors into which our race can fall about the devils. One is to disbelieve in their existence. The other is to believe, and to feel an excessive and unhealthy interest in them. They themselves are equally pleased with both errors and hail a materialist or a magician with the same delight.[8]

The time has now come for both materialist and magician to make way for the maven, or at least one who is more cautious about the evidences and what we are entitled to conclude from them.

A Natural Diabology: An Outline of This Book's Objectives

Philosophy of religion is dominated by talk of "the God of classical theism" by which its participants seek to discuss and debate the existence of God *so conceived*. This is to say that the God of classical theism is, to use the philosophical vernacular, "the Greatest Conceivable Being" whose attributes include transcendence, aseity, omniscience, omnipotence, omnibenevolence, and so forth. The overall objective of this work is to explicate and defend a particular view of the existence and nature of the gods of this world.[9] The use of the little "g" is deliberate, for here we mean to contrast the indestructible and immanent God of classical theism with the malleable and finite gods (so-called) of demonology.[10] Such gods are considered to be vastly inferior to the superlative deity of heaven though somewhat superior to the lowly creatures of earth.[11]

Our specific aim in talking about the gods of this world, then, is to enter into a discussion about a philosophy of Christian demonology that accords with all of the relevant evidence available in understanding whether such beings exist and what we are entitled to think about them in terms of their nature and powers. In so doing, I shall be arguing for the existence of Satan and his demons (viz., demonic realism) against the criticisms of anti-realists; and then I shall propose and argue for a particular way realists should understand them. In this section, I shall lay out a précis of the chapters that comprise this book in order to fill out a trajectory of this twofold objective a bit more.

In the inaugural chapter (chapter 2) that succeeds this one and launches Part I of the book's content, I shall survey the various concepts and terminology associated

---

8. Lewis, *The Screwtape Letters*, ix.
9. Cf., Deut 32.17; 2 Cor 4.4.
10. A similar use of the little "g" attends the relative status of Moses in the eyes of Pharaoh (Exod 7.1).
11. For a fuller treatment of "god(s) of this world," see chapter 2.

with talk of Satan and his demons (like "devil," "Beelzebul," and "Lucifer") along with the adjoining terminology and appellations associated with the good angels. Some of the tenets of a biblical demonology can be derived in rather straightforward, systematic ways bearing little controversy amongst conservative interpreters. Other tenets are not so straightforward, requiring some process of induction in order to tease out what is likely the case or not. Still, other tenets may be found to be utterly baseless, thus pressing one to consider their wholesale abandonment. Though the chapter seeks to be thorough in terms of providing the reader a grasp of what is often considered to be the traditional, conservative portrait of demonology as read in the Bible, it is not a mere parroting of previous declarations on the matter nor an unconscious adoption of official church teaching. And neither will I shy away from potentially important controversies about the identities of spiritual beings in the Bible, though I shall offer up some commentary on the controversial portions of Scripture wherein the identities of the beings in question may be unresolvable. As a chapter that not only sets the stage but provides the theological foundation for anyone's subsequent philosophy of Christian demonology, it communicates to the reader my understanding and arguments of what the Bible says and doesn't say about Satan, his demons, and their angelic *Brüder*. It is not intended to be a thorough recapitulation of biblical demonology, only a repository for the select data that populate the premises of the forthcoming philosophical arguments.

In chapter 3, I shall move on to survey the history of Christian philosophy regarding those who have forged and molded Christian demonology. As the subject matter is vast, I have selected a representative sample of some of the most influential philosophers who have shaped the competing views in demonology's philosophical history. Chapter 3 thus begins by tracing Christian demonology back to the ancient Greeks and Jews and shows how their perspectives did and did not influence the development of Second Temple and New Testament demonologies. I then proceed to discuss the earliest Christian philosophers as well as medieval philosophers, from Augustine to Aquinas, who wrote on the subject. The post-New Testament aggregate of Christian philosophers by and large considered demons to be quasi-material, though spiritual, beings. This is to say that they acknowledged that demons are bodiless, but may still possess subtle, material properties imperceptible to observers. It is in later medieval thinking that the notion of their being purely immaterial–being divested of any material properties whatsoever–really takes root. Ontological immaterialism's most influential catalyst is arguably Thomas Aquinas, but his assertion of pure immaterialism is preceded by that of the Pseudo-Dionysius. Accordingly, three ontological views of demons ultimately surfaced–that demons are material, quasi-material, or purely immaterial. And each has found able defenders going into the modern and contemporary periods. This prompts a rummage through some of those representative Christian philosophers of these later periods to show that, despite some materialist resistance (e.g., Thomas Hobbes), there is an increasing dominance in the notion

Introduction

of pure immaterialism amongst conservatives. All of the surveys undertaken shall also consider the mainstay notion that demons also have the special ability to interact with matter, sometimes in extraordinary ways–a power attributed to demons that seems to go unchallenged. In short, the chapter evidences the metaphysical problems seeking resolution.

In Part II, I shall be considering whether there can be a "natural diabology"–that is, whether there are any arguments to show that Satan and his demons *simpliciter* exist or not. I begin by interacting with arguments offered in support of demonic anti-realism (chapter 4). Following that, I shall critically assess those arguments that seem to support demonic realism (chapter 5). Finding some of those arguments to be less than compelling, or in need of something else to add, I shall offer up an argument that I do find compelling–one that is based on similar (historical) arguments enlisted for establishing the historicity of other extraordinary features pertaining to Jesus of Nazareth (chapter 6). I shall argue that Jesus's being an exorcist along with the particular descriptions given of alleged demonic activity imply the existence of Satan and his demons.

As we move into Part III, we shall venture into the quagmire of the nature of demons as spirits. Beginning in chapter 7, I shall present and defend the notion that Satan and his demons are purely immaterial creatures and that the earlier notions of the demons's being quasi-material, or fully material, is less likely to be true. By drawing upon the pneumatic vocabulary used in Scripture along with an insistence on uniformity and simplicity in the employment of that vocabulary, I argue that Satan and the demons are best understood to be purely immaterial. But such pure immateriality raises questions about the feasibility of being a personal being without any material attributes. I interact with some of those concerns therein and conclude that the pure immateriality of the demons is veritably understandable and probabilistically defensible.

In chapter 8, I discuss the candidates for what consists of the other-interacting powers of Satan and the demons. Almost all demonic realists affirm that they possess the ability to interact with (viz., commune with) other spirits and minds. I refer to such communicability as *cognitive interaction* as opposed to interaction by and through some other means. According to tradition, demons are also endowed with special matter-interacting powers (viz., psychokinesis) with which to wreak physical havoc on creation. Some theodicies and defenses of God's existence rely on the plausibility of having such a psychokinetic power. If the demons are purely immaterial, then they do not have the natural ability to interact with physical objects on their own as, say, air can. But if demons wish to interact with the world, and for demonic realists they reportedly do, then it would seem that their only means to do so would be through the agency of a psychokinetic power. But I shall offer up a cumulative case in chapter 9 for supposing that the demons probably interact with the world only through their cognitive interaction with the rational souls of others. And, thus, we no longer have any reason to posit the extraordinary and seemingly *ad hoc* notion that demons have the additional power of psychokinesis. I present an explanatory argument that shows that cognitive interaction is the best interpretation of the demons's ability–indeed their *only* ability–with which to interact with the physical world.

As we move into Part IV, chapters 10–11 handle a series of scriptural and philosophical objections to the conclusions of the previous three chapters. I respond to each to show that none of them gives us any good reasons to either deny the pure immateriality of demons or the theory that demons interact with this world exclusively via their cognitive interaction with human beings. The Scriptures covered span the Old and New Testaments and pertain to prominent episodes of alleged direct diabolical activity seemingly contrary to the metaphysical conclusions drawn in the previous Part. The scriptural episodes covered are touted as paradigm examples of either the demons's quasi-material nature or of some undisclosed psychokinetic ability. They include the appearance of a serpent in the Garden of Eden, the primeval sexual exploits involving human women, occurrences of atmospheric disturbances and the infliction of skins sores on Job, the temptation of Jesus in the wilderness, the infliction of blindness and muteness by Satan, the infliction of a morphological ailment on a woman, the Apocalyptic-Pauline notion that Satan can appear as an "angel of light," and the Pauline notion that Satan performs "signs and lying wonders." My views are shown to accommodate all of these instances of demonic interaction with the world without sacrificing a literalist hermeneutics and, thus, do not fare as successful objections.

In chapter 12, I anticipate some philosophical objections that may be given against the idea that demons are purely immaterial or can only interact with this world through the medium of cognitive interaction. Finding that none of them pose any real threat to my approach, I consider my arguments set out in the previous chapters to be ultimately successful and that any reservations posed by philosophical reflection are of no consequence.

Chapter 13 concludes the book by summarizing the cases that have been made in favor of the existence of Satan and his demons, what their ontology is, and what they can do. I follow up with a discussion about how such a demonology can be understood in the modern world and that, upon further reflection, the doctrine is both plausible and intellectually inoffensive. I close by discussing the future of the philosophy of demonology vis-à-vis the conclusions defended in this book and the impacts they make on other areas of study and practice. As such, this book is intended to begin the conversation, not to end it. For there is no doubt that our world will continue to be possessed by the spirit of skepticism and will require an exorcism, not at the hands of the clergy, but from the minds of the academy.

Our journey beings in the next chapter wherein I shall set the stage by explicating some terminology based on the Bible and to what extent such terminology elucidates a biblical demonology. It is a chapter devoted to foundations–foundations that are essential to going forward in making sense of the cast of characters known only by their familiar, though imprecise, diabolical referents. Accordingly, we shall explore an important cross-section of relevant terms used including those pertaining to the good angels.

Part I

Background

"Any doctrine that will not bear investigation is not
a fit tenant for the mind of an honest man.
Any man who is afraid to have his doctrine investigated
is not only a coward but a hypocrite."

—Robert G. Ingersoll, *Col. R. G. Ingersoll's Famous Speeches Complete* (1906)

2

Theological Foundations for a Christian Philosophy of Demonology

CHRISTIAN ORTHODOXY ADVOCATES A partisan conception of God that distinguishes its theism from those of other religions and nonreligious traditions. Among other doctrines, it speaks of God as the unity of three centers of self-consciousness (viz., the doctrine of the Trinity), however that might be cashed out. Unless one was in contact with special revelation such as to disclose the trinitarian nature of God, it is not considered by most to be a belief that neither has nor would have arisen from the bare philosophical work of natural theology. One turns to the canonical works of revealed theology in which to find this understanding of God divulged. Such is the case in pursuit of a Christian philosophy of demonology. For neither would most tenets of demonology arise from a bare philosophical work of natural *diabology*.[1] Instead, if one wants to advocate and defend a partisan conception of Satan and his demons, such a conception must also derive from its revealed theology. That there might be an originating principle of evil or a cause *in fieri* of temptation and suffering derivable from philosophical speculation would only evince a bare diabolism at best. And yet there are ancillary doctrinal commitments attached to one's diabolism (e.g., such as his being a rebellious angel).

It is, thus, necessary to take a foundational approach by first examining what Christianity's Scriptures, the presumptive *regula fide* of the church, have to say about Satan and his cohorts.[2] Accordingly, Scripture is being stipulated as the canonical and unimpeachable, even if incomplete and fallible, source *ultimo* of the distinguishing tenets of Christian demonology. That being so, the objective of this chapter is to introduce how Satan and his cohorts are portrayed within its pages. As such, we shall be attending to the explicit sayings of the Bible regarding these gods of this world

---

1. I stumbled upon the phrase "natural diabology" in the works of Jeffrey Burton Russell. E.g., Russell, *Satan*, 24.

2. I am borrowing from how Alvin Plantinga has referred to demons in his philosophical work. See his *Warranted Christian Belief*, 302 and his *God, Freedom, and Evil*, 58.

and other related beings while being conscious of the limitations of that information. Henry Ansgar Kelly does not exaggerate when he laments the irony that "even the Scripture-Only adherents have unwittingly accepted a doctrine of Satan which is based on a tradition that has displaced Scripture and disguised itself as Scripture."[3] Kelly's concern is that the church has bought into an inaccurate portrait of Satan that is nonetheless considered to be on a par with the very teachings of Scripture. Such a concern forces one to systematically revisit those original descriptions with which to adjudicate the tenets of demonology. And where the Bible is not explicit, reasonable inference and careful reflection will be offered in filling out those tenets.

However, a biblical demonology does not obtain in a vacuum. Indeed, one of its well-known appurtenant doctrines is that of angelology under which demonology is subsumed. Suitably, we shall incorporate what Scripture has to say regarding that subject. The particular objectives of this chapter, then, are to introduce, codify, and defend what Christian demonic realists are entitled to conclude about the initial portrait of the nature of Satan and his cohorts and their angelic affiliates. For such is necessary in laying the theological foundations that will inform my subsequent philosophy of demonology.

Biblical Angelology

Augustine once defined "angel" in a way that focused on the activity of a certain race of created (nonhuman) beings and not so much on their nature. He wrote:

> "[A]ngel" is the name of a function, not of a nature. If you inquire about the nature of such beings, you will find that they are spirits; if you ask what their office is, the answer is that they are angels. In respect of what they are, such creatures are spirits; in respect of what they do, they are angels.[4]

In accord with Augustine's understanding, "angel" is a designating term meant to describe, more or less, what they *do* and not so much what they *are*. This is quite right, especially considering certain biblical texts will identify angels as "spirits" (Heb 1.14). If an "angel" was a reference to one's ontology, we would have the vacuous notion that "spirits are spirits." I note this because Scripture indiscriminately utilizes the term "angel" across the board in a variety of different contexts for a variety of different kinds of being. Consider that the Hebrew word for "angel(s)" in the Old Testament is *mal'ak(im)*[5] and the Greek word in the New Testament is *aggel(oi)*.[6] The words themselves are generally translated as "messenger" in order to capture the notion that one

---

3. Kelly, *Satan*, 4.
4. Augustine, *Enarrationes in Psalmos*, 103(I).15:125.
5. Gen 19; 28.12; 32.1; Pss 78.49; 91.11; 103.20.
6. Matt 4.6, 11; 13.41; 24.31; Mark 1.13; 13.27; Luke 4.10; 16.22; Gal 3.19; Heb 2.2, 7; 13.2; 2 Pet 2.11; Rev 3.5; 7.2; 9.15; 12.7; 16.1; 17.1; 21.9.

is a representative and dispatcher of information and services. It is no different than one's being a "courier" whereby *anybody* could potentially qualify for such a position. The messenger-tasks ascribed to angels typically involve some kind of communicative intercourse with human beings. We are, for example, told that angels perform various ameliorating, ministerial duties in service to human beings (e.g., Matt 4.11; Heb 1.14, 2:2). But they also seem to have non-messenger-related, intra-heavenly duties. For example, they worship and sing songs unto God (Heb 1.6; Rev 4.8). And not all of their duties are for the *benefit* of the recipients. For they also have a role in meting out judgment on behalf of God (Rev 8.2—9.18).

No commitment can be made as to what their nature is purely on the basis of their vocation as messengers/ministers; that they might be immaterial or material or something in between is simply unrelated to their mission and will have to be derived by some other means of information. The diversity of the "angel" is simply unrestrictive. In the Old Testament, for example, the Patriarch Jacob is said to have had "messengers" (*mal'akim*) which were sent to his brother Esau (Gen 32.3, 6). In the New Testament, John the Baptist is said to have "messengers" (*aggelon*) of his own that were dispatched to Jesus (Luke 7.24). So, whether spirits or humans or whatever, no ontological implication or identification is offered by the uses of *mal'ak* and *aggelos*. Hence, angels *simpliciter* have no substantively essential properties other than that they are finite persons of a sort capable of distributing messages and the like. If they are indeed the spiritual agents of popular lore, this cannot be derived from the Bible's use of "messenger" alone.

The curious description of God's angels as "ministering spirits" in Heb 1.14 is an altogether different matter. The concept of being a ministering spirit might not be something the author of Hebrews is attributing to human beings but to some other persons of creation. This seems especially true given verse 14's immediate reason for the designation of angels as ministering spirits, viz., that they are "sent out to serve for the sake of those who are to inherit salvation." The verse seems to set apart the angels from these heirs of salvation. Moreover, in 2.16, merely one chapter over, the author explicitly adds that "surely it is not angels that he helps, but he helps the offspring of Abraham" since "the children share in flesh and blood [and] he himself likewise partook of the same things" (v. 14). Angels do not partake of flesh and blood, which is why they are not helped in a salvific way (cf., v. 15).

That angels are elsewhere described as beings that find the inheritance of eternal life a foreign though attractive notion (1 Pet 1.12) further underscores the distinction between angel and humankind hinted at in Heb 1.14.[7] Though more will be said about the spiritual natures of angels and demons in subsequent chapters, here we need only have a vague understanding that that which is ontologically "spirit" is not to be taken as referring to the same thing as that which is earthly, for "a spirit does not have flesh

---

7. For a different take on this subject, see the historical survey by C. A. Patrides in his "The Salvation of Satan," 467–78.

Part I: Background

and bones" (Luke 24.39). On the other hand, being a "spirit" does not always mean one is an otherworldly, discarnate substance (e.g., 1 Cor 15.45; *possibly* 1 Pet 3.19). Perhaps the notion that they are otherworldly is more secured if we consider that the only human beings created in the Garden of Eden were Adam and Eve wherein angels seem to have a presence (Gen 3.24). *What else would these angels–these Cherubim–be if not human beings?* If these angels are part of God's otherworldly divine council (Ps 82.1) and that collective council is being implied in some way by Gen 1.26 and 3.22, it is hard not to see angels as discarnate spiritual agencies that are beyond and even prior to the earthly.

These spiritual messengers of God are thought to be ranked akin to how human soldiers in the various branches of the military are.[8] While the rankings are not necessarily limited to those explicitly mentioned in Scripture, we have only a handful of texts that parse out angels as being distinguished from each other in this way. At the top of the hierarchy we have the familiar "archangel" (1 Thess 4.16; Jude 9) for the very term (*archangelou*) means "chief angel."[9] But any "lower" rankings are rather indistinguishable from each other in terms of who outranks whom. In fact, we are not even sure if the other designations do not connote a differentiation of *species* rather than ranks. For example, we are told about the "cherubim" (Gen 3.24; Ezekiel 10; Heb 9.5) and the "seraphim" (Isa 6.2, 6) but lack any explicit relation between these two classifications or of what "office" these might describe. "Cherubim" (*kerûbîm*), plural for "Cherub," has no definitive meaning (though it is thought by some to be rooted in the Akkadian term *karābu* which means "bless, praise"[10]). "Seraphim" (*śerāp̄îm*), plural for "Seraph," *does* have a connotation and means "fiery (flying) serpents," which is perhaps a reflection of their having a burning zeal ("fiery"), moving swiftly ("flying"), and possessing considerable wisdom ("serpent"). But, again, nothing is evident in the terms that show how such designations distinguish them (rank? species?) from their fellow angels other than that they do, in fact, distinguish them.

The archangel is Michael. But there is another named angel and is perhaps the only other named angel in the Hebrew Bible, Gabriel. This identification also occurs in Daniel (8.16; 9.21), but his rank, if he has one, is undisclosed. The Apocryphal Book of Tobit includes one other angel: Raphael. Elsewhere within the Apocryphal corpus we have other angels named "Uriel" (2 Esdras 4.1; 5.20; 10.28), "Gabuthelon," "Aker," "Arphugitonos," "Beburos," and "Zebuleon" (all in the Revelation of Esdras). There may be other implied exegetical details about additional names and ranks,[11] but we need not

---

8. Such a notion derives primarily from the sixth-century work *The Celestial Hierarchy* by Pseudo-Dionysius.

9. In some translations, "archangel" is used to describe Michael in Dan 12.1. Michael is described there as *haggāḏōwl haśśar* which means "the great/chief prince."

10. Steinmann, "Cherubim," 112.

11. See Olyan, *A Thousand Thousands Served Him*.

settle that here. Nothing regarding our focus on demonology hangs on probing angelic monikers any further; thus, we move on to the identities of the gods of this world.

Biblical Demonology

"Demons" and "devils," in the plural at least, are used as synonyms in the Bible.[12] The distinction is strictly in the Greek in that "demons" (*daimonion*) vaguely represents "divine ones" while "devils" (*diaboloi*) represents something more adversarial, viz., "slanderers." Though some New Testament translators use "devils" in certain passages, they are not necessarily translating a cognate of *diabolos* but, rather, they are translating a cognate of *daimon*. The Greek term *diabolos*, being used as a singular, is itself only used in reference to Satan, a being we have yet to formally introduce from Scripture. Yet all the while "demons" and "devils"–as plurals–generally represent the same subordinate, villainous entities found in the Gospels.

Whether demons or devils (or both), these beings are portrayed as *de facto* harassers of God's human creation. They seem to make themselves known exclusively through their interactions with human beings–from temptations to possessions (or demonizations). The New Testament's portrayal of them seems to suggest or imply that their harassments obtain across diverse demographics. Demons afflict the elite (John 6.70; Rev 2.9; 18.2) as well as the marginal (Mark 1.32; 5.2; Luke 8.27), the infirmed (Mark 6.13; Luke 4.40–41) as well as the healthy (Mark 8.33; John 13.2), and the anti-religious (John 13.27; 1 John 3.8–10) as well as the pious (Mark 1.13; Matt 16.22–23; Luke 4.33; 8.12; Acts 5.3; Eph 6.11). They also afflict both male victims (Acts 19.16) and female ones (Luke 8.2; 13.11), both adult (Mark 5.18; 2 Cor 12.7) and child (Mark 7.26–30; 9.20–21; Matt 17.15–18), both Jew (Luke 4.33) and non-Jew (Matt 4.24; 1 Cor 7.5; Rev 3.9; 9.20), and both Christian (1 Thess 3.5) and non-Christian (2 Cor 4.4; Rev 12.9). It is quite apparent that they are equal opportunity assailants. Despite their ubiquitous harassments, there is no explicit reference to demons, or to their chief, as ever manifesting as specters or as corporeal beings,[13] though a number of Christian theologians suppose otherwise.[14] In addition to their cognitive power utilized against their victims, they do appear to have knowledge that supersedes the ordinary (Mark 1.24; Matt 8.29), yet there is unambiguous indication that they are not omniscient (Acts 19.15).

Now, demons (or devils), according to tradition, are thought to have been good angels at one time (more on this in a moment). As such, they are thought to have

---

12. The only exceptions would be in those passages where merely human slanderers are implied (e.g., 1 Tim 3.11; 2 Tim 3.3). That having been said, it is evident that the term is akin to "angels" in that it denotes activity and not ontology.

13. "There is no biblical reference to demons's manifesting themselves physically" (Oropeza, *99 Answers*, 74).

14. E.g., Unger, *Biblical Demonology*, 64; Dickason, *Angels*, 176–77.

Part I: Background

been good, Godly messengers and ministers along with their angelic brethren. Having reputedly fallen from some state of grace,[15] some medieval thinkers thought that part of their punishment included their having been cursed by being given a degraded nature, perhaps even one that was grotesque in appearance.[16] But if the demons's original state was that of the good angels, then their new diabolical "occupation" would not itself establish that they have taken on a different ontology. Changing jobs, so to speak, does not change one's nature any more than the apostatizing of Alexander and Hymenaeus in the first century changed theirs (viz., that they would have become somehow not as human as Paul or Timothy!).[17] For those who pursue it, the absence of any descriptions about the demons's appearance thus imposes a burden on those who think otherwise.

However, it is a fair thing to wonder as to whether or not demons are in fact derivative of the good angels. There are two traditions that are thought to be ascertained from Scripture. First, it is conjectured that Isaiah 14 and Ezekiel 28 refer to, or imply, the fall of Satan. But such a view depends on whether the "Lucifer" and "anointed cherub" of these passages are indeed alternative designations of Satan (this will be assessed in the next section). But never mind. For even if these passages evince a Satanic fall, it would not follow that an aggregate of angels joined him. Those passages do not disclose whether the rebellion of Satan was a solitary incident or not. A second tradition points to Gen 6.1–4 as a possible indication of a corporate angelic fall. But it is considered almost axiomatic amongst interpreters that the "sons of God" does not conclusively refer to fallen angels or demons. For Genesis 6 is very much an opaque passage.[18] So, we would be remiss to consider it a resolute pointer to any angelic fall.

The New Testament would seem to be equally unhelpful. Some appeal to the Lukan reference where Jesus of Nazareth reports to have seen "Satan fall like lightning from heaven" (Luke 10.18).[19] But the context seems to indicate that this is a description of the authority of Jesus's name being used successfully to subdue and expel demons through exorcism (v. 17). It is a reflection of the superlative invading authority of the Son of Man. As such, it is more likely that Jesus is saying that the fall of Satan is due, not to some historical cosmic event, but to the conferment of authority and victory now underway (vv. 19–20). Others prefer a more explicit passage found in Rev 12.7–9 wherein it speaks of a "war in heaven" where Satan and Michael along with their respective angelic minions have engaged in battle. Having

---

15. Augustine, *De Civitate Dei* XI. 13; Anselm, *De Casu Diaboli*; Aquinas, *Summa Theologiae*, I.63–64.

16. E.g., Dickason, *Angels*, 176–77.

17. 1 Tim 1.19–20.

18. We shall explore this passage in some detail in chapter 10.

19. Craig S. Keener and Robert H. Stein, for example, both insist that Luke 10.18 does not relate to a precosmic fall of Satan (Keener, *The IVP Bible Background Commentary*, 217; Stein, *Luke*, 310). Also see Russell, *The Devil*, 1977), 194–97 and Henry Ansgar Kelley's response in his "Review: The Devil at Large."

been defeated, "the deceiver of the whole world ... was thrown down to the earth, and his angels were thrown down with him" (v. 9). But Revelation 12 is not depicting events of a distant cosmic past but of a recent one where Satan's struggle ending in his defeat is meant to correspond with the history of conflict between Satan and God, one that culminates in the victory of the martyrs who stand triumphant in the salvific power of the crucified Jesus.[20]

Nevertheless, there *are* some other biblical clues that suggest that an angelic fall likely occurred–clues that do not depend on the above problematic passages. Consider, first, Jude 6 (which is possibly based in part on the related 2 Pet 2.4) which reads:

> And the angels who did not stay within their own position of authority [*archēn*], but left their proper dwelling [*oikētērion*], he has kept in eternal chains under gloomy darkness until the judgment of the great day.

The "angels" (*aggelous*) are the supernatural messengers of God given the immediate context. It is three verses later where the more iconic figures, Michael and Satan, are locked in dialogue (Jude 9). Moreover, the context (v. 14) and background of Jude show that it is an allusion to the non-canonical book of 1 Enoch which overtly centers on God's rebellious angels. What is not addressed, however, is *to what extent* Jude (unconsciously?[21]) intimates the material of I Enoch. This has been a matter of much scholarly debate. If Jude means to endorse all of I Enoch's teachings, then we have clear-cut evidence of the angelic fall, for 1 Enoch paints a rather clear and dramatic picture of that fall–case closed. But not all readers and commentators–this author included–are willing to find Jude's comments as a full-fledged endorsement of I Enoch.[22] As such, the question that remains is: Is there enough evidence contained in Jude 6 to establish an angelic fall without relying on the legitimacy, or lack thereof, of I Enoch's inspiration?

It would appear so. *Archēn* in verse 6 denotes "position of authority," where such is revoked via an abandoning of one's *oikētērion* ("dwelling"). While *oikētērion could* refer to one's body (as it does in 2 Cor 5.2), that is not the likely rendition here for three reasons: First, we already know that angels are *incorporeal* things because they are "spirits" (Heb 1.14; cf., Luke 24.39) and, so, *oikētērion* cannot be in reference to the angels's bodies. Second, the angels abandon their *oikētērion* by doing so *willingly* (implied by their having "left" [*apolipontas*] their *oikētērion*), which–outside of suicide–is

---

20. Blount, *Revelation*, 233–34; Bauckham, *Climax of Prophecy*, 228.

21. I suppose it is possible Jude is not directly citing 1 Enoch but is simply reporting a well-known tradition otherwise captured in 1 Enoch and other Pseudepigrapha.

22. J. Daryl Charles admits that it is possible that "Jude is borrowing from Jewish apocalyptic imagery without necessarily endorsing its theological content, employing the imagery for his own purpose" which is "strengthened by the fact that the 'Watchers's of Dan 4:13,17, and 23 are *holy* and servants of God, whereas in *1 Enoch* they are fallen and take on mythological proportions" ("The Angels under Reserve" 47); Also see Keating, *First and Second Peter, Jude*, 211; Donelson, *I and 2 Peter and Jude*, 167; Coder, *Jude–Everyman's Bible Commentary*, 85.

Part I: Background

not possible to will. Thirdly, it would be quite an overreach of justice for the angels to be condemned for simply becoming disembodied! Given that *oikētērion* is tied with *archēn* makes *position of authority* a likelier understanding of what was abandoned. Hence, we can tease out of Jude 6 that there are angels who have willingly abandoned their position and, so, left their dwelling place in an act that culminates in their condemnation by God. Consider that Paul elsewhere warns his Galatian audience that an "angel from heaven" could potentially preach a false gospel (Gal 1.8). In the context of his warnings lodged elsewhere wherein fallen angels *qua* demons are the sources of false gospels and false doctrines (2 Cor 11.4; 1 Tim 4.1; cf., 1 John 4.1), such *may* provide independent support for the said Galatian "angel from heaven" in its being a cryptic reference to a heavenly expulsion. But the question that now imposes itself is, *Are these fallen angels in fact demons?* After all, some representatives of the early church understood them to be separate beings.[23]

We can infer from Scripture a satisfactory answer to this question. First, we observe that there is consistent mention of "the devil and his angels" (*diabolō kai tois aggelois autou*) according to certain passages (Matt 25.41; cf., Rev 12.9). There is no third category of satanic spiritual followers in the mix ever mentioned. The assumption is that the New Testament writers (Peter and Jude included) committed to other teachings contained in I Enoch, not the least of which is the notion that God's angels copulated with human women and had offspring who became the demons. How this was accomplished is described in I Enoch–a book that commentates and allegedly expands on the antediluvian world-scene of Gen 6.1–6 and its aftermath.[24]

In I Enoch, the angels are said to have taken human women as wives and corrupted them by teaching them all manner of carnal and bewitching practices. But in their union, they procreate a race of giants. These giants are killed off by God in the deluge of Noah thus releasing their spirits to roam the earth which they now do as discarnate, accursed demons. Unless one is willing to accept the currency of I Enoch, or other Pseudepigrapha like Jubilees, there is just not enough in the Bible itself to warrant parsing out a distinction between fallen angels and demons. One must assume that 1 Enoch offers an appropriate and accurate, if not inspired, commentary on Gen 6.1–6, and that is certainly far from being uncontroversial. So, the most natural and parsimonious reading of Scripture accords best with the notion that demons are themselves the fallen angels.[25]

Therefore, by way of summary, there is good indication in Scripture that the demons were once good angels who sinned and thus abandoned their original position of authority. By doing so, God condemned them to exile.[26] This would reflect the

---

23. E.g., Justin Martyr, *The Second Apology*, V; Lanctantius, *The Divine Institutes*, II.15.
24. Refer to the classic work by Charles, *The Book of Enoch*.
25. Dickason, *Angels*, 161.
26. The angelic exile of 2 Pet 2.4 and Jude 6 do indeed refer to some form of restrictive judgment: "[cast into] Tartarus" (*tartarōsas*) and "chains of gloomy darkness," respectively. "Casting" denotes

current independence of the demons from God and why they stand in enmity with him. It is, therefore, plausible that Jude 6 and 2 Pet 2.4 refer to the demons having once been angels and that their fall harmonizes with the greater New Testament that sees Satan's cohorts, along with their chief, as the ultimate harassers of God's people. And if the serpentine villain in the Garden of Eden in Genesis 3 is an iteration of Satan or some demon (more on this in a moment), then, on pain of sullying God's moral perfection, the best explanation for the arrival of this figure would be in the tradition that envisions all of God's heavenly entourage as created good but with the free will to do otherwise. Having exercised that free will for impudence, Satan and his cohorts would have incurred a punishment in accord with their effrontery of the supreme justice and goodness of God. The larger portrait of an angelic fall now looks to be elegantly supported both by scriptural testimony and by a measure of abductive reasoning. But this is all we can say at this juncture.

Let us now turn to the identity of this "chief," or Satan, in order to understand this key player further.

Biblical Diabology

(The) Satan

The name "Satan" derives from the Hebrew word *śāṭān* which is often translated as "adversary" or "accuser." Such a term *could* be in reference to a proper name, but it may not be. (In fact, just about *any* descriptive Hebrew word could be used as a (nick)name,[27] so such a word's mere occurrence in Scripture does not necessarily mean that

---

expulsion (i.e., Matt 25.29–30) and "chains" denotes some level of restriction (e.g., Ps 149.8). Regarding chains, it is important to note that such an image is not always literal or physical but sometimes metaphorical (e.g., Job 36.8; 38.31). The destination of their expulsion, the Tartarus of 2 Peter, is certainly not a reference to the final state of the wicked for they are merely "kept [there . . .] until the judgment of the great day"–Jude 7. Though it surely invokes the Greek notion of a subterranean underworld where the immortal Titans, or the most wretched of supernatural beings, are said to be literally chained and tormented in a misty, gloomy darkness (i.e., Hesiod, *Theogony*, 721–819), that Tartarus is being literally referred to by Peter and Jude is questionable. It is possible that they are merely using such familiar imagery only as a literary device. In this sense it is analogous to how one today might use the expression "imprisoned in my own home" in order to express intense restrictions to one's freedom in their home even though being "imprisoned" invokes the historical idea of being held in a cell lined with iron bars. Thus it is possible that *tartarōsas* is not being used literally, a notion reinforced by the idea that spiritual beings lack spatiality and that Tartarus does not obviously correspond to any New Testament notion of hell (viz., Hades and Gehenna). For those who insist on taking it more literally, I suppose that it could be that Peter is *reassigning* the usage of Tartarus's "chains of gloomy darkness" to have them refer to something less pagan. On this understanding, they are simply *importing* familiar terminology in order to refer to an *actual* place of condemnation that does not bear all or many of the same features originally ascribed to the term. Either way, the *tartarōsas* of Peter and the "chains" of Jude are not necessarily full endorsements of the Tartarus of Hesiod.

27. As Bauckham indicates (*Jesus and the Eyewitnesses*, 81), some "names" are actually nicknames that sometimes substitute for the agent's true appellation. This is the case for Simon who is later called "Peter" (*petros*) where *petros* simply means "the rock" and is used in a number of places to refer to

it is a personal appellation.) The particular term "Satan" (or "satan") can be used in reference to a temporary function of any personal agent whether human, angel, or otherwise.[28] We have only a handful of passages that utilize some form of *śāṭān* which could be interpreted in any of these noted ways. In 1 Chron 21.1 ("Then Satan stood up against Israel and moved David to number Israel"), we are given no interesting information about the identity of this personal adversary. The same goes for the parallel account of 2 Sam 24.1 which states:

> Now again the anger of the LORD burned against Israel, and it [or *He*] incited
> David against them to say, "Go, number Israel and Judah."

This Samuel passage suggests that God and not Satan is the ultimate agent behind David's numbering of Israel, which leaves the impression that the *śāṭān* of 1 Chronicles 21 is an agent of God in God's heavenly council (cf., Ps 86.1) like a good angel. But not necessarily. The Chronicler seems to insinuate that the Satan of 1 Chron21.1 is someone who seemingly "acts independently of divine permission"[29]–an agent having little or nothing to do with God. For in the New Testament, Satan is mentioned in a way that makes him explicitly executing the will of God (2 Thess 2.7–11), and by then the Satan figure is perceived as an independent agent who is (no longer) a part of the divine council.

In Job 1–2, the noun is used with the definite article in describing the adversary (*haśśāṭān*, or "the satan"). Herein we have the presence of *haśśāṭān* before God. This *haśśāṭān* acts as a courtroom accuser and, given the fact that the angelic hosts are with him in company (1.6; 2.1), suggests that *haśśāṭān* is just one of the good angels that is carrying out a legal role.[30] There is nothing definitive here that requires that *haśśāṭān* is himself a fallen angel or the chief of demons, even though this notion was developed in extracanonical and later demonologies.[31] Nonetheless, the constant stipulation of the *haśśāṭān* of Job as a mere member of God's good angels seems equally presumptuous if not more so. Job 1.6 prefaces that "there was a day when the sons of God [*bənê ĕlōhîm*] came to present themselves before the LORD, and Satan [*haśśāṭān*] also came among [*bətōwḵām*] them." There is much ado about the fact that Satan "came *among them*," that is, among the sons of God which are presumably the angels (cf., 38.7). Accordingly, it is supposed that *haśśāṭān* is merely a recruit from among the angelic entourage tasked with the burden of prosecuting the case against Job that his righteousness is solely contingent upon his life of comfort and luxury

inanimate things that are not Simon (e.g., Rom 9.33).

28. Compare with the fact that *diabolos* in the LXX takes on the additional meaning of "slanderer" and could refer to someone other than the devil himself.

29. Forsyth, *The Old Enemy*, 121.

30. Num 22.22 designates the "angel of the LORD" as *śāṭān* which might further suggest that *śāṭān* was more of a role than a proper name.

31. E.g., Origen, *Contra Celsus*, VI.42–43; cf., Forsyth, *The Old Enemy*, 88, 376–83.

(1.9–11).³² But one's merely coming from "among" some group hardly implies that the being is (merely) *one of them*.³³ For example, Exod 7.5 notes that the Israelites are to come out "from among [*mittôwkām*] them," that is, the Egyptians, and yet the Israelites were hardly anything like their Egyptian captors! Furthermore, *haśśāṭān* is not only "among them," but his point of origin is seemingly different from those of the *bǝnê ĕlōhîm*. For when the Lord asks Satan, "From where have you come?", the answer is, "From going to and fro *upon the earth*" (1.7; emphasis mine). Couched in the language of surveillance,³⁴ Satan's response seems to indicate that he later joins the *bǝnê ĕlōhîm* in their officiating before the Lord.³⁵ And the residential location of these sons of God–this "divine council"–is putatively thought to be in heaven in the midst of where God himself governs (Ps 82.1; cf., Ezek 1.5–13). However, John Walton contends that given the fact that it is God and not Satan who inaugurates the court proceedings, and that the Satan takes no delight in Job's torment, then the passive and dispassionate Satan envisioned here is not "homogeneous" with the one who acts preemptively elsewhere.³⁶ But Walton then walks this back a bit by acknowledging that "the pictures are not contradictory" and that "they may even be complementary."³⁷ This goes to show that the depiction of *haśśāṭān* in Job is not inconsistent after all with Satan being the chief of demons. Minimally, whether poetic or symbolic or literal or whatever, the Book of Job likely indicates that *haśśāṭān* is a supernatural being who is a key adversarial player in the famous drama that unfolds.³⁸ And if Satan indeed does exist as traditionally understood (or close enough), then no doubt this is the being who should be identified in Job as God's legal, if not also moral, adversary.

---

32. Walton, *Job*, 63–67; Alter, *The Wisdom Books, Job, Proverbs, and Ecclesiastes*, 12 n. 6; Pagels, *The Origin of Satan*, 39ff.

33. "Whether the Satan is a regular member of the council or an unexpected visitor is left ambiguous" (Habel, *The Book of Job*, 89).

34. Satan is thus considered a "roving intelligence agent" (Pagels, *The Origin of Satan*, 41). Also, the phrase "to and fro" does not necessarily indicate a spatial roving but, rather, is merely an idiom that can refer to one's conducting a *thorough* investigation (2 Chron 16.9).

35. Wray and Mobley, *The Birth of Satan*, 64.

36. Walton, *Job*, 66–67.

37. Walton, *Job*, 67.

38. Oddly, Kelly does not think of the *haśśāṭān* of Job to be adversarial at all. This is most curious given the very meaning of *haśśāṭān* as "the adversary." Kelly argues that in Job, Satan merely "advises extreme measures" and, upon divine approval, executes them (*Satan*, 27). Of course this sentiment is already guided by the widespread assumption adopted by Kelly that *haśśāṭān* just is one of God's good angels in service to the cause of vindicating the righteous servant through trial and tribulation. But if one does not assume that *haśśāṭān* is but a legal arm of the divine government, such a conclusion would be utterly *non sequitur*. For an adversary can serve as God's unwitting instrument for bringing about God's design plans for creation. This is, after all, how one is to understand the crucifixion of Jesus at the hands of the most adversarial regime: Rome. To wit, the Romans were unsuspecting pawns in bringing about the salvation of mankind (cf., Acts 2.23), but the Romans were certainly adversaries in the most exemplary way and were not part of God's government.

Part I: Background

Zechariah 3.1–2 may provide another Old Testament indication of the *śāṭān*'s being a unique adversary to God who is not part of the angelic community:

> Then he showed me Joshua the high priest standing before the angel of the LORD, and Satan standing at his right hand to accuse him. And the LORD said to Satan, "The LORD rebuke you, O Satan! The LORD who has chosen Jerusalem rebuke you! Is not this a brand plucked from the fire?".[39]

At least by the first century AD, Jews believed (and perhaps Jesus no less) that Satan had at one time been an angel of heaven out of which he was cast.[40] Nevertheless, the New Testament makes the identification of Satan here plausible, for Jude tells us about Michael the archangel's dispute with the devil (*tō diabolō diakrinomenos*) wherein Michael declares, "The Lord rebuke you!" (Jude 9). That Jude connects the reprimand of the devil with that of Zechariah 3 may suggest that the original "Satan" of Zechariah 3 is indeed "the devil."

In the New Testament, Satan himself plays the role of one who opposes Jesus, from his temptation in the wilderness[41] to his betrayal by Judas.[42] The Apostle Paul, having written most of the New Testament outside of the Gospels, treats the Christian believer as though he were in a direct state of war with this satanic kingdom.[43] John the Revelator (who may or may not be John the Apostle and beloved disciple) also discusses the role Satan has for both the present world (Rev 2.13, 24) and the eschatological one to come (Rev 12.9; 20.2, 7). As Revelation seeks to offer a peek behind the veil of the material world, Satan is seen coaxing or manipulating earthly regimes into the wholesale slaughter of God's people along with spearheading the advancement of worldwide doctrinal deception. Martyrdom and heresy are construed as a dual assault on the people of God. But eventually Satan is to meet his terminal doom (as are all the demons) upon being conquered by the returning Jesus (Rev 21.10) whose initial coming was to provide spiritual victory whereas his subsequent coming provides complete (body and soul) deliverance.

Satan is also likely to be identified with other nomenclatures sprinkled throughout the New Testament. The Gospels speak of "Beelzebul" (from *beelzeboul*) or, less accurately, "Beelzebub."[44] In all of the Synoptics (Matthew, Mark, and Luke), "Beel-

---

39. I recognize that "the usage of the verb is not sufficient to establish that 'the *śāṭān*' in Zech. 3:2 is the Devil, or even a devil figure, with implacable opposition to the will of God" (Tate, "Satan in the Old Testament," 464). However, by the time Judaism matured in the second century BC, *śāṭān* eventually became a proper name.

40. By the second century, there was already a fully developed demonology designating such beings as having 'fallen' from their original status. I make mention here specifically of Satan. For further discussion, see Marx, "La chute de 'Lucifer'"; Youngblood, "Fallen Star."

41. See Matt 4.1–11 and Mark 1.12–13.

42. See Luke 22.3 and John 13.27.

43. See Rom 16.20, 2 Cor 2.11, and Eph 6.11–20, just to name a few. Cf., 1 Pet 5.8.

44. *Beelzeboul* is likely a deliberate slight against Jesus in that He is being accused of drawing on the power of the primary enemy of the Israelite religion, the fertility god of the Canaanites better

zebul" is associated with "the prince of demons" (*tō archonti tōn daimoniōn*).⁴⁵ This "prince" is perhaps the same one Paul refers to in Eph 2.2 who is "the spirit that is now at work in the sons of disobedience." Furthermore, the identities of "the Evil One" (*ho ponēros*), "Ruler of this World" (*ho archōn tou kosmou toutou*), and "the Tempter" (*ho peirazōn*) would also appear to be Satan (Matt 13.19, 38, John 16.11, and Matt 4.3 respectively).

As to whether Satan was ever a good or benign creature in a previous state, we turn now to some of the posed possibilities on record.

Lucifer and the "Anointed Cherub"

Though it is not without controversy, many philosophers and divines, past and present, have appealed to another possible title-description (and even a *name* in some quarters) of Satan, namely "Lucifer" (Hebrew: *hêlêl*). As a referent to *someone*, it connotes one's being a "son of the morning" or "day star" and derives from Isaiah's condemnatory narrative in Isaiah 14. But the controversy surrounds precisely *to whom* the following threat of Isa 14.12–19 belongs:

> How you are fallen from heaven, O Day Star [or *Lucifer*], son of Dawn! How you are cut down to the ground, you who laid the nations low! You said in your heart, "I will ascend to heaven; above the stars of God I will set my throne on high; I will sit on the mount of assembly in the far reaches of the north; I will ascend above the heights of the clouds; I will make myself like the Most High." But you are brought down to Sheol, to the far reaches of the pit. Those who see you will stare at you and ponder over you: "Is this the man who made the earth tremble, who shook kingdoms, who made the world like a desert and overthrew its cities, who did not let his prisoners go home?" All the kings of the nations lie in glory, each in his own tomb; but you are cast out, away from your grave, like a loathed branch, clothed with the slain, those pierced by the sword, who go down to the stones of the pit, like a dead body trampled underfoot.

While the narrative sounds very much how Satan's fall from heaven is traditionally described, Isaiah 14 explicitly identifies this as a punitive "taunt" that is railed specifically "against the king of Babylon" (v. 4). In addition to the overt target of the taunt, Kenneth Allen argues the following:

> If the prophet begins his discourse with the burden of Babylon (13:1) and defines Babylon as the glory of the Chaldeans's pride (13:19), it would seem

---

known as Ba'al. And pagan gods were often associated with Satan as evidenced by the Septuagint's translation of Ps 96.5. For more on this, see Twelftree, "Demon, Devil, Satan," 164.

45. Matt 12.24; Mark 3.22; Luke 11.15.

exegetically sound to maintain that in chapter 14 he is still referring to the same literal city and land.[46]

Aside from the obvious, Robert Alden further presses for disparate characteristics between Satan and the King of Babylon:

> Has the accuser fallen from a position of power? Has the adversary ceased from ruling this world with "unceasing blows and unrelenting persecution" (v. 6)? To the contrary, Satan is very much in power. He is the god of this world (2 Cor. 4:4) and the prince of the power of the air (Eph. 2:2). In no sense is he fallen from a position of kingship in this world. The king of Babylon is gone and heard from no more. Not so Satan. His "fall" marked the beginning of his wicked reign. The king of Babylon's fall marked the end of his wicked reign. Lucifer cannot be Satan. Isaiah is not speaking of Satan in chapter 14.[47]

If it turns out that connections between Satan and the Lucifer of Isaiah were not made until well after even the birth of the Christian church,[48] the probability that there might have been a connection at all diminishes in the wake of these considerations.

On the other hand, the Bible often uses *obviously human* referents as typological representations of supernatural beings (think of the Messianic foreshadowings of the Old Testament such as that found in Isaiah 9 or the plausibility of the Edenic serpent being an iteration of Satan[49]). That the King of Babylon is the addressee in Isaiah 14 may be inconsequential given that in a typology one's identity is not the same as its antitype. Additionally, the passage declares that the condemned one is called a "Day Star" who is said to have "fallen from heaven" for having sought equality with God. This "Day Star" had a seemingly cosmic-level influence in that he "shook kingdoms" and was ultimately "cast out." Now, the star motif sits well with the association of angelic beings who are elsewhere described as "stars" (Job 38.7; Dan 8.10). And then there is the New Testament. According to Luke 10.18, Jesus says that he envisioned "Satan fall from heaven like lightning." John also writes that the "ruler of this world" (John 12.31; cf., 2 Cor 4.4), who also resides on a "throne" (Rev 2.13), has been "cast out"–a possible connection to the regal antagonist's being "cast out" in Isa 14.19. Paul himself warns that new converts are privy to being "puffed up with conceit" thus making them susceptible to falling under "the condemnation of the devil" (1 Tim 3.6)–a warning that might imply that new converts are susceptible to the same kind of sin as the devil's thus further implying the characteristics noted of the King of Babylon .[50] Add to this the obvious fact that kings do not actually fall "from heaven." This seems

---

46. Allen, "The Rebuilding and Destruction of Babylon," 23.
47. Alden, "Lucifer, Who or What?," 38.
48. Kelly, "The Devil in the Desert." Though Jeffrey Burton Russell demurs in his *The Prince of Darkness*, 43–44 and 79–80.
49. The identity of the serpent in the Garden of Eden is discussed below.
50. Scott, *The Existence of Evil Spirits Proved*, 139ff.

rather interesting when conjoined with the previously established conclusion[51] that 2 Peter and Jude imply a corporate, angelic fall that occurred at some point in the past. Collectively, these points seem to indicate that Satan may be in mind. However, it is equally plausible that just *any* demon could be in view if at all. And beliefs about a chief of demons being exiled from heaven was already woven into the Jewish conscience.

Regardless of whether or not Isaiah 14 refers to Satan, there are enough biblical indications that he was indeed expelled, or "fallen," from heaven. The only relevant, additional detail supplied in Isaiah 14 that would make it an interesting passage is its description of the infraction that was the catalyst for the expulsion of the king, namely his enterprising ascendancy over God. But as Bernard J. Bamberger has expressed, in following a similar sentiment by Friedrich Schleiermacher, "even we mortals know that such an ambition was, not only wicked, but ridiculous; could not great angels, with their lucid minds, understand and refrain from such tragic folly?"[52] If Isaiah 14 is designed to apply to Satan in any way, one must imagine the passage to be more of a poetic representation. Accordingly, the king's ostensive lust for power will have to be understood more along the lines of something like pride or injustice[53] which could arise in a being who knew he could not successfully implement a usurpation of the dominion of God. And if that much is granted, one must consider the alleged fall of the angels in Gen 6.1–6, being due to an entirely different matter, to be a separate event.

Let us now turn to the Old Testament passage, Ezek 28.13–16, which is cited as frequently as Isaiah 14 in attempting to proffer Satan as a rebel angel. It reads as follows:

> You were in Eden, the garden of God; every precious stone was your covering, sardius, topaz, and diamond, beryl, onyx, and jasper, sapphire, emerald, and carbuncle; and crafted in gold were your settings and your engravings. On the day that you were created they were prepared. You were an anointed guardian cherub [*mimšaḥ kərūḇ*]. I placed you; you were on the holy mountain of God; in the midst of the stones of fire you walked. You were blameless in your ways from the day you were created, till unrighteousness was found in you. In the abundance of your trade you were filled with violence in your midst, and you sinned; so I cast you as a profane thing from the mountain of God, and I destroyed you, O guardian cherub, from the midst of the stones of fire.

In this passage, the recipient of this condemnation is identified as the Prince (or King) of Tyre (v. 2). But what was said about Isaiah 14 applies here, namely that the addressee may typologically refer to Satan or not. Robert Morey argues for its unequivocal identification with Satan when he says with a great deal of confidence that

---

51. See the above section, "A Fallen Angel?"
52. Bamberger, *Fallen Angels*, 203.
53. Anselm, *De Casu Diaboli*, XV–XVIII; cf., 1 Tim 3.6.

nothing in the passage could be literally applied to the king of Tyre. The king of Tyre was not a model of perfection. Neither was he full of wisdom and perfect beauty. He wasn't in the Garden of Eden, nor was he created sinless. He wasn't kicked out of heaven and sent to earth.[54]

We could add, on behalf of Morey, one's being an "anointed cherub" is typically a designation reserved for a subset of the good angels of God (Gen 3.24; Ps 80.1; Ezek 10.1–20). Marvin E. Tate explains why such terminology, though, is used of someone who does not *literally* fit this description:

> In these verses, the problem of the hubris and rebellion of the "prince of Tyre" is set forth in plain language. The prophetic speaker draws from the mythical stock of traditions to give the condemnation of worldly powers meta-historical dimensions. Such powers as Babylon, Egypt, and Tyre transcend the ordinary in both good and evil. In the language of the New Testament, they are the agents of the "cosmic powers of this present darkness" and "the spiritual forces of evil in the heavenly places" (Eph. 6:12). The Ephesians passage links these powers and forces with the Devil (6:11), which is not the case in Ezekiel.[55]

According to Tate, such a description, while bathed in the language of Diaspora Judaism, imports references to Satan from its traditions in order to add a cosmic significance to the condemnation of the Prince of Tyre. It was primarily through later Christian writings that the "fallen" of Isaiah 14 and Ezekiel 28 would be overtly associated with the personal Satan of the New Testament.[56] If Satan is being typologically referred to by Ezekiel 28 as a way to deliver a grand insult to the Prince of Tyre, it is certainly not self-evidently clear. Therefore, caution must be exercised in looking to Ezekiel 28, as with Isaiah 14, for definitive theological clues about Satan's rebellion.

Even if these Old Testament identities in no way elucidate a prelapsarian Satan, this is not enough to dissuade us from considering whether Satan was ever a good angel at all. It is to this straightforward notion we now turn.

A Fallen Angel?

We shall now consider Satan's alleged association with his fallen angels and to what extent he is, like his brothers-in-arms, a fallen angel despite have little to no help from discussions about Lucifer and the "anointed cherub" above. This is not quite so easy to answer notwithstanding our assessment of 2 Pet 2.4 and Jude 6 above. For there appears to be no *explicit* mention in all of Scripture about Satan's being a fallen angel. In fact, with some possible exceptions (to be addressed), there is little about whether

---

54. Morey, *Satan's Devices*, 45.

55. Tate, "Satan in the Old Testament," 470.

56. Most notably Tertullian (*Against Marcion*, V.11), Origen (*De Principiis*, I.5), and the later influential John Milton (*Paradise Lost*, I.34–39, 157–168, 249–263).

Satan was ever *not* the enemy of God. In John 8.44, Jesus declares that the devil "was a murderer from the beginning" (*anthrōpoktonos ēn ap' archēs*) perhaps implying that the devil has always been a malevolent creature of destruction. However, the referent of "beginning" (*archēs*) does not itself necessarily connote a commencement of that being's existence. For the passage does not say "from the beginning *of that being's existence*." Consider that the combined use of *ap'* with *archēs* is elsewhere indicative of a beginning, not of one's existence, but of some situation or circumstance. This is elsewhere evident in John's and Luke's writings:

> "And you also will bear witness, because you have been with me from the beginning [*ap' archēs*]" (John 15.27).

> "My manner of life from my youth, spent from the beginning [*ap' archēs*] among my own nation and in Jerusalem, is known by all the Jews" (Acts 26.4).

> "That which was from the beginning [*ap' archēs*], which we have heard, which we have seen with our eyes, which we looked upon and have touched with our hands, concerning the word of life" (1 John 1.1).

> "Beloved, I am writing you no new commandment, but an old commandment that you had from the beginning [*ap' archēs*]. The old commandment is the word that you have heard" (1 John 2.7; cf., 2 John 1.5–6).

In John 15.27, the disciples were with Jesus, not from the beginning of his existence, but from the beginning of his ministry. Likewise, Acts 26.4 refers to Paul's beginning of his "manner of life" in his youth and not to the actual commencement of his existence. First John 1.1 speaks of the incarnate Jesus as "from the beginning," knowing full well that Jesus was not incarnate at the beginning of time or from eternity past. And John's "new commandment" in 1 John 2.7 is clarified to be an old commandment, not from the beginning of that commandment's existence *per se* (as if it were the first commandment ever), but from a time when that and other commands were originally being issued. These uses of "from the beginning" all seem to impress upon the reader some notion of a commencement to a subsequent series.

That the devil is construed as "murderer from the beginning" may be only to disclose that he is a murderer from the beginning of a series of murderers, thus making him *the* murderer. And this perhaps means to communicate that murder is not only basic or fundamental to the devil's nature, but that in being the first murderer of a series he became the metric or paradigm (primary cause?) for all murderers to come. It is not likewise suggesting that he *qua* murderer has always been one (cf., Matt 19.4 and 8). So, it would appear that John 8.44 is most likely unhelpful in adjudicating whether Satan ever fell from a propitious state.

We have already discussed the fact that little can be teased out of Isaiah 14 and Ezekiel 28 in support of the notion that Satan is a good angel gone rogue. But, as already hinted at, there are other grounds for reasonably inferring Satan's prior status as a good angel who is now fallen. There may yet be philosophical grounds in support of there being a rebellion of Satan. To this we now turn.

According to what is biblically uncontroversial, Satan, whoever he is, is considered to be a purely evil being–one relentlessly bent on theft, murder, and destruction (John 10.10). Accordingly, it seems unconscionable that he would have been directly created by an all-good God.[57] While God can and does *permit* beings to freely become evil, say by allowing them to succumb to temptation, God Himself is never responsible for directly tempting anyone into transgression (James 1.13). But if God created Satan initially as a tempter, it would seem that God *would* be directly responsible for any such temptations. Now, consider again that there were angels who willfully abandoned their original positions of authority by sinning (2 Pet 2.4; Jude 6). It is reasonable to suppose, as Augustine, Anselm, and Thomas Aquinas did,[58] that Satan was also originally innocent but likewise fell as a result of some initial sin(s). This would explain how a devil could come to exist in world where there is no evil. As an elegant explanation for the origin of the first transgression–one rooted in a morally innocent being–it augurs well for thinking that the rebellion of the other angels includes their chief.

Furthermore, it is difficult to consider just what *else* Satan would have been if not an angel of God. Of course one could simply say that Satan was an innocent being whose existence and classification are completely distinct from those of the good angels. But why assume that? It is a simpler explanation to think of *all* finite created spirits as belonging to the same category of being (vis-à-vis ontology) and to not assert an *ad hoc* tertiary category of being without independent reasons for doing so.[59] Suppose for a moment that Satan was actually a fallen "shmangel" instead

---

57. This is true unless one is willing to adopt a strong notion of a divine command theory of ethics wherein God can decree *anything, regardless of his nature and character*, and have it be good. Moreover, on such a model, it is possible that something that is *now* good has not always been so. A good at t1 might be decreed to not be good at t2. Or, God can decree at t1 that creating satans is morally neutral, and then can create any satans, and then decree that any subsequent creation of satans at t1+n (where n is any number greater than 1) is evil. But such extreme voluntarism is not held by the vast majority of divine command theorists. And if God is essentially good, then "good" cannot be a variable or placeholder for "that which God commands," for that would entail that God's commands must logically precede his essential goodness, which is absurd.

58. E.g., Augustine, *De Civitate Dei*, XI.15; Anselm, *De Casu Diaboli*, XVIII; Aquinas, *De Malo*, XVI.

59. I should mention Michael S. Heiser (e.g., "Monotheism" and "אלהים"). For Heiser, there are genuine "gods" who constitute God's heavenly council (cf., Pss 82.1, 6; 86.8) and are not angels, but neither are they beings coequal with God himself. He has also double-downed on this notion in his books, most notably *The Unseen Realm*. However, even if one grants Heiser's view, there is no reason to think that this pantheon would be ontologically distinct from God and angels–a notion Heiser heartily cedes. Aside from any theological misgivings Heiser's talk of a pantheon brings, the point remains that even if there is a "species uniqueness" ("Monotheism," 29) between the pantheon and God, there are still no grounds for a tertiary *metaphysical* category (viz., something "between" God and angel) in the biblical portrait of heavenly dwellers (just as no two distinct species of material objects are made of anything less than physical particles).

of an angel–some tertiary, *sui generis* category of created spirits that are neither human nor angel. Given the backdrop that an "angel" is merely to describe a being's vocation and not its ontology, it is reasonable to assume that anyone else in God's entourage would also be the same kind of being as those designated "angels" in the absence of reasons to the contrary. Similarly, identifying Satan as a "shmangel" should not itself lead us to think that there is indeed some tertiary, *sui generis* category of created spirits in the absence of counter-evidence. To wit, why think of shmangels as constituting a unique ontological category different from angels? The burden of proof would surely be on the side of establishing a new kind of being relevantly different from that of angels. Otherwise, just what is the difference between what an angel is and what a discarnate, finite, created spirit is apart from God and human? Since other finite, discarnate created spirits (i.e., Gabriel, Michael, Cherubim, and the Seraphim) are never designated as anything but beings belonging to the category of angels, it is simpler to think Satan is, or was, one of those kinds of beings (viz., angels). This is especially compelling if Satan is clearly not a member of the human race, for we will have reduced our options to angels or God himself. And it is, I take it, uncontroversial to affirm that Satan is not God.

Perhaps one ambitiously considers Satan to belong to another category of ontology *sui generis* in that he is a being who exists *a se* in the same sense as, or something similar enough to, God. One may construe Satan as a kind of counter-God, something akin to the later-developed figure of Angra Mainyu of Persian Zoroastrianism. In such a scenario, one imagines that Satan was never created but is, like his counterpart God, self-existent. But as with other discussions about angelic and demonic beings, if one adopts the totality of Scripture on the matter, there are probably no existents outside of God's creation and God himself.[60] For God's unparalleled and superlative status are replete throughout the Old and New Testaments (e.g., 1 Chron 17.20; Jer 10.6–7; 1 Cor 8.4). And God's being the creator seems also to be the sole preserve of God (Isa 44.24; John 1.1–4; Col 1.15–17) with no indication of an opposing equal. It seems reasonable, provided one accepts the testimony of Scripture, that if Satan exists that he would be a created being–particularly since God does not directly create moral evil (Gen 1.31; Job 34.10; 2 Cor 5.21; 1 John 3.5). On the other hand, the only other personal beings we are told about are the created terrestrial beings like humans and animals (Gen 1.21–27) as well as the supra-terrestrial ones, the angels (Ps 148.2, 5). By inference, then, Satan would not be a God. Thus, Satan would be a created spirit. If Satan is indeed a created spirit, then such would rule out his being terrestrial. If he is supra-terrestrial, then if we accord with Occam's Razor and resist formulating a tertiary category of existing personal spirits (like shmangels), then Satan is, and so *was*, an angel. This seems to be a reasonable deduction based on disjunction.

There is one final consideration. Satan's position is as one who is in charge of fallen angels and as one who commands them for his own purposes. In Revelation, for

---

60. Craig, *God Over All*, chapter 2.

instance, this apparent position directly corresponds to Michael's commanding of the good angels (see Rev 12.7–9). If the Revelator means to pit these two forces together, it is likely due to their being correlative in status. Furthermore, in 12.9 and 20.2, and perhaps also in 13.2, 4, 11, and 16.13, Satan is even called a "dragon" (*drakōn*). Such imagery could suggest a sort of dark counter-image to the angels being portrayed as winged creatures (Exod 25.20; Isa 6.2; Ezek 1; 10; 11.22; Rev 4.8; 9.9) that are, incidentally, also associated with "fire" (Heb 1.7). The fact that Satan's effectual combat only leads to "a third" being numbered among his casualties (12.4) also corresponds to the "third" of the human casualties the good angels can amass (9.15). That Satan is Michael's counterpart is subtly present elsewhere in the New Testament (cf., Jude 9) and perhaps hinted at in Dan 10.20.[61]

On the other hand, as I discussed above, Rev 12.9 has served as a commonly-cited proof-text for the historical fall of Satan. The passage reads in full:

> Now war arose in heaven, Michael and his angels fighting against the dragon. And the dragon and his angels fought back, but he was defeated, and there was no longer any place for them in heaven. And the great dragon was thrown down, that ancient serpent, who is called the devil and Satan, the deceiver of the whole world–he was thrown down to the earth, and his angels were thrown down with him.

Though the passage speaks explicitly of Satan and his angels, it refers to an event contemporaneous with Rome (or perhaps a future Roman antitype). It is likely an expression of the victory of Jesus on the cross in the first century. Or, it could be an expression of the effortless demise of Satan and his minions at some point in the future. Either way, it cannot possibly be hearkening back to the original angelic fall, for that event is to be located in the distant (pre-earthly?) past. Kelly's assessment is more aggressive, for he thinks that the passage's context (vv. 10–12) "decisively refutes the theory of a primeval Luciferian fall"[62] because it implies that "Satan has remained in his position as Heavenly Accuser of Humans since the time of Job and Zechariah's vision."[63] But verse 10's reference to Satan's having been "thrown down" from heaven is not necessarily incompatible with his having been previously discharged from an original angelic post (cf., the *archēn* of Jude 6), for it means only to convey in apocalyptic terms how the crucifixion of Jesus has now rendered ineffective Satan's "new" vocation to successfully accuse the righteous in times past.[64] One can be jettisoned from a position of authority and subsequently relegated to more limited functions only to have those functions later undermined. Nevertheless, my judgment, as noted

---

61. Cf., Collins, "The Son of Man," 55–56.
62. Kelly, *Satan*, 153.
63. Kelly, *Satan*, 154.
64. Keener, *IVP Bible Background Commentary*, 795; Blount, *Revelation*, 237.

before, is that 12.9 does not seem to speak of any pre-Edenic fall. But neither does chapter 12 mitigate against it.

While this investigation is not demonstrably conclusive, it seems more probable than not that Satan was indeed one of the good angels and perhaps one of the more high-ranking angels given his authority over the fallen ones. And if this is true, then he, like his fellow fallen comrades, was among those who were "cast out." This scenario seems to do the most justice to God's perfection and is reinforced by Satan's governing of the fallen angels as a corresponding reality to Michael and the good angels under his charge.

The Edenic Serpent

The Book of Genesis is home to the chronicles of the temptation of the first humans, Adam and Eve, in its opening chapters. As the narrative goes, the "serpent" tempted Eve to eat of the fruit of the tree of knowledge of good and evil–a tree of which God explicitly forbade Adam and Eve from partaking. Though Satan is not mentioned by name in Genesis 3 (i.e., that no cognate of śāṭān is used), later Jewish tradition came to (implicitly) identify the "serpent" with Satan as possibly evidenced by the Wisdom of Solomon 2.24 ("but through the devil's envy death entered the world, and those who belong to his party experience it"; RSV[65]) and the later John the Revelator's explicit connection in Rev 12.9 and 20.2 ("the old serpent [who is] the Devil and Satan"). Though we must consider that the Revelator may only be, or *is also*, making a connection with the chaos serpent of Ps 74.13, Isa 27.1, Job 3.8, and 41.1–22.[66] But in terms of its original content, Genesis 3 does not explicitly tie itself in with the Satan of the later-developed (apocalyptic) Judaism that gave rise to the Revelator's identification. As some commentators point out, it is difficult in its original context not to see that

---

65. One might surmise, as did Clement of Rome (d. 99 AD), that this is a reference, not to Adam and Eve's partaking of the fruit, but to Cain's murdering of his brother Abel. While it may seem difficult to see how Cain can be construed as the origin of death when Genesis already makes clear that the introduction of death was due to the Edenic curse of mankind (3.19), that "death entered the world" could also be merely descriptive of death's first historical occurrence. Kelly (*Satan*, 71ff) thinks that the *diabolos* of 2.24 is likely someone other than the familiar Satan, especially since death's introduction is due to the *diabolos's envy* (74–75)–a motivation not obviously present in the serpent of Genesis 3. One might surmise, as did Clement of Rome (d. 99 AD), that Cain–whose motivation accords well with envy–is the one to have introduced death into mankind, viz., that mankind has first come acquainted with its reality through Cain's action. On the other hand, the Pseudepigraphal writings suppose that the Edenic serpent was indeed motivated out of envy of Adam's special status over creation (Apocalypse of Moses 16.1–5; 2 Enoch 31.3–6). Add to this the canonical Paul's contention that the introduction of death is due the original rebellion of mankind (Rom 5.12–19) and these reasons make it more likely that Wisdom 2.24's *diabolos*, which is also another title-description of Satan, refers to the serpent.

66. See Jones, "Lions, Serpents, and Lion-Serpents in Job 28:8"; Lewis, "CT 13.33–34 and Ezekiel 32"; Murison, "Serpent in the Old Testament."

the "serpent" *just is* a beast of the field (3.1).[67] Indeed, this is the oldest recorded view of the serpent. We may refer to this as the literal view (*peshat*), for it takes the account at face value.

Nevertheless, there are some textual clues *within* Genesis itself that make the so-called literal view questionable.[68] First, the serpent should not be one of the beasts of the field for the simple reason that God had made everything–human and animal included–"good" (1.31). That a serpent who is presumably established to be an adversary of God should be one of the "good" members of his creation is too awkward for the story. Second, based on many translations of 3.1, the serpent is considered shrewder "than any *other* beasts of the field," and yet "other" is not present in the original Hebrew. So understood, 3.1 no more requires that the serpent be one of the beasts of the field than the Psalmist's declaration that "I have more understanding than all my teachers" (Ps 119.99) makes the Psalmist one of the teachers. Given that the curse imposed on the serpent was a curse "above all [other?] livestock and above all [other?] beasts of the field" (Gen 3.14), the addition of "other" would seem to imply that the other animals were likewise cursed, which is out of place in and unwarranted by Genesis 3. This likely means that since the structure of 3.1 is similar to 3.14, 3.1 makes more sense on a reading that intends to set the serpent *apart* from the beasts of the field instead of as one *of* the beasts of the field. In other words, 3.1 merely conveys the serpent's "otherness" as one opposed to the (non-shrewd) beasts of the field. All of this is just to emphasize that nothing about 3.1 makes the literal interpretation the correct one.

However, more can be inferred. The explicit mention of the angelic Cherubim (v. 24) along with God's cryptic pronouncement that "the man has become like one *of us* in knowing good and evil" (v. 22; emphasis mine) suggest to the reader that the serpent might be a part of a wider celestial company. This is especially intriguing when one considers that part of the angelic company includes the Seraphim (Isa 6.2–6) which, as we have already seen, means "fiery (flying) *serpents*." They have among their attributes, even if metaphorically, "feet" and "wings." That the serpent is cursed to move only "on [its] belly" (Gen 3.14) might be a subtle reference to the revocation of its angelic wings and feet. Alternatively, it could also allude to the serpent-lion-dragon motif of the ancient Near East in which case the recipient of God's curse is not necessarily a literal serpentine creature. Such would be to connect the primordial chaos monsters that are themselves quadrupedal to the undisclosed villain in the Garden.[69] Either way these serve to underscore the Revelator's connection of the Satanic serpent-dragon. Otherwise its being cursed to move on its belly seems rather vacuous

---

67. This view was held by the majority of rabbinic Jews as well as the Jewish historian Josephus. See his *Antiquities of the Jews* I.4. For more recent support on this interpretation, see Davidson, Stibbs, and Kevan, *New Bible Commentary*, 79.

68. Ronning, "Curse of the Serpent," 127–35.

69. See Jones, "Lions, Serpents, and Lion-Serpents in Job 28:8"; Lewis, "CT 13.33–34 and Ezekiel 32"; Mowinckel, "לחש."

Theological Foundations for a Christian Philosophy of Demonology

for a creature that already moves about this way. (It is no wonder that rabbinic Jews, in insisting on a literal interpretation, imagined the serpent as having legs and walking upright![70]).

Now the New Testament, outside of Rev 20.2, seems to draw some connection between Satan and the serpent of Genesis 3 in other ways. For example, Matthew and Paul speak of "the tempter" which is equated with Satan (Matt 4.3; 1 Thess 3.5). The use of the definite article might smuggle in a subtle connection with the Edenic serpent. That the devil is called a "murderer from the beginning" and the "father of lies" in John 8.44 perhaps hearkens back to the Garden of Eden as "the beginning" (cf., Gen 1.1), especially since it was the serpent's temptation that inaugurated mankind's death (cf., Rom 5.12) by means of a lie (Gen 3.13). Paul notes that the "God of peace will soon crush Satan under your feet" (Rom 16.20) which may be a deliberate approximation of the *protoevangelium* of Genesis 3 wherein the serpent's defeat is threatened to obtain at the hands of Eve's future descendant(s) (v. 15). Add to this the Synoptic fact that the temptation of Jesus himself (Matt 4.1–11; Mark 1.12–13; Luke 4.1–13) serves as an apparent counterpart to the temptation in the Garden of Eden. For Jesus, as the *last* Adam (1 Cor 15.45), successfully wards off the temptation of Satan unlike his Edenic predecessors. It is not surprising that Jesus had subsequently promised that his disciples shall "tread on *serpents* and scorpions" in Luke 10.19 (emphasis mine), especially after having just mentioned Satan in verse 18! This also dovetails nicely with the aforementioned statement by Paul in Rom 16.20.

While none of this is definitive, we have *some* indication cobbled from certain scriptural passages that allow us to infer that the serpent in the Garden was, in some sense, the devil himself. Given the entirety of Scripture and its fuller developments embodied in the New Testament, particularly once we arrive at Revelation, it is difficult *not* to see the serpent of Genesis 3 as Satan. But then the lurking, unanswered question presents itself: *In what sense was the devil a serpent?*[71] We *could* say that Satan *possessed* a serpent.[72] But since the serpent apparently has vocal cords and limbs, this does not seem to be the simpler interpretation (especially if one imagines Satan to have powers that enable him to morph a serpentine creature into a quadrupedal orator). Perhaps the serpent was an *apparition* of a snake.[73] But such a view fails to account for why Satan would choose to appear as a *detestable* creature rather than as a welcoming one like a kitten or a koala bear. This is especially questionable when tradition has it that Satan always appears "as an angel of light" (2 Cor 11.14).

---

70. E.g., *Genesis Rabbah* 19, on 3.1; 20.5; Abraham Ibn Ezra, *Ibn Ezra's Commentary*, 65–67; Rabbi Eleazar of Worms, *Midrash we-Perush 'al ha-Torah*, 1, Genesis.

71. We shall revisit the various nuances of how the devil could be, or could assume, the serpent of Genesis 3 in chapter 10.

72. Augustine, *De Genesi Ad Litteram*, XXVIII.35; Schaeffer, *Genesis*, 75–80; Delitzsch, *Genesis*, 146–49.

73. Heiser, "The Nachash (הַנָּחָשׁ) and His Seed."

Part I: Background

It turns out that serpent imagery is replete throughout ancient Jewish and other ancient Near Eastern cultures. It is quite prominent in all of the major civilizations familiar to Israel, including Egypt, Akkadia, Babylon, Greece, and Rome. Moreover, most of these regimes were outright oppressive to Jews. That these oppressive regimes would have used the image of a serpent to underscore the alleged divine and sage characteristics of their leaders makes exploiting that imagery as iconographically representative of the villain in the Garden of Eden rather appropriate.[74] For the regimes that tempted and oppressed God's people were consistently thought to be governed by Satan himself (cf., Dan 10.20; Rev 12–13). That Satan is described as a serpent (as well as a dragon, Rev 12.9) reflects what John Walton calls "imagistic" thinking.[75] He likens the use of "serpent" to Vincent van Gogh's *The Starry Night* wherein such a representation is not meant to be a literal "scientific" description, as if Van Gogh were doing astronomy, but rather an artistic representation used to highlight certain characteristic(s) of the participants in the narrative. On such a model, one imagines that Satan merely tempted Eve in the same way demons are alleged to tempt believers to this day–through internal, mental influence (cf., Acts 5.3). And that such an encounter draws upon ancient iconography in impugning the enemies of Israel, and so the enemies of God. I find this to be the most plausible way to construe the serpent of Genesis 3, though nothing crucial at this stage hangs on it.[76] At the very least, there are some good reasons for connecting the Satan of lore with the serpent of Eden.

The God of this World?

In 2 Cor 4.4, Paul tells his readers that there is a "god of this world [who] has blinded the minds of the unbelievers, to keep them from seeing the light of the gospel of the glory of Christ, who is the image of God." While most commentators think this is an explicit reference to Satan, some have demurred. One such dissident is Donald Hartley who has argued that Paul speaks cryptically of Yahweh's, and not Satan's, "non-transformational withholding of salvific wisdom."[77] He argues that the "blinding" of unbelievers to salvation is deprivational, along the lines of the previous chapter, 2 Corinthians 3, wherein Paul notes the Israelites's "hardening" of their

---

74. For example, if one accepts the traditional interpretation of Mosaic authorship, then on might see an Egyptian motif here since Egypt represents its god Atum as a serpent. But if a communal redaction of Genesis occurs in a later Babylonian context, as a number of Old Testament scholars think, there remains a serpent motif here since the supreme Babylonian city-god Marduk is symbolically represented as a snake-dragon. Either way, the ancient enemies of the Hebrews utilized serpents as icons of power and wisdom and such imagistic thinking does not change regardless of who (finally) authored Genesis.

75. Walton, *Lost World of Adam and Eve*, 137–39.

76. We shall revisit the notion that Satan is the serpent again in chapter 10.

77. See Hartley, "2 Corinthians 4:4," 1; cf., Kelly, *Satan*, 66–67.

hearts as something that results in a perpetual "veil" (2 Cor 3.14–15). Given that such veiling seems reminiscent of Isa 6.9–10's reference to Yahweh's "dulling" and "dimming" of people's understanding, along with Yahweh's being responsible for the "hardening" of Pharaoh's heart (Exod 9.12; 10.20, 27; 11.10; 14.8), identifying such veiling as God's doing seems a reasonable connection. Add to this Hartley's unsurprising contention that every argument promoting a Satanic identity "finds scant support."[78]

It seems to me, however, that since Paul explicitly connects demons to the *tous kosmokratoras* ("rulers of this world") of Eph 6.12 who are elsewhere said to engage in consistent deception (2 Cor 11.14; Gal 1.8; 1 Tim 4.1–2), we might find that a Satanic identification is more at home with the "god of this world" as historically proffered by Tertullian and Origen. The wider Jewish context that comprises the backdrop for Pauline thinking is, of course, the Torah. And the Torah indicates that there are "demons" (*šēḏîm*) which are the nefarious "new gods [*ĕlōhîm*]" of a perverse generation (Deut 32.17).[79] Furthermore, that Satan presumes of himself a certain kind of ascendancy over "the kingdoms of this world" and seeks the worship of no less than the Son of God himself (Matt 4.1–11; Luke 4.1–13) only makes the "god of this world" portrait an accurate moniker. The later, independent Johannine confession that "the whole world lies in the power of the evil one" (1 John 5.19) stands as external testimony to the "god of this world" as that which is evil. Even if 1 John's author is merely echoing a Pauline sentiment and not acting under any kind of divine inspiration, the understanding here accords better with a Satanic identification. For it finds solidarity with Paul's own identification of "the evil one" with Satan (Eph 6.16).

As an added testimony from outside the canonical Scriptures, the apocryphal Martyrdom of Isaiah (1.8–12) makes mention of a "Sammael" (or "Samael") who was later equated by some rabbinic commentaries (midrashim) with Satan (e.g., the Pirke d'Rabbi Eliezer). That "Sammael" means something like "god of the blind"[80] and was understood by Jewish Gnostics to be a blindness of intellect serve to increase the connection with the "god of this world" who specifically "has blinded the minds of unbelievers." This *may* be external verification that the "god of this world" is in fact Satan, but no doubt one that would not be so apart from the internal evidences noted above.

Though demonology neither stands nor falls on this identification, that Satan is in some sense a "god of this world" bears a truth in its own right even if it is not what Paul intended: that Satan is the unelected anti-God whose deceptions vie for the spiritual submission of the denizens of this world as if to a god.

---

78. Hartley, "2 Corinthians 4:4," 20.
79. See Heiser, "Deuteronomy 32.17."
80. Kotrosits, "Social Fragmentation," 183; Black, "Etymology for Jaldabaoth," 71–72.

Part I: Background

Conclusion

Theological foundations are important in understanding a religious object of philosophical speculation. It also allows us to narrow the scope of the data to be considered to a particular narrative rather than attempting to incorporate what every religion or outsider has to say on the matter. Hence, we have sought to undertake a sensible biblical survey of who Satan and his demons are as well as the good angels from whom they derive in accord with Christian orthodoxy. By way of summary, it appears that Scripture speaks of an aggregate of seemingly nonhuman, finite spirits residing in a transcendent world that intersects with and influences ours. These intermediary beings, which are the good angels, were directly created and deployed by God in partial support of carrying out his will for creation. At some point in the distant past, some of them abandoned their original posts and were condemned for their willful (and perhaps irredeemable) transgression. The chief of these fallen angels–these devils or demons–is known by various title-descriptions with the most notable being "Satan." Satan is the *de facto* ruler of his demonic clan.

We have not concerned ourselves with unessential questions that have no bearing on the metaphysics of these beings. For example, we have excused ourselves from any discourse about whether or not there are such things as *guardian* angels or whether there are such things as *vice* demons (i.e., a "demon of lust," a "demon of pride," etc.). I leave it to the theologian or the speculative philosopher to ruminate elsewhere on these unimportant, even if perennial, mysteries. Our attention here has been focused more on the penultimate core material regarding Satan and his demons and the necessary auxiliary tenets that set the stage for understanding the basis of demonic realism.

In the next chapter, we shall explore those in Christian history who have proffered some version of demonic realism in one form or another. Since the objectives of this book are primarily philosophical, and acknowledging that much ink has already been spilled by theologians who have written on the subject, we shall be highlighting particularly philosophy's relevant history and contribution to that realism. Following that survey, we shall explore reasons to think that such beings exist in contrast to reasons to think otherwise. And following that, we shall engage postulations for a particular way of understanding the ontology of demons and what powers and abilities they likely have as well as the arguments proffered for them.

3

Demonic Realism in the History of Christian Philosophy

IN THE PREVIOUS CHAPTER, we became acquainted with the theological foundations for a realist's construal of demonology and angelology. Therein was a preliminary examination of the Bible as to how angels are understood in the economy of God and how Satan and his rebellious angels figure as the putative architects of villainy and evil that oppose God and his human creation. But before the epic tales of demonic enmity were cast in the canons of the Old and New Testaments, belief in demons actually saturated the neighboring religious and non-religious cultures of antiquity. Of present interest is not another frolic through the literature of the ancient world and its measurable impact on the developing Christian church's narrative. For this has been accomplished in sundry book-length treatments many times over.[1] Rather, we are narrowly interested here in the specifically *philosophical* lineage found in diverse intellectual sources that helped give rise to a philosophical demonology amongst the evolving Christian church. One reason for this is to show, and perhaps even appreciate, that demonic realism has an impressive intellectual pedigree apart from, but not necessarily independent of, its theological heritage. Another reason is to reveal that, even amongst philosophers, there has been no clear univocal understanding of who and what Satan and his cohorts are and of what kinds of powers they can enact. And this is despite a recognition of Scripture as the definitive source for the church's demonology. As we shall see, these thinkers unwittingly knitted a confused tapestry of demonic realism has been bequeathed to the current generation of believing philosophers for elucidation.

---

1. E.g., Thuswaldner and Russ, *The Hermeneutics of Hell*; Almond, *The Devil*; De La Torre and Hernández, *Quest for the Historical Satan*; Kelly, *Satan*; Kelly, *The Devil*; Wray and Mobley, *The Birth of Satan*; Stanford, *The Devil*; Pagels, *The Origin of Satan*; Russell, *The Prince of Darkness*; Russell, *Mephistopheles*; Russell, *Lucifer*; Russell, *Satan*; Forsyth, *The Old Enemy*; Bamberger, *Fallen Angels*. These are some of—to borrow a phrase from Samuel Taylor Coleridge—the "devil's biographers" of the contemporary world (see *The Poetical and Dramatic Works*, 137).

Part I: Background

In this chapter we shall explore the development of the historical, metaphysical concepts of demons as advocated by (apparent) demonic realists throughout philosophy's history. I shall begin by highlighting those conceptions posed by the ancient world, specifically the Greek philosophers. Following this, I shall cover the subsequent Christian demonologies offered by its more partisan philosophers from the church Fathers to the present day. It will be apparent that the speculations of the early, premodern, and modern Christian thinkers on the subject of demonology continued to be metaphysically confusing at best and *prima facie* self-contradictory at worst. If Christians want to take the metaphysics of the demonic realm seriously, and so formulate a coherent but systematized philosophy of demonology within a conservative context, then they will need to amend or transcend the interpretive theories posed by their predecessors. Christian thinkers must opt for a theory that can at least accord with the sacred writings along with our relevant philosophical predilections. We shall begin by surveying the Greek landscape.

Early Greek Views of (Apparent[2]) Demonic Realism

Many of the ancient Greek philosophers are known for positing an animating substance–a soul (*psuchê*)–that resides in human beings and animals that can survive the death of the body. Similarly, the soul likewise constitutes the monistic ontologies of divine beings (viz., gods) in that they are *un*embodied. Concerning the genesis of views regarding the nature of the soul, it was common for pre-Socratic philosophers to think of the soul as a quasi-material, polymorphous substance that was (normally) imperceptible to bodily senses. This primal substance was, according to some of its most well-known pre-Socratic proponents (e.g., Anaximander, Anaximenes, Anaxagoras, Archelaus, and Diogenes of Apollonia), "air" (*aer*).[3] Such an aerial constitution was considered to be a reasonable fit since it explains how the soul could be inside the body, present throughout the body (or, in the case of unembodied souls, spatially located), and invisible.[4] Moreover, upon the death of any human person, "the soul aspires to the [ether], which is fiery air, whereas the body, because of its telluric nature, rejoins the earth."[5] Though the soul was not understood to be a material substance

---

2. Here as in forthcoming places I bracket "apparent" since the demonic realism putatively present in the works and sayings of the representatives may not have necessarily been actual. For example, as understood in the writings of Origen, the pagan Celsus thought that the Greeks did not hold to such realism despite using the language of such realism (Origen, *Against Celsus*, VI.42).

3. I.e., Anaximenes is reported to have said that "our soul, being air, holds us together, so do breath and air encompass the whole world" (Burnet, *Early Greek Philosophy*, 77); Diogenes says that "humans and all other animals live upon air by breathing it, and this is their soul and their intelligence" and that "the soul of all living things is the same, namely, air warmer than that outside us and in which we are, but much colder than that near the sun" (Burnet, *Early Greek Philosophy*, 361).

4. Sandywell, *Presocratic Reflexivity*, 182.

5. Mihai, "Soul's Aitherial Abode," 558.

in the sense of being corporeal and (*ceteris paribus*) susceptible to the senses, it was understood to be a quasi-material substance of a higher, divine order that could still interact and intermix with the corporeal world–an ontic distinction that appears to be one merely of degree.[6] Perceptive of the awkward implications here, Frederick Copleston had once pointed out that "the antithesis between spirit and matter had not yet been grasped" by the pre-Socratics and so "they were not fully conscious of the distinction, or at least did not realize its implications."[7] Nonetheless, the ontic substances of both divine and earthly souls are surely comprised of air. Consequently, specific things like demons would likewise be aerial beings.

Now the concept of *demon* (from the Greek *daimon, daimonion, daimoniou*) had undergone a period of evolution within the wider, thinking cultures of antiquity. In some narrower cases it was overlaid with religious motives and in others it was merely conforming to the conventional wisdom of the time. It is tempting for moderns to consider such talk of *daimonion* as a religious or literary device for handling the sinister aspect(s) of creation,[8] or perhaps as a convenient nomenclature for clever stories of superstition bent on explaining the seemingly unexplainable.[9] But these would not be the views of the intellectually-driven cultures of the time in that they are replete with discussions about intermediary beings as concretely existing, supernatural agents. It is also equally wrong and historically naïve to suppose that the *daimon* was consistently understood to be merely an agent *of evil* or the mere villain of a supernatural hero story. As far as the intellectual representatives of ancient Greece were concerned, the *daimon* was a variegated referent for a divine or superhuman power or activity, and it possessed none of the negative or evil associations which it had for later thought.[10]

Everett Ferguson discusses in his important study on Christian demonology and its Greek ideological backdrop how "demons" could refer to a wide range of possibilities: gods, agents of destiny, deceased souls, intermediary messengers, and divine guardians.[11] In the context of *daimonion* as a referent for "god," such a designation was used to refer loosely to a god either when the identity of the god was unknown or if one were emphasizing the general supernatural power coming into expression on

---

6. Aristotle wrote that air was a substance that could be used to reflect light under the right conditions: "Sight is reflected from all smooth surfaces, such as are air and water among others. Air must be condensed if it is to act as a mirror, though it often gives a reflection even uncondensed when the sight is weak" (Aristotle, *Meteorologica*, III.4.373b1: 601). This, Aristotle goes on to say, is what explains how someone may mistakenly see an apparition that turns out to be a reflection of himself.

7. Copleston, *History of Philosophy*, 20.

8. E.g., Tillich, *Systematic Theology*, 94ff; Pagels, *Origin of Satan*; De La Torre and Hernández, *Quest for the Historical Satan*.

9. I.e., Strauss, *Life of Jesus*, 21–52.

10. Ferguson, *Demonology*, 36. Perhaps Aristotle's use of *eudaimonia* (often translated simply as "happiness") is iconic evidence of the benign use of *daimon* amongst the Greeks.

11. Ferguson, *Demonology*, 36.

Part I: Background

a particular occasion.[12] It was common for *daimonion* to refer to something's being "heaven-sent," when one did not know what caused some wondrous power or event for which god may have been responsible. The invoking of *daimonion* would be used to reflect the generic notions of fortune, luck, or chance–something divine but imprecise nonetheless. It is therefore unsurprising that a variant, *daimoniou*, would also come to describe fate and sovereign destiny, which could be bad or good depending upon the context. As for demons being heroic souls in some sense, Plato's *Republic* makes mention of the "greatest, finest, and first of laws" which are described as the laws "having to do with the establishing of temples, sacrifices, and other forms of service to gods, daemons [*daimonion*], and heroes . . ."[13]

It is apparent that Hesiod (c. 750 to 650 BC), among many others, understood demons to be the proper designation of disembodied *human* souls, a fairly common Greek notion during this time.[14] For Hesiod in particular, demons figured as the classification of a deceased race. According to Hesiod himself, this deceased race is a "golden race of men" who lived without any suffering.[15] That Christian writers in the second century made frequent mention of demons as the souls of the departed would not be without precedent in the ancient Greek world as evidenced here. Such is a testament to Hesiod's influence.

For Socrates (c. 470 to 399 BC), it was not uncommon for him to speak of a personal *daimon* that would influence his behavior. For him, it was a sort of negative voice restraining him from doing certain actions.[16] This is a theme picked up by his student Plato (c. 427/428 to 348/347 BC) who goes so far as to suggest that every person *chooses* his own demon: "your daemon or guardian spirit will not be assigned to you by lot; you will choose him."[17] Early Stoic philosophers adhered to the idea that

---

12. Ferguson, *Demonology*, 37–38.

13. Plato, *The Republic*, IV.427b: 144.

14. Ferguson, *Demonology*, 41.

15. Ferguson, *Demonology*, 40. Hesiod says that "they are called pure spirits [*daimones*; 'demons'] dwelling on the earth and are kindly, delivering from harm, and guardians of mortal men; for they roam everywhere over the earth, clothed in mist and keep watch on judgements and cruel deeds, givers of wealth; for this royal right also they received" (Hesiod, *Works and Days*, II.121–139: 6). Hesiod also writes, "And Eos bare to Tithonus brazen-crested Memnon, king of the Ethiopians, and the Lord Emathion. And to Cephalus she bare a splendid son, strong Phaethon, a man like the gods, whom, when he was a young boy in the tender flower of glorious youth with childish thoughts, laughter-loving Aphrodite seized and caught up and made a keeper of her shrine by night, a divine spirit [viz., 'demon']" (*Theogony* II.984–991:54). Based on these, Hesiod's association of the demons with the souls of the deceased is apparent.

16. See Plato, *Thaetetus*, 151a; *Apology*, 24c, 40a. Plutarch has written on Socrates's demon (Plutarch, *A Discourse Concerning Socrates's Daemon*, 378ff); also see Ferguson, *Demonology*, 43. Merrill F. Unger notes how some have interpreted Socrates's *daimonion* to be merely the personification of the voice of God or conscience (see his *Biblical Demonology*, 57 n. 40), something that seems captured in Plato's *Timaeus* (e.g., 90a–90c).

17. Plato, *Republic*, X.617d: 1220; cf., Ferguson, *Demonology*, 43.

demons were supervisory spirits that might also serve as individual consciences for each person to tap.

It was also acknowledged by Plato that the demons were beings whose nature was in some sense a hybrid between the gods and man—a sort of intermediary ontology.[18] This notion would come to influence subsequent demonologies, particularly those within the Hellenistic and Christian traditions, for numerous centuries to follow. For Plato, the very nature of demons would be somewhat of a hybrid between an upper and lower class of being (something like Heracles was as the offspring of Zeus and a mortal woman). They also served as *messengers* between distinct parties (something like Hermes, a messenger and emissary of the gods) akin to the role typically assigned in the Old Testament to the *mal'akim* (Hebrew for "angels")[19] and in the New Testament to the *aggeloi* (Greek for "angels").[20] This is to say that there are intermediary beings or envoys commuting between the divine and human realms in order to communicate and carry out certain duties from God to humankind.[21] Their nature, according to Plato, is a synthesis of divine and terrestrial substances rendering it possible for demonic intercourse between the two worlds. As such, they are substantially composed of something between body and spirit. As a consequence, it was thought that demons might conceal themselves behind iconic statues and images until such a time as they would infiltrate the human priests.[22] Sympathetic to their being of an elevated status over humans, Plato speaks of "Cronus, who was well-disposed to man [and] placed us in the care of the [demons], a superior order of beings."[23]

Others, such as Pythagoras (c. 570 to 495 BC), Xenocrates (c. 339/8 to 314/3 BC), and Chrysippus (c. 279 to 206 BC), also share a common demonology with Plato from

---

18. Plato writes: "'What is [Eros] ... Diotima?' 'He's a great spirit, Socrates. Everything spiritual, you see, is in between god and mortal.' 'What is their function?' I asked. 'They are messengers who shuttle back and forth between the two, conveying prayer and sacrifice from men to gods, while to men they bring commands from the gods and gifts in return for sacrifices. Being in the middle of the two, they round out the whole and bind fast the all to all. Through them all divination passes, through them the art of priests in sacrifice and ritual, in enchantment, prophecy, and sorcery. Gods do not mix with men; they mingle and converse with us through the spirits instead, whether we are awake or asleep. He who is wise in any of these ways is a man of the spirit, but he who is wise in any other way, in a profession or any manual work, is merely a mechanic. These spirits are many and various, then, and one of them is [Eros]'" (*Symposium*, 202d–203a: 486).

19. Gen 19; 28.12; 32.1; Ps 78.49; 91.11; 103.20.

20. Matt 4.6, 11; 13.41; 24.31; Mark 1.13; 13.27; Luke 4.10; 16.22; Gal 3.19; Heb 2.2, 7; 13.2; 2 Pet 2.11; Rev 3.5; 7.2; 9.15; 12.7; 16.1; 17.1; 21.9.

21. There are some important distinctions worth noting. For example, the Greek concept of the intermediate regarding such beings is one of necessity because "Gods do not mix with men" (see n. 18). As such, they were the necessary medium of any bidirectional commerce between mankind and God. The biblical concept does not describe such intermediaries as necessary but simply as unidirectional, *de facto* messengers from God to man.

22. See Conybeare, "Demonology of the New Testament," 607.

23. Plato, *Laws*, IV.713d: 1400.

which Plutarch (c. 46 to 120 AD) later systematizes into a demonology.[24] These intermediary beings are entities of the divine order even though they share in the nature of man's soul and surpass human nature. As a result, such demons possess "perceptive faculties of the body . . . with a susceptibility to pleasure and pain" varying in "degrees of virtue and vice."[25] Grecian demonology eventually was developed to emphasize demonic actions as salient causes of sinister human actions as evidenced by the works of Plutarch (specifically his *Morals*) in reporting on Chrysippus and the later Stoics.[26] Plutarch elsewhere discusses the familiar phenomenon of demonic possession (or *demonization* as it is sometimes referred).[27] That demons would inhabit humans and wreak havoc and insanity on them was an already-established belief among these and earlier Greek representatives.[28] It is not surprising that belief in demonic possession led to efforts to expel demons by the use of magic.[29] Further evidence of higher demonology among the Greeks also comes from the Hermetic tradition.[30] According to an apt summary by Ferguson, "[w]e have thus reached elements of Greek thought which clearly are in the background of New Testament times and influenced Christian thinking in the post-biblical times."[31]

Though there exist similarities between the demonological pneumatologies of the ancient Greek understanding and the ante-Nicene Christian understanding with its New Testament backdrop, there are undoubtedly stark contrasts of thought–not the least of which is the construal of demons as deceased persons or as demigods working for God. But, given the variations of Greek thought on demons, one can only conclude that though demons were genuine, present personalities with a marked influence on human conscience, they were far from being captured by any consistent metaphysical description. Curiously, the Greek *daimonion* has more in common with the Catholic doctrine of the intercession and invocation of saints than with the wider Christian doctrine of angelology. As we will see in the Jewish and Christian portraits of demonology below, the Greeks were not alone in their ambiguous understanding of this realm.

---

24. Plutarch writes: "[O] of certain grand Daemons, whom Plato, Pythagoras, Xenocrates, and Chrysippus (following herein the opinion of the most ancient theologists) affirm to be of greater strength than men, and to transcend our nature by much in power, but not to have a divine part pure and unmixed, but such as participates of both the soul's nature and the body's sensation, capable of receiving both pleasure and pain, and all the passions that attend these mutations, which disorder some of them more and others of them less. For there are divers degrees both of virtue and vice, as among men, so also among Daemons" (*Of Isis and Osiris* 25. 360d–e, 86).

25. Plutarch, *Isis and Osiris*, 25.360e: 86.

26. *Dinner of Seven Wise Men*, 7.153a; *Stoic Contradictions*, 37.1051c; *Roman Questions*, 51.277a.

27. *Life of Marcellus*, 20.5f.

28. See Euripides, *Hippolytus*, 141ff.

29. Ferguson, *Demonology*, 54.

30. *Corpus Hermeticum*, XVI.10f.

31. Ferguson, *Demonology*, 51.

The Old Testament and Early Jewish Views of (Apparent) Demonic Realism

In terms of explicit designation, the Old Testament has very little to say concerning demons. The Greek translation of the Old Testament (the Septuagint, or LXX for short) utilizes *daimoniois* for the Hebrew root *shed* ("devils") in only two places: Deut 32.17 and Ps 106.37. And in both of these instances it seems that *shed* refers to pagan idols. It is unclear from the immediate context of those passages, however, whether the understanding of *unembodied, intermediary beings* is to be adopted as the nature of the power or identity behind the icons.[32] Isa 13.21 and 34.14 speak of the "satyr" (Hebrew: *sa'iyr*; "[hairy] he-goat") and are translated as *daimonia* in the LXX.[33] Theologian Merrill F. Unger, who did his doctoral work on demonology, explains that "Israelites considered these demonic conceptions to be goat-like in aspect or attributes" and that the Septuagint's use of *daimonia* is evidence that "Alexandrian Jews considered them to be demons."[34] Moreover, Leviticus 16.8–10, 26 speak of a cryptic *ăzāzēl* (or "Azazel" if it is the name of a demon) that has been popularly understood to be merely a goat used in a purification ritual–the so-called "scapegoat."[35] However, as evidenced by the Pseudepigraphal I Enoch,[36] a number of post-Exilic Jews came to think that this *ăzāzēl* refers to the name of a demon, in which case the sins of the community were heaped onto this goat and sent away unto the demon Azazel in contradistinction to the goat sent unto the Lord.[37] Regardless which is the correct understanding of *ăzāzēl*, the point is that by the time Jewish apocalypticism set in, demons were perceived to

---

32. Unger seems to think so (*Biblical Demonology*, 59–60). On page 60, Unger points out that the Psalmist's statement that "all the gods of the peoples are idols, But the LORD made the heavens" in Ps 96.5 has *'eliyl* ("worthless," "good for nothing," or "idols") translated in the LXX as *daimonia*. This would seem to support Unger's overall conclusion that "the demons behind them are the real existences" (61) even if Ps 106.37 or Deut 32.17 themselves do not. The same can be said about Isa 65.11: "But you who forsake the LORD, Who forget My holy mountain, Who set a table for Fortune [*daimoni*; LXX], And who fill cups with mixed wine for Destiny . . ."

33. Leviticus 17.7 and 2 Chron 11.15 mention the *sa'iyr* ("[hairy] he-goats") which some translations read as "demons," but the LXX simply translates these as *mataiois* ("idols") instead of *daimonia*.

34. Unger, *Biblical Demonology*, 60.

35. The word "*ăzā'zēl* could be a compound term, consisting of the noun *'ez* ('goat') and the verb *'azal* ('go away, disappear'), that is, a 'goat that departs/goes away' (cf., lxx). This leads to the traditional rendering of *scapegoat* (av, niv), since the goat departs bearing all the Israelites's sins" (Sklar, *Leviticus*, 209). Sklar also stipulates that "the Lord typically tells his people to have absolutely nothing to do with false gods (Exod 23:24; 34:13; Deut 12:3), as he in fact does in the very next chapter (17:7). One wonders whether he would involve a demon in this rite, even in such a negative way, and risk the Israelites turning the rite into some form of appeasement to this demon."

36. E.g., 1 Enoch 8.1; 9.6; 10.4, 9; 13.1; 54.4; 55.4; 69.2–3.

37. Milgrom, *Leviticus*, 1020.

be goat-like.[38] It is perhaps unsurprising, then, that corrupt leaders and nonbelievers would later be metaphorized as "goats."[39]

Apart from arguments and inferences that can be made from the Hebrew Scriptures as standalone testaments for teasing out a more developed demonology,[40] the explicit notion of a race of rebellious angels headed up by an archrival may not have been in view during the (initial) writing of the Pentateuch and Job. The more familiar portrait of disenfranchised, fallen angels being superintended by their chief, Satan, is not something that appears to be obvious or even likely simply given the Hebrew corpus at the time. Even less so any notion that demons should reside in dybbuk boxes, possess human beings, and be directly summoned for nefarious purposes. What *is* apparent is that at some time during the Babylonian Captivity or Exile of the sixth century BC, such views were certainly beginning to bloom. And it is not until the intertestamental literature does one find the more fanciful demonologies as espoused by later Jewish mystics. Since the views that came out of the Exile are reflected in subsequent Christian thinking, let us now turn to the relevant literature.

In the intertestamental literature we find that it is filled with examples of evil spirits (yet another designation of the demons) interacting with human beings. In fact, there are references to one of the offences of the demons as having sexual intercourse with human women–a Pseudepigraphal reference based on the canonical writings as commentated on in the Pseudepigrapha. In the original passage giving rise to such commentaries, Gen 6.1–4, we have an oft-cited story concerning a race of beings with the appellation "sons of God" who are said to take the "daughters of men" as wives and produce offspring as a result of a conjugal union. But it is surely awkward if not downright contradictory to the Jewish understanding that marriage and subsequent childbearing would not be considered consecrated practices. It also seems incommensurate with the Old Testament (as well as the New Testament)[41] that the practices of men given in marriage would inevitably result in such widespread judgment.[42] Consequently, Jews inevitably interpreted this passage as a reference, not to men, but to angels, viz., fallen angels (and/or demons). Certain Pseudepigraphal

---

38. It may be tempting to suppose that this understanding was influenced by the Greek god Pan who is often depicted as having a similar appearance to that of a faun. However, it is also possible that the 'ăzā'zēl of Leviticus 16 along with the connotation of 17.7 collectively might indicate that the Semitic understanding preceded those of ancient Greece so that the direction of influence was perhaps reversed.

39. See Daniel's discussion of *tsaphiyr* ("goat") as the envisioned eschatological King of Greece in Daniel 8 and Jesus's overt usage of "young goats" (*eriphion*) for the inhospitable in Matt 25.32–46 vis-à-vis the hospitable who are contrastingly represented as "sheep."

40. See chapter 2.

41. Cf., John 2.1–2.

42. The passage goes on to emphatically declare this judgement that ultimately culminates in the story of Noah: "And the LORD said, 'I will blot out man whom I have created from the face of the land, from man to animals to creeping things and to birds of the sky; for I am sorry that I have made them'" (Gen 6.7).

writings (i.e., Jubilees and 1 Enoch), completed no later than the first century BC, suggest that the sons of God of Genesis 6 were actually conspiring angels who were condemned for their wickedness and corruption through their unnatural unions with human women and their consequential offspring as physical "giants" of a sort.[43] The author of 1 Enoch saw demons as being the spirits of the giants which resulted from the forbidden sexual intercourse between those angels and women.[44]

Other stories, those not predicated on interpreting any portion of Torah or the broader Old Testament, are told about *specific* demons who villainously engage in human affairs. For example, in the book of Tobit, the demon Asmodeus is said to have interrupted the consummation of the marriages of Sarah (daughter of Raquel) on seven occasions by slaying the groomsmen. Asmodeus is said to have loved Sarah and so would not let anyone even approach her.[45] Parallels with stories about the Greek pantheon surely come to mind, and this is due to the obvious anthropomorphizing of demons that seemingly occurs here.

Therefore, the unfolding of Jewish demonology seems to indicate that as we go from the earlier canonical writings to the later non-canonical commentaries on various canonical accounts and beyond, we see an evolving understanding of the demons that were later described in familiar terms as sinister spirits that would interact with humans in physical and personal ways (*how* this can be is never countenanced). But in the canonical works, demons tend to be described in ways that are not clarified, e.g., that they might be "hairy goats," that they *may* have been involved with or are a result of the "daughters of men," and that they are the concrete forces behind the idols of Israel's enemies. Even more elusive is the identity and role of Satan outside of the cryptic references of certain angels being described as *functional* adversaries. As such, there exists an obvious hermeneutical danger of retrojecting later interpretations onto previous passages from which no clear exegesis can manifest. There is no doubt, then, that the intrusion of the demonic in the material universe according to Jewish thinking is surely a pervasive feature. But it is the non-canonical writings that tend toward a portrayal of direct demonic interaction with human beings in order to explain such invasions. Yet given the power of angels to appear before and interact with human observers, perhaps the evil counterparts may be doing the same in their mating shenanigans with human women.

The scriptural portions, left uncolored by commentary, do not necessarily envisage a clear materialistic ontology for demonic beings (if the relevant passages even refer to such things as superhuman villainous realities) and so a thorough Jewish demonology seems to tend toward ambivalence. Moreover, there is no clear explanation

---

43. See 1 Enoch 6.1–6; 15.8–16.2; 2 Enoch 18; 29.4f; Jubilees 11.5. The Hebrew term *nəp̄îlîm* along with *gibbôrîm* in Gen 6.4 is often translated as "the fallen ones–the giants." For more on Genesis 6 and the identity of the *nəp̄îlîm*, see chapter 10.

44. Ferguson, *Demonology*, 70.

45. Ferguson, *Demonology*, 77.

as to how these demons go from being "spirits" to creatures that are overtly physical and sensate.

Let us now consider the Christian traditions which have further shaped demonology amongst the philosophers.

The New Testament's Portrait of (Apparent) Demonic Realism

During the period represented in the New Testament, the demonology of first-century Palestine (shaped in part by both Jewish and Greek sources) is already a matured system that affirms an unspecified number of adversarial fallen angels called "demons." These sinister spirits roguishly influence the behavior of human beings and are convivial with earthly governments and movements in some undisclosed way. As was believed at the time of Jesus, demons were responsible for social, moral, and even physical ills wrought upon individuals and nations under the supervision of Satan, their chief and leader in the struggle to oppose God and his creation. Satan and his demons seem to have become a kingdom of their own–a perfidious aggregate of spiritual beings forever bent on undermining the trajectory of God's plans. As the true agents behind the oppressive Egyptian, Sumerian, Persian, Assyrian, Babylonian, Seleucid, and Roman empires of times past and present, the demons are malicious creatures determined to destroy the ones created in the image of God, viz., human beings. Human beings are, thus, the privileged of creation to share in the fellowship of God at the eschatological restitution of earth and so are the prime targets of demonic oppression (cf., 1 Pet 5.1–11).

In contrast to the Old Testament, the New Testament is quite imbued with references to demons, Satan (or the devil), and their active engagement with God and humanity.[46] Matthew chapters 8–12 contain reports of demonic exorcisms performed by Jesus (and mirrored by both his followers as well as his admirers) followed by criticism of such by the detractors of his day. Mark and Luke are equally pregnant with intermittent discussions about Jesus's victory over demons and the kingdom of Satan. Satan himself plays a primary and intimate role in opposing Jesus, from his temptation in the wilderness[47] to his betrayal by Judas.[48] The Apostle Paul himself, having written most of the post-Gospels New Testament with some of his works ranking as the earliest to be produced, treats the Christian believer as though he were in a direct state of war with this satanic kingdom.[49] John the Revelator also discusses the role Satan has for both the present world (Rev 2.13, 24) and the eschatological one to come (Rev 12.9; 20.2, 7).[50] Consistent with that, the New Testament describes demons as spiritual

46. Recall chapter 2.
47. See Matt 4.1–11 and Mark 1.12–13.
48. See Luke 22.3 and John 13.27.
49. See Rom 16.20, 2 Cor 2.11, and Eph 6.11–20, just to name a few.
50. The eschatological world of judgement has been interpreted to be either the generation of Jesus (precipitated by the destruction of the Jewish Temple in 70 AD) with the binding of Satan as a present

beings, candidly calling them evil "spirits"[51] and identifying their (original) abode as otherworldly.[52] The New Testament further describes the "spirit" as something that is naturally understood to be incorporeal[53] and "invisible."[54] Jeffrey Burton Russell offers a summary description of Satan as he appears to be described in the New Testament:

> The Devil of the New Testament is the prince of this world of space (*kosmos*) and time (*aiōn*), as opposed to Jesus Christ, whose kingdom is not of this world. To some extent, Satan is the lord of matter and flesh as opposed to spirit. . . . Satan is the prime adversary of Christ. He tried to tempt Christ but failed. He sought Christ's death, yet at the same time tried to avert the act of redemption. Following the death and ascension of Christ, the Devil tries to thwart the Lord's victory by attacking and perverting humanity. Satan tempts people; he causes illness and death. He obsesses and possesses individuals and tempts human beings to sin. He is the leader of a host of evil spirits. He and his followers will be defeated and punished by Christ at the end of the world.[55]

Beyond that, continues Russell, the New Testament has "left a great many questions of diabology open to future theologians."[56]

We have already seen that the antecedent Greek views of demonology were often inconsistent in their descriptions of demons (advocating the "spiritual" nature of demons while affirming their having various physical properties, and supposing them to be discarnate human beings and also demi-gods). We are about to see that the Christian views, beginning with the early philosophers of the church, were no different and that the following tide of Christian demonology itself engendered an equally confusing portrait. The Patristics seemed to acknowledge likewise the spiritual nature of the demons but ultimately their demonology also incorporated some aspect of physicality in describing that spiritual nature. Though such demonic creatures are considered to be (fallen angelic) *spirits*, they have also been conspicuously described as beings that could be physically perceived.

In the next section, we shall explore a sampling of some of the most influential Patristic philosophical thinkers regarding Christian demonology.

---

reality or a later conflict merely foreshadowed by the destruction of the Temple that has not yet been realized.

51. See the consistent use of *pneuma* ("spirit") in describing the demons in Luke 7.21; 8.2; Acts 19.12–13, 15–16; 23.9.

52. See Luke 8.31; 10.18; Eph 6.12; Rev 12.9.

53. See Luke 24.39.

54. Compare John 4.24's description of God as *pneuma* ("spirit") with 1 Tim 1.17's affirmation that God is invisible. However, it seems implied in Luke 24.37 that spirits *could* be seen. But this can be explained by suggesting that visibility was divinely induced (cf., Matt 17.1–9) and, so, not necessarily the inherent natural property of the spirit itself. Or, perhaps the disciples's expectation that a soul would be visible was just an understandable mistake on their part.

55. Russell, *Satan*, 27.

56. Russell, *Satan*, 27.

Part I: Background

Patristic Views of Demonic Realism

Justin Martyr's (100 to 165 AD) view of demonology is central to his world view,[57] and according to Ferguson, it not only "introduce[s] but also [outlines] much that is to be said about early Christian demonology."[58] In *The Second Apology*, Justin's demonology is inaugurated by his affirmation that the demons just are "evil spirits."[59] His interpretation of Genesis 6 later in the same work supposes that these "spirits" are not at all devoid of material properties. He says that the sons of God of Genesis 6 are fallen angels that "were captivated by love of women, and begat children who are those that are called demons."[60] The later Lactantius (c. 250 to 325 AD) shared this view thereby showing how pervasive and influential this understanding was.[61] These deviant angels and their birthed demons went "among man [and] sowed murders, wars, adulteries, intemperate deeds, and all wickedness."[62] A contemporary of Justin's, Athenagoras the Athenian (c. 133 to c. 190 AD), similarly affirmed that "the souls of the giants . . . are the demons" and even adds that they "are eager for the blood of the sacrifices [made to idols], and lick them."[63] All of this seems to clash with the modern *prima facie* idea that the demons are spirit (*pneuma*). For the Greeks, that a *daimon* might be "spirit" and (finely) material at the same time was not problematic. But in Christianity, God is also a "spirit" (cf., John 4.24) and it has been customary to insist that God is devoid of *any* material constitution–fine or otherwise–whatsoever. So what is not problematic for the Greeks is very problematic for Christians.

Tatian the Assyrian (c. 120 to 180 AD), another contemporary of Justin Martyr, adds to Justin's view that "none of the demons possess [*sic*] flesh; their structure is spiritual, like that of fire or air."[64] In chapter XVI of his *Address to the Greeks*, he would later identify the constitution of demons to be a species of *matter* to be distinguished from the "lower matter" of humans. Thus, someone like Tertullian (c. 155 to 240 AD) is able to describe them as "invisible and intangible, [and so] we are not cognizant of their action save by its effects, as when some inexplicable, unseen poison in the breeze blights the apples and the grain while in the flower."[65] According to Tertullian, they also have location in that they "[dwell] in the air [in] nearness to the stars [and have]

---

57. Barnard, *Justin Martyr*, 107.

58. Ferguson, *Demonology*, 106. As an example, Athenagoras (c. 133 to 190) agrees with Justin and the matured Jewish demonology as described in I Enoch.

59. Justin Martyr, *The Second Apology* I: 188. Justin uses the phrase again in chapters VII and XIII.

60. Justin Martyr, *The Second Apology* V: 190. This view is also shared by Lanctantius (see his *The Divine Institutes*, II.15).

61. See Lactantius, *The Divine Institutes*, II.15.

62. Lactantius, *The Divine Institutes*, II.15: 64.

63. Athenagoras, *A Plea for the Christians*, XXV and XXVI: 407–8.

64. Tatian, *Address of Tatian to the Greeks*, XV: 21.

65. Tertullian, *Apology*, XXII: 39.

commerce with the clouds."⁶⁶ Origen (184/185 to 253/254 AD) suggests additional geographical locations where the demons "haunt the denser parts of bodies" as well as the "unclean places upon earth" and yet all the while they are devoid of "bodies of earthly material."⁶⁷ In solidarity with his Christian contemporaries, Origen believed that demons possessed an incorporeal nature. But, also like his contemporaries, he thinks that such a nature is to be identified as a "material spirit"⁶⁸ *qua* an aerial substance such that it exhibits certain physical properties like weight.⁶⁹ Origen supposed that demons, which also reside in the air, could breathe in the vapors of earthly sacrifices and of blood from which they may acquire nourishment.⁷⁰ This function implies that they would have olfactory senses and some kind of digestive system.

The Fathers also comment about what the demons can *do*–specifically what they can do *to others*. Justin Martyr said that the demons are capable of "effecting apparitions of themselves" and so have "both defiled women and corrupted boys, and showed such fearful sights to men."⁷¹ He states that they can variously appear "in dreams, and sometimes by magical impositions."⁷² According to Tatian, demons "are seen . . . by the men possessed of soul, when, as sometimes, they exhibit themselves to men" whether to deceive or to destroy.⁷³ Tertullian speaks of how dynamic and intimate their interaction with the world is in that "[demons] inflict, accordingly, upon our bodies diseases and other grievous calamities."⁷⁴ He says "by an influence equally obscure, demons and angels breathe into the soul, and rouse up its corruptions with furious passions and vile excesses."⁷⁵ They can even heal diseases they themselves create:

> For, first of all, they make you ill; then, to get a miracle out of it, they command the application of remedies either altogether new, or contrary to those in use, and straightway withdrawing hurtful influence, they are supposed to have wrought a cure.⁷⁶

---

66. Tertullian, *Apology*, XXII: 39.
67. Origen, *Against Celsus*, IV.92: 538.
68. Origen, *De Principiis*, III.4.2: 338.
69. Russell, *Satan*, 125ff. This view is also in agreement with the pre-Socratics and Plato. While being an incorporeal substance that is supernatural, one cannot help but imagine "material spirit" to not be anything other than paradoxical and oxymoronic on its face.
70. Origen, *Against Celsus*, VII. 5; VIII.30–33, 60–61. According to VII.5, the constitutional makeup of a created being can actually be altered on the basis of that being's moral behavior.
71. *The First Apology*, V: 164.
72. *The First Apology*, XIV: 167.
73. Tatian, *Address of Tatian*, XVI: 22.
74. Tertullian, *Apology*, XXII: 39.
75. Tertullian, *Apology*, XXII: 39.
76. Tertullian, *Apology*, XXII: 39. Tertullian later says that demons inflict bodily ailments on people for the sole reason of validating themselves to others as bringers of miracles. See Tertullian, *Apology*, XXIII.

Part I: Background

By the end of the third century, there was no clear and uncontroversial theory as to who the demons are or from what they are composed. They are described as intelligent, incorporeal spirits but are also composed of a material, aerial substance. They are "material spirits" that are otherworldly but this-worldly at the same time (i.e., in the air or underground). They are invisible but potentially visible. They lack a corporeal, animal nature but are sexually arousable and interactive with nature. A comfortable border between matter and spirit has not been satisfactorily delineated and this metaphysical problem is uncritically embraced and handed off to medieval philosophers, to whom we now turn.

Medieval Christian Views of Demonic Realism

The early Fathers had developed their philosophy and theology thanks in part to the detracting heretics of their time. And, not surprisingly, the intellectuals who carefully sculpted the doctrinal and philosophical positions of Christianity were called to the task of defending them. As a result of their rigorous defences, the various budding doctrines were facing new challenges. Demonology was among them to be challenged. But, unlike the Christological controversies at the time which were driven into codification, there was not as much of a pagan resistance to force demonology into any sort of standardization after Augustine of Hippo (354 to 430 AD) boldly wrote on that very subject in a number of his works. Curiously, beliefs about demons went virtually unchallenged for eight centuries following Augustine. This period of doctrinal stagnation, telescoped as the "Dark Ages," gave rise to newer challenges while beckoning that the older challenges still needed to be met.

From about 500 AD to 950 AD the Christian church, insofar as it was the state religion of the Roman Empire at the time, was decreasing substantially from its position of prominence. With the Germanic invasions and the eventual fall of the Empire, Christianity became increasingly sparse as a political and social force in the world. The newly-arrived Arabic religion, Islam, was thrust upon the world-scene and eventually–and quickly–conquered Sicily, southern Italy, and Crete.[77] When Islam's founding prophet Muhammad ultimately seized Medina (Yathrib) and subsequently conquered Mecca and Arabia with his newly acquired military power (all during the seventh century), Islam became a substantial contravening force against the perpetuity of the Christian and Jewish religions. Unlike the paganism of Rome's invading enemies, Islam would not share the fate of these neighbors who abandoned the paganism of their ancestry in favor of Christianity. Indeed, it proved to be more successfully intimated into the borders of the Empire. It wouldn't be until the eleventh century that military counterforce would be implemented to stave off the spread of Islam and the expansions inaugurated by Muhammad.[78]

77. See Latourette, *History of Christianity*, 269–377.
78. See Watt, *Muhammad*.

Demonic Realism in the History of Christian Philosophy

By the twelfth century, with the advent of Scholasticism and the resurgence of Christian intellectualism (particularly among the current "Doctors of the Church"), demonology had made a roaring comeback. Such a renaissance of thought occurred at the budding development of angelology, its parent field. Since earlier works prior to the twelfth century generally and briefly discussed what was already believed, it appears that the credit for this burgeoning discussion of demonology goes primarily to Peter Lombard (under the influence of Peter Abelard) and his massive contribution to the doctrinal heritage of Christianity, the *Four Books of Sentences*, written around 1150.[79] It was this work that became a standard corpus for subsequent theology students in Paris as a work worthy of intellectual commentary. Though very little personal didactic additions were provided on Lombard's part of the *Sentences* (and that it was devoid of any philosophical reflection as well), the book was a compilation consisting of biblical passages and commentaries by the earlier church Fathers. Lombard's contribution here is so significant and impressive that later medieval graduate students did not hesitate to identify him simply as "The Master."[80]

When those students pursued their own masters in theology, it was customary for them to critically engage the work as the standard and decisive treatise on Christian dogma. Since the second book of the *Sentences* contains doctrinal statements on angelology (and, consequently, demonology), the theologians and philosophers were primed to clear away the cobwebs of those long-forgotten subfields and to provide some discursive reflection that would substantially elevate talk of angels and demons over the course of the next century like never before. As a result, such flourishing in all likelihood contributed to the amplified "demonomania" that would fuel the exaggerations of witchcraft and heresy beginning a century later.[81] As an occasion for further development of Christian theology and the newly developed natural theology, the subsequent commentaries on the *Sentences* by Lombard's readers proved to be dialectical and philosophically speculative. It wasn't until Bishop Stephen Tempier's Condemnations of 1277 that the scholastic fecundity set forth by Lombard's commentators would soon come to a screeching halt.[82]

---

79. David Keck notes the "outline of angelological topics treated by Lombard in his *Sentences* [includes] . . . The fall and confirmation of the angels . . . The location and powers of the fallen angels . . . The attributes (cognitive, moral, and physical) of angels and demons [and] . . . The corporeality of angels and demons . . ." (*Angels and Angelology*, 90).

80. For specific laudatory comments on Peter Lombard along these lines, see Colish, *Peter Lombard*, 30–32.

81. See Hopkin, "Thomas Aquinas"; Bailey, "Late-Medieval Crisis"; and Boureau, *Satan the Heretic*. It is from Boureau's work that I borrow the appropriate term "demonomania" (9).

82. Bishop of Paris, Stephen Tempier, published his Condemnations of 1277 which concerned the disparity between what the theologians felt compelled to affirm, viz., biblical doctrine, and what the scholastic philosophers were speculating on. Keck himself has observed that "the great angelologists of the Middle Ages developed their angelologies not only from Scripture and exegesis but also from philosophy and metaphysical reasoning" (*Angels and Angelology*, 70). Since much of what the commentators wrote on vis-à-vis the *Sentences* concerned the incorporation of, *inter alia*, Aristotelian

Augustine, then, was one of the first of the medieval Christian philosophers to offer up a serious attempt at a philosophical framework for understanding intermediary beings of either kind. Augustine writes that angels are indeed spiritual beings. Though "angel" itself denotes a functional role, regarding "the nature of such beings, you will find that they are spirits."[83] He adds that such creatures possess an "ethereal body."[84] Interestingly, such an ethereal body is then equated to the post-resurrection bodies of the future saints–something quite physical though supernatural.[85] Regarding demons, Augustine does not sculpt a new view inasmuch as he seeks to systematize and apply the diverse theological (and pagan) perspectives that he finds grounded in some way in the Bible and sacred Patristic tradition. Since the angelic nature is the original nature of demons, they are spiritual, too.[86] But when Augustine goes on to describe the demons, he is not thinking of them in terms of being pure spirit as God is; rather, he is aligning himself with (or at least ceding for the sake of argument) familiar views that acknowledge that demons possess "one [attribute] proper to themselves, their aerial body."[87] This airy nature is heavier than and more inferior to the ethereal nature of the angelic ontology.[88] Elsewhere he adds that such creatures were fashioned from "spiritual matter" (something reminiscent of Origen's "material spirit"). Evidently Augustine believed that they were anything but purely spiritual beings.[89] Once again, being a "spirit" no longer appears to be clearly segregated from one's being an utterly immaterial intelligence or entity. While Augustine attempts to offer up God's necessary existence as an essential distinguishing characteristic of "spirit" from the kind of "spiritual matter" angels and demons are,[90] we lack any clear taxonomy of a spiritual ontology–particularly one that delineates between spirit and matter in a way that is analytically satisfying.[91] According to an apt summary by Inta Ivanovska, Augustine

---

philosophy then it was pronounced in Tempier's letter that where the Bible does not speak, one should not speculate. Articles 34–61, to be precise, concern Tempier's condemnations of the philosophical speculations on angelic beings. See Thijsson, "Condemnation."

83. Augustine, *Enarrationes in Psalmos*, 103(I).15: 125.

84. Augustine, *Epistula*, IX.3.

85. Augustine, *De Diversis Quaestionibus*, 47.

86. Augustine, *De Beata Vita*, III.18; *Confessions*, III.3.6.

87. Augustine, *De Civitate Dei*, IX.13: 260. Also see his *De Ordine*, II.9.27 and *De Genesi Ad Litteram*, XIII.17; for some follow-up comments in the secondary literature, see Kelly, *Satan*, 244; Ivanovska, "Demonology of Saint Augustine," 51. According to Ivanovska, the "airy" nature is an exclusive property of demonic bodies and not something the good angels are said to have for their constitution is distinctively "ethereal" ("Demonology of Saint Augustine," 249). She speaks of Augustine's "hesitation" and "conjecture" in cautiously using the terminology of "air" to describe demonic bodies at all (248), something that cannot be said about Augustine's predecessors.

88. Augustine, *De Genesi ad Litteram*, III.10.15.

89. See Augustine, *Confessions*, XII.17.25.

90. *Confessions*, XII.

91. E.g., how is the air of a demon's ontology any different than the air of our atmosphere?

makes "[t]he issue of the 'bodies of angels's . . . one of the most knotted challenges of [his own] angelology."[92]

Augustine's affirmation of demons being aerial creatures and interacting with (or with*in*) the bodies of human beings would officially make the quasi-materialism of his demonological metaphysics an almost creedal baseline for subsequent thinkers. But it is a permanent fortress built on unmitigated ambiguity. Yet Augustine and the earlier Fathers do not stand alone. Thanks to the rising influence of Aristotelian hylomorphism, quasi-materialism takes a somewhat different connotation in later medieval Scholasticism that, alas, ends up being no less obscure.[93] Bonaventure (1221 to 1274 AD), a Franciscan and contemporary of Thomas Aquinas, adopted the view that intermediary beings exist as a requisite (*oportuit*) of a world divinely designed and created.[94] This is a return to the ancient Platonic and Aristotelian views of the Great Chain of Being. While human beings are composites of material and immaterial substances intrinsically united to each other, angels are ontologically closer in being to God and so do not have any intrinsic pairing with their material bodies.[95] As such, their constitution is closer to the spiritual (in the sense of not being composed of the stuff that rocks and animals and other concrete objects are made) though not purely immaterial. All created things that exist must themselves have a hylomorphic composition and so the angelic *compositum* can be immaterial and yet have material properties.[96] Given the complexity of the incorporeal-yet-material status of angels,[97] there is a fundamental agreement with the ethereal/aerial ontologies of the Fathers and Augustine. And what is true ontologically of the angels is true of the demons.[98]

Contrary to the various species of quasi-materialism as revealed above, Pseudo-Dionysius (c. sixth century) goes against the grain and supposes that since God is himself pure spirit, it must also be the case that those closest (ontologically) to him are also pure spirits. Angels, being closest to God, naturally share in that pure spirituality. This conclusion is what sets Pseudo-Dionysius apart from his quasi-materialist counterparts for he, as David Keck notes, "seems to have been the first Christian to

---

92. Ivanovska, "Demonology of Saint Augustine," 238. His metaphysics of angels in general and of demons in particular, says Ivanovska, is "a daunting challenge" (245), a product of "random patchwork and loose stitching" (251) leading to an overall "systematically problematic" demonology (252).

93. Already in the twelfth century, angels were considered to be quasi- in more than just their constitution. They were also understood to be quasi-temporal (aeviternity; *aeviternitas*) in that angels exist "between" the timelessness of God and the temporality of material creation. It was a way to explain how angels are not quite as permanent (mutable) as material beings but at the same time they are not quite as impermanent (immutable) as God. See Keck, *Angels and Angelology*, 23.

94. Bonaventure, *Commentaria in Quatuor Libros Sententiarum*, II.1.2.1.1.

95. Bonaventure, *Commentaria*, II.1.2.3.2 and 3.1.1.1; Also see Gilson, *Bonaventure*, 222–23.

96. Bonaventure, *Commentaria*, II.3.1.1.1; cf., Gilson, *Bonaventure*, 222.

97. Gilson says that "the angels [are] presented to us as spiritual substances, wholly independent of bodies, [and yet] composed of matter and form" (*Bonaventure*, 226). Also see Keck, *Angels and Angelology*, 31–32.

98. Bonaventure, *Commentaria*, II.4.I.2.

have argued for the pure spirituality of the angels."[99] This view would go on to thrive in the Dominican wing of Scholasticism while the Franciscans, following Bonaventure, would opt for Aristotelian, universal hylomorphism for both angelic and demonic beings.

Concerning the demons specifically, in further contrast to Augustine and (the later) Bonaventure, Pseudo-Dionysius affirmed the incorporeality and pure immateriality of both angels and demons. He writes:

> Through these all Spiritual Beings and faculties and activities (whether perceived or percipient) began; through these they exist and possess a life incapable of failure or diminution, and are untainted by any corruption or death or materiality or birth, being separate above all instability and flux and restlessness of change. And whereas they are bodiless and immaterial they are perceived by our minds, and whereas they are minds themselves, they possess a supernatural perception and receive an illumination (after their own manner) concerning the hidden nature of things, from whence they pass on their own knowledge to other kindred spirits.[100]

He seems to have never compromised this understanding with muddled talk of ethereal or aerial bodies.[101] Unfortunately, he never works out any of the biblical scenarios from Genesis to Revelation that describe how demons and their chief are able to interact with this world.

As a contemporary of Bonaventure's, Thomas Aquinas (1225 to 1274 AD) parts ways with his fellow Scholastic in defending the Dionysian sentiment that both angels and demons are indeed purely immaterial creatures.[102] He writes that "the higher substances, that is, the angels, are totally apart from bodies, subsisting immaterially and in intelligible existence."[103] They are endowed with rational faculties that can subsist wholly apart from any kind of material bodies–including the *hyle* of hylomorphism. Regarding demons specifically, he also agrees with Dionysius that "devils do not have bodies joined to them by nature."[104] Aquinas, himself a Dominican, came to represent the prevailing viewpoint on angels and demons well into the contemporary period.

---

99. Keck, *Angels and Angelology*, 31.

100. Pseudo-Dionysius, *On the Divine Names*, IV.1: 87.

101. As evidence of the clarity and perpetuity of this pure immaterialism, Thomas Aquinas later assures us that "angels and demons have not bodies naturally united to them, but are wholly incorporeal as Dionysius says" and that "[w]ithout doubt Dionysius maintained that angels and demons are incorporeal" (Aquinas, *De Potentia Dei*, VI.6: 198).

102. Aquinas's development of the metaphysics of angels requires him to reckon how an Aristotelian can come to see how the soul might subsist in a way Christians typically understand it as a form free of the hylomorphic baggage which is notably defended by Bonaventure.

103. Aquinas, "On Angelic Knowledge," *Summa Theologiae*, I.55.2: 379. Also see Aquinas, *De Spiritualibus Creaturis*, IX.2.

104. Aquinas, *De Malo*, III.4: 438.

Regarding the powers of the demons, we return to Augustine who taught, along with the succeeding Fathers, that the demons have some kind of supernatural ability to manifest to and deceive percipients.[105] But this capability need not necessarily be understood as a power intrinsic to the demonic nature in the way that being visible is to opaque corporeal objects.[106] Perhaps that power is extrinsic and one that is temporarily leased to them as the occasion demands. However, by means of "clarification," Augustine seems to suggest that demons *do* have an intrinsic physical sense perception and transmission mechanism that can pick up and manipulate the bodily traces of human thoughts.[107] It is through this medium that demons are able to stir the passions (even the subtle ones) within their victims. Thus, such internal agitations in human beings, being demonically induced, are physical movements of fluids inside the body (viz., "bile") as they affect the mind. Aquinas agrees and points out that Satan "sensibly appears to human beings in some form and sensibly speaks with them and persuades them to sin" as exemplified by the biblical accounts where Satan "tempted the first human being in the garden of paradise in the form of a serpent, and he tempted Christ in the desert in some visible form."[108] Elsewhere Aquinas insists that not only can demons interact with physical bodies, they can act as craftsmen and, so, can cause bodily transformations.[109] But this talk of extraordinary power appears to come out of nowhere in a seemingly *ad hoc* attempt to explain how immaterial demons can interact with the material world.

The conflicting metaphysical portraits of the medieval period along with their questionable intimations of having certain matter-interacting powers passes on to the modern era, the subject of our next section.

Modern Christian Views of Demonic Realism

After the waning of Scholasticism in the Christian church, any discussions about the reality of angels and demons that ensued became the sole province of theology (or were merely mentioned in passing by Christian philosophers). This was further solidified during the Protestant Reformation's impeachment of philosophy as a reliable vehicle to understanding all matters theological. As such, the sixteenth century saw no significant divergence from the antecedent views of the medieval thinkers.[110] Perhaps the most salient contributions come from significant non-philosophers like Martin Luther and Ignatius of Loyola who both perpetuated the idea that the devil was far

---

105. See Augustine, *De Civitate Dei* VII.35; also see Evans, *Augustine on Evil*, 105.

106. Cf., Augustine, *Adnotationes in Iob*, I.1 and *De Civitate Dei*, X.21.

107. See Augustine, *De Divinatione Daemonum*, IX; Also see O'Daly, *Augustine's Philosophy of Mind*, 122–24.

108. Aquinas, *De Malo*, III.4: 155–56.

109. Aquinas, *De Potentia Dei*, VI.5.

110. See Russell, *Mephistopheles*, 26ff.

more active in human affairs than originally thought.[111] The devil's actions ranged from individual affliction to institutionalized leadership. Demons would harass people through apparitions and possessions, enact sorcery and witchcraft in beguiling and enchanting the susceptible cultures, and even empower and control the very Pope of Rome who was declared by Reformers to be the apocalyptic Antichrist.

It was not until the eighteenth century, and the onset of the Age of Enlightenment, when philosophy began to challenge the canonical declarations of faith and tradition in its emphasizing and championing reason as the supreme indicator of truth and the disavowing of miracles as a real property of biblical events.[112] The emphasis changed from a focus on the otherworldly realm to the physical, present world. And when the fascination with witchcraft and magic had reached its zenith, having been rooted in medieval demonology and fed by Lutheran Protestantism, "[n]either the scientific nor the hermetic view of the world had much room for the Devil."[113] It is not surprising, then, that not much serious thought went into defining (much less defending) an ontologically realist view of demons, though many Christian apologists at the time certainly counter-argued in defense of the core miracle stories surrounding the person of Jesus. Those philosophers and thinkers that did tend to specifically address belief in demons during the time entertained conclusions that deviated not only from their Christian predecessors but also the Scriptures themselves–often citing legendary overlay or the linguistic devices of allegory and metaphor as enlightened explanations for the scriptural presence of demons.[114] Once Satan became demythologized as a mere symbol for radical evil, any talk of demonological metaphysics would be relegated to extraneous myth and superstition, though not a subject off limits to ongoing speculation.[115] Since this chapter seeks to chronicle specifically demonic realists in

---

111. Russell, *Prince of Darkness*, 168–73.

112. H. C. Erik Midelfort observes: "The 1720s and 1730s were also the decades of high dispute over the nature of miracles, and several of the demonologists took part in that debate as well, criticizing either the evidence for or the very possibility of New Testament miracles" (*Exorcism and Enlightenment*, 92).

113. Russell, *Mephistopheles*, 28.

114. Under the influence of Hermann Reimarus (1694 to 1768) and the rise of German Rationalism, David Friedrich Strauss (1808 to 1874) significantly influenced a notable stream of Christian scholarship in his demythologizing of the Christian faith in general and the Gospel portraits of Jesus in particular. Merrill Unger mentions Strauss's interpretation of the Gospel portrayals of Jesus as an exorcist when he succinctly notes that, according to Strauss, "the whole narrative of Jesus's demon expulsions is merely symbolic, without actual foundation of fact" and that "demon possession, so-called, is but a vivid symbol of the prevalence of evil in the world" (Unger, *Biblical Demonology*, 90). Strauss uses the demonic possession stories of the Gospels as evidence of legendary development in the Gospels. See Strauss, *Life of Jesus*, 426ff; Russell, *Mephistopheles*, 80.

115. Francis Bacon (1561 to 1626), contrary to those of the Reformation, was not opposed to one speculating about the nature of angelic creatures, emphasizing that such investigations are "neither inscrutable nor interdicted" and so "the sober and grounded inquiry, which may arise out of the passages of Holy Scriptures, or out of the gradations of nature, is not restrained. So of degenerate and revolted spirits ... The contemplation or science of their nature, their power, their illusions, either by Scripture or reason, is a part of spiritual wisdom" (*The Advancement of Learning*, II.6.2: 46). But

Christian philosophy, we shall focus on the handful of philosophers during this time period who made some sort of metaphysical contribution to a realist demonology.

The English philosopher and social contractarian Thomas Hobbes (1588 to 1679 AD) endorsed a full-blown materialism in his identification of the ontologies of angels and demons. This is in deep contrast to both the Patristic and medieval philosophers who either affirmed a sort of quasi-materialism or an outright pure immaterialism. The reason for Hobbes's overt materialism is because he finds the notion of an incorporeal and immaterial being to be incoherent.[116] Hobbes describes angels and demons thusly:

> I find in Scripture that there be Angels, and Spirits, good and evill; but not that they are Incorporeall, as are the Apparitions men see in the Dark, or in a Dream, or Vision.[117]

Hobbes's metaphysic certainly solves the problem of how angels and demons can interact with the world with ease. However, he has done so at the expense of the creedal affirmations that demons (and angels) are incorporeal, immaterial spirits.

This firm commitment would not be the conclusion of Hobbes's contemporary, John Locke (1632 to 1704 AD). Locke believed that "though we are told that there are different species of angels; . . . we know not how to frame distinct specific ideas of them"[118] except roughly through the analogy of the human mind. Locke did seem to think that angels, as well as demons, are in fact immaterial creatures and conceivably exist as such. He makes mention of the "nature and operations of finite immaterial beings [such as] spirits, angels, devils."[119] On the other hand, Locke seems content to affirm another possibility posed by the faith tradition of the Christian church, one that subtly evinces the church's inconsistency on this subject:

> The supposition, at least, that angels do sometimes assume bodies, needs not startle us; since some of the most ancient and most learned Fathers of the church seemed to believe that they had bodies: and this is certain, that their state and way of existence is unknown to us.[120]

Consequently, he is hesitant to speak of "[w]hether angels and spirits have any analogy to [figure, breadth, and thickness], in respect to expansion, [which] is beyond my

---

Bacon seems quite skeptical of their existence when he cryptically suggests that they are "fabulous and fantastical."

116. See Thomas Hobbes, *Leviathan*, III.34.

117. Hobbes, *Leviathan*, IV.45: 664. Hobbes does spend some time discussing demons, but not their metaphysics. His focus is on arguing against the ancient Greek misunderstandings of demons being segregated into good and evil beings; and he offers up some reasons for thinking that "demonic possession" is nothing but a metaphorical appellation.

118. Locke, *Essay*, III.6.11: 48.

119. Locke, *Essay*, IV.16.12: 279.

120. Locke, *Essay*, II.23.13: 250.

comprehension."[121] In short, Locke sees that there is an obvious metaphysical problem but no solution is forthcoming.

It was very apparent that, given the absence of any coherent creed or a singular metaphysical theory of demonology, a univocal understanding of the demons's ontology was still far from codification. Following Locke, the next step of the metaphysics of demonology was, essentially, to dismiss any further notions of realism. Once theology became increasingly influenced by deistic philosophers and progressive theologians, any realism pertaining to the intervention of supernatural beings (including the demons) was rejected.[122] The more conservative, realist theologians (like the mystics and the Reformers) did not dare to speculate about the metaphysics of demons other than to suggest that their presence was felt in the current harassment of Christians. Belief in demons had, once again, fallen into a period of developmental, philosophical stagnation. It remained behind the scenes and devoid of philosophical focus in anticipation of the contemporary period–a period which we shall now explore.

Contemporary Christian Views of Demonic Realism

As with the previous four hundred years (with the exception of those like Hobbes), Christian philosophers of the contemporary period did not add anything to demonology. This period of time marked a substantial diminution of speculations about the metaphysics of demons.[123] As a matter of historical fact, the prospect of belief in demons seemed to be kept alive, not so much by the philosopher's pen (for the rationalists had successfully relegated angelology and demonology to the world of mere faith) but by the artist's paintbrush in that it has moved from the world of fact to the world of literary fiction. Due to the legends of "Johann Faustus," European theatre, John Bunyan's *The Pilgrim's Progress*, John Milton's *Paradise Lost*, and a host of other Romanticist literature and art, such sources reversed the trend of wanting to mythologize demons.[124] Having been disenchanted with magic and the witch hunt craze fostered by such vivid storytelling (particularly once the targets of the famous witch hunts turned on some of society's elite), eventually a purely secular worldview began to dominate philosophical thinking commencing with the notable, skeptical influence of David Hume.[125] The rise of deterministic science (such as that espoused in Newton's *Principia*) essentially made demons irrelevant as explanatory causes. But

---

121. Locke, *Essay*, II.15.11: 324.

122. Voltaire is rumored to have described belief in the devil as a "disgusting fantasy" (Russell, *Mephistopheles*, 136).

123. "Daimonology died out, at least in the sense that later canonical Western thinkers did not occupy themselves with daimons or daimonology as such but addressed the order of spiritual life in different conceptual framings" (Smith, "Daimon Thinking," 183).

124. See Russell, *Mephistopheles*, 58–76, 91–127; Russell, *Prince of Darkness*, chapter 14.

125. See Russell, *Prince of Darkness*, 208–11.

it seems clear that those philosophers who persisted in the realist tradition and had bothered to write on the subject still tended toward some form of what I shall call the "Dominican view" as exemplified by Thomas Aquinas (that demons are real, post-angelic immaterial creatures being endowed with supernatural powers to materialize and/or manipulate physical objects).[126] While it is a reasonable view–one that is at least self-consistent–it requires that demons have (as a mere assumption) certain creative magical powers. This perception seems to be the prevailing interpretation for contemporary Christian philosophers and theologians who have flouted the trend toward demonic anti-realism. Accordingly, the Dominican view continues to be the prevailing theory of choice for realists.

Following a conservative theology influenced by (at least) Aquinas, Mortimer J. Adler appears to toe the Dominican line of reasoning when it comes to demonological (and angelological) metaphysics. Concerning the ontology of angels, he consistently and adamantly affirms that they are purely immaterial. Adler claims this mostly for scriptural reasons but also due to important sources of tradition like the Nicene Creed.[127] They are, he writes, "immaterial and incomposite" and, as a result, "angels are immortal."[128] It is uncontroversial for him, then, that demons would subsequently be described in a similar fashion when he writes that "the devils [are] fallen angels and so purely spiritual creatures."[129] Given the contributions of the rationalists of previous centuries, Adler thinks that philosophy cannot get us to a demonstration of the existence of angels and demons.[130]

Similarly, Peter Kreeft is also quite clear about the immateriality of angels. When equating human souls with angels, he stresses that both are "pure spirits" and so "[n]either one has size or color. Neither one has parts. . . . And neither one has weight."[131] Additionally, he continues, to be a spirit means to engender the "power of thinking-conscious, deliberate, rational understanding" along with the "power of willing and choosing and deliberately loving."[132] Moreover, angels are also "[n]ot in space. Space

---

126. Examples of such demonological realists spanning the seventeenth century through the twentieth century include Nicolas Malebranche (*De la Recherche de la Vérité*, II.3.6), Blaise Pascal (see his *Lettres Provinciales*, XIV), Samuel Clarke (see his *Discourse*, "The Evidences of Natural and Revealed Religion," Prop. XIV), William Paley (see his *The Clergyman's Companion*, IV-V), John Henry Newman (see his Easter sermon entitled "Victory of Good over Evil" delivered March 31, 1872), and C. S. Lewis (see his preface to the revised edition of *The Screwtape Letters*).

127. See Adler, *The Angels and Us*, 37–38, 79, 108, 122. On page 141, Adler does make a passing reference to heaven being "not a physical place" and so any spatial attributes, such as location, would be inappropriately applied to angels.

128. Adler, *The Angels and Us*, 159. Elsewhere he specifically says that angels are "incorporeal and, therefore, [have] the simplicity that belongs to anything indivisible . . ." (57).

129. Adler, *The Angels and Us*, 88.

130. See his four conclusions on 55.

131. Kreeft, *Angels and Demons*, 51. There are other places he makes explicit reference to angels as "pure spirits" (see 50, 85, and 133).

132. Kreeft, *Angels and Demons*, 50.

contains bodies, not spirits."[133] Naturally the devil also "is a pure spirit"[134] as are the demons, and they "do not have bodies."[135] As with Adler and Kreeft, Peter S. Williams supports the contention that angels are immaterial spirits and that "they have no bodies, and so no physically perceived sense data."[136] Also, since

> angels are bodiless spirits they have no appearance in themselves; they are invisible. It's not that angels have bodies that can't be seen . . . but that *they have no body to be seen*.[137]

A far more reserved analysis can be found in the work of Phillip H. Wiebe[138]–a philosopher with a Mennonite background. Instead of towing the Dominican line that demons in particular, along with spirits in general, are purely immaterial, Wiebe "wish[es] to remain neutral on the question of whether spirits are corporeal."[139] He reminds the reader less than twenty pages later that "we do not need to [. . . define] God and other spirits as nonmaterial and incorporeal" and that we should simply settle for the more modest view that spirits have "precise characteristics we will probably never know completely."[140] This includes the notion that such beings are even *supernatural*, for "we do not know enough about their 'real nature' to assert that they cannot be embraced within the natural order."[141] As to whether spirits are in any sense "observable," Wiebe once again suspends judgment.[142] Accordingly, he says that his views are closely aligned with those of "mysticism and the apophatic tradition."[143] Instead of ambitiously proffering characteristics and properties about demons and other spirits, his realism is motivated by a "theory of spirits," as he calls it, that should be informed by what we are (abductively) entitled to think vis-à-vis a non-aprioristic, Quinean sort of empirical approach.

When it comes to the kind of power demons have, Adler, like Pseudo-Dionysius, does not discuss *how* Satan (and the demons) interact with this world, though he

---

133. Kreeft, *Angels and Demons*, 68.

134. Kreeft, *Angels and Demons*, 131.

135. Kreeft, *Angels and Demons*, 91.

136. Williams, *Case for Angels*, 80; He also affirms this in his unpublished article, "In Defence of Angelology," 4–6.

137. Williams, *Case for Angels*, 90; emphasis his. In a note of clarification, Williams's use of "spirit" in application to angels (and disembodied humans for that matter) is not merely one to be described negatively (as, say, a mere synonym for "immaterial"), but as a positively embracing term that includes "capacities for thought, feeling, consciousness and active volitional power" (78) making them "persons" that are "self-aware" (80). Therefore, "it is perfectly possible for angels to exist in the absence of any space-time continuum (just as it is possible for God so to do)" (87).

138. Wiebe, *God and Other Spirits*; cf., Wiebe, "Finite Spirits."

139. Wiebe, *God and Other Spirits*, 142.

140. Wiebe, *God and Other Spirits*, 159.

141. Wiebe, *God and Other Spirits*, 151.

142. Wiebe, *God and Other Spirits*, 114.

143. Wiebe, *God and Other Spirits*, 150.

acknowledges *that* they do: "[The devil] is a mighty person with intelligence and will whose energies are bent on the destruction of the cosmos and on the misery of the creatures."[144] Adler just does not give us the specifics. Unsurprisingly, Wiebe is just as vague.[145] Kreeft is less so, for he says that demons have certain innate powers, including the "ability to move matter supernaturally"[146] which enables them to "manipulate any material vehicles on occasion, including animals."[147] Williams affirms that "they can apparently cause themselves to look like anything they want, either by manipulating our imaginations or . . . by 'assuming a body.'"[148] Moreover, he asks:

> Can angels act to produce effects in the natural world? It is strongly conceivable that if angels existed, they could interact with matter. Besides . . . spirit-matter interaction is perfectly intelligible in that it obviously takes place every day in humans.[149]

What is said to be true of angels is also said to be true of demons (right in line with Williams's contemporaries): "Demons are both *like* Angels in being naturally unembodied spirits."[150] In terms of sparsely documented cases of demonic interaction, Williams makes a passing mention of "reports of demonic levitation,"[151] which would presumably be a case of a spirit interacting with matter. But, concerning the ability of demons to manifest themselves, it is worth noting that Williams seems to break from tradition when he declares the following:

> It would seem to be the case that demons cannot assume bodies. . . . God refuses to manufacture bodies for demons to assume. On this explanation the idioplastic difference between Angels and demons is extrinsic . . . [and] Occam's Razor enjoins us to accept [this view] because it is simpler to assign the power of creating bodies to God alone than it is to attribute it to angels as well.[152]

Conclusion

I have surveyed a notable selection of influential pre-Christian and Christian sources who have shaped and contributed to the philosophical narrative surrounding a realist ontology of demons; understanding that much that arises in such discussions is the focus on the primal angelic nature first and the demon second. It is apparent that the

144. Adler, *The Angels and Us*, 301.
145. Wiebe, *God and Other Spirits*, 128ff.
146. Kreeft, *Angels and Demons*, 114.
147. Kreeft, *Angels and Demons*, 123.
148. Williams, *Case for Angels*, 90.
149. Williams, *Case for Angels*, 85.
150. Williams, *Case for Angels*, 101.
151. Williams, *Case for Angels*, 140 n. 87.
152. Williams, *Case for Angels*, 92.

thought and speculation concerning such beings has either been *prima facie* self-contradictory (i.e., advancing and defending the spiritual nature of such creatures while simultaneously affirming their (quasi-)material status) or inconsistent with other authoritative voices. This is to say that various representative metaphysical views are sometimes at odds with what other fellow philosophers have developed (i.e., consider how Pseudo-Dionysius's pure immaterialism sits in tension with Bonaventure's and Hobbes's (quasi-)materialism). Here is a summarization of each thinker's perspective on the demonic vis-à-vis their metaphysical status as "spirit":

	Demons are "spirit"	Demons are material	Demons are immaterial
Justin Martyr	X	X	
Tatian the Assyrian	X	X	
Tertullian	X	?	
Origen	X	X	
Lactantius	X	I	
Augustine	X	X	
Pseudo-Dionysius	X		X
Bonaventure	X	X	
Thomas Aquinas	X		X
Thomas Hobbes	X	X	
John Locke	X	?	?
Mortimer J. Adler	X		X
Peter Kreeft	X		X
Peter S. Williams	X		X
Phillip H. Wiebe	X	?	?

?=Unknown; I=Implied; The empty cells represent "at least not likely."

For all of these philosophers, demons are indeed spirit as the Bible and tradition say. Most take the term to be a line of demarcation separating beings that are incorporeal (or "finely material") from beings that are corporeal (or "grossly material"). This intimates the antecedent Greek view that regarded the *daimon* as an ontologically intermediate subject composed of an aerial substance. Perhaps this notion was absorbed into Christianity to explain how demons could be called spirits and yet interact with the physical world and facilitate an episode of human procreation. But this leaves the impression that one is attempting to have it both ways, viz., that something can be spirit and material at the same time–something that appears to compromise what it means for God himself to be a spirit (cf., John 4.24). To salvage this disparate use, consequentially, one must consider "spirit" to be an ambiguous term in that it would equally apply to at least one *purely* immaterial being (God) as well as to any quasi-material being.

For Hobbes this is not a problem at all, since in his opinion the Bible's use of "spirit" does *not* designate or describe incorporeality; rather, it is something of a linguistic device–a metaphor. Hobbes's view is much more elegant in its consistency and univocal terminology, but it achieves this at the cost of making "spirit" *always* a metaphorical, non-ontological description (something that defies at least *some* of the biblical uses as seen in Luke 24.39, "a spirit does not have flesh and bones as you see that I have"). However, since the medieval period, some have sought to clarify the notion of spirit by insisting that it refers exclusively to *purely* immaterial creatures with no kind of material composition whatsoever. Only when we come to the contemporary era, perhaps motivated by Aquinas's influential abandonment of Bonaventure's universal hylomorphism, do we see more of a consistent affirmation that demons are purely immaterial creatures. This fidelity to the immateriality of demons leads those partisan thinkers to a position even more elegant than that championed by Hobbes, that is, a position that not only endorses a univocal use of "spirit" when applied to God, angel, and demon alike, but also a non-metaphorical use of the term. But such a resolution also comes at a cost: it must now accommodate the biblical testimony of demons interacting with the physical world. As we saw, their resolution is just to ascribe to the demons a supernatural/mysterious power to manipulate and interact with nature. Still others, like Tatian, John Locke, and Phillip Wiebe withhold any definitive opinion on the matter.

As our survey of the diversity and inconsistency of Christian philosophers across the board indicates, there is a real need for a theory that harmonizes the fact that the Bible speaks of the "spiritual" nature of demons (and God alike) as well as their ability to somehow interact with this physical world. The scriptural data on their alleged physical interactions with the world are taken as undisputed. The pure immaterialists endorse a vague and *ad hoc* "magical powers" hypothesis in order to account for how immaterial spirits intercourse with the world. The (quasi-)materialists do not need to flounder in accounting for their physical interactions except that they do compromise what it means to be an incorporeal spirit–no lighter a problem. It seems to me that if one were to undertake to form a careful creedal statement of demons, equipped with the hindsight of the corpus of Christianity's philosophical history, no coherent answer would be forthcoming. Moreover, it is not really until the contemporary period do Christian philosophers (i.e., Adler, Kreeft, Williams, and Wiebe) offer up reasons to think that such beings exist. This is no doubt due to the fact that anti-realism did not quite surface until the modern period and the Enlightenment. Accordingly, philosophical arguments for the existence of Satan and the demons became more of a reactionary endeavor. This is quite understandable. And we shall endeavor in this book to settle on the realist's conclusion that such beings exist. But it is nearly unforgiveable that no coherent understanding of the metaphysics of demons has been codified. This, too, shall be remedied as we explore later on a way to reconcile a strong metaphysical view of the demons's spiritual immateriality with how they might nonetheless interact with the physical world.

In the next chapter, we shall begin our journey through the metaphysics of demonic realism by taking a look at whether it is a doctrine that can be maintained or not under the weight of scrutiny. We shall being by first taking a closer look at the arguments against the existence of Satan and his cohorts followed by a chapter that shall explore arguments in favor.

Part II

Existential Matters

"We are really faced with a cruel dilemma. When the humans disbelieve in our existence we lose all the pleasing results of direct terrorism and we make no magicians. On the other hand, when they believe in us, we cannot make them materialists and sceptics."

—Screwtape (from C. S. Lewis's *The Screwtape Letters*)

4

Philosophical Arguments for Demonic Anti-Realism

GOD IS THE UNDISPUTED objective of discourse in the philosophy of religion. Whether one follows the literature, professional conferences, or both, it is evident that these philosophers are heavenly minded, so to speak. But while the scene is dominated by talk of God–*and why not?*–we hear very little, if anything, about God's putative enemy, the devil. This may be because those of us siding with the traditional view have not been informed of the Nietzschianesque obituary unofficially issued by the Ivory Tower: *Satan is dead*.[1] But for the few who have insisted that reports of his death are greatly exaggerated, still not much of a defense had been subsequently offered by those on the other side. Instead, demonic realists simply have retreated into the sheltered confines of its partisan theology–insisting that the devil is indeed alive and well even if he has already been eulogized by the self-proclaimed curators of science and philosophy. The realist's fideism is likely rooted in the fact that some doctrines in Christianity hinge on its tenets. For example, those siding with certain (original?) views of the atonement of Jesus, like that of Christus Victor or the Ransom Theory, cannot have Jesus rescuing or ransoming mankind while denying the one from whom humanity had been rescued or ransomed.

Despite demonic realism's important ancestry in this regard, the existence of Satan and his cohorts fuels other doctrines, namely that Jesus genuinely delivers those afflicted by such beings and that Jesus himself escaped the temptation by Satan which serve as forms of accreditation for his messiahship. That demonic realism is a notion accompanied by an abutting intellectual awkwardness to it is incontestable. But for those who self-identify as orthodox Christians certainly must come to terms with the prospect that at least its flagship demon, Satan, must actually exist–intellectual warts and all. Demonic realists believe from Scripture that, as discussed in chapter 2, the

---

1. According to Miguel A. De La Torre and Albert Hernández, Satan's dying process actually began at 9:40am on November 1, 1755 when a massive earthquake in Lisbon, Portugal decimated much of Catholic infrastructure amidst its (ironic) celebration of All Saints Day. See *Quest for the Historical Satan*, 182.

devil is an actual spiritual,[2] non-human person who at one time was possibly one of God's most prestigious and powerful angels. Ever since his fall from grace, the devil has had and continues to have enmity with the God of the universe. Consequently, if the devil truly exists, then we have an opposing non-natural force in the universe. And if there is an opposing non-natural force in the universe, then such a being is an object of philosophical, and not scientific, speculation. Such speculation could be as the interest one may have in the metaphysics of abstract objects. One can debate a being's existence, or lack thereof, without thinking much about one's own existential position in relation to it. (I doubt anyone thinks the universe has more meaning for oneself if it should be that the number 1 exists in a Platonic reality rather than as a mere linguistic fiction, and yet debates about abstracta rage on.)

In fact, the existence of the devil should get more attention amongst philosophers of religion beyond merely being a convenient character in a fleeting thought experiment (such as by René Descartes who loosely speaks of an "evil demon" [*genium malignum*] who can lead the epistemologist to doubt certain incorrigible mathematical truths[3] or Alvin Plantinga's invoking of "Satan and his cohorts" in order to demonstrate how natural evil can logically arise in a universe created by an all-good God[4]). There is at least one way to think about how the existence of a devil plays an important philosophical role. Specifically, there is a rising number of contemporary thinkers who are invoking the devil as a serious possibility in accounting for the existence of animal suffering among other natural evils prior to the Fall of mankind.[5] Others are even more ambitious in supposing that a full-blown theodicy can be crafted whereby Satan's existence actually serves to *explain* evil's origin.[6] Talk of abstract objects hardly has these kinds of sundry implications for the philosopher, and yet Satan gets far less academic press.

This chapter, then, inaugurates an attempt at settling the most primary question of whether demonic realism is believable or not. First, I shall discuss and object to the arguments against the existence of Satan and his demons (viz., demonic anti-realism). Second, I shall show that there is at least one good argument for the probability of their literal existence (viz., demonic realism). This chapter and the two that follow consist of Part II and officially launch our excursion into what Jeffrey Burton Russell

---

2. Christian philosophers in the past have disagreed as to what it means to be ontologically "spiritual." Some, like Justin Martyr and Augustine, have thought that demons are quasi-material beings composed of air. Others, like Pseudo-Dionysius and Thomas Aquinas, have thought that demons are purely immaterial. It is not crucial to have that cashed out a satisfactory meaning for "spirit" here.

3. Descartes, "Meditation I."

4. Plantinga, "Supralapsarianism," 16; Plantinga, *God, Freedom, and Evil*, 58.

5. E.g., Murray, *Nature Red in Tooth and Claw*, chapter 3; Kelly, "The Problem of Evil"; Penelhum, *Religion and Rationality*, 246; Lewis, *The Problem of Pain*, chapter 9; Mascall, *Christian Theology and Natural Science*, 301–2; Trethowan, *Christian Philosophy*, 128.

6. Boyd, *Satan and the Problem of Evil*, chapters 9–10.

has rightly called a "natural diabology."[7] While it is true that some philosophers sympathetic to the existence of the devil and/or good angels are quite pessimistic of such a project,[8] I shall argue here in Part II that there is some promising justification for demonic realism, though I will point out that some affirming arguments are not all good or at least could use some more attention and development. We shall explore those arguments that are questionable in the chapter that follows this one followed by an argument that, I think, shows the existence of Satan and his demons to be probable. The present chapter shall focus narrowly on taking on a series of arguments in the promotion of demonic *anti*-realism (or *adiabolism* if we are talking strictly about the devil only). I shall respond to each argument by showing that none of them pose good reasons for that adiabolism.

Arguments for Demonic Anti-Realism

If it should turn out that no Scripture or Holy Book truly speaks of the existence of demons as a fact, in and of itself this would not entail that such beings do not exist. This is supported by the fact that a number of people who believe that demons exist are not necessarily associated with any religious tradition.[9] Similarly, there are a number of people who affirm some form of theism who are likewise not a part of a religious tradition. As ancient Greek philosophy displays, one can come to believe in the existence of God/the gods wholly apart from appeals to any special revelation (think Plato and Aristotle). While Scripture-*as-history* can serve as viable evidence for some historical figure, its dismissal does not entitle one to conclude that such a figure does not exist. (One may doubt, for example, the historical reliability of the Gospel portrayals of the high priest, Caiaphas, but the archaeological discovery of his ossuary, *inter alia*, independently confirms his existence.[10]) Unlike the philosophical arguments lodged by atheists against their theistic detractors, arguments enlisted in service to promoting adiabolism contain far fewer candidates. From my reckoning, there are approximately three arguments that have been or can be formulated against the existence of Satan and his demons that have been offered in the literature. Two of them are *a priori* arguments and the third one is *a posteriori*.

While the following may not exhaust all of the (would-be) arguments for adiabolism or demonic anti-realism, they comprise the known ones already replete in the literature in one form or another. To be frank, demonic anti-realists think little of needing to engineer sophisticated arguments against Satan and his demons (one is free to insert their own speculations as to why this is so). Accordingly, in presenting

---

7. Russell, *Satan*, 24.
8. E.g., Adler, *The Angels and Us*, chapter 4.
9. E.g., the forensic psychologist and demonologist Lynne Campbell. See Vázquez, "Interview with a Demonologist."
10. Greenhut, "The 'Caiaphas' Tomb."

the arguments, it is often necessary for me to develop them on their behalf. I contend that none of these three arguments for an anti-realist approach to demonology are ultimately successful, and my complaints are aired immediately following a charitable presentation of each.

The Incoherence Argument

The Enlightenment foisted upon religion an aggregate of challenges to its numerous traditional supernatural beliefs. From religion's philosophical speculations to biblical interpretations, prominent thinkers were beginning to reevaluate the import of metaphysical conclusions drawn in previous centuries. One among many of the consequences of such thinking was the disavowing of angels and demons as genuine forces at work in the universe. Apart from the abuses of Western demonology awash in the fourteenth century and beyond, talk of spiritual agents as intervening causes of physical and psychological effects was being displaced by a more "reasonable" paradigm due in part to the influential thinking of Baruch Spinoza (1632 to 1637).[11]

Spinoza was rather clear and bold about his objection to the existence of Satan or anything like him in a short piece he wrote entitled "On Devils." Therein he writes:

> [L]et us just see whether such a wretched thing could even exist for a single moment. And, if we do so, we shall immediately find out that it cannot; for whatever duration a thing has results entirely from the perfection of the thing, and the more essence and godliness things possess, the more lasting are they: therefore, as the Devil has not the least perfection in him, how should he then, I think to myself, be able to exist?[12]

Spinoza's critique is surely on *a priori* grounds, complaining that a devil–a "thinking thing" that opposes God–cannot possibly be brought into existence by a perfect Creator (i.e., God). He continues by pressing the point that since "persistence or duration of a mode of the thinking thing only results from the union in which such a mode is, through love, joined to God," then given that demons are "the precise opposite" of God, "they cannot possibly exist." One obvious solution is to denounce Spinoza's hard determinism (and that everything is an extension of one Being) and to consider a full-fledged demonology that recognizes that these demons were originally created as good angels but were also endowed with the free will to fall from grace.

However, in his 1830 to 1831 work, *Der Christliche Glaube* (*The Christian Faith*), the German theologian Friedrich Schleiermacher anticipates this rejoinder and argues that realism fails nonetheless. He complains that even if *per* a traditional Judeo-Christian demonology Satan and his demons were originally created good and free, the problem is simply relocated to how there could be such a thing as an angelic fall

---

11. Almond, *The Devil*, 211–13.
12. Spinoza, "Of Devils," 143.

that explains the arrival of demons in a universe created and governed by an all-powerful and sovereign God. He writes:

> [A]s to the so-called fall of the good angels: the more perfect these good angels are supposed to have been, the less possible it is to find any motive but those presupposing a fall already, e.g., arrogance and envy.... [I]f after the Fall the natural powers of the devil remained undiminished, it is impossible to conceive how persistent evil could exist side by side with superlative insight. For such insight must, in the first place, have shown every conflict with God to be an entirely useless undertaking[13]

Schleiermacher's argument here is that no morally perfect being, or someone near enough, would have entertained the passions of "arrogance and envy" since it obviously would have been "an entirely useless undertaking" for a being with "superlative insight." Bernard Bamberger, a twentieth-century Jewish theologian, has more recently built on these sentiments when he asks,

> [H]ow could angels, created all good, have yielded to such sin? What was the difference by virtue of which some fell from grace, while others stood firm? Either there was some weakness in the original nature of the rebels—which means, God did not create them good—or else He did not bestow on them the same grace through which the others resisted temptation—in which case the fall was God's doing, not Satan's. Moreover, it is generally held that Satan's sin was the desire to usurp God's place. But even we mortals know that such an ambition was, not only wicked, but ridiculous; could not great angels, with their lucid minds, understand and refrain from such tragic folly?[14]

From Bamberger, the objections become clearer: First, angels are not the kinds of things that can rebel on pain of making an all-good God ultimately culpable for things he shouldn't be, thus tarnishing his moral perfection; second, no angel, being in proximity to God and with a certain amount of elevated knowledge above humans, would ambitiously seek so impossible a task such as the unseating of an omnipotent God. Altogether we shall consider this to constitute the *incoherence argument*. That is to say, the incoherence argument renders improbable demonic realism no matter if demons are directly created or are the result of a fall from grace.

However, there are a number of reasons why this argument fails to deliver. We shall consider these reasons now.

1. *It is reasonable to suppose that good angels could freely rebel against God*

First, the incoherence argument consists of an indictment against a certain kind of *narrative* about demonic realism, not of the existence of demons *per se*. Scripture does

---

13. Schleiermacher, *The Christian Faith*, 161.
14. Bamberger, *Fallen Angels*, 203.

not indicate that the angelic rebellion is due to either "arrogance and envy" or "the desire to usurp God's place." One not committed to Origen's or Tertullian's theses that Isaiah 14 and/or Ezekiel 28 describe Satan's fall need not think that Satan acted out of either of those passions. I argued previously *that* there was an angelic fall, but at no point do we know for sure on what basis that fall obtained.[15] All that is required to make sense of a fall is that there is the possibility of a morally innocent being either having a reasonable desire that can overwhelm or circumvent that being's ability to act (morally) appropriately[16] or that such a desire can deceptively appear to the acting agent as good.[17]

To justify this, we must understand that there is a fundamental difference between a being that is morally *innocent* and one that is morally *perfect*. The former does not entail the latter, though the latter certainly entails the former. A being that is only morally innocent is one who simply lacks (at the time) any history of moral impropriety. A being that is morally perfect is one who is functionally incapable of any moral impropriety. If a prelapsarian devil is a species of mere moral innocence and not one of moral perfection, then there is nothing *prima facie* about its ontology that entails its being incapable of acting against that state of moral innocence. Satan can be morally innocent at any interval from his creation to some time prior to an initial act of moral impropriety. Theologians consider Adam and Eve to have been in just such a situation. And yet the doctrine of a human Fall does not engender any such difficulty vis-à-vis the original "good" nature of being human.

However, the incoherence argument is not raised in a vacuum. That is to say that the problem arises not out of a context that only considers the innocence of Satan's nature but also that he is in *ontological proximity* to God. After all, someone could contend, *pace* Augustine,[18] that when human believers enter into the heavenly beatific vision, they will be incapable of acting contrary to God's moral perfection. This, I think, is what the challenge of the incoherence argument is forcefully aimed at. For if one's nature is in proximity to God, it is impossible or incredible to think that one could and would deviate from that sublime original state. Whether one thinks that human free will is forgone or intact, all seem to think that once in the beatific vision, that heavenly denizen will be indefinitely kept from any subsequent moral deviation.[19] Whence cometh an angelic fall?

Now, an unqualified comparison with the heavenly state of post-mortem believers will not do. For such believers have been made righteous as a consequence of

---

15. See "Biblical Demonology" in chapter 2 of this book.
16. Anselm, *De Casu Diaboli*, IV.
17. Aquinas, *De Malo*, I.3.
18. Augustine, *De Correptione et Gratia*, XXII.33.
19. See, for example, the back and forth over the so-called "problem of heavenly freedom": Pawl and Timpe, "Incompatibilism"; Cowan, "Compatibilism"; Pawl and Timpe, "Heavenly Freedom"; Brown, "Making the Best Even Better."

Philosophical Arguments for Demonic Anti-Realism

their receiving of Christ during their earthly trials. The problem of an angelic fall is dramatically intensified if angels were, in fact, in a beatific vision in their prelapsarian state. As the medieval Doctors of the Church taught, it is possible that angels were not enjoying the benefit of full grace such as that entailed in the notion of the beatific vision offered to human beings.[20] In fact, as in the case of human beings, being given the benefit of full grace may be better seen as the *result* or *reward* for having opposed unjust desires and falsehoods. Anselm writes, "whatever [this benefit the angels received] was, it suffices to know that it was something toward which [angels] could grow and which they did not receive when they were created, so that they might attain it by their own merit."[21] Perhaps angels were created deliberately with a certain amount of epistemic distance–being positioned "at arm's length" so to speak–so that they would be capable of choosing to be forever in the company of God's favor (not too dissimilar to the Edenic testing grounds of Adam and Eve).

Though possible, the mystery of the details persists: *Why* would God arrange things that way when the results are disastrous? In answering this question, we must tackle both the context in which morally innocent and free beings can fall under sublime conditions and why God might knowingly create such a world. Let us examine these in order. If it is reasonable to suppose, as Anselm thinks,[22] that God is morally permitted to withhold perseverance and justice from free creatures so that they only act out of a desire for self-happiness, then we should expect that any evil that arises in the creature is truly and justifiably self-made. Elucidating the details will prove difficult, but not impossible. William Wood has recently filled out Anselm's insights and suggests a model that provides a workable, even if nascent, solution.[23] In Wood's Anselmian construction, Satan and his demons are able to choose perseverance, even rather easily, but instead desire more an incompatible but "highly desirable good that confers a considerable advantage on those who possess it," which he just calls a "forbidden good."[24] Desiring this good *simpliciter* is not itself wrong, but it is incompatible with desiring perseverance. In fact, Wood argues, both demons and angels have relative desires weighed differently between perseverance and forbidden goods. Furthermore, these beings have inclinations toward justice and benefit and they weigh for themselves the value of the different goods. Supposing that acquiring the forbidden good is incompatible with acquiring perseverance, then such an acquiring of the forbidden good may perpetuate them into a downward spiral of a sort of unquenchable consumeristic thirst for more forbidden goods that ultimately enslaves them to oppose God at every turn. To wit, Satan "makes himself a voluntary slave, in utter

---

20. E.g., Anselm, *De Casu Diaboli*, XXV; Aquinas, *Summa Theologiae*, Ia.62.1.
21. Anselm, *De Casu Diaboli*, VI: 227.
22. Anselm, *De Casu Diaboli*, III and XVIII.
23. Wood, "Anselm of Canterbury."
24. Wood, "Anselm of Canterbury," 228.

thrall to his own desires, and completely cuts himself off from justice."[25] Apart from any non-trivial objections to Wood's suggestion, it seems plausible that free angelic beings could fall even under sublime conditions.

And now a word about why God might have intended such a world where free angelic beings fall. We must consider what might have been the case if at least one angel did not freely deviate from his original position. If no angel rebelled, then there would not have been a tempter in the Garden of Eden. Perhaps that sets off a chain of possibilities that look very much different than how things actually turned out. With such a change, there might not have been a world with as many believers as that which we actually have (due, perhaps, to fewer people reproducing in that world or that fewer people are convinced by that world's Gospel). So, in order for there to be a trajectory of a satisfactory amount of redeemed human beings, it might be necessary that there be some kind of antecedent angelic fall. In addition, there might be no actualizable world that God could create with the specific design plan he has where only one angel ever ends up rebelling. While it is possible, of course, that only one angel rebels, perhaps in the range of actualizable worlds this is just not the case. As such, the number of angels that do rebel perhaps are just as many as is necessary to bring about the right number of saved human beings who will have been guilty of Original Sin and subsequently will have responded freely to God's grace. The fact of the matter is, like all theological tensions associated with divine foreknowledge and creaturely freedom, we just do not know what is truly broadly logically possible for God and what is not. Therefore, it is possible that in a broadly logical world where multiple angels do not freely rebel does not yield a world where an optimal number of the saved obtains. Being so possible, the incoherence argument does not appear to show God and devils to be logically incompatible things.

But the scenario is not complete. For though human beings are given the possibility of redemption, fallen angels, by contrast, are not thus making an angelic fall a far graver concern than originally construed.[26] It is now incumbent upon the demonic realist to defend this entire fallen-angel portrait as to whether it, *mutatis mutandis*, accords with God's perfect goodness and omniscience. With the incoherence argument so amended, let us consider why the argument is still not triumphant.

2. *It is reasonable to suppose that fallen angels could be refused redemption*

As to the unavailability of angelic redemption, I would insist that no person's freely choosing to rebel–whether human or angel–should have any kind of veto power over another person's freely choosing to be saved. If such a fall is due to the free decisions of the angels, then they justifiably inherit their unfortunate lot. And can one reasonably insist that God is *obligated* to save any creature who freely rebels or freely avers from

---

25. Wood, "Anselm of Canterbury," 243.
26. 1 Pet 1.12; 2 Pet 2.4.

God's redemption? As long as the creaturely world was not "rigged" in an unfair way, that God permits angels to fall without redemption is morally unproblematic at least on incompatibilist grounds. If eternal separation is the consequence of one's rebellion, one can hardly impugn God for not having brought about what could only be a supererogatory act that would serve to overturn one's just desert.

There is a second thing to consider here, too. It is a clarification of the *teleology*–the purpose and function, and so the entitlements–of the angels. If angelic teleology is significantly different from that of human beings, then God would not be obligated to save them even if he was somehow obligated to save a species like human beings. Consider vertically differing teleologies in the distribution of benefits. Take the telos of a child *qua* child. A child's telos is one that excludes him or her from enjoying the rights and privileges of adulthood (e.g., signing contracts, joining the military, driving a vehicle, being a college professor, etc.). Or, consider horizontally differing teleologies where something like a lion is such that his teleology excludes his enjoying the benefits of sustaining himself underwater for long periods of time whereas a whale can. Scripture portrays angels as "ministering spirits" (Heb 1.14) and, so, are more or less God's "support staff." They are not entitled to the benefits of being human (i.e., glorification; resurrection) simply because their teleology is such that they were not *intended* to be human-like benefactors. This is God's prerogative, and who else but God is licensed to designate such intrinsically disparate teleologies?

One could retort that angels are ontologically superior to human beings (cf., Heb 2.7, 9) and, so, they would have teleologies that should minimally encompass those of any "lower" beings, including the benefits of human redemption. But the analogical comparison of angels to children can be modified by flipping the analogy, i.e., make adults and not children analogous to angels. And it is evident that there are benefits and privileges enjoyed by children that adults are not entitled to despite their "higher" status. For example, children enjoy the benefits of not paying taxes. They also have the freedom to indulge in fatty foods and dessert with fewer consequences to health. This shows that the teleologies of "higher" beings does not necessarily include the benefits and privileges of those of "lower" beings. (I note that being a child is not to be ontologically inferior to an adult, only that the child-adult relation is *analogous* to the human-angel relation.) Similarly, it is unobjectionable that the telos of angels is such that they are not a race of beings created to enjoy and participate in the intra-trinitarian relationship of God that is otherwise intended for human beings.

There is a third justification one can offer for why angels are never redeemed. To borrow language from Anselm, perhaps such lack of redemption is not because God does not offer it but because the fallen angels do not freely accept it. For angels who have been in a delimited form of grace in God and still choose to rebel, it is possible that those angels simply *will* never seek redemption even if it were to be offered. Perhaps the angels that choose that rebellion will perseveringly lock themselves in that state of rebellion no matter the consequences (and I cannot imagine they would not have known about the consequences of their rebellion). While this may seem like an irrational thing to do, consider that some people in this world made privy to the consequences of their decisions will nonetheless find certain causes worth the self-sacrifice. If these causes are desirable for someone and such desires overwhelm or skew one's sense of right and wrong, then it is conceivable that something like an angel could desire an ignoble cause even if it entails that angel's self-ruination. Suppose, for example, that one desired to oppose immorality. Without careful thought and reflection, that person's desire leads them to enlist as a protestor for the odious Westboro Baptist Church. If a naïve and perhaps innocent Westboro congregant desired to champion holy living, then if their passion overwhelms or skews their discursive reasoning, it is possible that that person ends up desiring a cause that is deplorable (for "holy living" for a Westboro member includes "being homophobic and anti-Semitic and . . .").

In a fascinating episode in Scripture, there is a point at which Moses himself is willing to forego his own eternal life if it means that there are certain others who will not have their sins forgiven (Exod 22.32). Moses no doubt was only using his own life as leverage and not directly willing his own expulsion from eternal life, but he is desiring a cause that may well be inappropriate (particularly if the people for whom he is pleading are unrepentant) and is willing to embrace the eternal consequences if need be. C. S. Lewis has imagined that human beings condemned to an eschatological hell of conscious torment are not actually kept there by force; rather, they indirectly choose their ongoing fate simply because their hatred of God is proportionately increased with every passing moment they suffer.[27] If this is a plausible scenario that can justify the traditional view of hell, then such reasoning can certainly apply to the angelic fall. That is to say, the angels that rebel indeed suffer the consequences, but they continue in their hateful rebellion with every passing moment that they suffer in their state of expulsion from God's presence, for their desire to oppose God goes unabated.

But here Schleiermacher raises another salient point:

> The fallen angels . . . out of hatred to God and to relieve their feeling of distress, engage in active opposition to God, while yet they are unable to effect anything except by God's will and permission, and thus would find far greater alleviation for their distress as well as satisfaction for their hatred of God in absolute inactivity.[28]

He suggests that if the fallen angels *truly* want to oppose God and satisfy their desire to hurt him, then they should do nothing lest they be unwittingly aiding and abetting God's overarching plan of creation. In the pithy words of Henry Ansgar Kelly, if demons really want to oppose God effectively, they "should refuse to do God's dirty work for Him."[29] We shall consider a response to this now.

---

27. Lewis, *The Problem of Pain*, 115.
28. Schleiermacher, *The Christian Faith*, 162.
29. Kelly, *Satan*, 310.

Philosophical Arguments for Demonic Anti-Realism

3. It is reasonable to suppose that fallen angels would not be idle

If the rebellious angels were to do nothing, God would have known that and would not have created *those* angels. Instead, he would have created other angels whom he knew would actively engage with creation in the ways necessary for his plans to obtain. But this is not quite sufficient to handle Schleiermacher's other objection, for it seems improbable that *any* would-be fallen angel would actively engage creation in the ways that would fulfill God's plans. Here I want to suggest that the cognitive abilities of the fallen angels might have been corrupted. While *as good angels* they would think that acting positively to offend God would unwittingly fall in line with God's plan, their status as demons leads them to erroneously act in ways lucid thinkers would deem illogical. It is no different from a dismissed boyfriend whose sense of logic and reason is overwhelmed by his heartbreak and anger that he should engage in a "crime of passion" in not considering the consequences.

It might also be the case that demons come to think that they can trick God out of fulfilling some of his punitive plans because, upon further reflection, they become as open theists thinking that God's *modi operandi* can be railroaded.[30] And open theists, like theologian Gregory Boyd, believe that opponents of God can truly take God by surprise.[31] According to open theism, God does not know the future because the future is not something that exists (yet). Since omniscience entails only knowing what is true, and there is nothing that is or can be true about the future (yet), then God does not know the future. Accordingly, the future is not a fixed trajectory. This is not to say that God is *unprepared* for the unforeseeable circumstances (for he may be, as Boyd acknowledges,[32] prepared to carry out his plan once he knows what demons will do). None of this is to insist that open theism is true or that demons are in fact open theists, only that demons themselves might come to be convinced of an aggressive sort of open theism that ignores Boyd's stipulation that God is nonetheless prepared for any such contingency.

It is intriguing that in the episode of the Gerasene demoniac in Matthew 8, the possessing demons encounter Jesus and ask, "What have you to do with us, O Son of God? Have you come here to torment us before the time?" (v. 29). Two things are evident here. First, the demons are relatively ignorant. This is to say that they are apparently unaware of Jesus's mission and whether he will renege on this "torment . . . before the time." Second, the suggestion of reneging on this "torment" supposes that Jesus is at liberty to change the course of God's fixed plan (i.e., of "the time"; *kairou*). Again, it doesn't matter that this is true or not, only that this is how they think. Thus, they might (falsely) come to think that they can undermine God's plans. And if they

---

30. *Pace* Anselm who seems to think that all angels are now "certain that this kind of punishment follows this kind of guilt" (*De Casu Diaboli*, XXV: 257).

31. See Gregory Boyd's two complementary books on the subject: *God at War* and *Satan and the Problem of Evil*.

32. Boyd, *Satan and the Problem of Evil*, 128–29.

believe that, then that might be sufficient motivation for them to positively act on creation–even war with God. As a possibility, and I think a plausibility, the ignorance of the demons and their being (possibly) open theists of a sort provides an avenue as to why demons would not remain inactive, for they think (wrongly?) that the future is not a fixed reality.

The notion that there is a fallen angel in such proximity to God is indeed a difficult thing to explain but not impossible. And yet that reality may actually provide some unexpected support of the notion. Let us look at this final point now.

4. The fallen-angel narrative may be indicative of its historicity

That there would be an angelic fall at all seems like an embarrassing detail in the hegemony of God as described in Scripture. For the angelic fall supposes that God's government is in such disarray that there is a segment of the divine council that sees fit to rebel despite the consequences. It is precisely due to the incredulity elicited by the incoherence argument that should, ironically, delay a wholesale abandonment of demonic realism from the standpoint of the historicity of the Bible. While a world with demons–counterforces to God's design plan–calls into question a coherence within the divine government, on a deeper level it conveys a hard reality in the hearts of free creatures espoused elsewhere in Scripture (cf., Jer 17.9). From the hard-heartedness of Pharaoh in the face of the Egyptian plagues (Exod 8.19) to the declared hard-heartedness of the rich man's brothers in the face of a resurrected Lazarus (Luke 16.27–31) to the company of eyewitnesses to Jesus's resurrection who remain in disbelief despite the evidence of their eyes (Matt 28.16–17), the stubborn hearts of humankind will evidently lead many to not be open to *any* amount of divine enlightenment.

Proponents of the so-called Divine Hiddenness argument against God's existence wonder why the evidences for God are so ambiguous so as to be missed by a casual but sincere sojourner, particularly since the stakes are high and God loves and wants all people to be saved.[33] But even if the evidences are ultimately embraced, this is not a sufficient condition for one to move into a salvific relationship with God, for "even the demons believe–and shudder" (James 2.19). Pharaoh did not deny Yahweh's existence, and yet his rebellion is very much a central obstacle in the Exodus narrative. All of this is to say that while the angelic rebellion may be an awkward tenet of demonic realism, it accords with the larger biblical schema of human stubbornness evident in other unrelated contexts. But if the incoherence argument is supposed to be an obvious problem, one wonders why the notion of an angelic rebellion was neither omitted nor squelched (that a keen fictional author might have had angels cast instead as creatures *outside* of God's abode). Thus, the embarrassing inclusion of an angelic

---

33. See J. L. Schellenberg's most recent iteration of the argument in his *The Hiddenness Argument*.

fall (which is likely taught at least in Jude) adds a certain and unexpected historical credence to the story.

Therefore, the incoherence argument does not support demonic anti-realism since a world with an optimal amount of believers may, in part, hinge on whether that world also contains rebellious angels who positively act on creation. Moreover, it is conceivable that beings in proximity to God and are not in any sort of beatific vision (yet) may still rebel if they feel that their cause is to be desired more than their personal welfare. This is enough to deflect the incoherence argument. But we can add that, assuming that Scripture preserves the notion of an angelic fall, such a fall possibly serves to indicate that its authors were not writing fiction, for they most certainly would not have mentioned an angelic fall to avoid the obvious embarrassment that being in God's company is nonetheless not enough to secure and sustain one's perpetual moral innocence.

We shall now move on to one of the most contentious arguments for demonic anti-realism, the *ethical argument*.

The Ethical Argument

There are two forms this next argument could take. First, some have supposed that positing Satan as the primary cause for the ills in human civilization–specifically human-based atrocities–potentially exonerates wrongly the real perpetrators of their crimes. If one appeals to her being influenced by demonic conspirators, then she, like a child acting under the orders of her parents, can hardly be responsible for her actions. As Don Cupitt writes, any "[e]xplanations of moral phenomena which have recourse to the Devil or devils must be repudiated because they are a device for shuffling off responsibility."[34] Since this is unacceptable, Satan cannot exist for he, and not the alleged perpetrators themselves, would be culpable for the heinous actions attributed. On this, Miguel de la Torre and Albert Hernández muse:

> The devil made me do it, and Jesus cleaned up my mess. As a new creature in Christ "I" can move on without really addressing the consequences of or restitution for those sins the devil made me do. Hence, Nazi concentration guards can torture all week long and still attend worship services on Sunday mornings. Politicians can lead armies to war under false pretenses without addressing the tens of thousands, if not hundreds of thousands, who are killed or maimed because, after all, our intentions were pure–it was the enemy who was really evil.[35]

They go on to note an extended consequence that results from this devil-made-me-do-it mentality in that the

34. Cupitt, "Four Arguments against the Devil," 413.
35. De La Torre and Hernández, *Quest for the Historical Satan*, 198.

illusion of Satan as the father of all evil not only excuses and absolves God of any responsibility for evil but also excuses and absolves those with power and privilege who benefit from the status quo that causes suffering for many who reside on the margins of society. Satan is the cause of all the world's hunger, disease, and oppression–instead of those humans who are enriched by such misery.

When one considers all of history's atrocities, particularly those committed in the name of God, Satan appears to look more like a convenient scapegoat that can be invoked to absolve the perpetrator of her egregious sins. As Neil Forsyth sums up, "[o]nce human life is viewed as conditioned by a struggle between divine forces, it becomes difficult to insist on human responsibility."[36]

If the original portrait of Satan is as *the father of lies* or as the primary cause of every ungodly human action,[37] then it is difficult if not impossible, so the argument would go, to attribute any blame to the human agents who are nothing but the unfortunate victims of manipulation. De la Torre and Hernández themselves suggest a different role for Satan to play, that of "trickster."[38] This is to say that Satan's shenanigans can have a positive role such that he, at the behest of God, aids the plight of the hero in providing the testing grounds that allow for this hero an opportunity to exhibit virtue in establishing his or her credibility. I should say that the same problem above also attends the "trickster" motif since one could appeal to the hero's would-be failed response to be due to a careless overextension of Satan's testing power. One could insist that her "testing grounds" were too irresistible thus exonerating the human "evildoer." This suggests that such attempts at self-exoneration are no less problematic than the so-called traditional view.

It would thus appear that true justice can only be upheld if society does not take Satan and his demons to genuinely exist. And despite the few who claim "voices in my head" or some kind of equivalent appeal to demonic manipulation and/or entrapment, the vast majority of perpetrators are indeed acting on their own. That there are those who perform virtuous acts and yet do not think or believe that their actions are under compulsion by God or his angelic delegates are added reasons for disavowing any form of diabolical determinism. Since this version of the ethical argument sees malevolent acts at the hands of human beings to be the fault of alien agents (viz., demons), then let us call this species *the ethical argument from scapegoating*. We can schematize this as the following:

---

36. Forsyth, *The Old Enemy*, 10.

37. Even if the demonic realist were to delimit Satan's involvement and say that he is only the primary cause of *some* ungodly human actions, the problem would remain. For an outside observer would still be unable to demarcate which actions are diabolical and which properly belong to the human perpetrator. Possession states provide the most obvious iterations of demonic agency that would avert culpability from the victim.

38. They are only salvaging an overarching theology here, they are not defending demonic realism, for "ontologically, there is no Satan" (De La Torre and Hernández, *Quest for the Historical Satan*, 179).

Philosophical Arguments for Demonic Anti-Realism

1. If demons exist, then they, *ex hypothesi*, causally determine the atrocities enacted by some human beings (from without).

2. If demons determine the atrocities of some human beings (from without), then those human beings are not culpable for those atrocities.

3. Those human beings are culpable for enacting any atrocities.

4. Therefore, demons do not exist.

Premise 1 is assumed to be a tenet of traditional demonology. We might stipulate that not all atrocities committed are caused by demons, however. This premise speaks only to those scenarios where, for argument's sake, it is the demon(s) determining the actions. Premise 2 assumes that some form of incompatibilism is true. This means that if anyone's actions are determined by another agent or an event, then the actor is not morally responsible (for she was not free to withhold the action). Premise (3) is predicated on the unacceptability of human actors to appeal to scapegoating in order to be exonerated for their crime(s). The conclusion follows from denying the consequent of 2, and so of 1, which in turn negates the antecedent of 1.

Now, there is another species of the ethical argument that takes a different approach based on something else unscrupulous, namely that there is an identity crisis in the human actor herself that permits one to justifiably punish the actor. It is argued that given the alleged ability of Satan and his demons, again *ex hypothesi*, to morph into spiritual and physical opponents of Christianity (i.e., doppelgängers), then though such a scenario locates the blame to the human actor, it turns out that this human actor is no human at all: she is a devil or demon who has merely assumed the identity of the human actor. In a twist of fate, one *can* properly punish, even to an extreme, the "human" offenders given that they are not really human beings. In fact, no amount of "punishment" could ever be considered cruel or unusual for demons deserve anything punitive that can be thrown at them. That this notion was believed has some *a posteriori* support as evidenced by the abuses and bloodshed from the Crusades to the witch-craze to the more recent "satanic panic" of the late twentieth century. Such practices are ultimately influenced by a Christian demonology shaped in part by its medieval predecessors.[39] If a human being is believed to be a demon in actuality, or is a special agent of Satan, then it is not wrong, so one might assume, to harm or execute that particular manifested demon. Bamberger writes:

> Those who recognize a Devil often hold that some group or nation or sect are the Devil's own—the witches, the heretics, the Jews, the capitalists, the communists—and these enemies of God are no longer entitled to the rights,

---

39. I am setting aside the subset of atrocities committed that may not depend on demonology but, rather, on the uncritical application of certain Old Testament texts, viz., "You shall not permit a sorceress to live" (Exod 22.18). Cf. Hopkin, "Thomas Aquinas."

the just dealing, the simple humanity which are the heritage of all created in the divine image.[40]

But knowing this leads to one having to adopt an imperfect and awkward discernment of just who is a demon or an emissary of Satan and who isn't. As a result, those that are innocent (all of them?) are harmed or executed wrongly. But it is divinely sanctioned abuse.

Such a portrait adds fuel to the so-called New Atheists's complaint of theistic (religious) belief that supposes that religion "poisons everything."[41] Though the atrocities committed are considered by many to be mostly due to the recent rise of terrorism committed in the name of Islam,[42] such "poison" is often juxtaposed with the aforementioned atrocities committed in the name of Christianity. And Christian atrocities, regardless of whether they are comparable to those of other religions or are exaggerated in the contexts in which they occur, are easily mined from certain unambiguous episodes found in religious history. As such, they are egregious enough in their own right. In many ways the demonic anti-realist David Kyle Johnson is actually not far off the mark when he says that "[w]hen it comes to belief in demons, it's not the demons who are dangerous–it's the believers."[43] Thus, it may not be so much about demonic realism *simpliciter* as much as it is having a certain doxastic attitude about demons and their powers. But if demons are believed to mimic or manifest as human agents, the origin of such beliefs possibly derives from the nearly three millennia of an evolving demonology.

Let us call this species *the ethical argument from dissimulation*. I frame the argument thusly:

5. If demons exist, then, *ex hypothesi*, they manifest as human beings.

6. If demons manifest as human beings, then it is not wrong to bring harm or death to those "human beings."

7. It is wrong to bring harm or death to those "human beings" because they are actually innocent human beings.

8. Therefore, demons do not exist.

Premise 5, as with the previous species of the ethical argument, once again posits a traditional view of Christian demonology. Premise 6 predicates the permissibility to

---

40. Bamberger, *Fallen Angels*, 251.

41. Hitchens, *God Is Not Great*.

42. Consider how certain Islamic leaders and followers have considering America to be "the great Satan," Israel the "little Satan," and the old Soviet Union the "lesser Satan" in their more recent attempts at justifying their jihad against Westerners. As Elaine Pagels has observed, Jews and Christians have also engaged in the demonizing of their opponents (literally, even) as it imbues a sense of moral justification for the inordinate harms they inflict. See Pagels, *Origin of Satan*.

43. Johnson, "Justified Belief in the Existence of Demons is Impossible," 187.

bring harm and/or death to certain "humans" on their *really* being demons (and it is further assumed that harming or killing a manifested demon is not wrong). Premise 7 is considered true because if all of the victims of Christian abuse were actually demons, then there would (presumably) be no argument here. On the one hand, the force of the argument appears to rest on a question-begging assumption by contemporaries, namely that those abuses and deaths actually involved (innocent) human victims and not demonic assailants. But the premise could reasonably be taken as an attempt at a Moorean shift–i.e., it being more obvious to think that anyone harmed or killed are in fact humans rather than to think that demons can manifest in that way. As with the scapegoating species, a denial of the consequent of 7 ultimately leads to a negation of the antecedent of 5, namely 8.

Below are some reasons for why both species of the ethical argument are unconvincing.

1. Both species of the ethical argument fail to disentangle the existence of demons from (wrong) beliefs about them

As with the previous argument for demonic anti-realism, much that underscores the ethical argument in its various forms is a certain assumption had about beliefs about demonic interaction and not about the existence and practices of demons *simpliciter*. Obviously one can deny that demons have any kind of causal efficacy in the actions of human beings, but this would not be sufficient to abandon demonic realism. This was, after all, one of the hallmarks of the Deist controversy, namely that God might not be active in the world despite having initially created it. That God might not perform miracles or involve himself in any way with human history after the creation event is no swipe against the existence of God *qua* Creator. Some variations of hard Platonism posit concretely existing abstracta that have no causal intercourse with the material world at all. But again, being causally effete is insufficient grounds for such things's nonexistence. As a matter of mere logic, the demonic realist can simply deny the opening premises to both arguments, viz., 1 and 5. But this strategy will have to square with its scriptural and doctrinal foundations.

Now, such a mere logical move need not be the only push-back here. There actually have been some demonic realists who have denied that demons can do the sorts of things often attributed to them (i.e., 1 and 5) despite a highly evolved, post-medieval demonology. In other words, it is unfair to assume the truths of 1 and 5 on the basis that such notions are necessary or uncontroversial tenets of demonology. Counterexamples abound. For example, the sixteenth-century theologian, Reginald Scot, argues the following in opposing the notion that things like witches are empowered by Satan:

> Seeing therefore that some other things might naturallie be the occasion and cause of such calamities as witches are supposed to bring; let not us that professe

the Gospell and knowledge of Christ, be bewitched to beleeve that they doo such things, as are in nature impossible, and in sense and reason incredible. If they saie it is done through the divels helpe, who can work miracles; whie doo not theeves bring their busines to passe miraculouslie, with whom the divell is as conversant as with the other? Such mischeefes as are imputed to witches, happen where no witches are; yea and continue when witches are hanged and burnt: whie then should we attribute such effect to that cause, which being taken awaie, happeneth neverthelesse?[44]

Other demonic realists who, following Scot, distanced themselves from the notion that demons can causally and miraculously act on the natural world include the Cartesian theologian Balthasar Bekker,[45] William Fleetwood,[46] and even philosopher John Locke.[47] As Christian demonology continued its maturation throughout the modern period, it is evident that there still had been no monolithic understanding about the demons's powers and manifestability. In fact, to derive conclusions about the entirety of Christian demonology on the basis of an extremely small chapter in human history of fantastical thinking is irresponsible.[48] What one should conclude from the premises of these ethical arguments is, at best, that such common beliefs about demons can and should be dismissed. Rehabilitating such beliefs happens to be the project taken on in Part III, and so I refer the reader there for further consideration.

2. Even if 1 is true in the ethical argument from scapegoating, the move from 1 to 2 is controversial

The assumption behind the kind of free agency said to be had by the human actor smuggles in the assumption that incompatibilism (i.e., that acts borne out of causal determinism by outside agents or events are not done freely; but if they were done freely, they could not have been causally determined) is true. But the demonic realist can enlist all of the philosophers and theologians in support of various compatibilist versions of free will as *at least* a logically possible alternative; she would not even have to endorse those positions herself. Compatibilism is not only a live option amongst philosophers, it is statistically the preferred model of free will.[49] The defender of the

---

44. Scot, *The Discoverie of Witchcraft*, 11.
45. Bekker, *The World Bewitch'd*, 249, 253, and 256–57.
46. Fleetwood, *An Essay Upon Miracles*, esp. 85ff.
47. Locke, *A Discourse of Miracles*.

48. "In spite of the great interest that the prosecution of Sorcery has received in the history books, it was actually of fairly limited scope and duration. Only a very small percentage of persons suspected of Sorcery were executed, and mass arrests occurred mainly during the seventy years between 1550 and 1630" (Kelly, *Satan*, 299).

49. David Bourget and David J. Chalmers report that a whopping 59.1 percent of the philosophers in their study affirm compatibilism where the percentage of libertarians is only 13.7 percent, the number of those denying free will altogether is 12.2 percent, and those subsumed under "other" comprise

Philosophical Arguments for Demonic Anti-Realism

ethical argument will instead have to insist on and defend some form of incompatibilist free will (e.g., libertarian free will) before warrant can ultimately be afforded the ethical argument's conclusion. Unless and until this is accomplished, the demonic realist has affirmative reasons to side with 1 without necessarily agreeing with 2 and, thus, rejecting this version of the ethical argument.

Another possibility exists for the committed demonic realist who is an incompatibilist. Perhaps it isn't that demons causally *determine* human-based actions but, rather, that they merely *influence* their human actors (i.e., something less causally constraining). It is conceivable that demons only *suggest* or *prompt* human beings to do certain things but do not overwhelm them. This notion has some direct and indirect biblical support (John 8.38, 44; Acts 5.3–4; 1 Cor 10.13; 1 Pet 5.8–9; James 1.14–15; 4.7). Such an indeterminist view would be no different from the ordinary promptings of a neighbor, friend, family member, or even God himself but would still have causal efficacy in cooperation with the human actor. As the eighteenth-century devotional work *The (New) Whole Duty of Man* makes clear, blaming the devil for one's giving in to temptation "is an error arising from a very false notion of the devil's power of tempting men; it being nothing more, but like that of wicked men tempting one another."[50] Thus, the mere fact that these sources of influence exist are in no way *prima facie* grounds for dismissing the acting agent's culpability. For such an agent is never constrained to act as she does.

As a matter of observation, most demonic realists past and present have always thought that demons engage in less deterministic forms of influence on their human victims in ways that are resistible (excluding of course those instances that are considered episodes of demonic possession).[51] Even if one met the demands of establishing incompatibilism as suggested above (and I note that I am an incompatibilist), the point being made here is that there are good reasons for thinking that demonic determinism need not be true. This is to say that the *modus operandi* of the demons is not one that constrains the human agent to enact things like atrocities. Accordingly, the demonic realist, as an incompatibilist, can deny the truth of 1 altogether.

Since neither species of the ethical argument successfully supports demonic anti-realism, let us move on to an *a posteriori* argument for such anti-realism and why it is unconvincing. This is the last argument for demonic anti-realism we shall consider.

14.9 percent ("What Do Philosophers Believe?," 476).

50. Allestree, *New Whole Duty of Man*, 326–27.

51. E.g., Boa and Bowman, *Sense and Nonsense*, 111ff; Unger, *Biblical Demonology*, 68–70; Augustine, *De Civitate Dei* XVIII.18; Augustine, *De Genesi Contra Manicheos* II.14.21; Aquinas, *De Malo* III.4; Origen, *De Principiis* III.2.2.

Part II: Existential Matters

The Devil-of-the-Gaps Argument

A third line of reasoning, one that now ventures exclusively into the *a posteriori*, plays heavily on the corresponding God-of-the-gaps objection often leveled against defenders of the existence of God. It is explicitly, though briefly, defended by Don Cupitt.[52] The demonic anti-realist avails herself to the fact that science has progressed in such remarkable ways that fewer non-scientific hypotheses have had any currency in the West since the Enlightenment. Here is a recent example of this particular accusation being carried out: On April 4, 2009, atheist Christopher Hitchens engaged Christian philosopher and theologian William Lane Craig in a public debate over the existence of God.[53] In Hitchens's opening statement, he had set up his atheism in opposition to an ancient and medieval cultural milieu of scientific ignorance. He gave an example of the occurrence of disease that would by today's standards be attributed to a germ theory. He said that, in their historically primitive contexts, such occurrences were often met by religious adherents who believed that "maybe evil spirits caused disease."[54] During the cross-examination period, Craig appealed to Jesus's use of exorcisms as evidence for Jesus's understanding of himself as the special revelation of God. Hitchens quickly exploited the subject again: "When you say exorcism, do you mean that you believe in devils too?"[55] Craig parried the question, but the rhetorical effectiveness of tethering Craig's theism to demonic realism certainly imposed on the audience the veneer that appeals to gods of any sort are, in effect, appeals to ignorance.[56]

Hitchens's criticism is not without merit. For it is an understatement to declare that there have been many instances of seemingly inexplicable events, or events given pseudo-explanations, that have obtained throughout history only to be demystified by subsequent investigation and analysis. The level of knowledge humanity holds today is obviously not the level of knowledge held yesterday. As such, history is replete with examples of scientific ignorance–ignorance that sometimes has given rise to fanciful alternative hypotheses that no self-respecting modern would entertain. That pain relievers and not leeches assuage fevers, that gravity and not angels move planets, and that microscopic bacteria and not the luminescent moon cause epidemics all give rise to a more universal expectation that the less extravagant (read: naturalistic) hypothesis is bound to be the correct one even if the evidence is incomplete or unavailable.

The same is said to be true about explanations in some of the cognitive sciences such as those found in clinical psychology. Consider specifically historical attempts to account for certain mental health maladies. It is no secret that many had believed

---

52. Cupitt, "Four Arguments," 414.
53. "Does God Exist? William Lane Craig vs. Christopher Hitchens."
54. Hitchens, "Opening Speech."
55. Hitchens, "Cross Examination."
56. I note that William Lane Craig is in fact a demonic realist. See his "Doctrine of Creation," §8.20–26.

that demons possess their human victims and make them convulse and/or perhaps manifest in the form of multiple personalities. With the advancements in psychology and psychiatry, these so-called mental harassments by demons are now considered better accounted for by natural etiological conditions subsumed under known professional diagnoses.[57] That these cognitive sciences have offered explanations that have displaced contrary religious accounts is further bolstered by the fact that a number of people today who think they are afflicted by demonic possession have been professionally diagnosed with more "ordinary" maladies and have had some measure of success when followed up with psychological and psychotropic treatments and coping strategies. To wit, mental disorders are no longer considered by most to be engineered by evil spirits.

And then there is the mired world of (alleged) paranormal activity. Whether one believes to see a ghostly specter or spook appear before one's eyes or thinks that a UFO has managed to trek across the night sky, many of the evidences that lie behind these occurrences tend to find better explanations in a pool of more ordinary and mundane causes. Such patterns of *faux* numinous explanations being overturned by naturalistic ones in inquiries where the supernatural *should* be a consideration is perhaps one of the major reasons science is heralded as the paradigm of truth. In fact, in some quarters science is even the *summa disciplinae*–the most exalted if not the sole means of acquiring reliable knowledge.[58] It is not surprising, then, that when it comes to belief in God, angels, or demons, a skeptic will demur on grounds that for whatever reason one might invoke the supernatural as an explanation, science will inevitably replace that explanation with a soon-to-be-discovered naturalistic alternative.[59] To insist on any supernatural explanation is to insist on a surrogate for a more reasonable, evidence-based conclusion. David Kyle Johnson summarizes the problem thus far: "Such poor reasoning . . . is what led to belief in demons in the first place; the inability to find an explanation for diseases and weather is that for which the demonic was invented."[60]

Accordingly, so it is alleged, past phenomena once attributed to the gods over nature and conscience have all been refuted at the hands of the physical and behavioral sciences. And, so, the devil-of-the-gaps charge is fundamentally no different than those of the God-of-the-gaps: Any explanation that alleges that Satan or his demons are somehow responsible for certain physical or psychological phenomena is likely false since previous allegations of demonic activity have been and continue to be better accounted for by naturalistic alternatives. Explanations that entail demonic realism

57. E.g., Henderson, "Exorcism and Possession in Psychotherapy Practice"; Joshi, "Mental Health in a Historical Perspective."

58. E.g., Rosenberg, *Atheist's Guide to Reality*, esp. 5–8; Hawking and Mlodinow, *The Grand Design*; Wilson, *Consilience*; Midgley, *Science as Salvation*.

59. E.g., Richard Dawkins says as much when he anticipates that a scientific explanation for the fine-tuning of the universe will eventually replace creationist theories and those of intelligent design. See his summary in *The God Delusion*, 157–58.

60. Johnson, "Justified Belief in the Existence of Demons is Impossible," 180.

are then expected to always be wrong. But for the so-called lazy thinker entrenched in a mythologized universe, devils remain as convenient explanatory surrogates in accounting for mysterious negative phenomena with no immediate, apparent natural causes. Richard Dawkins's assessment is most caustic: "Those people who leap from personal bafflement at a natural phenomenon straight to a hasty invocation of the supernatural are no better than the fools who see a conjuror bending a spoon and leap to the conclusion that it is 'paranormal.'"[61] Cupitt's is equally so as his comments pertain specifically to "[e]xplanation by devils" which is something he thinks "must be rejected on scientific grounds . . . because it is slothful and cowardly."[62]

The best way to construe a devil-of-the-gaps argument, then, is to insist that demonic realism implies that certain facts obtain, namely that some physical or psychological occurrences are best explained by demons. Since all of these explanations have been (allegedly) displaced by naturalistic alternatives in the past, then, given such a track record, demonic realism is not likely going to be vindicated as an explanation for anything forthcoming. This argument appears to be making its case in the following way:

9. If demonic realism is true, then some mysterious events are best explained by demons.

10. No mysterious events in the past (i.e., gaps) have been best explained by demons.

11. There remain some mysterious events yet to be explained.

12. Demonic realism is unlikely to explain those remaining mysterious events.

13. Therefore, demonic realism is (probably) not true.

The principle thrust of the argument has to do with demonic realism, as an explanatory hypothesis, meeting certain expectations about the mysterious events in question. If observations do not confirm those expectations, then the hypothesis is considered not likely true. Now, the "mysterious events" of the argument has a twofold connotation. First, there are certain *physical* events like astro-geological disasters, biological maladies, and alleged paranormal activity all of which are mysterious by virtue of lacking any known physical causes. Let us collectively refer to these as ϕ-occurrences. Second, there are certain *psychological* events like dysfunctional or abnormal behavior often associated with mental disorders and/or mental illnesses which are mysterious by virtue of lacking any known psychological causes. Let us refer to these as ψ-occurrences. I contend that, regarding both types of occurrences, the demonic realist can successfully push back against premises 10 and 12. Moreover, there is a reasonable way to push back on premise 9 as well. Let us look at the objections now by focusing first on problems with premise 9.

---

61. Dawkins, *The God Delusion*, 129.
62. Cupitt, "Four Arguments," 414.

Philosophical Arguments for Demonic Anti-Realism

1. Premise 9's assumption that demonic realism implies that demons cause φ-occurrences is not necessarily true

The reason why demonic realism appears to imply that some physical events (such as putative occurrences of paranormal activity and biological maladies) are caused by demons is because most adherents think that demons can indeed directly interact with the physical universe. While most representatives of demonic realism have thought this way, it is unclear that a *biblical* demonology, or a bare demonic realism, in any way entails the ability of demons to directly intercourse with the physical universe. One could thus argue that it isn't the failure to find demons as causes in certain physical events that shows gaps once filled by devils are shrinking to nothing, rather it only shows that demonic realists *should not have appropriated diabolical hypotheses in those instances to begin with*. Maybe demons do not cause physical events at all. As such, not finding them in the gaps would hardly constitute evidence for demonic anti-realism.[63]

2. That φ-occurrences are best explained by naturalistic alternatives to demons is not obviously true

As it turns out, there is a way for the traditionalist who insists on the ability of demons to intercourse with nature to reply here as well. For it is unclear whether one is failing to consider whether, like God, demons can utilize secondary causes in actualizing their diabolical objectives. It may be that the presence of demonic agents is not directly evident in the analyzed causal chain, but such an analysis may not have any currency toward showing no demonic agents in the causal chain whatsoever. In the case of God, if, say, biological evolution best explains the arrival of *Homo sapiens*, it is certainly possible that God utilizes the mechanisms of the evolutionary process in ultimately bringing about *Homo sapiens*. One would not find God, so to speak, in the forces of natural selection or adaptive radiation, but it does not mean that God is not or cannot be the source of those forces. The same could be said about the forces behind the more cosmic occurrence of stellar evolution.

Let us return to the opinion that demons can indeed move upon physical mechanisms. If a slamming door is best explained, say, by the presence of a wind tunnel, it is possible that, in supposing that a demon were somehow responsible, the wind tunnel itself may have been diabolically engineered. While one may not have direct evidence for a spiritual cause of wind tunnels, that something like that is possible even in light of the observations made shows that it is not obviously true that no φ-occurrences have a spiritual genesis. In discussing X-of-the-gaps reasoning in general (where X

---

63. For, as I shall argue in chapter 9, I think it is false that demons have the capability of interacting with objects in the physical world.

is the placeholder for some posited explanatory cause not known to be confirmed by other evidence), Robert Larmer writes:

> The failure to find something can only be considered good evidence that it is not present if it is reasonable to suppose that one's search procedure was adequate to detect it. What constitutes an adequate search procedure will vary depending upon the phenomenon in question.[64]

Consequently, the demonic realist can doubt that "an adequate search procedure" has in fact been employed.

As for the general hope or expectation that any currently unresolved mysteries that invoke demonic explanations will and should be overturned, it should be noted that just about any mysterious thing science cannot currently explain could be waived away on similar grounds. For example, eliminative materialists, like Paul and Patricia Churchland, fully expect that consciousness itself with its properties of intentionality, beliefs, and desires (i.e., "folk psychology") will and should be displaced by a better, soon-to-be-offered neurobiological explanation.[65] For the Churchlands, it does not matter that we human beings see the world from the standpoint of self-consciousness, for they argue that the self's beliefs and desires are just consciousness-of-the-gaps reasoning–that consciousness itself is a prescientific postulate that irrationally supplants a good, though nascent, scientific alternative. But for the majority who in fact think that self-consciousness is a real thing, no X-of-the-gaps push-back would displace it as a sufficient explanation for explaining self-motivated activity. In other words, the notion that consciousness does not actually exist is not obviously true (and is more likely obviously false) despite its rather "unscientific" approach to explicating human behavior. Like eliminative materialism, the devil-of-the-gaps objection is only as convincing as the evidence warrants. And one cannot presume in advance, armed only with prejudice and lack of evidence, that demons are not ever sufficient explanations for some mysterious events. For that is a gap of reasoning in itself that has not been adequately filled.

3. That ψ-occurrences are best explained by naturalistic alternatives to demons is greatly exaggerated

It goes without saying that modern society considers the phenomenon of demonic possession to be a prescientific (mis)understanding of mental disorders.[66] This is to say that all of the alleged demonic possessions of antiquity were actually an aggregate of misdiagnoses of various human behaviors that are now better understood in

---

64. Larmer, "Is there Anything Wrong?," 136–37.
65. Churchland and Churchland, *On the Contrary*.
66. Magiorkinis, Sidiropoulou, and Diamantis, "Hallmarks in the History of Epilepsy"; Loschen, "Psychiatry and Religion"; Joshi, "Mental Health in a Historical Perspective."

the light of modern cognitive science. Proponents of a devil-of-the-gaps argument regarding ψ-occurrences think that alleged demonic possessions are (by and large) better explained as iterations of schizophrenia or as manifesting episodes of Dissociative Identity Disorder (formerly known as Multiple Personality Disorder) with some symptoms being attributed to neurological disorders like epilepsy. Indeed, on the presumption that current demonic possession cases are best understood as episodes of cognitive or mental disorders of a certain kind, treatments of these cases have been overall–so the perception goes–more ameliorating for the patients than has exorcism. In other words, on the probability that such symptoms are the results of ordinarily classified disorders, a diagnosis based on something like, say, Dissociative Identity or Transitive Disorder or schizophrenia or some other mainstream disorder has led to more rehabilitative success in patient recovery.

Given the obvious impact of Enlightenment thinking, the prospect of demonic possession as a diagnosis has fallen out of favor in the West. The result is, as the devil-of-the-gaps argument implies, that the notion of spirit possession as a genuine phenomenon is perceived as outright unreasonable–a vestige of a superstitious culture long overcome. And since treating certain symptomatic behaviors as mental disorders seems to have made such conditions more amenable to mainstream care (e.g., medication), and perhaps far less stigmatizing than being the innocent victim of an otherworldly kidnapping, it is no surprise that demons are no longer seen as real entities that contribute to the erratic behavior in putative possession cases.

While we should always prefer, *ceteris paribus*, a more naturalistic interpretation of the cause of some event (i.e., within the physical universe there should be a preference for the natural in the absence of any mitigating evidence to the contrary), it is unclear that any mental disorder pathology does the explanatory job that is assumed of it. When someone is diagnosed with, say, Dissociative Identity Disorder, it sounds technical enough to the uninformed to give the impression that we have a known neurological etiology with which to engage and potentially cure as if it were a concise medical diagnosis that enables one to isolate the offending cause(s). Just what is the explanation for someone's suspected dissociative behavior? Presumably, it is because the person is suffering from Dissociative Identity Disorder. But what is *that*? In and of itself it is not a cause.[67] According to the *Diagnostic and Statistical Manual of Mental Disorders* (fifth edition), a Dissociative Identity Disorder is a

> [d]isruption of identity characterized by two or more distinct personality states, which may be described in some cultures as an experience of possession. The disruption in identity involves marked discontinuity in sense of self and sense of agency, accompanied by related alterations in affect, behavior, consciousness, memory, perception, cognition, and/or sensory-motor

---

67. As emphasized by Thomas S. Szasz, mental illness in general "is not literally a 'thing'" ("The Myth of Mental Illness," 4.

functioning. These signs and symptoms may be observed by others or reported by the individual.[68]

What is notably lacking in this description is reference to any causal explanation whatsoever. If one were to say that one is suffering not from demonic possession but from Dissociative Identity Disorder, it would not be an attempt to relocate the cause of one's condition to some naturalistic etiology. No doubt this is how the diagnosis will be read by those who believe demons do not exist, but it should be clear that no causal pathway is being traced here. Rather, such a diagnosis merely describes a family of relevant symptoms exhibited by the patient. In fact, many cognitive scientists hesitate even to speak of causation at all in classifying mental disorders, for it is often controversial as to whether there even exist sufficient and necessary conditions for some putative disorder. Philosopher of cognitive science George Graham reports that "there are no successful causal explanations of (exemplary) mental disorders that cite a single main cause or a final common pathway for their pathogeneses."[69]

Thus, the causes of mental disorders *in general* are hotly disputed in the literature and, contrary to the hopes of those skeptical of demonic possession, do not bode well in leading one away from the possibility of demonic possession as a possible contributing cause in some of those cases. One might insist that demons are not ever to blame when considering a psychological malady like Dissociative Identity Disorder, but this amounts to nothing more than a misreading of what the *DSM* itself actually says since it only observes that the condition "may be described in some cultures as an experience of possession." That this is how some cultures may describe it hardly counts as a refutation of its being a genuine possession case. By signaling a "disruption in identity" it leaves open to interpretation what the cause may be in a, quite frankly, spiritually friendly manner!

As Graham explains, the *DSM* has been known to "[classify] disorders through the description of syndromes or syndromal clusters . . . quite regardless of surmises about possible underlying or antecedent proximate causes."[70] It is an exaggeration, to say the least, to insist that psychologists and psychiatrists have somehow *solved* the mystery of so-called possession cases when, in fact, they have merely *categorized* it according to a "cluster" of symptoms only. Analogies readily exist in medicine. Take tinnitus (i.e., "ringing in the ears") for example. One's being diagnosed with tinnitus is not to say that their condition has this or that cause. Tinnitus can be brought on by any number of factors including hearing loss, vascular diseases, tumors, loud noises, or disturbances of the eardrum. To have tinnitus is not to have ruled out some causes and favored others. No more should be the case when it comes to the more controversial field of clinical psychology.

68. American Psychiatric Association, *DSM-V*, 292.
69. Graham, *The Disordered Mind*, 55.
70. Graham, *The Disordered Mind*, 65.

Philosophical Arguments for Demonic Anti-Realism

If that was not enough to undermine the force of the devil-of-the-gaps objection, it gets even worse for its proponents. For, despite the forceful rhetoric of modernity, psychologists and psychiatrists have not even settled on whether mental disorders of any sort are even *mental*.[71] One school of thought, fueled by those primarily within psychiatry, think that a disorder's etiology is to be found in a cause or set of causes that is/are merely biological.[72] Others–that is, those generally within psychology–think that this is nothing short of false.[73] Furthermore, according to Rachel Cooper, "'[m]ental' disorders frequently have multifactorial causes."[74] It is not as though there is only one cause per disorder (though this is certainly possible) and that a diagnosis that locates one cause somehow excludes the possibility of there being any other contributory causes. Instead, it is apparent that there is often a presence of multiple factors and this fact convolutes a diagnosis. All of this creates a web of ambiguity in the hunt for any particular cause. What precludes demons, then, from being possible contributory causes in some possession cases?[75] Beyond an *a priori* prejudice against the supernatural, I cannot think of any. The fact that demon-possession cases *qua* demon possessions have been getting a serious second look in academia is a credit to the demonic realism naturalists disparage.[76] Thus, the notion that demon-possession cases can never be spiritually caused is not only dubious but overdrawn. If the industry cannot even adjudicate what causes or even constitutes a conventional mental disorder, shame on the anti-realist for insisting that there is some kind of unprecedented certainty that demonic agents cannot ever be causal candidates!

Having presented and assessed three arguments for demonic anti-realism, let us now consider a summary and some concluding thoughts to this chapter.

Conclusion

This chapter has sought to cover three main arguments, or classifications of arguments, that seek to establish that Satan and his demons do not exist: (i) the incoherence argument, (ii) the ethical argument, and (iii) the devil-of-the-gaps argument. The first argument proposes that the tenets of a Judeo-Christian demonology are not compossible with the existence of an all-good, all-powerful God. But I argued that if the good angels could freely rebel against God, and they can reasonably be refused redemption, then a scenario where demons obtain and push-back against God and

---

71. See Garson, *The Biological Mind*; cf., Stein et al., "What is a Mental/Psychiatric Disorder?"

72. Insel et al., "Research Domain Criteria (RDoC)"; Kandel, "A New Intellectual Framework for Psychiatry."

73. See Olbert and Gala, "Supervenience and Psychiatry."

74. Cooper, "What's Special About Mental Health and Disorder?," 490.

75. L. Stafford Betty bluntly says that "we do not have . . . indubitable evidence (the 'slam dunk') we need to overturn the claim of Western medicine that infesting spirits are not the cause–ever–of mental illness" ("The Growing Evidence for 'Demonic Possession,'" 25).

76. E.g., Montgomery, *Demon Possession*.

his creation is plausible. Moreover, that God's semi-divine servants should rebel at all seems too embarrassing a narrative, for these reasons the critics highlight, to have been invented as a fiction. This suggests that if the notion of an angelic fall was obviously an offensive concept, then surely it would have been cast differently if not deleted altogether from the canons of orthodoxy.

Second, the ethical argument proposes that those committing atrocities can always evade justice through scapegoating; and that since demons can allegedly manifest as human beings, one can justify and has justified harm against those human beings whose only "crime" is sorcery. In either case, belief in demons appears to sanction unacceptable moral consequences. That is to say, one can both exonerate a tyrant while bringing disproportionate harm to a "witch," neither of which is ethical. But I charged that this twofold argument fails to disentangle incorrect beliefs about demons with the existence of demons. It also assumes a certain version of human agency that is philosophically controversial, i.e., incompatibilism. But even if one accepts incompatibilism, the ethical argument still does not license an assailant to avoid moral culpability.

And third, the devil-of-the-gaps argument suggests that scientific explanations have displaced demonic explanations. Proponents suppose that even if physical and psychological mysteries remain, science will inevitably offer a better explanation for any seemingly inexplicable maladies as it has done in the past. Anti-realists insist that appeals to the demonic are irrational for realists are merely appealing to primitive notions in want of a good explanation. I objected to this argument by pointing out that its demonological assumptions are dubious. And the idea that naturalistic explanations have in fact displaced demonic ones is either not obviously true or is greatly exaggerated. In all cases, the devil-of-the-gaps is an unsuccessful charge.

Having surveyed a series of arguments designed to support demonic anti-realism and reasons why they fail to support their conclusions, we move on to the next chapter wherein we shall consider a series of arguments in support of demonic realism.

5

Philosophical Arguments for Demonic Realism (I)

IN THE LAST CHAPTER, we began our exploration of natural diabology by first looking at three main arguments for the nonexistence of Satan and demons. Accordingly, I showed why each failed to offer any good support for the thesis of anti-realism/adiabolism. Of course this alone does not suppose that demonic realism is true by default, for the failure of the arguments against demonic realism only implies that it is those arguments alone that do not lead to anti-realism. A clever argument may yet be waiting in the wings. Even in showing that multiple arguments that share a common conclusion fail does not entail that their shared conclusion is, therefore, not true. This is especially evident in the previously-discussed case for demonic anti-realism. What my responses to each of those arguments indicates is that it merely remains possible for demons to exist despite the particular objections that were lodged. A case must still be made for demonic realism to bridge the gap from its being a survivable hypothesis to being a believable one.

Now, the kinds of arguments one might consider for the existence of a Satan seem to parallel some of the kinds of arguments for the existence of God (just like some of the objections to the existence of Satan seem to parallel atheistic arguments against God). This fact was recently brought to light by a creative essay authored by Paul McNamara who attempted to show how putative arguments for Satan's existence show up theistic arguments to be inadequate justifications for God's existence, for something like Satan just does not exist. And any argument that would lead to the proposition that Satan exists would serve more as a *reductio* against its theistic sibling rather than as a genuine piece of natural diabology (for, as McNamara takes it, Satan doesn't exist).[1] McNamara's essay consists of a fictional dialogue between a clinical psychiatrist and a patient who is plagued by a nightmare he had about revisiting a previously completed philosophy of religion course. In the nightmare sequence, the student hears all of the classical arguments re-lectured to him by his professors but

---

1. McNamara, "A Theist's Nightmare," chapter 9. Cf., Law, "Evil God," 18.

Part II: Existential Matters

with subtle tweaks made that convert them into arguments for the existence of the devil. Seeing that the same arguments for the devil have been previously enlisted as evidences for God, and that identical arguments cannot yield contradictory conclusions, the student sees this as a categorical defeater for the employment of all such arguments for theism.[2]

But what McNamara has intended for ill, God may have intended for good. That is to say, there may be some warrant to similarly constructed arguments that give credence to belief in the devil that do not necessarily defeat or dismiss arguments that offer up evidence for God's existence. They may coexist in perfect philosophical harmony and, hence, provide independent streams of reasoning that secure some kind of demonic (minimalist) realism. However, as will be made evident later in this chapter, I do not think that *all* such arguments can be converted into successful reasons for the diabolical. If Satan is not the First Cause of all contingent beings or is not the locus of all (im)morality, then surely there are some kinds of theistic reasoning that are incommensurate with diabolical reasoning.

It is the purpose of this chapter and the next to survey more serious philosophical attempts to argue for the existence of Satan (and his demons). I do think that the ones in this chapter end up being either unconvincing on their own or are in need of supplementation or full-on rehabilitation. However, the next chapter surveys one argument that seems pretty good even if on its own; and having one good argument for demonic realism is still better than having none. Accordingly, I expect–nay, I *hope*–that the work embodied in these pages will prompt further research on this and its related matters. But it is currently serving only as a "state of the union" that either begs for further discussion or stands as a monument for attempts that should not be revisited. As such, I bequeath this chapter to readers to draw their own conclusions on the matters discussed herein.

In what follows, we shall survey three main arguments for the existence of Satan and his demons that do not depend on any biblical data. Like the arguments for anti-realism, these arguments also range from the *a priori* to the *a posteriori* with some combining these approaches. I have deliberately labeled the arguments so as to coincide with their familiar theistic counterparts.

The Ontological Argument

The ontological argument for God's existence is enjoying a bit of a renaissance amongst sympathetic theistic philosophers today. Those familiar with its various formulations since Anselm know that it is the most well-known *a priori* argument for God's existence. According to most iterations of the argument, one is led to deductively infer the existence of God by appealing to the necessity of there being the greatest conceivable

---

2. "If the reasoning is parallel in both cases, and the conclusions are incompatible, then the reasoning itself has gotta be flawed" (McNamara, "A Theist's Nightmare," 131).

being whose non-existence would be *ex vi termini* impossible (or, not true in every possible world). And because such a being would be that which none greater could be conceived, then that being would be no less than God. Therefore, God exists necessarily and this entails that God exists actually. Despite the argument's success–or lack thereof–one might wonder if there is a correlative argument for the existence of an anti-god, or Satan, along these lines. Since one of the key premises of an ontological argument for God's existence pertains to some maximal quality (viz., greatness), Satan would likewise possess a maximal quality of a different sort (viz., worseness).

There have been some published philosophical works on the subject of ontological arguments for the existence of the devil.[3] However, such formulations are not usually written to prove the devil at all. Instead, the authors have designed such arguments in attempts to show why ontological arguments for God appear to either not work or work inconsistently. Specifically, it is alleged that such arguments fail to establish the existence of only one kind of Being (viz., God) since they can also be co-opted to imply the existence of other kinds of being–viz., devilish kinds that are radically antithetical and contradictory to the traditional Being.

It is this irony that makes the ontological argument for the devil so shocking. As such, if one can use the same formulation of an ontological argument for the devil as one can for God's existence, then an antinomy arises. That is to say, we would now have two omnipotent, all-knowing, etc., beings. But this cannot be. Therefore, either the beings concluded by the mutual arguments are the same being that need to be understood in some non-dualistic, transcendent sense or the ontological argument's strategy or axioms on which it is based are flawed altogether. Either way, the ontological argument delivers *neither* deity nor devil.

If there *is* an *a priori* argument to be made, and one wants to take it seriously, then let us consider a construction such as that found in the following:

1. I have a concept of something "than which nothing *worse* can be conceived."
2. If that "something" did not actually, or in fact, exist, it would not be "that than which nothing worse could be conceived," because something could always be conceived to be much worse, viz., something that actually exists.
3. This "that than which nothing worse could be conceived" we shall call the devil.
4. Therefore, the devil exists.[4]

To adopt the usual terminology, we might refer to that which adds to the degrees of *worseness* as *bad-making properties*. But what sorts of bad-making properties would there be such that it would lead to "that than which nothing worse could be

3. Richman, "Ontological Proof of the Devil"; Richman, "A Serious Look at the Ontological Argument"; Haight and Haight, "An Ontological Argument for the Devil"; Power, "Ontological Arguments for Satan"; Haight, "What Have We Learned from Ontological Devil-Arguments?"

4. This is a slight modification of the argument as originally stated in Haight and Haight, "An Ontological Argument for the Devil," 218–19.

conceived"? One might reason that since a being with bad-making properties can be conceived, and so would obviously be bad, it would be *worse* if that being with bad-making properties actually existed. Therefore, the worst possible being exists.

Now this formulation is predicated, more or less, on St. Anselm's original construction in his *Proslogion* II. Since existence as a great-making property is not to be necessarily equated with that which adds to the *goodness* of something (viz., that greatness and goodness are not synonymous with each other[5]), then the greatest possible being and the worst possible being will have existence, for Anselm's contention was that the greatest possible being that actually exists (*in re*) is greater than one that merely exists in the understanding (*in intellectu*). Likewise, a being is *worse* (or is a worse possible being) if he exists *in re* rather than merely *in intellectu*.[6] Of course if greatness and goodness *are* to be equated, thus making the principle that existence is a perfection true, then the ontological argument for the devil is not sound. Since this seems too quick, as one can readily deny it, let us not suppose that the two are equivalent.

There are other reasons why this ontological argument fails. For one, if the argument were sound, we would have an omnipotent devil in the universe if being the worst possible being also entails having omnipotence. This awkward implication seems right since a bad being with more power is seemingly *worse* than a being without as much power (e.g., it is not as bad to be on the receiving end of an evil peasant than of an evil king!). And if the worst possible being is omnipotent, then God cannot be. Thus, one would have to insist that God does not also exist. But God's existence is established by the same kind of ontological proof and, so, an omnipotent God also exists necessarily! Hence, we have an unresovable antinomy. While the co-existence of God and the devil may not be compossible, they *should* be if both ontological proofs work. Or, alternatively, there would have to be a non-binary understanding of the mutual arguments's conclusions in that they somehow refer to the *same* ultimate being (viz., that the greatest conceivable being *just is* the worst possible being, but is neither good nor bad).[7] But it is hard to make much sense of this. Such a holistic conclusion amounts to nothing more than an attempt to force a reconciliation of a contradiction.

There is another problem with the ontological argument for the devil. While we were quick to assume that a being that exists *in re* is worse than a being that only exists *in intellectu*, it is not an assumption that is *ultima facie* true. Why not? Because

---

5. Perry C. Mason is "not convinced that Anselm uses 'greater' to mean 'better' . . . despite the fact that he does identify the greatest possible being (that than which no greater can be conceived) with the perfect being (that that which no better can be conceived)" ("The Devil and St. Anselm," 8).

6. Mason writes: "one might assume that, while existence itself is neither a perfection nor a defect, it does intensify the good and the bad aspects of things. In that case existence in reality would make a good thing better and a bad thing worse than either would be if it existed only in the understanding or not at all. The best possible being, therefore, would have to exist in reality to be as good as possible, and similarly in the case of the worst possible being" ("The Devil and Saint Anselm," 9).

7. Haight, "What Have We Learned from Ontological Devil-Arguments?," 304 n. 18.

Philosophical Arguments for Demonic Realism (I)

once we consider in what sense something is said to be worse, it will turn out to not necessarily be the case. When one says that it is worse for something to exist, she must be referring to some state of affairs wherein a bad being exists *in re*. Thus, one is really saying that some state of affairs containing a bad being existing *in re* is worse than a state of affairs where a bad being exists only *in intellectu*. But this is neither obvious nor probable. Let us suppose that an α-type evil is a certain, unambiguous kind of evil. There is a possible world where the state of affairs consists of a bad being who exists *in re* and α-type evils obtain (perhaps those evils are caused by the bad being) only on odd-numbered years. Likewise, there is a possible world where the state of affairs consists of a bad being that only exists *in intellectu* but α-type evils obtain *every* year (perhaps due to other bad agents, or the sum total of all other bad agents). Accordingly, the world where the bad being in question exists only *in intellectu* is actually worse than the world where the bad being in question exists *in re*.[8] Conversely, a possible world containing a certain amount of evil does not entail that any member of that world is worse than any member of some other possible world where the amount of evil is not as much. And that, of course, strips the key premise of the ontological argument of any force.

Finally, even if an ontological argument for the existence of the devil were to be made successful, say by reformulating the argument along the lines of the Kripkean semantics of possible worlds, the conceptual implications of such a necessary being of the sinister type are theologically aberrant to a so ramified theology as Christianity. If the devil is the worst possible being (a la Anselm) or a maximally evil being such that he exists in every possible world (a la Kripke), he would possess properties that would far exceed those of the biblical devil. As explicated in chapter 2, Satan is likely a fallen angel–a finite though semi-divine being. Biblically, Satan's powers are mitigated by those of God and of those whom God has empowered (e.g., Luke 9.1; 10.19; 1 John 2.14; 4.4). A Zoroastrian-Manichean portrait of Satan as a polarizing but equal anti-power in opposition to God is not supported by either Old or New Testament demonologies.

Perhaps one is willing to bite the bullet on this one. For, the notion of an anti-God who is maximally evil, though offensive to Jewish and Christian demonologies, is, nevertheless, demonstrably existent. But this is to mistaken what evil actually is, at least according to the classical understanding. Evil is, as classical metaphysicians from Plato to the Scholastics explain, a *privation* of the good. Evil as privation means that it is a defect–a failure in attempting to actualize its potentialities. This notion is predicated on *essentialism* which is a viable option in the philosophy of religion. This is to say that every kind of thing that exists tends toward actualizing its potentialities all of which are entailed or dictated by its essence. Essences are what makes things what they are and serve as the archetypal blueprints for how something is to function in fulfillment of its nature–a nature that is mapped by its essence. If an object fails to realize its potentialities or is impeded from being able to function well in accord with its

---

8. See Mason, "The Devil and St. Anselm," 10.

essence, such an impediment or privation is construed as an evil (either being brought about by itself or at the hands of another). A dog that barks and runs on four legs and laps up water in an effort to quench its thirst are examples of this dog functioning properly in accord with its essence. If the dog should go hoarse, lose a leg, or sever its tongue, it would not be in a position to optimize its essence as a dog. As a *maximally* evil being, this being would be, in Aristotelian terms, an unmoved mover of evil. If it had any potentialities left unrealized, it would not be a maximally evil being.

By now it might seem obvious why there can be no maximal being that is essentially evil. For if a maximally evil being exists necessarily and is himself necessarily evil *qua* the unmoved mover of evil, then the being's essence consists of his acting in accord with the very essence he necessarily has. That such a being may end up engaging in acts of torture or treachery against defenseless creatures would be doing precisely what such a being ought to be doing vis-à-vis the dictates of its essence that it has necessarily. Evil, so understood, would not be a privation of its being and, so, lacking a good; rather, his torturing and abusing would just be the actualization of a good, namely the fulfillment of the nature it necessarily has. On such an understanding, it is impossible to conceive of a necessarily existing being who is essentially and necessarily evil so construed. For it is impossible that such a being is actually doing anything wrong when he tortures and abuses innocent victims–the actualization of which successfully optimizes his nature.[9] In fact, it would actually be his *failure* to torture and abuse that would constitute an evil. And that is just absurd. Thus, if one co-opts the classical notion of evil as privation, as most philosophers of religion do, then the notion of the worst possible being as a necessarily existing and essentially evil being is incoherent given that evil entails the lacking or privation of being. In the absence of another, more suitable notion of evil, there can be no such thing as a maximally evil being *qua* an unmoved mover of evil that exists necessarily.

Therefore, an ontological argument for the existence of the worst possible being is not only unsuccessful, it is theologically egregious and philosophically absurd. Accordingly, it is actually fortunate for the orthodox that ontological arguments of this sort do not work, but it is not so fortunate for the demonic realist who seeks a philosophical demonstration of the diabolical. Perhaps these defects can be overcome in a clever reformulation, but I cannot imagine what that would be.[10]

---

9. I cannot help but note the irony for moderns that Aristotle should label the successful achievement of one's essential *telos* as *eudaimonia*. For that term derives from the two Greek words *eu* ("good") and *daimonia* ("demon"), words that, today, do not belong together.

10. At this point, someone might be tempted wrongly to enlist Stephen Law's novel defense of an "evil god" ("The Evil-God Challenge"). But his "argument" is not intended to demonstrate the existence of a malevolent deity or a demon but to argue that, contrary to the tenets of theism (vis-à-vis perfect being theology), a world containing evil undermines the supposition of God's maximal goodness. On a classical notion of theism, however, this seems like an impossible notion especially for a being whose essence just is his existence (viz., pure actuality).

Philosophical Arguments for Demonic Realism (I)

The Cosmological Argument

Cosmological arguments for God's existence may be the most discussed family type of arguments used in support of a natural theology. Though they are quite diverse, they share in common the fact that *at least* one contingent thing exists. This evident truth sets the foundation for its crucial, though variegated, form of reasoning: If there is no metaphysical possibility of an infinite temporal and/or hierarchical regress, and no explanation for the contingent thing(s) that exists, then there must be some ultimate cause and/or explanation for the existence of that thing(s). To be more colloquial, as long as there is a creation there can be a creator inferred from it.

One of the major strengths of cosmological arguments is its relatively recent intimation of astrophysics (e.g., that Big Bang cosmology provides additional evidence for the contingency of our universe). Ever since Edwin Hubble's 1929 empirical validation of an expanding universe, astrophysics has continued to confirm that our universe began to exist some 13.77 billion years ago. This is not to say that classic hierarchy-based cosmological arguments such as those championed by Aristotle and Aquinas are somehow less useful. Quite the contrary. Those arguments infer a dependence of creation on God *regardless* of whether or not the universe has a temporal beginning.[11] But if the universe *did* begin to exist at the moment of the Big Bang, one adds to their argumentative repertoire additional support for the contingency of the universe. Obviously a cosmological argument for the devil requires a bit more to its inference than a mere appeal to the existence of some contingent thing. In fact, a cosmological argument for the devil is really an extension of and one that follows an established cosmological argument for God as the creator-cause. In inferring the existence of a devil, one simply takes an additional step (or two) toward making inferences. What, then, would such an argument look like?

I shall present a cosmological argument for the existence of the devil in the vein of those who formulated a version of it, viz., medieval Scholastics, so that we can consider whether it is a successful piece of natural diabology. Let us consider the following argument schema to be adequately representative (note: I am using the term "universe" below to refer to the existence of at least one contingent thing):

5. If God creates any universe at all, then He will create a universe with at least one angel in it.

6. God created a universe (this one).

7. Therefore, at least one angel exists in it.

8. If natural evils exist, then the first natural evil(s) is caused by either God, a human being, or at least one angel.

---

11. For more on the success of classical arguments for God's existence not predicated on temporal causation, see Edward Feser's *Five Proofs of the Existence of God*.

9. Natural evils exist.

10. The first natural evil(s) is caused neither by God nor human being.

11. Therefore, the first natural evil(s) is caused by at least one angel (and this we call Satan).

Notice that premise 6 adopts a conclusion set out in some cosmological argument or other for God's existence. It is the first premise (5) that makes a rather surprising connection, namely that merely having a universe created by God implies that at least one angel exists in it. No doubt this is one of the argument's crucial and most controversial premises. Although premise 8 involves a different controversy because it assumes that a particular Augustinian tradition is true, namely that natural evils only arise as either a consequence to or as a punishment for moral evil.[12] And, presumably, moral evil requires or entails free will–something that only autonomous beings have. Premise 9 just states the obvious. Premise 10 eliminates two candidates from the disjunction as likely inaugurators of natural evil. Statement 11, as the conclusion, follows from the others and identifies the culpable angel, aside from whatever other features it may have, as Satan.

This argument would appear to have at least three vulnerabilities. First, premise 5 makes a whopping supposition that having an angelic realm is entailed by God's creating at all which doesn't seem obvious. God might have created a universe where only animals exist or no animals exist, and this would not appear in and of itself to be contrary to God's omnibenevolence. Secondly, premise 6 assumes more than just that the universe exists, it also supposes that *God* is the creator of the universe. As such, the project of natural diabology is naturally going to be *after* the project of natural theology. But it is important to point out that one cannot just show that God exists, one must show that he is also the creator of the universe. And there are few argument types that accomplish this, one of which is indeed a cosmological argument. Thirdly, premise 8 attempts to exhaust all possible candidates of free agents for the origin of the first evil(s). That may be harmless enough except that, as already noted, the premise implies that the Augustinian tradition is true. The defender must offer some positive support for the Augustinian thesis.[13] In addition, one must undermine the plausibility of alternative explanations for the origin(s) of natural evil such as that found in Irenaeus and John Hick (viz., that natural evils are inaugurated by God in order to prepare beings to be suited for eternal life[14]).

If that much can be established–which is no small task–then and only then can one move on with the argument's other salient claims. Since, given premise 8, evil is something God does not (cannot?) directly will, then it is necessary to find

---

12. Augustine, *De Genesi Ad Litteram* I.3.

13. Some have pointed to various Old and New Testament passages as evidences for the tradition. See Michael Murray's presentation of them in his *Nature Red in Tooth and Claw*, 73–81.

14. Hick, *Philosophy of Religion*, 44f.

an alternative source (with free will) for the origin of natural evil. And if the evil in question exists prior to human beings, as the various historical sciences seem to indicate, then human beings obviously cannot be the source of the first natural evil(s) either. That leaves a being (or beings) that is neither God nor human as the one(s) responsible (by disjunction); QED, it was an angel. But now circle back to the most controversial premise of them all, namely that there even is such a thing as angels. Since much hangs on the existence of there being at least one angel, we shall focus on premise 5 next.

Premise 5 obviously has the limited goal of establishing merely the existence of the angelic realm. This is certainly a good thing as long as one accepts the traditional notion that Satan was indeed one of the good angels God created. The strength of premise 5's implication for angels derives from an old controversy amongst medieval philosophers. This controversy centered on whether God had any free will in creating the universe given his moral perfection. What stimulated the debate was the insinuation, if not outright accusation, that God *necessarily* created *our specific* universe (viz., the universe that we in fact have).[15] Such a notion was fueled by speculation about Plotinus's doctrine of emanation in that it was *thought* (perhaps wrongly) that the mere existence of the One entailed its diffusion into the rest of reality.[16] Such a view derives from Plato's notion of the Great Chain of Being wherein all of reality can be arranged into an ontological hierarchy with brute matter at the "bottom" and an abstract Good at the "top" with all of the ranked intermediates obtaining "in between." Aristotle also accepted this notion and employed it in his famous argument for an ultimate cause, the Unmoved Mover.

The problem then presented itself to medieval Christians who adored the metaphysics of Plato or Aristotle: if it was necessary that this universe obtained as the natural diffusion of God, then there is no such thing as the metaphysical possibility that there be no universe or a universe distinct from the actual one. Accordingly, God had no freedom to withhold from creating this universe any more than the sun has for its radiating light in the way dictated by its essence. If God exists, then a universe necessarily exists too. And not just any universe, but *this* one. Without getting bogged down in whether this was indeed the medieval Christian view or not,[17] even if it is a sound argument against the freedom of God, it may not be enough to establish the existence of specific things like angels. Michael Heiser has recently argued for a sub-trinitarian pantheon of gods that reside in heaven.[18] These would be beings, says Heiser, distinct from God and would be a wider aggregate of gods than the angels. But never mind

---

15. See Kretzmann, *The Metaphysics of Theism*, 217–25. Kretzmann sees the necessity of creation in Aquinas's metaphysics. For a reply, see Wippel, "Norman Kretzmann," 287–98.

16. See Rist, *Plotinus*.

17. Thomas Aquinas seems to have overtly denied that God creates the universe out of the necessity of His nature. See his *Summa Contra Gentiles* II.23, 27.

18. See Heiser, *The Unseen Realm*, esp. chapter 3.

the nuance, for this means one should only speak of gods rather than (only) angels. This alone doesn't change the argument's force, only the broader identity of those intermediates (of which Satan could still be one).

For some medieval philosophers, the existence of the angelic realm helps complete the upper hierarchy of the Chain of Being (viz., the *scala naturae*).[19] But in order to be an *argument* for the existence of the angelic realm, one would have to argue for the notion that *if any universe at all is created by God*, then its various contents as we have them (with angels being among them) are entailed *a priori*. Needless to say, if these points can be adequately supported, one would have an interesting argument for the existence of angels. And if angels must exist given God's creation of a universe, then one is well on her way toward an argument for the existence of Satan. Can the angelic realm be inferred in this way then?

Let us turn to what Arthur Lovejoy has called the *principle of plenitude*.[20] Plenitude refers to the notion that anything that could possibly exist in fact does. Leibniz has been one of its most notable and recognizable modern champions of this. He writes in his *Monadology*:

> It follows from the supreme perfection of God that he has chosen the best possible plan in producing the universe, in which there is the greatest variety together with the greatest order; the best arranged situation, place, and time; the greatest effect produced by the simplest ways; the most power, the most knowledge, the most happiness and goodness in creatures which the universe could allow.[21]

Appeals to Leibniz tend to focus on notions of a qualitatively-perfect universe model. But Leibniz adds to his dossier of such an ideal universe a range of beings that includes,

---

19. E.g., Augustine, *De Libero Arbitrio*, III.5.13–14; Aquinas, *Summa Theologiae*, I.50.1; Bonaventure, *Collationes in Hexaemeron*, V.23–27.

20. Lovejoy, *The Great Chain of Being*.

21. Leibniz, *Monadology*, 275. He says elsewhere: "I have good reasons for believing that all the different classes of beings whose assemblage forms the universe are, in the ideas of God who knows essentially their essential gradations, only like so many ordinates of the same curve whose unity does not allow us to place some other ordinates between two of them because that would be a mark of disorder and imperfection . . . Now the Law of Continuity demands that when the essential determinations of one being approximate those of another, as a consequence, all the properties of the former should also gradually approximate those of the latter. Hence it is necessary that all the orders of natural beings form but a single chain in which different kinds like so many links clasp one another so firmly that it is impossible for the senses and imagination to fix the exact point where one begins or ends; all the species which border on or dwell, so to speak, in regions of inflection or singularity are bound to be ambiguous and endowed with characters related equally well to neighbouring species. Thus, for example, the existence of Zoophytes, or as Buddaeus calls them Plant-Animals, is nothing freakish, but it is even befitting the order of nature that there should be such. So great is the force of the Principle of Continuity in my philosophy, that I should not be surprised to learn that creatures might be discovered which in respect to several properties, for example, nutrition or reproduction, could pass for either vegetables or animals" (Leibniz, *Philosophical Selections*, 187–88). Many thanks to Lloyd Strickland for pointing me to these references.

or entails, "the greatest variety." Here is what this seems to look like. It is evident that rocks, plants, animals, and human beings exist. For theists, God is also something that exists. But God is the kind of thing that exists quite differently than humans, animals, plants, and rocks. For these things that aren't God are things that share one property in common: materiality. Plants seem to be a slight step up from rocks (being entirely material but differentiated in terms of being organic or not while they both share in lacking any autonomy). Animals seem to be a slight step up from plants (having a quasi-autonomous nature). And humans seem to be a slight step up from animals (having a fully autonomous nature). Regardless of whether human beings are only material things or not, there is surely a profound ontological gap between us and a God who is purely immaterial not to mention superlative in every way. If angels do not exist, then we seem to have a variety of material objects and then a stark leap to God–something wholly immaterial, superlative, non-composite, and quite removed from the sort of thing a human being is. As the argument would go, such a world would be neither orderly nor the most variegated and, so, would not be the one God created on pain of imperfection.

Consider an analogy. Between the colors red and yellow there exist many gradations of color ranging from red-orange, to orange, to yellow-orange. And one can inch toward one color or another by simply adding a minute shade of red or yellow to the mix. Thus, in a color wheel that includes red and yellow, it would be odd (read: disorderly) to have a gap between, say, orange and yellow while all of the gradations between yellow and red are filled in. One would expect to have the potential of all of the colors in between without any break whatsoever. And if all potentialities get realized in a perfect world, then each of the gradations of colors in fact are realized. Hence, *every* shade of red + yellow exists on that color wheel in addition to their extremities: red and yellow. Consequently, there would be no color gaps between red and yellow and it would be perfectly balanced if laid out in a spectrum (consisting of equal amounts of the various shades of red-orange and yellow-orange on either side of the mean color: orange). If the color wheel in the analogy represents the universe created by God, then we might expect that *every gradation of being conceivable exists*. Like the color wheel, one can imagine all sorts of gradations of being that could exist in between human beings and God. If a universe will consist of all realized gradations, then there will be no gaps. If there are no gaps, then there are beings that exist "between" human beings and God.[22] To not have such beings would be tantamount to not

---

22. Such an argument may imply more than one kind of intermediate being between humans and God. It may require that in order to balance the gradations that have obtained on the material side, it is necessary to add more than one kind of intermediate being on the spiritual side. As a result, it may not be just angels that would be implied by the Chain of Being. Even so, this would not constitute a refutation of premise 5. First of all, even if other intermediates were implied, angels are still part of the Chain, which is enough to send the argument forward. But, secondly, why not think that *each angel is a different gradation of being*? Perhaps angels are ranked in accordance with their ontological proximity to God (or lack thereof). One could combine the notion of rank (cf., Pseudo-Dionysius,

having orange-yellow on the color wheel. And these beings occupying the "between" slot are what we would simply call "angels" for they are the lower spirits that fill in the missing gap.[23]

There are, however, some challenges to this line of reasoning. First, if *all* gradations must be realized (if one accepts the analogy of the color wheel), then we have a potentially infinite number of beings that would exist in between humans and God (not to mention elsewhere). We would have everything from "mostly human" to "mostly divine," and it is difficult–if not impossible–to consider that some angels in the range would be situated as being almost humanly physical when the Scriptures seem to make clear that they are categorically all spirit (Heb 1.14). While the implication of being partially material might delight followers of the early Greek Church, if we attempt to delete these almost-human angels from the hierarchy (say, due to the pronouncements of special revelation), then we cannot insist that all gradations get realized after all. And if we cannot insist that all gradations get realized, we no longer can infer *a priori* that angels are inevitable in God's creation for the same reasons these almost-human angels do not.

One could respond by arguing, as one does in support of the *Kalām* Cosmological Argument for God's existence, that an infinite number of things cannot exist in reality (viz., that there are no actual infinites).[24] But some range of gradations are indeed implied by the principle of plenitude if understood in the above way. Consequentially, it is simply *impossible* to have an infinite number of gradations realized, so we should not expect an actually infinite number of gradations. Assuming that the totality of existents in the universe cannot refer to all possible gradations of being, there could still be talk of different, though finite, *kinds* of being that occupy all the *non-trivial* gaps in ontological creation (something closer to how Aristotle and Aquinas understood the Great Chain of Being). In other words, plenitude need not imply every single conceivable gradation of existence but only a member(s) of every distinct kind.

That kinds and not sheer number may be more important seems right. It is difficult to think that *Star Wars* (1977) would have been better simply by being longer and having additional scenes that exhibit only trivial differences with another (e.g., suppose Han Solo shoots Greedo again in another scene but the only difference is that Han does not have a scar on his chin). To multiply nearly identical beings is,

---

The Celestial Hierarchy) with the notion of each angel being a species unto himself (cf., Aquinas, *De Spiritualibus Creaturis*, VIII). One could argue that the former is predicated on the latter. Moreover, the unintended advantage with this maneuver is that the Chain of Being implies the existence of *multiple* angels and not just one–something orthodox Christians can appreciate.

23. We could follow the Scholastics further and assert that *each angel* occupies a rung in the "lower spirit" category since each angel is considered to be a species unto himself (e.g., Aquinas, *De Spiritualibus Creaturis*, IX.2). Correlatively, there are numerous species of insects, plants, and animals that would occupy the "lower matter" category. But it is not important to the overall portrait here that we leave out the delineation of each species of "lower spirit" and "lower matter."

24. E.g., Craig, *The Kalām Cosmological Argument*, 65ff.

to cite Hugh McCann, "a boorish exercise in running up the score that simply fails to understand perfection."[25] Mortimer Adler uses the examples of the sequences of whole numbers and geometric shapes to illustrate the better notion that kind, and not sheer number, is the right perfection-enhancing feature. Adler writes that, despite the fact that there are fractions in between the whole numbers, "[t]here can be no intermediate whole number between 1 and 2 or between 3 and 4."[26] Likewise, there can be "no intermediate polygon between a triangle and a square or between a square and a pentagon." As such, he says of Aristotle that he "viewed nature as an orderly arrangement that is a scale of beings differing in kind, not in degree." Thus, if there are upper and lower bounds to the hierarchy, there is no reason to suppose that the hierarchy would necessarily consist of an infinite number of intermediates. So, the idea that there might not be almost-human angels is of little to no consequence.

Nonetheless, there is a second problem that arises. Even if we charitably affirm that the plenitude of reality is solely about kinds of being, then we are still left to wonder *which* kinds succumb to such plenitude. For example, one can agree that there cannot be an actually infinite number of colors on the color wheel. As such, the decision to just refer to orange and forego any talk of the other intermediate shades of orange on the red and yellow sides would end up yielding a finite number of colors. In this schema, there is *one* kind of color in between red and yellow (viz., orange) that happens to have an indefinite amount of shades. While this scenario would seem to save the hypothesis (that there are no non-trivial gaps in the hierarchy) without invoking an impossible metaphysical series, there does remain the problem of arbitrariness. Returning to the color wheel example, there is no reason to insist on including such secondary colors as orange *at all*. One could simply forego talk of orange altogether by opting, instead, to just talk of the three primary colors: red, yellow, and blue. The decision to do this instead of including the secondary colors would appear to be just a matter of prejudice. The same could be said about the Chain of Being. Why not just talk of kinds of being in terms of "all things material" and "all things spiritual"? And if one is an anthropological dualist, one could add "all things material + spiritual" in the middle. On this schema, "all things material" would be satisfied by the instantiation of rocks, plants, insects, and (some) animals. "All things spiritual" would be satisfied by God's existence. And if there are "all things material + spiritual," then this would be satisfied by the instantiation of human beings. In either schema, there would be no gaps in the Chain of Being needing to be filled with an angelic realm. So, if choosing which level of the kinds of being one decides to schematize is arbitrary, then there is, alas, no hard *a priori* inference to the angelic realm.

But even if one could circumvent that and find a non-arbitrary set of ontological categories that would complete a universe, it is not at all obvious that such a universe is a preferable option for God to create than one in which one kind of being (i.e.,

---

25. McCann, *Creation and the Sovereignty of God*, 163.
26. Adler, *The Angels and Us*, 62.

angels) does not exist. For if angels are never created, neither are demons. And it is hard to imagine that such a world might not have been a better world. But even if it was truly not a better world after all, we are in no position to know that. If Adam and Eve were not beguiled by a demonic being, then, if they are not prevented from sinning, might have inaugurated a human Fall nonetheless. And yet we *have* to know if that's true or not if we want to say that it is better for a universe to have all of the non-trivial, non-arbitrary categories realized. Consequentially, it is not necessary to settle the notion of a "best possible world." Because even if there was such a thing, we could never know if that world was the one that was an ontologically complete one.

Despite the challenges to the *likelihood* of the cosmological argument, one thing seems apparent: if angels, and so demons, do exist, then if God created an optimal world (whether it be the best possible world or merely one within a range of better worlds), the existence of intermediary beings certainly seems a more *elegant* construction.[27] What I think we are entitled to say, then, is that if we had some other reason–apart from plenitude–to think that angels were in fact created, then a certain kind of non-trivial plenitude has been achieved. And this would indicate that among the worlds God has chosen to actualize, there arises an ontologically elegant one–an aesthetically pleasing system where, at the level of God, human, animal, plant, and earth there is a kind of being between God and human. In and of itself, this does nothing to advance the cosmological argument. But if we thought for a moment that good reasons existed elsewhere, considerations of plenitude make the demonic realist's hypothesis more plausible because such an elegant ontology would help to unify the entire aggregate of data. For another argument that establishes the existence of demons, and so, *a fortiori* angels, plenitude would then enhance our understanding as to why such beings exist.

Nevertheless, such a cosmological argument for the existence of Satan, and so demons, *as an isolated argument* immediately stalls at premise 5 regarding plenitude. But there is a loveliness to the picture painted by plenitude. We could go on to discuss the challenges to the other premises (i.e., pushing back against the notions that natural evils originate in some agent or other and that Satan was in fact a good angel), it would appear that the argument cannot even get off the ground in establishing on its own the existence of the good angels from which Satan is said to derive. Consequently, on the traditional understanding, if there are no angels, then there can be no Satan. And, despite my sympathies to the conclusion, I am not currently optimistic that a satisfactory resolution is forthcoming.

A fully *a posteriori* argument for the existence of Satan and his cohorts to be considered remains, the *argument from (diabolical) experience*. In our final section below, we shall consider its (de)merits.

---

27. Cf., Lipton, *Inference to the Best Explanation*, 59ff.

Philosophical Arguments for Demonic Realism (I)

The Argument from (Diabolical) Experience

Ever since the days of Rudolf Otto and William James, modern philosophers have taken seriously the phenomenon of mystical, religious experiences as comprising some level of justification for belief in God. More recently, epistemological arguments supporting demonic realism have been amassed to the effect that if one should have a particular numinous and non-sensory experience that one feels is supernatural (or mystical), then those experiences, and what they imply, could reasonably be accepted as credible unless there are mitigating reasons that reduce their credibility in a non-trivial way.[28] Such internal experiences are analogous to, though not identical with, sensory experiences of the external world. Since it is circular to assume the reliability of the five physical senses in order to justify the doxastic results of those senses, one must aver to some other criteria with which to certify those results. Richard Swinburne has offered up his Principle of Credulity in regard to experiences both present and past:

> If it seems (epistemically) to a certain subject that x is present (and has some characteristic), then probably x is present (and has that characteristic); what one seems to perceive is probably so. And similarly I suggest that (in the absence of special considerations) apparent memory is to be trusted. If it seems to a subject that in the past he perceived something or did something, then (in the absence of special considerations) probably he did.[29]

In natural theology, one may build her justification of an argument for God's existence by focusing strictly on *theistic* rather than broader *religious* experiences (for the latter could be a numinous experience that has nothing to do with a deity). A theistic experience would be an experience that, to some degree, involves the apprehension of God. According to the Principle of Credulity, which hearkens to an adverbial theory of experience, how something appears to be to a subject is probably, *ceteris paribus*, what it really is. We often think that the deliverances of the physical senses do this all of the time: if one is appeared to treely, then the subject can affirm that (probably) there is a tree. Accordingly, if a subject is appeared to Godly, then the subject can affirm (probably) that there is a God. Such an approach can offer a subject *prima facie* justification for God's existence on the basis of the immediate theistic experiences that subject has.

In a popular formulation of an argument from theistic experience, Alvin Plantinga, an epistemic externalist, thinks that those experiences may be classified as *properly basic beliefs* (beliefs that do not depend on other beliefs in order to be rationally held).[30] In building his case, he points out that it is widely recognized by theist and

---

28. E.g., this approach finds a contemporary champion in Phillip H. Wiebe. See his *God and Other Spirits*.

29. Swinburne, *The Existence of God*, 303.

30. My thanks to Tyler Dalton McNabb for some discussion about an earlier draft of this section.

non-theist alike that there are properly basic beliefs one is entitled to affirm. Plantinga argues that certain beliefs about God (or caused by being appeared to Godly) can and should be included in this category. But, he points out, such beliefs would *not* include "the simple belief that God exists."[31] For that proposition alone would not be the direct result of an encounter with God but only that it would be *entailed* by such an encounter (much like how "that house exists" would be entailed by encountering a piece of real estate and forming the belief, "That house looks magnificent!"). As such, there are Christian beliefs–*prima facie* ones–that obtain as a result of some experience one has of God:

> God is speaking to me.
> God has created all this.
> God disapproves of what I have done.
> God forgives me.
> God is to be thanked and praised.[32]

By experiencing God in this personal way, one can come to know God wholly apart from the input of evidence with which to ground that knowledge. If any Christian belief happens to be formed within an agent whose belief-forming faculties are all firing appropriately and the agent is in the right circumstances in which that belief is formed (or triggered), then those beliefs are fundamentally reliable. Crucially, part of what grounds the reliability of such belief-forming is that God is the architect of human creatures and wants them to come to know him in an intimate way according to a design plan. Surely one should expect that God will see to it that humans will have noetic access, *inter alia*, to that God. As such, Plantinga borrows from the Geneva Reformer, John Calvin, the notion of a *sensus divinitatis* (an intrinsic sense of the divine) which is a sort of God-detection faculty or disposition all human beings are endowed with.[33] Accordingly, reliable Christian beliefs obtain apart from the promptings of arguments or evidences if detected through that *sensus*. And being appeared to Godly–in the ways noted above–is sufficient to justify our doxastic deliverances that naturally arise as a result of the experience.

Another model, one not necessarily unrelated to the previous, is to first consider the doxastic deliverances of any mystical experiences to be sufficiently analogous to the doxastic deliverances of sensory experiences, namely that they just are perceived. William Alston thinks that because we tend to accept the deliverances of our sensory experiences in the belief-forming processes we just happen to have, then we thereby take it, and are rational in believing, that the deliverances of our doxastic practices

---

31. Plantinga, "Is Belief in God Properly Basic?," 46.
32. Plantinga, "Is Belief in God Properly Basic?," 46–47.
33. Plantinga, *Warranted Christian Belief*, 188ff.

are, *ceteris paribus*, true.[34] And because this just happens to be what *I* do epistemically, then it is justification for *me* to accept it as a rational process (viz., that there is a latent "practical rationality"). This is not to say that such doxastic practices are, therefore, *reliable* for there is no noncircular way to assess this. But it would be odd to take a doxastic practice, like perceiving sensible experiences, and assume them to be unreliable from the start (that is, guilty until proven innocent). I am, nonetheless, rational to accept the deliverances of any and all relevant doxastic practices given such practical rationality. And this commits me to supposing that it is *prima facie* reliable, if the question should ever arise, even if there is no accompanying *justification* for its being reliable. If such practices, then, lead to me to believe that p then I am committed to the truth of p.

If mystical experiences are indeed sufficiently analogous to sensory experiences, then it is difficult for the skeptic to think that one is not rational in accepting the deliverances of mystical experiences. Now, unlike mystical experiences of God, experiences of the diabolical are going to be obviously different. But that difference will not in any way, on Alston's model at least, be substantively different from the divine ones. And yet diabolical experiences have an epistemic virtue that advocates of divine experiences cannot tout: that alleged divine experiences could be facilitated by deceiving devils, and so any "reasons for suspecting the experiences to be artificially induced, or the work of the Devil, . . . would, arguably, reduce or cancel their justificatory force,"[35] *but all the while diabolical experiences could never be facilitated by a deceiving God* in diminishing *their* justificatory force. For God's being incapable of deception is what precludes a diabolical experience from being derived from this (divine) kind of mystical source.

We should then be, for the most part, content to affirm the implications of sensory experiences of the external world as *prima facie* justification for having beliefs about the external world. Natural theologians simply want to extend that epistemic strategy to justify beliefs about God by those who experience him. I aim to assess whether one can take it a step further: Can a *diabolical* experience be justification for believing in Satan and/or his demons? One imagines that arguments from diabolical experiences would be similar to arguments from theistic experiences. For the most part I think that this is the case. And an argument from diabolical experience could potentially be as strong as any parallel argument from theistic experience to the existence of God if not more so. But before we can jump into an assessment of such experiences, it is incumbent upon me to explicate what a diabolical experience is.

A diabolical experience will not be quite like a theistic experience in the sense that there would not be characteristics that typify various theistic experiences such as love, unity, forgiveness, adoration, wonder, etc. I would not think that Plantinga-style beliefs like "Satan loves me," "Satan created all this," "Satan is to be praised," and so

---

34. Alston, *Perceiving God*.
35. Alston, *Perceiving God*, 94.

forth, would be formed in the presence of being appeared to Satanly. But surely "Satan is speaking to me" and perhaps "Satan disapproves of what I have done" could be the sorts of experiences one might expect to acquire under certain circumstances. (Benjamin McCraw recently identified this epistemic procedure—one no doubt intended as tongue-in-cheek—as "Reformed Demonology."[36]) In the case of Alston's model, I think that if one has a particularly sinister or traumatic mystical experience, it is going to look very different from divine experiences which tend to involve feelings of divine elation and communal oneness. However, even on Alston's model, a skeptic will consider divine as well as diabolical experiences to be just as inconclusive as on Plantinga's model. But, aside from any philosophical complaints about each model's approach, I imagine the epistemic inconclusiveness of religious experiences in general will have much to do with the vividness and clarity of the particular experiences in question. Without adjudicating all of the arguments for and against each model, which has already been done many times over, we shall instead focus on the nature of diabolical experiences in particular. Thereupon, if diabolical experiences are at least as authentic (whatever this means for one's epistemic model of religious experience) for perceivers as divine ones, then the argumentative success of one's model enjoins us to include the diabolical among what can be known by such acquaintance.

Hence, we shall focus in more detail on the kinds of diabolical experiences one can have. We may parse out two kinds of diabolical experiences that have a basis in real-life testimonies: Diabolical harassments and diabolical invasions. These are often construed as among the most common, if not exhaustive, experiences of the diabolical one can have. To these we now turn.

Diabolical Harassments

In this type of experience, one feels a sense of being harassed or distressed by a malevolent, and presumably spiritual, presence. In such a situation, one feels bothered or fearful when the subject allegedly hears (mentally or aurally) or sees or feels what appears to be the presence of Satan (or of some demon-person). Such harassment may even drive the percipient into acting in a way that either directly or indirectly leads to the harm of others[37] or of oneself[38] (or both). Such harm could be physical (i.e.,

36. McCraw, "Reformed Demonology?"

37. E.g., many serial killers have claimed to hear the other-destructive kind of demonic voice. According to Ronald M. Holmes and James E. DeBurger, the serial killer sometimes feels "impelled to murder because he has heard voices or has seen visions which demand that he kill a certain person or a category of persons. For some the voice or vision that is perceived may be that of a demon" ("Profiles in Terror," 31).

38. E.g., Former sex-trafficking victim, Annie Lobert, has publicly spoken of her alleged diabolical experience which serves to illustrate the self-destructive type: "A night came in my life where I faced death. I OD'd on cocaine because I hated myself and I kept hearing voices to tell me [sic] to kill myself– there was no reason to go on. And I know that wasn't coming from inside of me. There was a diabolical force speaking to me and I truly believe it was the devil and his demons" ("Does Satan Exist?").

substance abuse, violence, mutilation, etc.) or spiritual (i.e., separation from God, demoralization, fanaticism, etc.). Or, perhaps self-harm comes in a more subtle fashion via one's "hearing" accusations that one is guilty of or should be ashamed about some past action or thought. The modes of such experiences that could be had are twofold in that they can be either internal (as in having a telepathic encounter) or they can be external (as in having some kind of external, sensuous encounter). If the experiences are external, we may consider such experiences to be something along the lines of *paranormal*. For we imagine that such experiences come in the form of a sinister specter, a malicious-sounding voice, or a physical assault–all evidencing the presence of a malevolent, spiritual force. In either case, one is being threatened or coaxed by a spiritual agency with which to facilitate some measure of harm.

Regardless of where and how the experiences derive, both the internal and external versions of diabolical harassment are often all dismissed by skeptics as the products of psychological disorders, such as clinical schizophrenia, or as the result of some correlated mental deception (e.g., an auditory or visionary hallucination). The skeptic imagines the diabolical experiences to be, therefore, false because the victims are thought to always be in an unstable or an epistemically compromised state–a feature that does not, as far as we know, obtain in all those who claim to have experiences of God. Only a few cynics and iconoclasts would think *all* religious experiencers are outright delusional. But these harassing experiences are not the only kinds of diabolical experiences one can have. There is another kind that can also be observed both from within and without, namely *diabolical invasions*. Let us turn to this kind now in completing the picture of the sundry kinds of experiences of the demonic that are often reported.

Diabolical Invasions

These experiences thought to be caused by demons are far more dramatic than their harassment counterparts, for they do not merely threaten their victims through experiences but actually usurp *control* over them. As an internal phenomenon, the percipient is sensing more than just alleged communication or promptings from Satan or a demon. Her sense of autonomy is being overwhelmed by forces that cannot be resisted. This sometimes results in an unwilling transfer of control of the percipient's body to the alleged demonic presence. We may be familiar with its more familiar locution "demon possession" in describing a diabolical invasion. As an external phenomenon, there are often happenings occurring in and around the victim that are perceptible to outside observers. Consider the high-profile case of Anneliese Michel. Her situation exemplifies both the internal and the external phenomena quite dramatically:

> In 1968, aged 17, [Anneliese] began to suffer convulsions. Although initially diagnosed with grand mal epilepsy, she started experiencing devilish

> hallucinations while praying. By 1973, she was suffering severe depression and considering suicide. Voices in her head told her she was damned.... [G]radually, Anneliese slipped further into the abyss. She would perform 600 genuflections a day, eventually rupturing her knee ligaments. She crawled under a table, barking like a dog for two days. She ate spiders, coal and bit the head off a dead bird. She even licked her own urine off the floor and could be heard through the walls screaming for hours.... [She made] growls mingle[d] with throaty gurgles [and] screamed obscenities.... [Her exorcisms] often resulted in such brutality that Anneliese would be held down or chained to her chair.[39]

Anneliese's internal experiences consist of "devilish hallucinations" and "voices in her head." The external experiences entail the various incidences of peculiar behavior exhibited by Anneliese that prompt her to be restrained in a chair.

The skeptic can certainly pick apart Anneliese's case in particular since it turns out that (a) the priest responsible for her exorcism, along with her parents, were eventually charged with involuntary manslaughter upon her death, thus suggesting that Anneliese was the victim of a misdiagnosis; and (b) that her condition is consistent with ongoing bouts with epilepsy and forms of psychosis (along with perhaps other unnamed, natural factors). But Anneliese's case, though dramatic, is neither an isolated one nor is it rare. From antiquity to the contemporary world, a number of reports of demonic invasions abound.[40] Moreover, such possession cases transcend all kinds of demographic and social barriers. And many of these reports do not all include a diagnosis of a mental disorder or the presence of abuse. They are not even consistent with what one might expect of a mere psychological disturbance. Even if some of the allegedly possessed did concurrently suffer from certain mental and physical disorders, it is unclear how one could conclude that the putative demonic invasions did not operate in tandem with these preexisting conditions.[41] I may have acquired a paper cut, but it does not mean that someone else could or would never be able to aggravate it by throwing salt water on it. Could not someone with a mental disorder simply be a ripe environment for this kind of assault?

Both diabolical harassments and diabolical invasions evince a malevolent spiritual presence that, to some degree, bothers or manipulates its victim. Sometimes such experiences are exclusive only to the victim, sometimes such experiences are publicly

---

39. Day, "God Told us to Exorcise my Daughter's Demons"; cf., Goodman, *The Exorcism of Anneliese Michel*, chapters 4 and 5.

40. See Koch, *Demonology Past and Present*; Keener, *Miracles*, appendices A and B; Kay and Parry, *Exorcism and Deliverance*, esp. chapters 3–7. There is even an online research database housing 6,000 alleged "spiritual experiences," including exorcisms, available through an institution I once did postgraduate work at. See "Alister Hardy RERC Archive Database."

41. I may have a recent history of sneezing due to allergies, but if someone throws pepper in my face, I will no doubt have aggravated sneezing episodes. Having such preexisting conditions is not an immediate refutation of a pepper assailant. Refer back to our discussion on the anti-realist's devil-of-the-gaps objection in chapter 4.

manifest in one form or another. But do they constitute a credible source for a warranted or justified belief in demons? Immanuel Kant once wrote that traditional metaphysics is in no position to rule out the deliverances of testimony one might have of spirits acting on or within oneself.[42] But, he insists, neither could such metaphysics affirm such spirits. This returns us to the issue as to whether such first-hand experiences can ever be included as mitigating justification or warrant for belief in demons even without the aid of traditional metaphysics to guide us. To this question we shall now turn.

Assessment

There are obvious parallels between having a religious experience and having a diabolical experience. But there are also many differences. To the extent that those differences are *relevant*, I would say that they are not. After all, one's experiences of "My spouse loves me" and "My co-workers hate me," despite having clear differences, are not so different so as to make one kind properly basic and the other not. In fact, one's experience of the hatred of their co-workers may even be more vivid and intuitive than the love of a spouse given our skewed intrinsic desire to be loved–such that we may even exaggerate one's affection for us and misconstrue a familial love for a romantic one. I dare say that we have little desire in being disliked or disdained (though I am sure there are exceptions such as those harboring a so-called martyr complex). Seemingly, if all of the conditions for having genuine knowledge by means of being appeared to diabolically are met, whatever one might say in favor of a religious experience could be said in favor of a diabolical one. And yet there are some unique challenges to having diabolical experiences that will need to be surmounted if one is to take such experiences as properly basic or genuine.

First, if one takes Plantinga's Reformed Epistemology and thinks that the *sensus divinitatis* is the only way knowledge can be delivered up, then she will have ignored Plantinga's extended conversation on the subject. It is true that the *sensus divinitatis* is, when properly functioning, a belief-forming mechanism (or faculty) created by God. It is also, as the Reformers like Calvin have put forward, that by which one naturally forms beliefs in and about *God* and no other beings. Such God-knowledge obtains when the relevant belief-forming experiences under the right circumstances obtain. The *sensus divinitatis* of the Reformers, then, gives rise to McCraw's loosely proposed sister notion that one *could* correspondingly have a *sensus diaboli*.[43] But for reasons he himself points out, "the Devil doesn't create us and has no real causal input into what faculties we have and how they properly function."[44] Neither would they be *prima facie* reliable. As McCraw insinuates, a Satan-detection faculty would have to come

---

42. Kant, *Dreams of a Spirit-Seer*.
43. McCraw, "Reformed Demonology," 148–50.
44. McCraw, "Reformed Demonology," 48.

from another source, viz., God, and a bare theism does not itself supply the epistemic resources that would guarantee that he would create such a faculty. *Why would he?* For while one can easily see and affirm that God would want us to have knowledge of himself (otherwise why the fuss over "divine hiddenness"?), it is unclear that God would want to secure in us noetic access to Satan. In fact, our contact with Satan or his demons is unqualifiedly disastrous to our spiritual and even physical well-being. The sooner we lose the ability to detect Satan the better! Thus, if one wanted to construe diabolical beliefs as properly basic on the Reformer's terms, it would appear that one would have to offer up and defend why we should expect God to create in us something like a *sensus diaboli*.

But attempting to mount such a defense is unnecessary. For Plantinga himself acknowledges that apart from a *sensus divinitatis* vis-à-vis God's existence there actually is "a battery of faculties" among which includes the "instigation of the Holy Spirit."[45] William Lane Craig speaks of this as the "self-authenticating witness of the Holy Spirit."[46] In other words, the Holy Spirit directly impresses upon us and not necessarily through the medium of some specific *sensus*. The Holy Spirit would act in us in such a way that, if we are under the right circumstances, we will come to know God's presence directly and intimately no matter how cognitively damaged we are by our sins. Plantinga makes it clear that such (Christian) beliefs "come instead by way of the work of the Holy Spirit, who gets us to accept, causes us to believe, these great truths of the gospel."[47] We need not think *pace* the Reformers that a separate faculty was created in us that somehow spontaneously generates these properly basic beliefs about God when they are triggered by an appropriate circumstance. Accordingly, our more traditional belief-forming faculties are already equipped to form such beliefs. This permits one to construe diabolical experiences along the lines of an "instigation" by an *un*holy spirit, one that is even "self-authenticating." In this understanding, one need not be bothered by a God-*only* detection faculty by which we form the relevant beliefs, but a general *spiritual* detection faculty, so to speak. Thus, any concerns surrounding the notion of a *sensus diaboli* can be jettisoned.

However, another problem remains. For one can only consider that properly basic beliefs about Satan and/or his demons can be had if one's *belief-forming faculties are all functioning properly*. This would mean that in a Reformed Demonology, and quite unlike its Religious Epistemology counterpart, the existence of God is not part of the package. Positing the existence of God would be *wholly distinct* from one's experience of the diabolical. And this would be true even if Satan were *per impossibile* God. For if Satan were God, we might suppose that any beliefs churned up by apparent experiences of the diabolical might be noetic deceptions or *lies*. In what sense in Satan's universe would beliefs be *properly* basic? And just what would be the *right*

---

45. Plantinga, *Warranted Christian Belief*, 149.
46. Craig, *Reasonable Faith*, 43.
47. Plantinga, *Warranted Christian Belief*, 263.

circumstances? These things smack of a more exemplary foundation unavailable in the Satanic kingdom of knowledge. It would seem that some independent support for or confirmation of God's existence would have to be included. While properly basic beliefs about God may be warranted on their own, for God's existence putatively justifies the deliverances of those experiences, Satanic experiences apart from God would be about as reliable as expecting pleasure to be churned out from a torture chamber.

But why should *that* matter? If one has an immediate diabolical experience at all, it is still being caused by a *supersensible person*. And if that person is, *per impossibile*, God himself, then God is a demon. If God is not and/or cannot be a demon, then there just is the demon. Moreover, one could insist that a diabolical experience does double-duty in that the reality of a demon *implies* the reality of God by which to substantiate the reliability of the beliefs formed from the diabolical experience. For a thing like a demon would not or could not exist *a se*. Thus, the necessary foundational epistemic resources still obtain in a Plantingian universe of diabolical experiences. Furthermore, though the existence of God may be a necessary auxiliary fact in order to *ultimately justify* one's experiences, it is not so clear that one must appeal to God in order to accept the doxastic deliverances of those experiences. Unless one already had some positive reason to think that beliefs arising out of those experiences are unreliable, one's first-hand experiences of the diabolical could very well be good evidence nevertheless.

Actually, there is one unique epistemic *advantage* had by experiencers of the diabolical over those of the divine. For diabolical experiences can also be dramatically perceived by public observers–a feature not enjoyed by most accounts of religious experience (except maybe in the case of public miracles). As Phillip H. Wiebe writes: "The phenomena that provide the strongest intimations that a malevolent form of transcendent reality exists are those that leave traces in the spatiotemporal-causal world or are intersubjectively observable."[48] These tend to be reported by a cross-cultural variety of eyewitnesses that cannot be easily dismissed. Accordingly, continues Wiebe, "experiences that occur across cultures and are reported throughout human history ... deserve a significant place in theorizing about transcendent realities."[49] But are not alien abduction stories and anti-Christian miracle claims also reported "throughout human history"? While the victim of an alleged invasion may be entitled to her belief, what about those observers who are on the outside? It would seem that one must enlist the relevant criteria for what counts as a good explanation for possession cases. And this can, in principle, be done in the case of diabolical invasions. After all, there are numerous other situations where detecting diabolical agency in some state of affairs is a mainstay, including situations involving conspiracies, plagiarisms, and incidences of (cyber)terrorism. In a real sense, the quest for detecting whether the alleged possessed are truly being manipulated by a demon or not is really just

---

48. Wiebe, *God and Other Spirits*, 58.
49. Wiebe, *God and Other Spirits*, 219.

another quest for intelligent design (dare we call this *malevolent design*?). And many philosophers certainly think that such can be done even if not always successfully.

Alston's model also can be worked rather easily to accommodate diabolical experiences. In fact, his is a straightforward belief-forming context where one's spiritual experiences are analogous to one's sensible experiences. As long as that is reasonable, then any spiritual being could potentially give rise to one's spiritual perceptions. And those perceptions will yield appropriate beliefs just in case they are reliable. Furthermore, when we consider Alston's model of divine experiences, one's perception of the diabolical is not likely to be confused with any other deceiving experiences facilitated by God even though the reverse is possible. This certainly reduces the total number of causal candidates for the origin of diabolical experiences even if it does not eliminate them. So, while one may be concerned about mystical experiences being the illusory products of demons, one would not likely be justified to think that one's diabolical experiences are possibly the illusory products of the divine.

Aside from whatever model one may seek to employ, when it comes to the contribution of diabolical experiences as evidence at all, some demur. David Kyle Johnson, in a recent work, vehemently disagrees with the prospect that *any* kind of diabolical experience could ever justify or provide warrant for belief in demons.[50] He thinks that demonic realism cannot, even in principle, be evidenced from any experience one might have. He offers five reasons for his conclusion. First, he says that "such stories hardly ever involve unbiased observers."[51] Second, "such stories often involve less than reliable means of gathering evidence."[52] Third, though experiencers "may not be certifiably ill," he nonetheless thinks that "these people have been so religiously indoctrinated that they are convinced they're possessed and thus act out the part."[53] Fourth, "[e]ven with multiple eyewitnesses, collusion, exaggeration, and mass delusion are more common than many realize."[54] And fifth, "[b]y their very nature ... demonic explanations are not simple, conservative or wide scoping. Thus, they will always fall short when compared to the available natural explanations."[55] I submit that Johnson's conclusion is overstated and does not show all diabolical experiences to be unwarranted or unjustified.

The first reason he offers is hardly unique to diabolical experiences, for the problem of bias plagues just about any area of inquiry–including the natural sciences, as Thomas Kuhn and Paul Feyerabend have pointed out. Moreover, when Johnson himself decries the ethics of even the *right* to believe in demons, five of the eight sources

---

50. Johnson, "Justified Belief in the Existence of Demons is Impossible."
51. Johnson, "Justified Belief in the Existence of Demons is Impossible," 179.
52. Johnson, "Justified Belief in the Existence of Demons is Impossible," 179.
53. Johnson, "Justified Belief in the Existence of Demons is Impossible," 181.
54. Johnson, "Justified Belief in the Existence of Demons is Impossible," 182.
55. Johnson, "Justified Belief in the Existence of Demons is Impossible," 187.

he cites in support of this contention *are derived from an online "Skeptics Dictionary"*![56] How is *that* not an instance of bias much less of questionable scholarship? In support of the second reason he offers, he has in mind mediating sources like Ouija boards and séances.[57] But there are no mediating sources like these in the particular cases of diabolical experiences we have been considering. When he turns to the specific prospect of one's witnessing an exorcism, he commits a form of question-begging when he asserts that an exorcist "can't find a natural explanation for a supposed possession as good reason to conclude that a demon is the cause."[58] For one can only know that the means of gathering such (experiential) evidence makes the diabolical invasion an unreliable hypothesis if the beliefs produced are already prejudged to be mistaken or that better explanations exist for the experience, which is precisely at issue. The third reason fairs no better since it, too, presumes that the victim is mistaken about her diabolical invasion. The fourth reason provides no additional criticism of diabolical invasions than it does for any ordinary human defendant in a court of law who is indicted for a crime on the basis of multiple eyewitnesses.

The fifth reason, that "demonic explanations are not simple, conservative or wide scoping," is Johnson's best argument. However, I think that Johnson's explanatory virtues that he lists (viz., his adopted "criteria of adequacy"[59]) are all met. The hypothesis of diabolical invasion is only less parsimonious than certain rival explanations if and only if demons do not exist. But if, say, scriptural testimony about demons is true, then no additional entities are added to one's metaphysical inventory. For Johnson to be right about parsimony, he must already have a case against the existence of demons. Indeed, he thinks he does. He banks on the God/devil-of-the-gaps argument already critiqued in the last chapter.[60] But this means that parsimony of the kind Johnson is predicating his criticism on is only settled by virtue of his gaps-based reasoning which is not only controversial but does not actually support diabolical anti-realism. So, no help for him there. His principle of conservativism, while sensible, is only as good as one's background information. Again, if one's background information already includes demonic realism, then there is no added traction to his criticism. As for explanatory scope, not only would the hypothesis of diabolical invasion explain many possession cases where victims are not lying and are not suffering from any known mental illness, it would also explain the other species of diabolical experiences, viz., diabolical harassments, of perfectly lucid individuals. It also explains why multiple eyewitnesses often come to the same conclusion, even begrudgingly. If one

---

56. Johnson, "Justified Belief in the Existence of Demons is Impossible," 187–88.

57. I do think Johnson is correct on this particular point. See my postscript on the paranormal below.

58. Johnson, "Justified Belief in the Existence of Demons is Impossible," 179.

59. Johnson, "Justified Belief in the Existence of Demons is Impossible," 177.

60. See Johnson, "Justified Belief in Miracles Is Impossible"; For my response to the devil-of-the-gaps argument, recall chapter 4 of this book.

dismisses them as frequent mass delusions obtaining across the board in all cases simply because such is possible, then one wonders why anything we conclude on the basis of eyewitness testimony should be believable. It turns out Johnson's warmed-over Humean criticisms here are no better than when they were first delivered by that other famous David of the eighteenth century.

Since his in-principle objections fail, what can we say about the *de facto* evidence, namely what it is percipients actually report? Recently, there have been interesting experiences of diabolical invasions offered up with well-defined diabolical agency-detecting criteria that may be sufficient to raise the probability of demonic realism vis-à-vis demonic possessions. According to the recent testimony of psychiatrist and professor at New York Medical College (and former anti-realist), Richard Gallagher, some of these telltale properties of diabolical design that convinced him of demonic realism was his claim to have witnessed the possession victims's ability to "[speak] various foreign languages previously unknown to them," their ability to "exhibit enormous strength," and their "'hidden knowledge' of all sorts of things—like how a stranger's loved ones died, what secret sins she has committed, even where people are at a given moment."[61] Wiebe adds that, regarding other encounters of the same type, "finding that people regain their sight or hearing or mental wholeness after an exorcism in which evil spirits are commanded to leave a person, as though those spirits were causally responsible for producing the malady, adds credence to the claim that spirits might exist."[62] Obviously non-percipients cannot comment on the presence of such data in the various possession cases, but certainly if such data exist, especially if conjointly present on a singular occasion, one may think that there is little reason to doubt that such data is more probable given the hypothesis of a diabolical invasion than without. One way that such a probability could be lowered is for one to accuse the conclusion of demonic realism as not following from the reasons. Given the nature of the experience as merely the perceived presence of a foreign sinister agent taking control of a human victim, such an experience *could* elicit another interpretation. Perhaps it's not a demon but an extradimensional being from another universe or even a malicious extraterrestrial from our own. Are demons any less extraordinary or exotic than extraterrestrial and extradimensional beings?

Or, it may even be that the culprits are somewhat more mundane. That is, what appears to be diabolical or otherworldly is in fact maliciously *human* and *this*-worldly, namely that a deceased person has found the resources to return to his earthly abode to inflict petty but destructive abuse on the living. If survivalist arguments are successful (viz., that there are good reasons to think that souls survive the deaths of their bodies), it is especially unclear whether the harassing or invading entity is anything

---

61. Gallagher, "As a Psychiatrist, I Diagnose Mental Illness." Gallagher is not the first agnostic to be impressed by the firsthand experience of diabolical harassments. Also see Friedkin, "The Devil and Father Amorth."

62. Wiebe, *God and Other Spirits*, 39.

more "out of this world" than you or I. Perhaps Adolf Hitler or Nero or just an angry migrant worker (emphasizing, of course, that these figures share in common the speaking of languages other than English) have returned from beyond to harass the living. The point is that any one of these hypothetical causes for diabolical experiences is no predictor of said diabolical experiences. There is nothing about being a surviving spirit or a spirit from another universe or a demon that would increase our expectation that the properties of the experiences are the properties one would expect. Even if one is entitled to believe that a non-dimensional, spiritual agent is the right inference to make over naturalistic alternatives, there remain alternatives noted here that can equally account for any putative cross-cultural testimony. Even if one is "fortunate" enough to have a diabolical experience of one kind or another, without any other pieces to the explanatory puzzle, we are just not in a position to disambiguate the causal agent(s) involved.

All of this is to point out that if one is open to the possibility of any one of these kinds of causal agents, then the prospect of supporting demonic realism on the basis of diabolical experience looks grim. For such questions are just as those found in religious epistemology vis-à-vis theism in that one may query as to *which* god one may be in contact with. Add to that challenge the notion that these experiences are supposed to be with generally evil beings. If we are attempting to disambiguate which malevolent causal agents are at work purely on the basis of the experience itself, that we should expect the cause of such experience to have the moral rectitude to be forthcoming about its identity is borderline preposterous. I imagine even a malevolent, extradimensional being might even feign obedience to an exorcist's command to depart in the name of Jesus in order to facilitate a clever misdirection! Alas, such is the crippling epistemic limitations and liabilities of personal experiences of the sinister type.

What may serve to ultimately save the argument from diabolical experience, then, is to populate the background information of the percipient or to provide independent confirmation about what sorts of agents would most likely be responsible for these kinds of experiences. If we had *another* reason to help us think that demons and not extraterrestrials or surviving post-mortem despots were responsible for these kinds of activities, then the occurrences of diabolical experiences would serve, I think, to punctuate that evidence. But as a standalone piece of reasoning, it seems to be no more convincing to an outside observer than an alien abduction story. And for those who actually have such experiences, they are only in a position to make limited doxastic pronouncements–pronouncements that admit of ambiguity.

Postscript on the Paranormal

I should make brief mention of the prospect of utilizing paranormal experiences as part of the (external) diabolical experiences repertoire. While one could have enlisted all kinds of testimonies to diabolical paranormal activity–including hauntings, apparitions, Ouija board correspondences, séances, and poltergeist disturbances–these particular experiences would not be assessed any more successfully than the others mentioned. One could always accuse the percipient, as Johnson does, of overstepping her evidential boundaries by confusing fact-gathering with interpretation.[63] Thus, we *could* give honorable mention to paranormal experiences for the record, but it does not constitute a substantially different or even a better subcategory from those already mentioned. What would it mean to be appeared to *demonly*? We might imagine a grotesque figure with horns and red, glowing eyes. But there is nothing about that that is particularly demonly, for that could also be the apparition of a deceased angry goat! In point of fact, the experiences are decisively *less* direct, and so less reliable, than the others. There just is no adequate description of "being appeared to demonly" with respect to paranormal experiences.

Moreover, I, in solidarity with Johnson, am certainly less confident about object-oriented media like Ouija Boards and tarot cards. Specific occurrences such as hauntings and poltergeist activity do not themselves elucidate the alleged spiritual causes in the percipient's field of perception. When an object appears to move by itself or one hears voices and feels temperature changes in a room, these are unquestionably less decisive as pointers to the demonic (much less the disembodied). Accordingly, any conclusions drawn must be *inferred* in many instances–inferences that assume no deliberate deception is taking place. But these are supposed to be *evil* spirits of one kind or another we're talking about, which, like before, plummets the prospect of a positive ID. But never mind. Drawing inferences from the experiences are not quite how religious epistemologists envision their case, either for the divine or the diabolical. As such, this subset of paranormal experiences lacks the direct access that the other diabolical harassments and invasions have. If a case from diabolical experience is ever going to get a fair hearing, appeals to the paranormal will only stunt it.

Let us suppose, then, that there are some apparitions that appear as unambiguously self-confessed demonic entities. Would this allow the paranormal to be admissible as evidence? Wiebe thinks so and says that it can even provide us evidence "in some objective way."[64] But while it certainly can be evidence under this modification, it does not advance the argument past the complaint about the possibility of deception–that beings other than demons are causing the experiences. All of the virtues of good abductive reasoning apply here just as much. And there is nothing about the nature of a paranormal encounter that has an explanatory edge over the other kinds of

---

63. Many philosophers have suggested that the prospect of pure fact-gathering, viz., a theory-independent form of perception, is in principle *virtually impossible*. See Kuhn, *The Structures of Scientific Revolutions*, 16–17. Kuhn outright calls the distinction between "discovery and invention or fact and theory" to be "exceedingly artificial" because they are always "intertwined" in some way (52–53). Also see Cartwright, "How We Relate Theory to Observation"; Baergen, "The Influence of Cognition upon Perception"; Papineau, *Theory and Meaning*. However, I would not say that because experience is prone to interpretive ambiguity that it, therefore, has no justificatory value.

64. Wiebe, *God and Other Spirits*, 58.

diabolical experiences. In fact, as I shall argue in a later chapter, we actually have good grounds for thinking that demons cannot interact with the world in the ways that would give rise to diabolical apparitions or other kinds of extramental interactions.[65] If that is so, then the experiences of paranormal phenomena do nothing to add to the proponent's case from diabolical experience. In fact, they may even mitigate against them, for one should think that there are beings other than demons that are responsible for the paranormal. Those interested in further discussions about the evidential weight of paranormal experiences apart from what was said here are encouraged to consult the works of Stephen E. Braude,[66] David H. Lund,[67] and the aforementioned work of Wiebe (pro) as well as those of Antony Flew, Richard H. Schlagel, and Michael Sudduth (con).[68]

My conclusion about this is that adding these additional sources of data (viz., the paranormal) do nothing to enhance, and may even undermine, the argument from diabolical experiences. Perhaps if the other diabolical experiences prove veridical, one may have a better case in returning to the epistemic contribution of the paranormal.

Conclusion

We have explored a variety of arguments for demonic realism by focusing on arguments for the existence of Satan. As discussed, there are arguments that span both the *a priori* and the *a posteriori*. Among the *a priori*, we discussed an ontological argument for the existence of Satan. But such an argument fails on grounds that one cannot conclude that a world where the worst possible being exists *in re* is worse than one in which he exists *in intellectu*. And even if one could surmount this failure, the result would be, not the Satan of classical tradition, but an anti-God whose attributes would in many ways rival those of God. We then looked at a cosmological argument for the existence of Satan predicated on a principle of plenitude. But, as I pointed out, there is no reason to think that a requisite angelic realm could be confidently affirmed since the vantage point from which one can parse reality in terms of gradations of being is arbitrary. Moreover, it is unclear that there may not be other factors that mitigate against actualizing a world with angels since, if angels did not exist, the world might have been a better place. This is not to say that such a notion is true, only that it is possible. And if it is possible, then one cannot conclude deductively a world with angels from a principle of plenitude. However, there is no doubt that such a portrait of the universe–one where on the level of particular kinds of beings created we have

---

65. See chapters 8 and 9.
66. Braude, *ESP and Psychokinesis*; Braude, *The Gold Leaf Lady*.
67. Lund, *Persons, Souls and Death*.
68. Flew, *A New Approach to Psychical Research*; Schlagel, *Contextual Realism*; Schlagel, *The Vanquished Gods*; Sudduth, *Critique of Empirical Arguments for Postmortem Survival*.

such gradations "filled"–is a more elegant one. It's just not enough steam on its own to overwhelm the counter-possibilities.

The final argument we explored was an argument from diabolical experiences. These include diabolical harassments, such as temptations and oppressions, as well as diabolical invasions, such as possessions. While the argument parallels that of religious experience, its success is, at best, only as good as those for theistic iterations of religious experience. At worst, diabolical experiences do not entail that such experiences reliably point to any particular kind of cause of the experience(s) in question. While the line of reasoning has promise, as its theistic counterpart does, certainly more work needs to be done if the argument is to serve as a standalone piece of justification (or warrant). I do think for the person who has the experiences, she is entitled to believe that demons exist if there is independent evidence for or reason to believe that demons exist. But then that means the argument from diabolical experience can never be its own measure of support for demonic realism. And yet the occurrences of putative diabolical experiences would serve to strengthen the independent evidence for demonic realism should it arise elsewhere. More work needs to be done to disambiguate the transcendent, spiritual origin of such experiences from alternatives that can threaten such an inference. And if that requires a different argument to accomplish this, then demonic realists will not have as of yet made their case.

Thus far we have seen that arguments for demonic anti-realism are not quite successful as assessed in the previous chapter. And, for the most part, the arguments for demonic realism in this chapter fair no better than the anti-realist's, save the argument from diabolical experiences. One might prefer to say that they simply are in need of further (or better) development in order to be convincing. Maybe. But I leave that to others to pursue. I do, however, want to mention one other thing. It turns out that McNamara's implied criticism of natural theology in its proffering of evidence for theism ends up falling flat. For McNamara thinks he has illustrated a *reductio* against the deliverances of natural theology since it conceals transitive procedures that deliver up "clearly false" conclusions, namely Satan's existence. But that most of these sister arguments for Satan end up unsuccessful, as was shown, actually spoils the impact of his thesis. While the demonic realist may feel deflated about the lack of success or inconclusiveness of a natural diabology thus far, it shows that one cannot simply co-opt the arguments of natural theology for just any "wrong" hypothesis. Unlike McNamara, the theist will sleep well tonight.

In the meantime, it turns out that we have not yet exhausted the demonic realist's argumentative arsenal. There is a more promising case to be made that we have yet to discuss: the classic historical argument for the existence of demons. This argument shall take center stage in the next chapter. We shall consider a viable defense of it as well as objections that can be offered against it.

6

Philosophical Arguments for Demonic Realism (II)

THUS FAR WE HAVE explored unsuccessful arguments for demonic anti-realism as well as unsuccessful, or underdeveloped, arguments for demonic realism. After reviewing the last two chapters, one may find oneself in a form of agnosticism over the diabolical. However, there is one final argument to consider. It is an argument that has been employed by demonic realists in the Christian tradition in one form or another and, as one might expect, depends on the Bible as an ancient source of history, and so of reality. In formulating this argument, I shall craft a case for the existence of demons on the basis of events, sayings, and beliefs that are not only found in the Bible but are indelibly attached to the portrait of the historical Jesus. This latter point is significant, for if Jesus performed miracles and was indeed raised from the dead, and that these events enjoy historical confirmation, then anything he said, believed, or did are all confirmed to be historical, and so real, by no less an authority than God himself.

Following a presentation and defense of the argument, we shall consider objections leveled against it. Finding such objections unconvincing, and good reasons for thinking this historical argument a good one, I shall conclude that demonic realism is probably true after all. Some additional reflection about this argument considered in tandem with some of the previous ones will be offered as well.

The Historical Argument

This particular argument for demonic realism is an *a posteriori* argument that is based on the reliability and testimony of Scripture. This argument is perhaps the most well-known and the most widely circulated. In one form or another it is almost always the argument of choice, or at least is the most important among the choices,[1] for demonic

---

1. Merrill F. Unger ranks it among others as "the most important witness" (*Biblical Demonology*, 36–37; Cf., Adler, *The Angels and Us*, 36).

Part II: Existential Matters

realists who are Christians.[2] A typical, informal presentation tends to take the following (over)simplified form:

1. The Bible teaches that demons exist.
2. We should believe what the Bible teaches.
3. Therefore, we should believe that demons exist.

While the argument lacks sophistication and nuance, its essence is pretty much on point. That due to the reliability of the Bible, anything it declares as factual is to be believed. And yet its weaknesses are rather evident: Someone could think that the Bible is rather *un*reliable either as history or as doctrine (or both) and that the demonic realist's *interpretation* of what Satan and demons are is mistaken. These reveal unnecessary vulnerabilities in the argument one could avoid. Accordingly, if a successful version of the argument is to be advanced here it must undergo rehabilitation in order to meet these challenges.

It turns out that demonic realism is not alone in relying on the witness of Scripture as a premise to an argument on a topic in the philosophy of religion. Much ink has been spilled on attempts to establish the historicity of certain key events surrounding Jesus of Nazareth, most notably his miraculous resurrection from the dead following a lethal public crucifixion. And Jesus's resurrection has certainly been a topic particularly handled by professional philosophers ranging from those who sympathize with it[3] to those who oppose it.[4] This is so because even historical facts are subject to philosophical speculation if they are to serve as premises for philosophical conclusions. In particular, any explanatory argument whose *explanans* bears a supernatural feature is bound to invoke philosophical arguments about whether the supernatural is something that is metaphysically coherent and historically possible (e.g., the existence of God or the reality of miracles).

The biblio-historical argument for demonic realism, or just "the historical argument" for brevity's sake, benefits greatly from two millennia of discussions about the historicity of the resurrection of Jesus. For a sufficiently nuanced presentation that incorporates the conclusions already derived from defenses of Jesus's resurrection carry over into a more-developed argument for the existence of Satan and his demons. This is so because the historicity of the resurrection serves as a "divine vindication" of Jesus's self-understanding against the charge that he was a fraud and a blasphemer.[5] As the argument goes, if Jesus's resurrection probably occurred, then we have a superlative authority, namely God himself, vouchsafing the beliefs, sayings, and actions

---

2. E.g., Unger, *Biblical Demonology*, 36–37; Adler, *The Angels and Us*, 33ff; Dickason, *Angels*, 121–25, 161–63.

3. E.g., McGrew and McGrew, "The Argument from Miracles," 593–662; Swinburne, *The Resurrection of God Incarnate*; Craig, *Reasonable Faith*, 333–404.

4. E.g., Parsons, "The Universe Is Probable"; Cavin, "Is There Sufficient Evidence?"

5. Pannenberg, *Systematic Theology*, 363–66.

of Jesus. As God's unique representative on earth and the only one who can speak and act for God without qualification *qua* the incarnation of God himself, there is no room for Jesus having done and said things that are not endorsed or sanctioned by God. This is important not merely in establishing the historical goings-on of Jesus's activities as such, but that any interpretation by Jesus regarding those events are also justifiably established. Thus, it is the resurrection of Jesus that guarantees God's approval and endorsement of Jesus's own self-understanding. And what authority could be greater than that of God's?

The only remaining question that would deserve attention is: What exactly *is* Jesus's self-understanding? As a matter of (biblical) higher criticism, one must follow certain rules and guidelines in parsing out the New Testament witness of Jesus to discern which sayings and actions are in fact his and which are potential fabrications, exaggerations, poor recollections, or embellishments that have been penned by redactors and forgers and not really by Jesus himself or those originally writing about him. For example, Jesus's sayings and actions regarding his opposition to the Jewish high priest, the Pharisees, Scribes, and Sadducees are considered as belonging to the portrait of the historical Jesus, and so contribute to his self-understanding as one opposed to the religious establishment of the time. Hence, Jesus's self-understanding includes his believing that these individuals and groups really existed and were in some kind of opposition to him and his mission. If we suppose, contrary to fact, that there is no historical corroboration for any of these opponents of Jesus, it would seem that Jesus's self-understanding alone should vindicate the reality of those opponents particularly if Jesus was resurrected from the dead as a means of God's endorsement of his beliefs and actions. I cannot imagine God's endorsement of Jesus as his only begotten Son and the only true representative of himself not being a ratification of all that Jesus said and believed.

We can now bring in the doctrine of demonic realism. The historical argument for Jesus's self-understanding validates the existence of Satan and his demons if and only if part of Jesus's self-understanding includes beliefs, sayings, and/or actions that either explicitly or implicitly approbate the existence of such beings. The accusations and commentaries offered up by *others* (the Jews, Pharisees, Sadducees, Scribes, disciples, et al.) would not in themselves be justified by the resurrection unless Jesus speaks or acts in ways that clearly endorse their responses. (Consider that Jesus's accusers accuse him of being in league with Beelzebul, or Satan, in the exercise of his power over demons; this accusation would not be given approval merely by Jesus's resurrection for the reasons he himself has offered.[6] By contrast, some responses of Jesus's accusers are given implicit, if not explicit, endorsement as evidenced by the back-and-forth over Jesus's assuming himself to be in the position of being God.[7])

---

6. Mark 3.22–27.
7. E.g., John 10.32–39.

Moreover, it is crucial that our contemporary knowledge of Jesus's self-understanding on this matter be sufficiently disambiguated. In other words, it must be the case that if Jesus speaks or acts in support of there being "Satan" and "demons," he must mean by these terms *per* demonic realism that these are something like the evil spiritual beings discussed in this book in chapter 2. It is not enough to establish that there are accusations or claims or acts that explicitly or implicitly affirm "the existence of Satan and his demons," for the *interpretation* of such a claim must be such that it is an endorsement of the demonic realism we have previously codified. For example, Paul speaks of "the flesh" as a mutual enemy of God and the believer (e.g., Rom 8.3–13). He also seems to use language that makes "the flesh" sound almost as if it were a personal being, such as when he says that believers are to "make no provision for the flesh, to gratify its desires" (Rom 13.14) and that "the desires of the flesh are against the Spirit" (Gal 5.17). And yet one is not to properly interpret Paul as though "the flesh" is some kind of ultramundane, personal villain imbuing its human victims with sinful desires. Similarly, a figure of history might profess that there is such a thing as the existence of Satan, and that it is historically credible that that person indeed uttered the words "I believe there is a Satan." But it could be that what the person *meant* by that affirmation is that there is merely an abstract principle of evil shared by villains around the globe. This would hardly be the relevant demonic realism characterized in chapter 2. Jesus's interpretations will likewise need to be disambiguated as either explicit or implicit affirmations of demonic realism as we have understood it.

The task of the present chapter, then, is to explore the salient pieces of evidence that show demonic realism so understood to be part of the historical Jesus's beliefs and actions. But I will not be rehearsing the arguments for the resurrection of Jesus as God's "divine vindication" herein. Many excellent resources already abound that focus on defending it.[8] However, it is unclear that the inverse is true, namely that a lack of a resurrection and adjoining miracles themselves invalidate Jesus's witness. For, as will be made evident, *some* of the practices and beliefs of Jesus regarding demonic realism are too awkward or embarrassing to have been invented by even a fraudulent messiah who is seeking some kind of following. Alternatively, one could insist that Jesus is not a fraud at all; rather, it is his messianic claims and similar ones made about him that are unhistorical or inaccurately reported. As a mere prophet of God, Jesus might have been both God's legitimate spokesperson (like Moses and Elijah) and yet something less than the Son of God; but he would have had some measure of credibility nonetheless, particularly if it should turn out after all that Jesus has indeed performed miracles (especially the resurrection). Though the lack of a resurrection or any adjoining miracles would not themselves serve to *prima facie* falsify Jesus's beliefs

---

8. For a recent selection of impressive defenses, see Wright, *The Resurrection of the Son of God*; Habermas and Licona, *The Case for the Resurrection of Jesus*; Licona, *The Resurrection of Jesus*. Also see the aforementioned resources noted in this chapter in n. 3.

and practices regarding the demonic realm, their presence would certainly enhance the level of probability that would otherwise be attributed in their absence.

Let us begin by considering the following, more developed version of the historical argument for demonic realism which assumes a range of miracles performed by Jesus, including his resurrection, as an important component (Assume J = Jesus; $M1 \ldots n$ = a range of miracles performed):

4. For any action and/or belief by J, that action and/or belief by J is divinely approved by God by means of $M1 \ldots n$.

5. If J has beliefs and/or actions that imply proposition d, then d is approved by God by means of $M1 \ldots n$.

6. J has relevant beliefs and/or actions that imply a particular disambiguated proposition, d.

7. d is divinely approved by God by means of $M1 \ldots n$.

8. If d is divinely approved by God, then d is true.

9. Therefore, d is true.

Premise 4 establishes the general principle that anything Jesus does or says is endorsed by God by means of a number of miracles (including, but not necessarily requiring, the resurrection of Jesus from the dead). Premise 5 makes a bridge between all of Jesus's beliefs and/or practices and the propositions that are implied by those actions and/or beliefs. Any proposition legitimately implied by those beliefs and/or practices is also, by extension, being endorsed by God. Premise 6 affirms that there are beliefs and/or a practices that imply a specific unambiguous proposition, namely that demonic realism, so defined, is true. This premise will require that the reports of Jesus's beliefs and practices that imply such realism as we understand it are historically reliable and belong to the historical Jesus. If so, then 7's implication that demonic realism is endorsed by God follows. Premise 8 connects God's approval of certain propositions to the truth of those propositions, for it is obviously wrong to think that an infallible and omniscient God's endorsement of some proposition entails its not being true. From this it follows that 8.

It would seem that the most controversial premises are going to be 4 and 6. Since the literature is replete with defenses already available to the inquirer, I defer to those defenses in the substantiation of a resurrection which is one occurrence of a miracle *par excellence* in the range $M1 \ldots n$. As long as there are no *a priori* reasons for dismissing 4,[9] establishing 4 belongs to those defending the historicity of $M1 \ldots n$ (where

---

9. The resurrection of Jesus serves as the supreme validation of Jesus's life and ministry—including all that he said and did. Philosophers have historically pushed back on this notion by asserting the *a priori* impossibility of there being miracles in human history. But, as mentioned, true miracles in general serve as similar endorsements. If miracles are impossible—that the prior probability of miracles ever obtaining is zero–then no amount of posterior evidence for $M1 \ldots n$ can overwhelm that. But

the resurrection in particular has been widely defended on historical grounds). This brings us to premise 6 which is the premise of immediate interest. Hereafter, we shall focus on a defense of 6 in ultimately finalizing the argument from history for 9.

We shall consider four explicitly recorded exorcisms allegedly performed by Jesus in the Synoptic accounts which, as I shall argue, imply demonic realism. We shall also consider some relevant interaction Jesus has with his enemies in buttressing our case. If any or all of these passages are historically credible, then we have good evidence for 6. Let us explore each episode now.

Episode #1: The Demoniac in the Capernaum Synagogue (Mark 1.21–28; Luke 4.31–37)

In this particular episode, Jesus confronts a demon-possessed man in the synagogue in Capernaum on the Sabbath. Mark's version of the account, which New Testament scholars tell us is likely the earliest, reads as follows:

> And they went into Capernaum, and immediately on the Sabbath he entered the synagogue and was teaching. And they were astonished at his teaching, for he taught them as one who had authority, and not as the scribes. And immediately there was in their synagogue a man with an unclean spirit. And he cried out, "What have you to do with us, Jesus of Nazareth? Have you come to destroy us? I know who you are–the Holy One of God." But Jesus rebuked him, saying, "Be silent, and come out of him!" And the unclean spirit, convulsing him and crying out with a loud voice, came out of him. And they were all amazed, so that they questioned among themselves, saying, "What is this? A new teaching with authority! He commands even the unclean spirits, and they obey him." And at once his fame spread everywhere throughout all the surrounding region of Galilee.

This episode has at least four features or properties that, among others, underscore the historicity of the event. First, that the setting is in a Jewish synagogue is quite

---

there is no good reason to justify such a wholesale dismissal of the possibility of miracles just in case it is logically and metaphysically coherent that special divine actions can occur in a universe operating under physical laws and causes. Accordingly, if we follow Thomas Aquinas and assert that miracles are events that are caused by something outside the entire created order of nature (*Summa Theologiae*, I.110.4), it is difficult to see how such an event could not occur if the miracle-performer (viz., God) is simply not a member of or constrained by that created order of nature (*contra* Spinoza). Thus, it is not necessary to see miracles as "violations" of the created order as such, only that there are some events–viz., miracles–that circumvent the productive powers of nature (See McGrew, "Miracles"). For all of David Hume's notorious opposition to apriorism, it is odd indeed that he, or any of those who follow his thinking, should have an *a priori* prejudice against the metaphysical possibility of the miraculous. Thus, if there are no *a priori* objections to there being miracles at all, then the question of any given miracle redirects to whether or not that miracle has in fact occurred. (This, of course, does not preclude that one should not be cautious or skeptical of any given miracle claim; rather, only that the demerits of any given miracle claim should not be assigned on the basis of their being impossible.)

Philosophical Arguments for Demonic Realism (II)

embarrassing. The idea that a demon-possessed person, whose invader is described as "unclean," would be in a sacred place and submitting to the teachings of the Son of God himself seem inexplicable, especially given the traditional notion that God "dwells in unapproachable light" (1 Tim 6.16; cf., Exod 3.5).[10] Consequently, the proximity of the demoniac to the synagogue where Jesus is underscores his and the synagogue's sacredness. Such an episode also implicates the teachings of Jesus, for the demoniac seems undisturbed by them ("they were astonished at his teaching, for he taught them as one who had authority"). Despite what one would expect of this story if it were a fabrication, it accords with Satan's rather unfettered ability elsewhere to be in the presence of God and his Son (Job 1.6; Matt 4.1; John 6.70–71).

Second, the Capernaum confrontation in the synagogue occurs amidst a crowd–viz., in public–and would not likely have been an invention that could have been easily dispelled by naysayers and skeptics seeking to oust a fraudulent messiah. This is especially significant since Jesus scathingly rebukes the residents of Capernaum and declares her sins to be worse than those of the decimated city of Sodom (Matt 11.20–24; cf., Luke 10.12–15). As someone who undoubtedly picked up a few enemies along the way, this public spectacle was never challenged or denounced by those excoriated as never having happened. The most probable explanation is that it really occurred as a public spectacle.[11]

Third, that Mark's version has "unclean spirit" (*pneumatic akathartō*) instead of "demon" (*daimonion*) shows the account to be decisively pre-Markan and indicative of an ancient Palestinian/Semitic usage.[12] This is significant considering that Mark is likely written to a largely Gentile audience which is evidenced here by Mark's mentioning that this occurs in "*their* synagogue" (v. 23; emphasis mine) rather than in "ours."[13] Sometimes the Gospel writers–Mark included–preserve this usage and in other times update the references to "demon" or "evil spirit" or something else. That the later Gospel of John–also written to Gentiles–never uses "unclean spirit" bespeaks the preference that was given for the later Grecian designation over the more antiquated "unclean spirit" referent. Thus, the account is old and is not updated to the vernacular of the later church.

Fourth, as with "unclean spirit," another primitive Semitic expression is used. The invading spirit identifies Jesus as "the Holy One of God." This is significant for two reasons. First, the expression is an early and inchoate affirmation of Jesus's messiahship (John 6.69). Outside of the Gospels the expression is replaced with others and does not reappear on the lips of anyone else in the New Testament. Second, the demon is not merely affirming Jesus's messiahship but is, instead, reversing the

---

10. Raymond F. Collins reminds us that this notion, though a Pauline novelty, "is deeply rooted in Jewish tradition" (*I and II Timothy and Titus*, 168).
11. Witmer, *Jesus, the Galilean Exorcist*, 155–56.
12. Witmer, *Jesus, the Galilean Exorcist*, 156–57.
13. Boring, *Mark*, 62f.

commonly-understood role of the exorcist by attempting to ward off its opponent by revealing the opponent's identity. This practice by exorcists was a common feature in the ancient Mediterranean world as a way to overpower the invading spirits and take control.[14] That Jesus's power would have been openly challenged in this way and that the demon violently resists as it makes its reluctant exit (i.e., by "convulsing him"; *sparaxan auton*) seem too embarrassing for either Mark's theological motifs or the higher Christology of the later church.[15]

The accumulation of these factors suggest that the tradition is neither a Christian nor a Markan invention and contains elements that make it likely that it is a reliable memory of the events as they actually unfolded.

Episode #2: The Gerasene Demoniac
(Mark 5.1–20; Matt 8.28–34; Luke 8.26–39)

The Markan presentation of this exorcism is as follows:

> They came to the other side of the sea, to the country of the Gerasenes. And when Jesus had stepped out of the boat, immediately there met him out of the tombs a man with an unclean spirit. He lived among the tombs. And no one could bind him anymore, not even with a chain, for he had often been bound with shackles and chains, but he wrenched the chains apart, and he broke the shackles in pieces. No one had the strength to subdue him. Night and day among the tombs and on the mountains he was always crying out and cutting himself with stones. And when he saw Jesus from afar, he ran and fell down before him. And crying out with a loud voice, he said, "What have you to do with me, Jesus, Son of the Most High God? I adjure you by God, do not torment me." For he was saying to him, "Come out of the man, you unclean spirit!" And Jesus asked him, "What is your name?" He replied, "My name is Legion, for we are many." And he begged him earnestly not to send them out of the country. Now a great herd of pigs was feeding there on the hillside, and they begged him, saying, "Send us to the pigs; let us enter them." So he gave them permission. And the unclean spirits came out, and entered the pigs, and the herd, numbering about two thousand, rushed down the steep bank into the sea and were drowned in the sea. The herdsmen fled and told it in the city and in the country. And people came to see what it was that had happened. And they came to Jesus and saw the demon-possessed man, the one who had had the legion, sitting there, clothed and in his right mind, and they were afraid. And those who had seen it described to them what had happened to

---

14. Langton, *Essentials of Demonology*, 28–29.

15. Chilton, "An Exorcism of History: Mark 1:21–28," 226ff. That the Gospel of Luke downplays Mark's *sparaxan* of the victim by replacing it with *rhipsan* ("thrown down") demonstrates how likely uncomfortable the original report was. Cf., Twelftree, *Jesus the Exorcist*, 67f; Witmer, *Jesus, the Galilean Exorcist*, 160.

> the demon-possessed man and to the pigs. And they began to beg Jesus to depart from their region. As he was getting into the boat, the man who had been possessed with demons begged him that he might be with him. And he did not permit him but said to him, "Go home to your friends and tell them how much the Lord has done for you, and how he has had mercy on you." And he went away and began to proclaim in the Decapolis how much Jesus had done for him, and everyone marveled.

Regarding this particular occurrence, there are about three observations that can be made that suggest the historicity of this event.

First, if the story was an outright fabrication and grafted as an attempt to substantiate Jesus's authority over demons, then the presence of certain embarrassing and inimical details would surely not have been included. For one, the demon's response ("I adjure you by God, do not torment me") and the fact that it does not immediately leave after Jesus calls for its evacuation once again show that a demon can resist one no less than the Son of God.[16] Second, despite ultimately being a successful exorcism, the results are devastating to the community, for the transfer of the demons to two thousand pigs–the community's livestock–ends with their destruction in a watery grave.[17] Accordingly, the livelihood of the larger innocent community is openly ravaged. Third, the response of the community is one of hostility, namely that the eyewitnesses "began to beg Jesus to depart from their region." Such a response suggests that Jesus may have done more harm than good, a feature that would surely have been downplayed or omitted by would-be forgers of the account.

Second, there is the presence of one kind of "undesigned coincidence" that underscores the historicity of the event in an unexpected way. An "undesigned coincidence" is a descriptive phrase that was originally used by William Paley.[18] Such a coincidence is considered "undesigned" if the presence of one or more features of an alleged eyewitness account seems awkward or inexplicable on its face but is subsequently explained unintentionally by either another, independent eyewitness account of the same event or by some underlying fact that is later disclosed by another independent source that was not deliberately engineered to "fix" any tension prompted by the initial witness. What makes undesigned coincidences quite remarkable is that they are too subtle to have been picked up on by any casual reader. If an ancient

---

16. Witmer, *Jesus the Galilean Exorcist*, 183.

17. Some have suggested that the expulsion into the pigs does not belong to the original account. But, as Witmer argues, "[t]he problem with detaching the incident of the pigs from the rest of the story is that it becomes difficult to know where to separate the two parts, since so many of the elements are linked. . . . The story becomes unintelligible without all of the elements" (*Jesus the Galilean Exorcist*, 168).

18. Paley, *Horae Paulinae*; Paley, *View of the Evidences of Christianity*. The later John James Blunt wrote a more ambitious work on the subject entitled, *Undesigned Coincidences in the Writings Both of the Old and New Testaments*. For a recent discussion of "undesigned coincidences," see McGrew, *Hidden in Plain View*.

forger is colluding with other forgers, and wants to relieve any awkwardness left by the others, he would not bury his solution to or explanation of the awkwardness as an incidental feature to an unrelated story only to be found by scholarly eggheads nearly two millennia later. This is why such subtleties are undesigned, for we imagine that forgers do not want to leave any unnecessary awkwardness in the telling of their lies. Accordingly, an undesigned coincidence evidences the fact that an alleged eyewitness was not colluding with others in order to fabricate his testimony.

So, let us look to the particular case at hand regarding the Gerasene demoniac. In the present case, it is curious that herdsmen would have pigs as livestock feeding near the Sea of Galilee since they were unambiguously declared unclean (Leviticus 11.7). Most readers would simply gloss over that fact as a trivial though awkward feature of the story. But a curious scholar would wonder, if the author of Mark were inventing a Jewish story, why he would have mentioned this kind of animal as the basis of their livelihood in such a region.

The answer comes from the first-century Jewish historian, Josephus. Josephus reports as an aside in a completely unrelated context that "Gaza, and Gadara, and Hippos, . . . were Grecian cities, which Caesar separated from his government and added them to the province of Syria."[19] That Caesar annexed these cities, all a part of the region near the Sea of Galilee where the incident took place,[20] implies that the community would have become increasingly secularized and would have had more relaxed policies regarding livestock. Without meaning to do so, and without Mark's anticipating any later clarification of his account, Josephus unintentionally explains why there would have been pigs as part of the community's livelihood. A forger would not have anticipated that a Jewish historian would incidentally affirm why pigs might be part of the local economy. And neither was Josephus writing to justify the Synoptics's telling of the Gerasene demoniac which helps confirm Jesus as the messianic "Son of God" (why would he?). As such, this incidental whisper of congruity suggests that the event likely occurred in the way one might expect from an eyewitness uninterested in explaining every awkward detail of his forgery.[21]

Third, as with the earlier encounter in the Capernaum synagogue, the demon's (or demons's, "for we are many") responses invoke some interesting and familiar features. For one, the demon identifies Jesus as "Son of the Most High God." Like the demon's confession in Capernaum, its confession here "is on the margins of New

---

19. Josephus, *Antiquities of the Jews*, XVII.11.4: 568.

20. The Synoptics report different locations (i.e., the "region" of Gadara, Gerasa, and Gergesa), but, regardless of which is the case, all of these references fall within the relevant province. The specific location, whichever it is, is going to be the one near enough to the Sea where the pigs meet their fate. As Craig L. Blomberg argues, plausible solutions exist that need not call the episode into question on the basis of this apparent Synoptic confusion. See his *The Historical Reliability of the New Testament*, 74–75. John P. Meier considers Mark's mention of the Gerasene city and the Decapolis to be some of the "linguistic details" that "point in the direction of historicity" (*A Marginal Jew*, 653).

21. See Blunt, *Undesigned Coincidences*, 343.

Testament tradition [and] points to the improbability that Mark or the early church needed to introduce it into the demon's defence;" accordingly, "we can be reasonably confident that this title was included in the first report of this event."[22] Second, this demon, like the one in Capernaum, seeks to overpower Jesus ("I adjure you by God, do not torment me"). Demons exhibiting resistance is counterproductive to a Markan apologetic for Jesus that seeks to establish him as the unique Son of God that leave onlookers trembling in fear. Moreover, this "torment" that the demon fears is seen in Mark to be straightforwardly related to being expelled "out of the country" and not to any eschatological "torment" that is later implied by Matthew and Luke (Matt 8.29; Luke 8.31; cf., Rev 20.10). The intact dialogue in Mark shows that the later Christian community was not interested in clarifying as to what precisely the "torment" refers. This lack of clarification makes Mark's version likely reflective of the original in not being updated to fit with later theological (eschatological) motifs.[23]

Episode #3: The Syrophoenician Woman's Daughter (Mark 7.24–30; Matt 15.21–28)

Unlike the other episodes, this one is not found in the complete triple tradition of the Synoptics but is found only in Mark and Matthew. Here is Mark's telling of the story:

> And from there he arose and went away to the region of Tyre and Sidon. And he entered a house and did not want anyone to know, yet he could not be hidden. But immediately a woman whose little daughter had an unclean spirit heard of him and came and fell down at his feet. Now the woman was a Gentile, a Syrophoenician by birth. And she begged him to cast the demon out of her daughter. And he said to her, "Let the children be fed first, for it is not right to take the children's bread and throw it to the dogs." But she answered him, "Yes, Lord; yet even the dogs under the table eat the children's crumbs." And he said to her, "For this statement you may go your way; the demon has left your daughter." And she went home and found the child lying in bed and the demon gone.

For the first time we have a young filial demoniac who belongs to a marginalized family. But it is the second time we appear to have an exorcism of a Gentile. Regarding the circumstance of the demonic expulsion here, Amanda Witmer says that "it is the only case of exorcism recorded in the Gospels in which Jesus does not actually confront the demon, or even the possessed girl, directly."[24] Graham Twelftree is less certain about this when he suggests that "the daughter could have accompanied the

---

22. Twelftree, *Jesus the Exorcist*, 82.
23. Twelftree, *Jesus the Exorcist*, 86; Witmer, *Jesus the Galilean Exorcist*, 182.
24. Witmer, *Jesus the Galilean Exorcist*, 191.

Part II: Existential Matters

woman, perhaps on a stretcher (cf., Mark 2.3 and 9.14–29)."[25] Nevertheless, it is not out of character for Jesus to believe himself to heal from a distance (e.g., Matt 8.5–13). At any rate, observations regarding historicity of the episode can be made here despite some scholars, especially T. A. Burkill, as seeing this as the mere product of the early Christian (Gentile) community.[26]

First, we, once again, have Mark referring to the demon as an "unclean spirit" which, as we have already noted, indicates how likely primitive the account is. (See the fourth point in the Capernaum episode above.)

Second, the reference to the woman's being of Syrophoenician origin actually underscores, *contra* Burkill, its not being a later Christian invention since the woman is being identified as a pagan and Jesus disparages the Gentiles by calling them "dogs"–a particularly Jewish slander. That Mark otherwise portrays Gentiles in a favorable light mitigates against it as a mere invention. As Twelftree argues, because "Mark shows an interest in the Gentiles and Jesus's Gentile Mission, . . . he would hardly create this potentially offensive story."[27] Regarding the Gentiles being deemed "dogs," there is a further detail that is striking. The woman checks Jesus's prejudice in her response ("yet even the dogs under the table eat the children's crumbs"). Witmer thus argues that such an offensive saying makes it "difficult to imagine [for] the church wanting to portray Jesus as one who first insults someone and then is corrected for this hostile saying."[28] What Christian community seeking converts in Gentile communities would have arranged for Jesus to be this kind of anti-Gentile person who has his own prejudice challenged by a pagan?

Third, despite someone on the margins of society and who is also female, the expulsion of the demon is accomplished rather easily. If the exorcism was indeed at a distance, the effortlessness of the healing is not what one would expect of a pagan Gentile adversary. That certain pagan cultures are considered to be run by Satan himself (Dan 10.13, 20; Rev 2.13) and that they are often ground zero for the violently opposing demonic forces (Acts 16.14–18; 19.13–17) makes the ease of the confrontation here too peculiar. If an early Judeo-Christian community wanted to, for whatever reason, harshly disparage Gentiles or their practices from a particular region, it seems to me that they would have empowered or even pluralized the demon in their story a bit more. The circumstances and the ease of the remedy are probably the way they are because that is how it actually happened.

As it turns out, there are some elements in this story that mitigate greatly against its being an invention by the early Christian community. Accordingly, we have good grounds for the historicity of this episode. And now we shall consider one more exorcism.

---

25. Twelftree, *Jesus the Exorcist*, 175. However, I find it hard to reconcile Twelftree's opinion here with v. 30 which says that the woman "went home and found the child lying in bed."

26. E.g., Burkill, "The Historical Development"; Meier, *A Marginal Jew*, 660.

27. Twelftree, *Jesus the Exorcist*, 90.

28. Witmer, *Jesus the Galilean Exorcist*, 200.

Philosophical Arguments for Demonic Realism (II)

Episode #4: The Convulsing Boy
(Mark 9.14–29; Matt 17.14–21; Luke 9.37–43)

The Gospel of Mark leads us to another episode of exorcism that involves, like the incident in Capernaum, someone who is not on the margins of society and, like the Syrophoenician woman's daughter, this possession case involves someone who is not an adult:

> And when they came to the disciples, they saw a great crowd around them, and scribes arguing with them. And immediately all the crowd, when they saw him, were greatly amazed and ran up to him and greeted him. And he asked them, "What are you arguing about with them?" And someone from the crowd answered him, "Teacher, I brought my son to you, for he has a spirit that makes him mute. And whenever it seizes him, it throws him down, and he foams and grinds his teeth and becomes rigid. So I asked your disciples to cast it out, and they were not able." And he answered them, "O faithless generation, how long am I to be with you? How long am I to bear with you? Bring him to me." And they brought the boy to him. And when the spirit saw him, immediately it convulsed the boy, and he fell on the ground and rolled about, foaming at the mouth. And Jesus asked his father, "How long has this been happening to him?" And he said, "From childhood. And it has often cast him into fire and into water, to destroy him. But if you can do anything, have compassion on us and help us." And Jesus said to him, "'If you can'! All things are possible for one who believes." Immediately the father of the child cried out and said, "I believe; help my unbelief!" And when Jesus saw that a crowd came running together, he rebuked the unclean spirit, saying to it, "You mute and deaf spirit, I command you, come out of him and never enter him again." And after crying out and convulsing him terribly, it came out, and the boy was like a corpse, so that most of them said, "He is dead." But Jesus took him by the hand and lifted him up, and he arose. And when he had entered the house, his disciples asked him privately, "Why could we not cast it out?" And he said to them, "This kind cannot be driven out by anything but prayer."

Here we have a vivid set of symptoms that indicates a recurring series of convulsions or seizures. Witmer notes that "this is one of the times in the Gospels when the distinction between illness and spirit possession is blurred."[29] A number of scholars suggest that the boy may be suffering from some official form of epilepsy in accordance with the canons of modern medicine,[30] which obviously in itself is not a predictor of pneumatic possession. Whether the boy is to be formally diagnosed with epilepsy

---

29. Witmer, *Jesus the Galilean Exorcist*, 185.

30. E.g., Meier, *A Marginal Jew*, 655ff; Dunn, *The Christ and the Spirit*, 188. Cf., Matt 17.15's use of *selēniazetai* ("moonstruck").

or not,[31] nothing about this case precludes the possibility of his having a comorbid condition, namely the concurrence of a spirit possession.[32]

Nevertheless, there are some indications of historicity in this episode worth mentioning. First, the account lacks the usual characteristics found in the other exorcism stories. Specifically, the afflicting demon uses no Christological appellations in addressing Jesus, neither does it make any insinuations regarding eschatology; and the victim in this case is suffering from physical, even debilitating, symptoms.[33] As such, this is not a "cookie cutter" presentation of an event for the purposes of feeding any theological motifs held by the early Christian community. As a straightforward and theologically unadorned account, and one with little similarity with other exorcisms, it is likely authentic.

Second, the expulsion of the demon by Jesus is, once again, a struggle. So much so that "after crying out and convulsing him terribly, it came out." The difficulty of the expulsion is further punctuated by Jesus's reply to the disciples that "[t]his kind cannot be driven out by anything but prayer." That Matthew downplays the violent exit (17.18) and that neither Matthew nor Luke make mention of the renitence of "this kind" suggest that the Markan version empowered the demon beyond what early Christians would have been comfortable with. This makes his version a likely accurate account of what actually happened–warts and all.

Third, the post-exorcism debriefing is quite interesting. The admission of the inability of Jesus's disciples that they could not cast out the demon is an embarrassing feature for an early Christian community to invent. In fact, the longer ending of Mark's Gospel–being a likely interpolation by the early Christian scribal community–indicates that they thought quite differently about their community's expected abilities: "And these signs will accompany those who believe: in my name they will cast out demons; . . ." (16.17). Considering that such a power is broadened beyond The Twelve

---

31. Though I have no professional training in clinical psychology, it seems to me that a conversion disorder better accounts for all of the diverse symptoms as given in *DSM-V* (viz., the concurrence of the boy's seizure along with his deafmuteness and eventual paralysis/unresponsiveness). And conversion disorders do not tend to have any kind of organic or biological cause but tend to be psychogenic, which is certainly in line with there being an alien spiritual stressor.

32. Epilepsy is a chronic neurological condition that predisposes one to having seizures. Accordingly, some seizures can be provoked. For example, a photosensitive epileptic patient can have a seizure triggered by a strobe light. Consequently, having epilepsy is not incompatible with there being an external, provoking cause of one's seizure episode(s). And if that is true, then an external, pneumatic cause cannot be ruled out *a priori*. The only question that remains here is whether the account is an amalgamation of two separate accounts (Bultmann, *History of the Synoptic Tradition*, 211) or whether Jesus's treatment of the boy is predicated on prescientific ignorance and *just is* epilepsy (Dunn, *The Christ and the Spirit*, 188), both of which imply that there is no alien spirit provoking the seizures. But if this is a singular account and the diagnosis of a "mute and deaf spirit" is indeed Jesus's conclusion, and his being raised from the dead vindicates his beliefs and actions, then we either have concurrent conditions (epilepsy + pneumatic possession) or we only have the presence of an alien spirit that is merely causing the kind of seizures normally associated with epilepsy.

33. Witmer, *Jesus the Galilean Exorcist*, 191.

(cf., 3.15), the lack of success by any of Jesus's disciples runs aground against Mark 16's expectation. That Matthew explicitly attributes their failure to a "lack of faith" (17.17, 19–20; cf., Deut 32.5), where the later Synoptics only make this implicit (Mark 9.19; Luke 9.41), is also striking for their failure to exorcise in Mark is not clearly attributed to any inadequacy on their part.[34] The failure of Jesus's disciples, then, is likely too uncomfortable a fact to be a Christian invention. For, as Witmer notes, their failure is "difficult and embarrassing" for the early Christian community because in Mark it is not the case that "faith alone can cure the boy."[35]

All three points suggest that the event is likely a historically credible occurrence and belongs to the historical Jesus. And the convergence of all of the episodes discussed here increase the likelihood that Jesus at least *believed* that he could perform exorcisms successfully. There is one more consideration beyond these four well-established exorcisms, it is an exorcism story that is immediately followed up by criticism from the Scribes and Pharisees. Let us turn to the additional historical observations we can glean about the demonology of Jesus from this criticism often referred to as the "Beelzebul controversy."

Observations from the Beelzebul Controversy
(Mark 3.20–27; Matt 12.22–30; Luke 11.14–23)

This episode might qualify as a fifth exorcism, but it is not the exorcism itself that draws our interest here. Instead, the Synoptics refer to a critical response–a polemic, even–against Jesus's practice of exorcism. Once again we take Mark as our launching point:

> Then [Jesus] went home, and the crowd gathered again, so that they could not even eat. And when his family heard it, they went out to seize him, for they were saying, "He is out of his mind." And the scribes who came down from Jerusalem were saying, "He is possessed by Beelzebul," and "by the prince of demons he casts out the demons." And he called them to him and said to them in parables, "How can Satan cast out Satan? If a kingdom is divided against itself, that kingdom cannot stand. And if a house is divided against itself, that house will not be able to stand. And if Satan has risen up against himself and

---

34. Twelftree may be right to see an indictment of the disciples's faith also in Mark (*Jesus the Exorcist*, 94). But the noted unbelief is ambiguous, for it refers generically to the entire "generation" represented by the crowd. Even so, the putative unbelief of the disciples only serves to preface the exorcism (perhaps as to explain why there even is a demon-possessed boy in their midst). There is no doubt that the explicit reason given in Mark for the disciples's failure to exorcise is due, not to a lack of faith, but to the kind of demon involved. Moreover, non-believers are elsewhere considered to be successful in their exorcisms (Mark 9.38–39; Matt 7.22–23) which would make any "lack of faith" an awkward reason. Matthew and Luke may have simply harnassed Mark's "faithless generation" quip in order to deemphasize the implication that some demons are beyond the power of rebukes in Jesus's name.

35. Witmer, *Jesus the Galilean Exorcist*, 191.

is divided, he cannot stand, but is coming to an end. But no one can enter a strong man's house and plunder his goods, unless he first binds the strong man. Then indeed he may plunder his house.

It is noteworthy that the account, or something like it, appears to be implied by the independent Gospel of John (10.19–21). Regarding the Beelzebul controversy across the Synoptics, the variations of the details in Mark are a bit starker in comparison with those of Matthew and Luke. This is likely due to the fact that Mark is not the only source for the incident (for it is probably embedded in a source, such as Q, outside of the canonical Gospels). One notable contrast is Mark's omission of an exorcism that takes place just prior to the Beelzebul accusation which is otherwise reported in Matthew and Luke. But some observations can be made here that add credibility to demonic realism being among the beliefs had by Jesus.

First, that Mark's narrative begins with the accusation *by his own family* that Jesus is "out of his mind" and that they seek to "seize" (viz., restrain or overpower; *kratēsai*) him creates a sense of inner conflict between him and his family. Considering that his mother, Mary, is among them (v. 32) makes the episode far too embarrassing to have been fabricated by anyone seeking to show Jesus, much less Mary, in a favorable light. That Matthew and Luke omit this element evidences how uncomfortable this feature was thereby suggesting Mark's report was not being fabricated by the Christian community. Since the family's attempted seizure continues after the Beelzebul controversy (vv. 33–35), and the content or implication of the accusation provides the reason why Jesus would have been seen as "out of his mind," then the embarrassing features cannot be separated from the controversy, thus rendering the entire episode likely historical.[36]

Secondly, the accusation by Jesus's accusers and his response implies that he believed himself to be a successful exorcist. For Jesus does not deny the allegation *that* he casted out demons, only that he did so by the assistance of Beelzebul.[37] This is important to note for two reasons. First, Jesus confirms his own belief that he performs successful exorcisms. Second, the enemies of Jesus do not dispute his success. Rather than simply deny that Jesus did or can do these things, the accusers imply his success by offering up a counter-explanation to account for the healed victims. One might imagine Jesus's accusers preferring to say, "He didn't heal anybody. Those people were never possessed!" or "The victims are still afflicted by demons!" Presumably, the victims were available for cross-examination. Accordingly, the counter-explanation by the accusers implies the success of the exorcisms that Jesus himself believes to have been responsible for.

Thirdly, the event provides some missing details about Jesus's character vis-à-vis his harsh statements elsewhere about one's family (this may possibly be another undesigned coincidence between Mark and Luke). Specifically, Jesus provides a rather

---

36. Witmer, *Jesus the Exorcist*, 115; Twelftree, *Jesus the Exorcist*, 100.

37. "Beelzebul" is likely a circumlocution for Satan. See Witmer, *Jesus the Galilean Exorcist*, 113–14 and Twelftree, *Jesus the Exorcist*, 105–6.

unusual prerequisite for discipleship in Luke 14.26: "If anyone comes to me and does not hate his own father and mother and wife and children and brothers and sisters, yes, and even his own life, he cannot be my disciple." Why in the world would Luke have Jesus make hating one's family a mark of true discipleship given that Luke has Jesus submit to his parents (2.51) and has him repeat the Covenantal command to "honor your father and mother" (18.20)? Though it is true that, earlier, Luke's Jesus declares that his coming foreseeably divides family members (12.51–53), it is not something that is offered as a prescription for Jesus's followers to practice. Instead, it is merely stated as an unfortunate reality that will be *corrected* when he, in the spirit of Elijah, comes to usher in the "day of the Lord" (Malachi 4.5–6). Jesus's call in Luke to (hyperbolically) "hate" one's family in order to be a disciple appears to come out of nowhere. The character of Mark's Jesus exhibited in the preface to the Beelzebul episode as one who appears to be "out of his mind" and in need of restraint might explain this. It is noteworthy that the family's planned intervention is found only in Mark and not in Luke. After Jesus responds to his accusers on the charge of being empowered by Beelzebul in his exorcisms, he is told that his family is now there to get him (vv. 31–32). It is then that Jesus responds aloud that it is his disciples that are to be identified as his true family (vv. 33–35)! This part is also missing in Luke. If the author of Luke were a forger and wanted to place the call to hate one's family on the lips of Jesus, he surely would have incorporated Mark's family's adversarial reaction and the public declaration that his disciples are his true family in order to better contextualize his call to hate one's actual family. Without Mark, Luke's Jesus seems conflicted about family in loving and honoring them on the one hand and then insisting on hating them on the other. The witness behind Luke or Luke himself probably knew of these other events of Mark but, for whatever reason, felt they were not important to include in the telling of the Beelzebul controversy. And yet Luke's leaving out such information makes Jesus's call to hate one's family appear awkward. Thus, it is likely the full account given in Mark, including the exorcism, which provides the missing insight as to why Jesus gives such an odd prescription in Luke.[38] If Mark explains Luke in this regard which includes the family's reaction to his performing exorcisms, then we have additional reason (by way of an undesigned coincidence?) to think the Beelzebul controversy should be seen as an integral part of the historical Jesus.

For these reasons and others the Beelzebul controversy is likely a report of a historical occurrence that entails Jesus's belief, as well as those of his accusers, that he could perform successful exorcisms. It is no wonder that the Beelzebul controversy is considered by some to be one of the most firmly grounded traditions we have about the historical Jesus.[39]

It is possible to address other incidences and events that involve demons as further confirmations of Jesus's belief in real demons (such as the temptation narrative or

---

38. Cf., Witmer, *Jesus the Galilean Exorcist*, 111.
39. Witmer, *Jesus the Galilean Exorcist*, 118; Mann, *Mark*, 253.

his sayings in the Olivet discourse), but the case presented here is more forceful for it involves public events that were witnessed by multiple bystanders. They provide the best type of evidence for Jesus's beliefs and actions regarding demons. We shall now consider objections to this argument and some replies to them in the next section before consolidating some final thoughts about the case for demonic realism.

Objections

Following the rise of European rationalism and German idealism, theologians as well as philosophers were especially motivated to oppose demonic realism due to modernity's philosophical reluctance to entertain hypotheses involving the supernatural. This led to various theologians scrambling to find alternative ways to interpret the divine marvels reported in the New Testament. The same also went for the diabolical ones. While under the spells of David Hume and Voltaire, New Testament sympathizers needed to revisit their Scriptures through the fresh eyes of Enlightenment thinking. While one might think that such a paradigm shift toward metaphysical naturalism might prompt theologians to give up the ghost (pun intended), their apparent love and appreciation for the teachings of the New Testament in general and the Gospels in particular begged for a different form of reconciliation with the modern conscience–one that did not amount to abandoning Christianity *in toto*. Let us see what those historical options are and why they have failed as viable alternative interpretations of the exorcism accounts.

Option #1: Exorcism as a Prescientific Explanation

This first option has to do with the notion that though the underlying events of the Gospels are indeed historical (i.e., that some states of affairs described actually happened), the descriptions given about them are not to be taken literally, for they are merely prescientific ways of attempting to understand elusive phenomena like human behavior. If they were to be taken literally–that actual demons were involved–then they would amount to literal falsehoods about the events depicted. These theologians, instead, suppose that the concept of demonic possession was being imported as a prescientific and convenient context in attempting to explain people that were really suffering from physical and/or psychological maladies. As such, it was an effort to knowingly or unknowingly accommodate the primitive beliefs of the people of the region. Some notable representatives of this view include the German theologians

Heinrich Paulus (1761 to 1851)[40] and Hermann Olshausen (1796 to 1839)[41] as well as the American theologian A. Alexander Hodge (1823 to 1886).[42]

Despite the popularity of this approach, attempts at alternative naturalistic explanations fail to take into account the full scope of the narratives. For example, some attempts were made to explain one of the most complex episodes of the Gospels: the Gerasene demoniac. Some of them suggested that it was the storm that occurred over the Sea of Galilee just prior to Jesus's arrival (Mark 4.37) that drowned the pigs. Upon dealing "immediately" (5.2) with the demoniac Jesus encountered there, the coincidence that pigs nearby had drowned and Jesus's subsequent cure led to the telling of the story as an exorcism that (wrongly) related the cure with the pigs's meteorological fate at sea. What this explanation fails to account for is that the demons in the story are not the same things as the demoniacs (for one must imagine the demoniacs themselves or some aspect of their psyche had entered into the pigs). The story is clearly one of soulish transmigration. Moreover, the destruction of the local livestock caused considerable anger and outrage against Jesus. Such a climax to the story would not have led anyone to deliberately equate Jesus's cure with the pigs's destruction much less canonize them for Christian posterity.[43] That the alternative explanations fail to take into account all of the elements of the narratives plagues all of the various attempts at modernizing the exorcism episodes. By contrast, supposing demons to be real and acting in part on their own accord better accounts for all of the elements in the narratives just in case it is possible that demons exist.

The failure of this naturalizing approach did pave the way for another anti-realist consideration of an interpretation that would take all of the available information in the narratives into account. We turn to this option now.

Option #2: Exorcism as Myth

According to this option, it may be that the sayings of Jesus regarding his exorcisms of demon-possessed people should be taken at face value, but these sayings are not necessarily meant to be descriptions of *any* underlying events that might have taken place. In this view such descriptions are more like the parables of Jesus–stories that use familiar scenarios and imagery in order to bolster some kind of agenda regarding a particular real-life situation. It is the language of the myths of exorcism that provides the imagistic framework for apprehending human conflict in its sundry forms. That

---

40. Refer to his *Das Leben Jesu als Grundlage einer reinen Geschichte des Urchristentums*. Also see Schweitzer, *The Quest of the Historical Jesus*, chapter 5.

41. Refer to his *Biblical Commentary on the New Testament*.

42. Refer to his *Outlines of Theology*, esp. chapter 12.

43. It was Olshausen's contemporary, David Friedrich Strauss, who dismantled this thesis in the ways noted here. See his *Life of Jesus*, 424ff. In fact, Strauss has made it clear that he has no love for any attempts at finding alternative naturalistic explanations to any of the demon-possession stories (415ff).

Jesus talks of demonic possession on a particular occasion is his way (or the way of the Gospel writers/redactors) of advancing an agenda that enlists myth as a colorful way to punctuate the cosmic significance Jesus had over the struggles that ensnare human beings. These struggles range from the various kinds of personal and impersonal evils found in the world. Myths, then, colorfully tell us that Jesus can conquer our demons both within ourselves and within the world. So understood, attributing to Jesus the power of exorcism is narratively borrowed and appropriated from previous legends about Jewish mystics, like Rabbi Simeon ben Yose, and pagan ones, like Apollonius of Tyana.[44] This mythical view was held by the influential German theologian David Friedrich Strauss (1808 to 1874).[45]

But like the preceding option, such a view shoulders too many problems of its own. Perhaps the most damning criticism one could level against the mythical view is that there are obvious dissimilarities between the accounts of Jesus and those of the mystics. For example, Jesus does not use formulaic incantations in order to drive out demons. Nor does he invoke the authority of another sage or mystic but acts on his own authority. And, unlike the mystics, he does not use amulets and talismans. Other criticisms of the mythical view involve debates about the genre of the Gospels. For, as the evidence seems to indicate,[46] the Gospels are more akin to the genre of Greco-Roman biography. Attempts to dismiss the stories of exorcism as mere myth fail to take into account the literary style and intent of the Gospel portraits on these occasions.

Unless one has good reason to overturn the evidence set out in the historical argument, the only conclusion we should prefer in the wake of the failure of both the opposing options just covered is that the descriptions and the events they depict are literally and historically true. But that entails that demons exist.

A Cumulative Case

Now that we have seen a good though isolated argument for demonic realism, such a historical case provides some interesting background for some of the other arguments mentioned in the previous chapter. For one, we already saw that the notion of plenitude seems inadequate on its own merits to warrant the conclusion that angels, and so demons, exist. But now given the historical argument, the notion of plenitude, particularly the elegance it affords, makes the entire picture lovelier: the existence of demons may seem peculiar and even inexplicable as metaphysical creations when only considering the historical case, but plenitude about our world fills out our understanding about why intermediary beings exist at all.

---

44. See Twelftree, *Jesus the Exorcist*, 22ff.
45. Refer to his *Das Leben Jesu*.
46. See Blomberg, *The Historical Reliability of the New Testament*, 3ff.

Furthermore, consider also the argument from diabolical experiences. Now that history evidences the existence of demons, we have a context for modern-day possession cases. And if such possession cases resemble, indeed *conform* to, the patterns of possession we find in the New Testament, then we have more of a web of information that, when taken together, increases the overall probability of demonic realism. For the modern experiences become extensions of those experiences attested by history. Moreover, the historical argument helps us to adjudicate better the modern occurrences. For though the harassing or invading alien agents in the alleged diabolical encounters, if they are indeed personal agents, could still be buffaloing their perceivers to only *think* that demons are present, we now have a reliable context, thanks to the historical record, that provides the backdrop for hypothesizing more confidently about what kinds of agents might be responsible for those diabolical experiences. For example, we know that (from history) radical Islamic terrorism has been an adverse factor in certain segments of human history. This means that any contemporary incident, from 9/11 to the recent vehicular acts of terror in England and Spain, make the hypothesis of terrorism a more believable reality.

Furthermore, the causes of the experiences are not the only things corroborated by the historical argument, but so are our *expectations* about what demonic harassments and invasions would look like apart from the experiential data we in fact have. The diabolical experiences are what we would expect them to be given the historical situation in that the verisimilitude of possession cases today with those in the portrait of Jesus provides more of a web of support for an overall, even if persistent, demonic realism. And the current iterations of such experiences elucidate how such things might have obtained for those in the first century. For the picture is one of mutual support of its parts that fit together like a Jenga tower. And, like a fishing net, the evidential loops are tethered together to make strong the notion of demonic realism. Thus, what appeared to be a doubtful stream of random evidence in the last chapter now becomes, at least for the cosmological and experiential arguments, confirming pieces of evidence when conjoined with the historical argument of this chapter.

Conclusion

In this chapter, we have explored one successful, *a posteriori* argument for demonic realism based on the historicity of some of Jesus's beliefs and practices regarding exorcisms. If Jesus's beliefs and practices in fact imply demonic realism, and God's raising Jesus from the dead and/or his performing relevant miracles constitute an endorsement of those beliefs and practices, then Jesus's miracles imply demonic realism. The historical attempts at averting this conclusion by Enlightenment theologians included two options that did not lead to a wholesale abandoning of the Christian message. One option was to suppose that the stories of Jesus's exorcisms were prescientific explanations derived from the cultural milieu at the time. Another option was to think of the exorcism stories as mythical overlays on the historical Jesus in order to establish him as a hero. But, as was demonstrated, both options fail to take into account all of the available evidence. Given the evidential support for the historicity of Jesus's exorcisms, the historical argument thus constitutes a good case for the probability of demonic realism. And when we integrate some of the not-so-convincing arguments of the previous chapter, what appeared to be dubious or questionable as standalone arguments now seem to network together to embolden the historical testimony.

The conclusion may be a philosophical victory for the realist, but it's quite sobering to ponder our conclusion thus far: *that there are such things as evil spirits*. Establishing the existence of a terror cell, for example, may testify to the acumen of an intelligence community, but it subsequently invokes questions concerning their *modus operandi*. As such, demonic realism leaves us with another huge discussion that has to be engaged. If Satan and his demons in fact exist as the evidence seems to suggest, then what kinds of beings are they? Are they immaterial spirits? If so, do they have any causal or communicative powers over nature and human beings? We shall now turn to the problem of the metaphysics of demons in the next Part in an attempt to answer these questions.

Part III

Ontological Matters

"Regarding the devil and his angels, and the opposing influences, the teachings of the Church has laid down that these beings exist indeed; but what they are, or how they exist, it has not explained with sufficient clearness."

—Origen, preface to *De Principiis* (c. 225)

7

On the Spiritual Nature of Demons

IN THE PREVIOUS PART consisting of three chapters, we focused on demonic realism as a philosophical hypothesis worthy of disagreement. Therein we assessed arguments against the existence Satan and/or the demons (viz., the gods of this world) and concluded that anti-realists have not made their case. We then looked at reasons that, in part, successfully support the conclusion that they probably do exist. Consequently, humanity has a non-trivial kind of enemy–a supersensible terrorist organization of cosmic proportions. But if the gods of this world genuinely exist in the *prima facie* way discussed in chapter 2, then more work has to be done in attempting to establish what they are and ultimately what they can do. This is no easier task than that of arguing for their existence. This chapter, then, shall take up the first concern–what demons are– and will argue for thinking that demons are not spirits in a material or quasi-material sense, but are unequivocally *purely immaterial* spirits. We shall leave it to the chapters that follow this one to take up the second concern regarding what demons can do.

It is a historical truism that theologians have not always seen the data on demonic incorporeality and spirituality in the Bible to be *ipso facto* declarations of any sort of pure immaterialism. As surveyed in chapter 3, the early Eastern Church Fathers and the later Western Franciscans conceived of demons as "spirits" but not to the extent that they associated such a notion with a pure immaterialism. For example, the universal hylomorphism of certain immaterialists (like Bonaventure) seems to treat "matter" merely as an essential component for some undisclosed spiritual substratum (viz., the accidental conjunction of an actual and a possible).[1] This is puzzling since talk of "spirit matter," "spiritual substance," or an "aerial nature" smack of the conceptual problem of demarcating spirit from matter. Even some of hylomorphism's proponents among the ancient Greeks never thought to dissociate corporeality from the spiritual realm.[2] As such, all of these views just seem like different ways to designate lesser

---

1. E.g., Bonaventure, *Commentaria in Quatuor Libros Sententiarum*, III.1.1.1.

2. Tertullian singles out Greeks like Hipparchus, Heraclitus, Hippon, Empedocles, and Critias in his own assertion that the soul is a corporeal thing. See his *De Anima* V. Cicero has called the associations of the soul with physical elements to be a common view among the Stoics. See his *Tusculanae*

degrees of materialism. Consequentially, we can then stipulate that "pure immaterialism" is a reference to a simplistic, strict denial of *any* connotation of matter–"gross" or "fine."

Accordingly, I shall infer by means of argumentation no more than what the data (canonical or otherwise) justify. We shall thus see that pure immaterialism is the best explanation of the demons's ontology over the more confusing rival views. But because the notion of a purely immaterial person, so defined, seems difficult if not impossible to conceive, then I shall first focus on the coherence of pure immaterialism, arguing that there are no good reasons to think that the very concept of a purely immaterial demon-person is either impossible or improbable. Following that, I shall proceed to the pure immaterialism of demons on the basis of the simplest and most straightforward metaphysical understanding of all of the available biblical data.

The Logical Possibility of Pure Immaterialism

If one is an unqualified materialist but accepts the conclusions set forth in the preceding chapter, then one might come to infer that demons are, or must be, material substances. As such, the prior probability of some form of materialism under any modal interpretation would be 1 (or near enough) which is to say that the hypothesis is, in some modal sense, necessary (or something near enough). For most contemporary philosophers–materialists included–they actually do not think that there is anything *logically* incoherent (as in "A cannot simultaneously be ¬A") in the idea that an existent might be an immaterial substance. But some iconic philosophers of history, such as Epicurus and Thomas Hobbes, have attempted to show such incoherence by insisting that "immaterial" tacitly refers to "the absence of existence."[3] For Hobbes, the notion of an immaterial, incorporeal substance that exists is as incoherent as that of a round square. Hobbes says as much when he defines the nature of soul in his section on the "Christian common-wealth" where such serves as the typology for the secular common-wealth of a polis. Hobbes, who later explicitly discusses the demonic world, writes on the nature of substance as follows:

> *Substance* and *Body*, signifie the same thing; and therefore *Substance incorporeall* are words, which when they are joined together, destroy one another, as if a man should say, an *Incorporeall Body*.[4]

Disputationes I.9–10.

3. Epicurus and Hobbes take "incorporeal" to be similar to how I have defined "immaterial." Accordingly, their comments about the impossibility of an immaterial spirit rests on their problematic understanding of "incorporeal"; See Epicurus, *Letter to Herodotus*, VI.65–67; Hobbes, *Leviathan*, III.34.

4. Hobbes, *Leviathan*, III.34: 429–30. Describing "substance" as "incorporeal" was not previously held to be self-contradictory as we see in, for example, Augustine. Augustine, who lived over a millennium prior to Hobbes, claimed that "not everything which lacks body is an empty substance" (*De Anima et eius Origine*, IV.18: 362).

This conceptual impossibility, he continues, forces us to reconsider our understanding of

> *Spirits*; as when [some] call that aeriall substance, which in the body of any living creature, gives it life and motion, [and that] some . . . call them *Bodies*, and think them made of aire compacted by a power supernaturall, because the sight judges them corporeall; and some to call them *Spirits*, because the sense of Touch discerneth nothing in the place where they appear, to resist their fingers: So that the proper signification of *Spirit* in common speech, is either a subtile, fluid, and invisible Body, or a Ghost, or other Idol or Phantasms of the Imagination.[5]

This is in part motivated by the fact that the Greek word "spirit" is something often associated with "wind." But Hobbes wants to say something more forceful about what a spirit is when he says that spirits

> are not Ghosts *incorporeall*, that is to say, Ghosts that are in *no place*; that is to say, that are *no where*; that is to say, that seeming to be *somewhat*, are *nothing*.[6]

In noting some particular passages of relevance in the Bible where angels are discussed, Hobbes concludes that in many cases the word "*Angel* signifieth there, nothing but *God* himself."[7] But Hobbes himself is quick to confess that there are very compelling reasons to affirm in general the literalness of the angelic realm,[8] and that those beings (as real entities) simply must be corporeal substances:

> To men that understand the significance of these words, *Substance*, and *Incorporeall*; as *Incorporeall* is taken not for subtile body, but for *not Body*, they imply a contradiction: insomuch as to say, an Angel, or Spirit is (in that sense) an Incorporeall Substance, is to say in effect, there is no Angel nor Spirit at all.[9]

Unsurprisingly, if angels exist, then on pain of irrationality they must be corporeal in some way. Hobbes thus writes that "though [the New Testament] prove[s] the Permanence of Angelicall nature, it confirmeth also their Materiality."[10] Believing that the judgment of "everlasting fire" is reserved for Satan and his demons according to Matt 25.41, this substantiates the existence ("permanence") of evil angels, and that such

---

5. Hobbes, *Leviathan*, III.34.
6. Hobbes, *Leviathan*, III.34: 434.
7. Hobbes, *Leviathan*, III.34: 436.
8. He later writes, "I was enclined to this opinion, that Angels were nothing but supernatural apparitions of the Fancy, raised by the special and extraordinary operation of God, thereby to make his presence and commandments known to mankind, and chiefly to his own people. But the many places of the New Testament . . . have extorted from my feeble Reason, an acknowledgment, and beleef, that there be also Angels substantiall, and permanent" (Hobbes, *Leviathan*, III.34: 439–40).
9. Hobbes, *Leviathan*, III.34: 439.
10. Hobbes, *Leviathan*, III.34: 439.

infinite judgment would be "repugnant to their Immateriality; because Everlasting fire is no punishment to impatible substances, such as are all things Incorporeall."

Hobbes's contention that *substance* and *body* are synonyms is the ground for his disavowal of the possibility of there being such a thing as an incorporeal (immaterial) person. By "substance" he just seems to mean "materiality." Thus, to be an incorporeal person means for him that there is a substantial soul (which entails physical attributes) endowed with an intellectual capacity which *ex hypothesi* lacks location (viz., "Ghosts that are in *no place*; that is to say, that are *no where*"). He seems to build his case by equating "incorporeality" with an absence of substance. And if something is not a substance, then of course it does not exist. But his view of "substance" incorrectly assumes that to be a substance entails that that object–whether person or thing–must essentially possess physical attributes. Perhaps Hobbes is thinking of substances as *individuated* things which is, on an Aristotelian interpretation, only achievable through the inclusion of *hyle* ("matter"). Debates about substance have raged since Aristotle, but it is by no means a settled issue that "substance" should be taken as "body"–individuated or not. And if one adopts a deflationary account of substance, then she will not easily equate "body" with "substance." What we need from Hobbes is an argument to settle this, and there does not appear to be any.

For the vast majority of Christendom, God is a paradigm case of an incorporeal substance (a substance with three individuated egos, incidentally!). It is no wonder that Hobbes rescues himself of a potential inconsistency by calling the substance of God "incomprehensible."[11] Even if the evidence went against the existence of immaterial substances, it would not show that something like God or a Cartesian ego or a subsisting form (intelligence) cannot *in principle* exist.[12] But what about Hobbes's complaint that an incorporeal demon cannot suffer the physical punishment of hell? By way of response, there is nothing about the doctrine of hell that requires a literal understanding of physical torture and, thus, no need for thinking a demon to be capable of such suffering. Not all descriptions of the judgment of hell entail the use of literal fire. The language of fire is perhaps meant to capture in physical terms the strictly emotional torment of one's horrid separation from God.[13] Or, it could be that such language represents the prospect of being denied the condition of eternal life resulting in one's being annihilated forever.[14] This latter view accords well with the adjoining biblical notion that such judgment entails being a "second death" which involves one's "destruction."[15] But neither view implies that the "occupants" of hell must be corporeal things. Hence, Hobbes's contention that hell is "repugnant to their

---

11. Thomas Hobbes, *The Elements of Law*, XI.2–3.

12. The same could be said about abstract objects, for it is quite meaningful to talk about them given that they, too, could *in principle* exist. See Marmadoro, "Is Being One Only One?"

13. See Crockett, "The Metaphorical View."

14. See Fudge, *The Fire That Consumes*.

15. Rev 20.14 and 2 Pet 3.7, respectively.

Immateriality" leads one to avoid taking into account viable non-physical interpretations of the doctrine of hell. By contrast, philosophers are generally able to talk meaningfully about bodiless minds without any worries that such things, even implicitly, are like square circles or married bachelors.[16] Hobbes thus fails to support the notion that an incorporeal substance is incoherent.

Now the modern difficulty of conceptualizing an immaterial thing is certainly not unlike the difficulty of conceptualizing certain scientific ontologies within particle physics (consider the Higgs field of the Standard Theory in astrophysics). The so-called *phenomenalistic* approach in philosophy to consciousness is a possible mitigating factor against unremitting materialism. We might say that it is far from *obvious* at least that even an ordinary agential cause such as a *human* consciousness (if one does not eliminate the reality of mental states) must be *prima facie* an embodied thing or at least some kind of physical thing (i.e., a brain state or the vibrating of C-fibers).[17] Most materialist philosophers themselves recognize this point as evidenced by the literature.[18] This is why the materialist tends to reject immaterialism on the less forceful grounds that a personal, immaterialist ontology is either *metaphysically* problematic (such that persons cannot be actualized as purely immaterial souls) or not parsimonious.[19] For example, consider the prominent materialist philosopher of mind, David Armstrong, who forthrightly declares that "disembodied existence seems to be

---

16. Modern philosophers, despite their aversion to any type of dualism, think it quite rational and appropriate to refer to "immaterialism" (viz., *incorporeality*) as meaningful. For example, see Strawson, *Mental Reality*, 107–44. Strawson describes "immaterialism" as something that is not necessarily purely mental but that immaterialism *simpliciter* "is not material or physical [. . . and that] [a]ll it means is 'not material'" (117–18). Strawson goes on to give a very helpful taxonomy of the different types of monistic and dualistic views that one could affirm. But this entails the meaningfulness of incorporeality.

17. C. Lewy, for example, argues that once we disambiguate what the token "I" refers to, one can "understand the supposition that *I* may exist without a body" ("Is the Notion of Disembodied Existence Self-Contradictory?," 72).

18. Keith Campbell says it this way: "any orthodox current materialist 'equilibrium' is rather less stable than many suppose" ("Swimming Against the Tide," 176).

19. Of the metaphysical problems associated with persons as souls, there are classic objections that include mechanistic quandaries. For example, philosophers of mind often refer to the "pairing problem" whereby critics of substance dualism argue that the immateriality of souls lacks the necessary properties of being able to causally interact with spatio-physical objects including a soul's *own* body. But this specific problem attends anthropological dualism and not the metaphysics of intermediary beings for my theory is precisely at a distance from *any* material composition in its ontology. And since I have not yet engaged the arguments of whether angels and demons can and do directly interact with physical objects, then such objections would here be irrelevant to the establishment of unembodied souls *simpliciter*. Feasibly, one could reject substance dualism but cede the metaphysics of demons I espouse. Such a matter regarding interaction with this world will be discussed further in the next chapter and, per my theory, I do not endorse the traditional view that demons directly interact with any physical objects–organic bodies or otherwise. I should also note that Jaegwon Kim's specific approach to the "pairing problem," as previously mentioned, *is* relevant for he thinks it also excludes the metaphysical possibility of soul-soul commerce. More on this below.

a perfectly intelligible supposition."[20] William G. Lycan, an eminent philosopher of mind and a materialist who "cannot take [anthropological] dualism very seriously,"[21] recently confessed the following:

> To anyone uncontaminated by neuroscience or materialist philosophizing, the mental does not *seem* physical in any way at all, much less neurophysiological.... And now acknowledge the prevalence of weird quantum phenomena. Though there is as yet no theory for Cartesian interaction, microphysics gets more and more bizarre, and indeed itself resorts (on some interpretations of quantum mechanics) to quasi-mental vocabulary. We cannot possibly be sure that no theory for Cartesian interaction will emerge.[22]

Not long ago, naturalist Thomas Nagel raised the eyebrows of his materialist colleagues by expressing disenchantment with the view that evolutionary biology can and will solve the origin and nature of phenomenal consciousness.[23] But Nagel, as with most naturalists who find no appeal in theories featuring immaterial things,[24] nonetheless acknowledges: "I myself believe that . . . dualism of mind and body is conceivable" even if implausible.[25]

Materialist Jaegwon Kim does not *presume* that an immaterial substance is incoherent *on its face* but focuses instead on posterior considerations of "insurmountable difficulties,"[26] namely the problems of a soul's causal interaction with another soul or its psychophysical causal efficacy with (paired) physical bodies (at least in the case of human beings). He says that such a world could contain immaterial agents but that they would be existing in causal isolation.[27] The problem for Kim, then, is not the actual concept of immaterialism (as unsettling as being causally "isolated" would be) but with their ability to commerce with anything outside of each soul. And since dualistic philosophers are attempting to formulate a doctrine of mind that countenances the ability of consciousness to interact with something else, the problem is only one that takes away from immaterialism as a full and complete explanation of immaterial minds as causes. But nothing, so acknowledge the materialists, disturbs the mere formal conception of an unembodied, nonphysical mind. And that concession is enough

---

20. Armstrong, *A Materialist Theory of Mind*, 19.
21. Lycan, "Giving Dualism Its Due."
22. Lycan, "Giving Dualism Its Due," 553 and 558.
23. See Nagel, *Mind and Cosmos*.
24. Nagel says that for a naturalist to affirm dualism is to "abandon hope of an integrated explanation" (Nagel, *Mind and Cosmos*, 49).
25. Nagel, *The View from Nowhere*, 29.
26. Kim, "Lonely Souls," 38.
27. As Kim suggests, perhaps one might imagine souls living in a Leibnizian pre-established harmony of some sort.

to admit that the idea of demons as immaterial souls is logically coherent for demonological metaphysics to get off the ground.[28]

In the case where the metaphysics of immaterial persons and not the logic of them is contentious, such critics argue that substance dualism unnecessarily posits an additional substance.[29] Accordingly, dualism comes across as less parsimonious. But to make matters worse, in positing an immaterial soul as the explanatory base of mental activity, there is a fear that one is essentially positing in the common tongue a "God-of-the-gaps" or, to be more precise, a "soul-of-the-gaps" kind of extraneous ontology. The positing of an otherworldly soul is itself a mysterious thing. And so it comes off as an attempt to explain some mysterious activity by means of something even more mysterious (an *obscurum per obscurius*). So, even if such otherworldly souls do exist, positing them would do no explanatory work.[30]

But, are there any grounds for thinking that such things are not merely conceivable or logically possible but metaphysically possible? That is to ask, could such things actually be meaningfully instantiated in the kind of reality we have? We shall explore an answer to this question now.

The Metaphysical Possibility of Pure Immaterialism

Defenses of the existence of the human soul abound in the recent literature on the philosophy of mind.[31] While materialism, on the other hand, is surely in vogue with today's metaphysicians, there do not seem to be any strictly logical impediments preventing philosophers from speculating about how such a thing (viz., the soul) can possibly exist and interact with its body.[32] All such speculations seem to fall into what

28. It is worthy of note to mention that anthropological dualism *simpliciter* is not immediately contrary to materialism. Consider theologian David Rousseau, someone who is happy to uphold a non-Cartesian dualism of matter and "mental stuff," defends a theory he calls "Naturalistic Structural Dualism." He defends its naturalistic status by arguing that since such a mental substrate would be, presumably, causally active and spatial; thus, it should be theoretically "*analysable by science*, and hence a *natural* stuff" ("Understanding Spiritual Awareness," 45; emphases his). This perspective is similar to a view held by naturalist W. V. O. Quine who thought that if spirits existed and we could know about them, then such things would exhibit empirical attributes susceptible to scientific investigation. Refer to his "Naturalism" and *The Pursuit of Truth*.

29. E.g., Smart, "Sensations and Brain Processes."

30. This is not quite like the problem of *overdetermination* in which substance dualists (in anthropological metaphysics) are often accused of supplying two sufficient causes of spatio-physical events (such as the moving of one's right arm by a conscious thought). But so far I'm simply contrasting *monistic* ontologies and not dualistic ones. Demons are being explored as being either *merely* immaterial or *merely* (quasi-)material based on *a priori* considerations of one sort or another.

31. For examples, see Loose, Menuge, and Moreland, *The Blackwell Companion to Substance Dualism*; Farris, *The Soul of Theological Anthropology*; Swinburne, *Mind, Brain, and Free Will* and *The Evolution of the Soul*; Lund, *The Conscious Self*; Moreland and Rae, *Body and Soul*; Hasker, *The Emergent Self*; Eccles and Popper, *The Self and Its Brain*; Goetz, "Dualism, Causation, and Supervenience"; Foster, *The Immaterial Self*; Taliaferro, "A Modal Argument for Dualism."

32. John Perry, a self-declared "antecedent physicalist," sums up the usual sentiment thusly: "The

Gilbert Ryle has derisively codified as the "dogma of the Ghost in the Machine."[33] But one thing should be immediately clear: such pro-dualistic defenses are almost exclusively devoted to justifications of the existence of a *human* soul.[34]

Unlike human souls, the gods of this world are stipulated to be purely immaterial spirits that are not tethered to or paired with any physical body. They are endowed with consciousness and (presumably) an enduring identity for the continuity of their personhood, however that might be anchored. Despite materialist objections to anthropological dualism, there have been some post-Hobbesian objections raised against the metaphysical possibility of there being purely immaterial souls. The first category of criticism offered by materialists pertains to how the earlier stages of a self (however that might be defined) can be identified with its later stages without being confused with another self (viz., the problem of the continuity of the self). The second category of criticism by materialists pertains directly to the problem of the metaphysical conception (given all that we know) of an existing, immaterial self apart from some real dependence on a (quasi-)material ontology. The literature is indeed already replete with various defenses of how a purely immaterial thing bearing mental or psychological properties can maintain an enduring identity and a non-physical base.

In support of the metaphysical possibility of an unembodied spirit or soul, I shall now turn to traditional objections offered in these two categories and offer up responses to them.

The Challenge of Personal Identity

The first category of criticism–the problem of the continuity of the self–concerns a sufficient means of affording possible identity to any given demon-self as it endures through a succession of temporal events $t_1, t_2, t_3, \ldots t_n$ (where t_1 represents the first moment of the demon-self's existence and t_n represents the last)[35] in the demon's biography. Some materialists would argue that bodily continuity provides a sufficient

---

problem with commonsense dualism is not inconsistency but that the arguments for it . . . are simply not compelling in the face of arguments against it" (*Knowledge, Possibility, and Consciousness*, 79).

33. Ryle, *The Concept of Mind*, 22.

34. Many of dualism's detractors have generally levelled their criticisms against the plausibility of the mechanism of mind-*body* interaction (a feature unnecessary in my theory as demons do not have bodies with which to interact). This is a significant preface to my discussion here since I need not rehearse those defences of how a soul or mind can interact with its body since my theory is precisely to describe souls that do *not* interact with any material body. Objections to mind-body interaction would be red herrings in my defining and defending of demons as purely spiritual creatures. Such a stance is surely inconsequential to the core beliefs of the Abrahamic faiths, even those beliefs that include the prospect of intermediary beings whose interaction with this world is arguably non-physical. Since I am only interested in the *a priori* plausibility of an unembodied soul *simpliciter*, I thereby excuse myself from this bit of controversy and leave it to the anthropological dualists and materialists to settle.

35. Even if the demon-self should be immortal, one could easily imagine t_n to then see it as representing an open-ended maximal numeral, like infinity, to refer to some immensely distant future moment.

basis on which to ground personal identity. But counterexamples seem to arise at every turn thereby making materialist considerations of this sort inconclusive (and I will not rehearse them here).[36] One thing seems evident, at least for the theist, is that God is an ostensive case of an immaterial thing that retains its identity. While the theist may not *know* how such unembodied identity endures, she surely believes *that* it does with God.

I submit that we are under no *a priori* obligation to think that materialism, or any other *ism* for that matter, provides the essential basis for personhood. It may very well be the case that no criteria for an enduring personal identity under anyone's rubric are adequate, but this would not necessarily undermine the coherence of something's essentially being an immaterial soul.[37] As Trenton Merricks comments, "[i]t is consistent to maintain that criterialism is false and that persons . . . have essential properties."[38] Moreover, if God exists as an immaterial being himself, then *a fortiori* the theist has an additional reason to think that materiality is not essential to personal identity.

But something more needs to be said about the prospect of a purely immaterial subject as the essential locus of the self, a self endowed with enduring identity. I surmise that a necessary attribute for being a person is for it to be a concrete thing that is distinguished from abstracta. As a Cartesian, John Foster offers the appellation "subjectness" and "selfhood" as suggestions for identifying the immaterial, basic subject of particularly human persons.[39] This nature would at least ground or possess various attributes like consciousness, enduring identity, personality, thinking, reasoning, contemplating, imagining, etc. This is a notion that can be imported into talk of unembodied souls, for such attributes of personhood are not predicated on one having a conjoined physical body. Consider a thought experiment by John Locke who posits an intelligent, rational parrot.[40] Locke imagines that some random non-sentient animal, like a parrot, might possibly come to possess the accidental properties of being rational and intelligent. In this case it would have no properties that would make it *human* but it would have properties that might nonetheless make it a *person*.[41] Perhaps the same could be said about artificial intelligence and the prospect that a machine might eventually acquire a level of consciousness such that it, too, becomes a person. Immaterialism certainly makes it more palatable to see "selfhood" in things other than human beings in that the self transcends its contingent material constitution (if it has one). In those thought experiments where small portions of the brain are replaced

36. Braude, "Personal Identity and Postmortem Survival"; Nozick, *Philosophical Explanations*, 27–70; Swinburne, "Personal Identity"; Gale, "A Note on Personal Identity and Bodily Continuity."

37. For critiques of theories of identity, see Lund, *The Conscious Self*, 195–246.

38. Merricks, "There Are No Criteria of Identity Over Time," 118.

39. Foster, *The Immaterial Self*, 234.

40. Locke, *An Essay Concerning Human Understanding*, II.27.8.

41. The unsatisfactory part about Locke's identification of the self (whether human or rational parrot) is that he remains ignorant about just what that is. The Lockean self *just is* a material substratum—a substratum that grounds the exemplification of psychological properties.

piece-by-piece over time,[42] it is the immaterialist who can secure the intuition that the self continues or endures despite the body having been gradually replaced by a completely different material constitution.

Certainly the nature of "subjectness" might not be particularly clarifying in terms of helping us to imagine what this kind of thing is. However, we, as humans, are beings that are each attached to a body–being immersed in a spatio-temporal universe of materiality. As such, we might just be as the man who suddenly realizes he has been sitting on a fortune in valuables but cannot grasp what "being wealthy" is like having been entrenched in poverty his entire life. Something like "subjectness" would be the substantive anchor for that entity's various psychological properties (i.e., memories, knowledge, intelligence, emotions, etc.). And since it is somewhat apparent to see how such things can and do endure (even if certain things, like memories, might fade), this seems like a reasonable self-contained theory for how one can be a person without having to also be material. As for Foster, he believes to have established the conclusion "that mental items are attached to basic subjects and that basic subjects are wholly non-physical."[43] And if that is so, then positing a basic subject *qua* "subjectness" that would accommodate this will offer the immaterialist a way to envisage "subjectness" as the enduring possessor of psychological qualities while being substantially distinct from any material body. At least we can conclude that an immaterial ego so conceived is logically and metaphysically possible, and is referentially meaningful as a means to pick out the self apart from material properties. As a means of explicating a demon's ontology, it suffices to show that this conclusion renders the pure immaterialism of demons at least coherent as a metaphysic of persons.

Let us now consider another problem with the concept of purely immaterial persons, namely whether it is possible for such persons to be individuated. It may be that though an enduring, solitary self can be an immaterial person, it may yet not be metaphysically possible to be an immaterial person *distinct* from other enduring selves.

The Challenge of Individuation

If there are souls that are purely immaterial and have separate identities, then on what basis would they be individuated from each other since no appeal can be made to

---

42. For example, Lycan talks about "a normal human being" named Henrietta who undergoes microsurgery to have all of the neurons of her brain gradually replaced by neuron-like prostheses. The results would not, according to Lycan, cause her to lose consciousness or her personality. Despite such an overhaul with synthetic parts, Lycan insists that it "is hard to imagine how the boor, or any other chauvinist, would be able to draw a line and state with assurance that after the nth operation, Henrietta ceased to have a phenomenology (whatever she may think to the contrary)" ("Qualitative Experience in Machines," 174). Swinburne uses a similar theme and argues that "for many possible replacements of brain parts it is logically possible that the replacements take place and the person remains the same" thus implying that the "preservation of certain brain parts is neither logically necessary nor logically sufficient for personal identity" (*Mind, Brain, and Free Will*, 155).

43. Foster, *The Immaterial Self*, 231.

the obvious material boundaries provided by gross or fine matter? And if immaterial souls in general cannot be individuated, then how can demons individually subsist apart from any matter with which to individuate one from another?

I turn, first, to a solution offered up by Aquinas. His view is a possibility if and only if one is not squeamish about adopting a strong form of Platonism.[44] Let me explain. Aquinas is quite aware of the implications of Bonaventurian hylomorphism when it comes to his understanding of different angels (like Gabriel and Michael). For Aquinas, angels, as subsisting forms, would be *universals* and so "the angels cannot be many in one species."[45] On his view, declaring something as an "angel" is tantamount to identifying something as "humanity" or "whiteness." Just like there could not be any individuating of or means of speciation within "whiteness" or "humanity," neither can there be more than one species of the same angelic nature so understood.[46] Aquinas's solution to the problem of intra-angelic distinction is to posit each angel *as its own species*. This will accommodate not only the criticisms wrought by Bonaventure's insistence on *universal* hylomorphism (viz., that all created intelligences must, of some sort of necessity, be a hylomorphic composition), but it also accommodates the biblical data as to the multiple species of angels (and demons) that are both explicitly and implicitly said to exist in numerical separation.[47] Unfortunately, the Thomistic solution evinces a Platonism of universals. In what way, for example, would whiteness be existentially different from "Gabrielness" except to arbitrarily designate the latter as something that exists and the former as something that exists, say, only in the mind of God? If one is prepared to commit to Platonism, the Thomistic solution would appear to do the trick. Nonetheless, it may not, according to Nathan Jacobs, avoid "the basic category error of labelling a universal a particular."[48] Regardless, few are prepared to commit to Platonism and so, as Jacobs argues, there remains a lethal problem for Thomism. Let us turn to his brief criticism now.

Jacobs asks us to consider a computer (called "Computer 1") that has a particular game (*Adventure to Mars*) installed on its hard drive.[49] The computer analogously represents the *hyle* (or material body) and *Adventure to Mars* the *morphē* (or the soul *qua* form). To say that the soul is removed from its material body is akin to the removing of *Adventure to Mars* from its hard drive. Jacobs then asks the salient question, "Would the instance of *Adventure to Mars* on Computer 1 continue to exist? Clearly not."[50]

---

44. Some Thomists protest that Aquinas's explication of the individuation of angels is a reversion to Platonism (e.g., Feser, *Aquinas*, 160). Even so, it is very much non-Aristotelian if not *anti*-Aristotelian, and any thought of flirting with even a slightly modified Platonism may still cause one to aver.

45. Aquinas, *De Spiritualibus Creaturis*, XIV, Reply 2: 105; Cf., Feser, *Aquinas*, 160; Also see Keck, *Angels and Angelology*, 98.

46. Aquinas, *De Spiritualibus Creaturis*, VIII.

47. See "Biblical Angelology" in chapter 2.

48. Jacobs, "Are Created Spirits Composed of Matter and Form?," 93.

49. Jacobs, "Are Created Spirits Composed of Matter and Form?," 92.

50. Jacobs, "Are Created Spirits Composed of Matter and Form?," 92.

Part III: Ontological Matters

Similarly, once a human soul is removed from its body, it simply does not exist just in case Platonism is not true. However if souls do exist Platonically, Jacobs confesses, one may attempt to differentiate individual souls by appealing to John Scotus's notion of *haecceitas* (an object's "thisness").[51] On this view, an angelic soul gets individuated simply by being *this angel* as opposed to being *that angel*–a solution capitalized on by contemporaries like Alvin Plantinga and, in a more cautious manner, Richard Swinburne.[52] Despite any mutation of accidental properties a soul may bring about, the soul would still essentially be *this* soul and not *that* one. So, if Platonism is not an unsavory choice, then the Thomistic solution handles the individuation of purely immaterial souls.

Let us now consider another way to differentiate two immaterial souls. It seems that if private, subjective states are accepted as an epistemic means of differentiation between subjects, then the point of view had by each soul should constitute sufficient grounds for accepting its individuation from another soul apart from a requisite material ontology. For example, suppose that the angel Gabriel is a purely immaterial soul. Could not Gabriel rely on his first-person awareness that his experiences are his own and do not belong to, say, Michael? Gabriel may remember that he once spoke to Zechariah,[53] but he will never get confused as to whether he was the one who fought with the Prince of Persia (the one who did was Michael).[54] If one asked Gabriel on what basis he is not Michael, it is doubtful that Gabriel would have to appeal to a material or quasi-material constitution he did not have in order to be justified in making the distinction. Subjective states are sufficient for *someone*, namely Gabriel, to individuate himself from Michael even if no one else can.

Now it may be objected that I am just begging the question here, specifically that I am already assuming that there is no material distinction that renders it possible for Gabriel to have subjective states different from those of Michael. After all, awareness of one's own subjective states is just a criterion for identifying whose states those are. One could easily argue that if Gabriel is not constituted by any matter, he would not have subjective states that he could differentiate from Michael. Given that he does have different subjective states, he must be constituted by matter. However, it is not question-begging since the solution I am offering above is one of modality. To wit, it remains *possible* or *conceivable* to be Gabriel (or to be the possessor of Gabriel's experiences) and not Michael even though neither may be constituted by matter. There is nothing about Gabriel's subjective criterion for self-identity apart from Michael's that necessitates a material form of individuation. Such modality would be purely

---

51. Scotus, *Ordinatio*, II.3. For a good commentary on Scotus's *haecceity*, see Copleston, *A History of Philosophy*, 511ff.

52. See Plantinga, *The Nature of Necessity*, chapter 5; Swinburne, *Mind, Brain, and Free Will*, chapters 1 and 6.

53. Luke 1.11–20.

54. Dan 10.10–21.

epistemic and not metaphysical, which is to say that, *for all he knows*, Gabriel's own subjective experiences are not Michael's.

There is a feature about Gabriel's subjective experiences we are not fully considering here, namely, that there is a special kind of knowledge had by Gabriel that makes it *impossible* for him to be confusing himself with Michael. This can be seen by putting the experiences of Gabriel and Michael in the present moment. Gabriel, for all he knows, knows that he is not *now* fighting the Prince of Persia but is speaking with Zechariah. Michael is experiencing fighting the Prince of Persia now and not speaking with Zechariah. Gabriel *cannot fail to know what he is experiencing and is not experiencing* and so has that important differentiating property that does not itself rely on anything material–the awareness of not being the one who is fighting the Prince of Persia. Since Gabriel can be certain that he is not experiencing fighting the Prince of Persia, he can put this forward as what seems obvious: I am not Michael. Given the impossibility of confusing the two subjective experiences, no *a posteriori* identification of Gabriel with Michael can ever be successfully made. And this means that the individuating of the two angels is accomplishable wholly apart from any kind of material substratum. The only way I see out of this conclusion is to deny that *anyone* owns subjective experiences, viz., a Humean no-ownership view of consciousness. But since such views seem obviously false and have already been critiqued in the literature, I defer to those criticisms.[55]

Therefore, there are no good philosophical reasons to insist on a material composition in order to differentiate unembodied souls. Individuation of souls can be preserved simply by being "this" soul and not "that" one; and that private, subjective states confirm how individuation can be confidently maintained apart from matter. Certainly if conceivability is at all a metaphysical guide to the metaphysically possible, then this much has been accomplished.[56] Let us now turn to another important challenge, one raised by Jacobs, in that the Bible would appear to treat the realm of unembodied souls as existing in a "place."

The Challenge of the Bible's Apparent "Spatializing" of Unembodied Souls

Important for those who take the biblical data at face value, it is curious that deceased human beings–as unembodied souls–are said to be located in some sort of space, viz., Hades or "heavenly places." I return to Jacobs who takes notice of the language of spatiality used in scriptural descriptions of Hades in particular as the abode of deceased human beings. If souls are spatially related to one another, and only (quasi-)material things can be spatially located, then souls must be (quasi-)material. The implications for demonology are evident: if any kind of unembodied souls is treated spatially, this

---

55. See Strawson, *Individuals*, chapter 3; Lund, *The Conscious Self*, Part I.
56. Cf., Chalmers, *The Conscious Mind*, 65–69.

may suggest that demons, sharing the same ontology, may be (quasi-)material as well. According to Scripture, unembodied *human* souls are treated spatially; hence, demons may also be (quasi-)material.

Jacobs says that "the very concept of the intermediate state entails that the disembodied soul retains location and situation."[57] Why does he think this? Because "Christ identifies Hades as a place (*topas*) in Luke 16:28" in Jesus's presentation of the Parable of Lazarus and the Rich Man. Philosophers do take it that being purely immaterial is a sufficient condition, *ceteris paribus*, for being non-spatial.[58] But if that is the case, then if unembodied souls are spatially located somewhere (i.e., Hades or some other putative otherworldly topography), then they would not be immaterial. Such a move would also have profound implications for God's own omnipresence (something Jacobs is happy to concede).

Now, I have deep reservations about taking the Parable of Lazarus and the Rich Man as an unadulterated description of post-mortem existence. But even if the Parable's contents are to be taken in a *sensus literalis*, one could say that such spatial designations are simply due to the fact that God might re-embody disembodied souls in a uniquely created environment with bodies unlike those they will ultimately have in the eschatological resurrection of all believers. That God might do this in no way entails that such re-embodiment is *necessary for individuating souls*, however. And so what we would have in passages like Luke 16, if taken literally, are at best descriptions of how things *will* be, not how things *must* be.

More importantly, it is questionable whether such passages truly speak of spatiality at all. Being the central point here, are there good reasons to think that the *topas* of Hades is to be taken literally? I think not. Scripture consistently employs a non-geographical use of *topas* as we have in the case of the two apostolic candidates who were vying to "take the place (*topon*)" of Judas Iscariot (Acts 1.24–25). But, Jacobs might retort, such a usage is in the minority for in the vast majority of New Testament texts *topas* takes on a rather unequivocal geographical connotation. And this says

---

57. Jacobs, "Are Created Spirits Composed of Matter and Form?," 95.

58. See, for example, Hoffman and Rosenkrantz, *The Divine Attributes*, 39–41. Emily Thomas contests this entailment in her response to Hoffman and Rosenkrantz in "The Spatial Location of God." Thomas argues that thought experiments show how it's possible that Cartesian souls might conceivably be spatially located in a way similar to how ghosts are imagined to be. Thomas acknowledges that ghosts are not gaseous objects–thereby making them subject to atmospheric conditions and such–but bear all of the localizing properties of an ordinary object excepted by the fact that they are "completely invisible and incorporeal" and nothing like "gasses or massless particles" (57–58). As such, "the possibility of ghosts tends to imply that they *would* have spatial location" (60). I think Thomas is just imagining, in a circular way, souls to be *(quasi-)material* objects and is projecting those properties onto purely immaterial subjects. For me, ghosts just are not souls in the sense I've described them and, so, Thomas seems to be confusing the latter with the former. This would be like my imagining seeing something invisible like a musical note–imagining that it looks like a floating black golf club–and pressing for the possibility of the visibility of notes while maintaining that such notes just lack any visual frequencies that would otherwise make them visible. Thomas's overall mistake is modal: one cannot derive a metaphysical possibility merely from a strict logical possibility.

nothing about the *other* spatial designators found apart from using *topas* in Luke 16: "Lazarus ... is comforted *here*" (v. 25) and "*between* us and you a great chasm has been fixed" (v. 26). But this need not be a problem for considering *topas* to be non-geographical. For it is not uncommon for spatial descriptions to be used in a way that does not suggest a coordinate location of a physical subject.[59] For both the Old and New Testaments offer up many examples of the utilization of spatial language that does not necessarily connote a literal spatial relation. For examples:

> "... the Spirit of God was *hovering over the face of the waters*." (Genesis 1.2)

> "... the man and his wife hid themselves *from the presence of the LORD God* among the trees of the garden" (Genesis 3.8)

> "[God's] abode has been established in Salem, his *dwelling place in Zion*" (Ps 76.2)

> "[B]ehold, the kingdom of God is *in the midst* of you" (Luke 17.21)

> "But I know that you do not have the love of God *within you*" (John 5.42)

> "Believe me that I am *in the Father* and the Father is *in me* ..." (John 14.11)

> "Do you not know that you are God's temple and that God's Spirit *dwells in you*?" (1 Cor 3.16)[60]

In fact, we are told outright that the spatial attributions, when used of God in particular, *cannot* be construed literally:

> "But will God indeed dwell on the earth? Behold, *heaven and the highest heaven cannot contain you*; how much less this house that I have built!" (1 Kgs 8.27).

Therefore, there is no reason to suppose that unembodied spirits have a (quasi-)material nature on theological grounds. The biblical references to Hades as a *topas*, even if the story is taken literally, does not warrant such a conclusion. But even if it did, it is not clear that a spatial intermediary state exists by necessity rather than by God's desire. For it is conceivable that God embodies the denizens of heaven in the interim while awaiting final resurrection. Thus, we have no reason to deny that being a purely immaterial spirit is a live metaphysical option for the demons's ontology.

So far we have seen that pure immaterialism, as a theoretical description of the ontology of demons, is neither logically nor metaphysically objectionable. As such, there is no prior probability that spirits should be (quasi-)material if they in fact exist.

---

59. See Davis, "How Personal Agents are Located in Space."

60. At this point someone might object and say that I have begged the question. Why *not* think of God's dwelling *in* me as a literal spatialization? For one, God would need to be awkwardly understood in Davis's "repletive" sense (viz., being spatially diffused *everywhere*; see Davis, "How Personal Agents are Located in Space," 438) since the dative pronoun "you" of 1 Cor 3.16 is plural (*umin*). Secondly, things like "love" (cf., John 5.42) are surely not located in any "molecular" or "repletive" sense for love is not likely a concrete substance (as in "the love of God is 12 millimeters from your left lung").

I shall now put forth a positive argument based on three cumulative pieces of evidence that show that pure immaterialism is probably true.

The Probability of the Demons's Pure Immaterialism

In this section, I shall begin to argue for the probability of pure immaterialism by offering evidences–data that confirm such immaterialism–that lead us to infer that the (posterior) probability of pure immaterialism is increasingly higher than any materialism or quasi-materialism. In building my case, I shall emphasize and discuss three main evidences that I believe constitute part of a cumulative case for thinking so:

1. *Prima facie*, the Bible seems to imply cosmic and anthropological dualism.
2. The description of the ontology of angels and demons (as *rûaḥ* and *pneuma*) is the same as that of God.
3. There is a disproportionate set of manifestation stories in that angels manifest frequently to observers but demons never do.

I shall now discuss and support each point in turn. As such, I shall argue that each claim independently confirms the thesis of pure immaterialism. But more than that, if one combines the evidence, then they constitute a powerful, cumulative case for the immateriality of demons. Let us begin by turning our attention to the specific evidences before consolidating them.

Evidence #1: Prima facie, the Bible seems to imply cosmic and anthropological dualism

It is important to acknowledge up front that the Bible may not be *obviously* anthropologically dualistic just in case materialism can adequately accommodate the various descriptions of the ontology of human beings. But I find it of equal importance to press the related point that the Bible itself seems to speak of a *cosmic* dualism, viz., a duality of worlds where one is the physical world of terrestrial creatures and the other the transcendent realm of all spiritual agencies.[61] Curious enough, this kind of dualism is not contested by most contemporary materialist, Christian philosophers.[62] To see why this may be uncontested, consider how the following references on how reality seems to be partitioned consistently of at least two ontological polarities:

---

61. It is important to stress that I am not referring to the dualism of forces, viz., that there are comparable cosmic powers equally matched in the spiritual realm–one good and one evil (i.e., Zoroastrianism and Manichaeism).

62. Van Inwagen, "A Materialist Ontology of the Human Person," 206; Corcoran, "Human Persons are Material Only," 273; Murphy, *Bodies and Souls, or Spirited Bodies?*, 23ff; Merricks, "The Resurrection of the Body," 485; Baker, *Persons and Bodies*, 92.

On the Spiritual Nature of Demons

"Earth" and "the highest heaven" (1 Kgs 8.27)

"Above" and "below" (Jer 31.37; John 8.23)

"Visible" and "invisible" (Col 1.16; 2 Cor 4.18)

"This world" and "heavenly places" (Eph 6.12)

Frank Matera explains that the concept of the "highest heaven" in the Old Testament was understood to be the transcendent, spiritual realm of God by no less than the Apostle Paul.[63] "Above," as opposed to "below," equally signifies the transcendent realm of God as evidenced in Jewish apocalyptic literature.[64] And the "heavenly places" of Eph 6.12 refers to a realm where both God and other spiritual agencies reside–including demons! Harold Hoehner explains that these "heavenly places" span "from God's throne down to the sphere where cosmic powers reside and operate."[65] As indicated by Eph 1.20 ("[God] worked in Christ when he raised him from the dead and seated him at his right hand in the heavenly places"), it is the otherworldly province of God himself.

I now turn to some passages that, on their face, imply an anthropological dualism. But this shall require a bit more discussion. Let us first consider the following selection of passages:

"To depart [the flesh]" and "remain in the flesh" (Philippians 1.23–24)

"Body" and "soul" (Ps 31.9; Matt 10.28)

"Flesh" and "spirit" (Isa 31.3; John 3.6)

"Natural" and "spiritual" (1 Cor 15.44, 46)

"In the body" and "out of the body" (2 Cor 12.2–3)

The list could easily continue, but in terms of an apparent contrasting of the physical world with the world of spirit, it is difficult not to see how *pneuma* (spirit) and *sōma* (body) might not also be the ontological polarities of a bifurcated reality. *If* God and angels reside in a realm utterly different from our physical one, then it seems reasonable to suppose that the inhabitants indigenous to a heavenly, spiritual realm would likely have a different ontology from those of a terrestrial, corporeal realm. Hence, we would seem to have two *kinds* of things in our ontology. And whether this alone should lead to believing in a *compositum* of substances in human beings is not a question that need be resolved here.

Regarding the biblical portrait of intermediary beings (viz., both angels and demons) as residents of this otherworldly realm, the eminent New Testament scholar

---

63. Matera, *II Corinthians*, 280.
64. Cf., 1 Enoch 20–36; 2 Enoch 8–10; 67.2.
65. Hoehner, *Ephesians*, 169. Also see Fowl, *Ephesians*, 35–39, 203–5.

PART III: ONTOLOGICAL MATTERS

James D. G. Dunn reminds us that demons were once "all understood as experiences of personal forces from the spiritual realm" and that there are "[o]ther forces operating on humanity's world from the spiritual realm [that] are thought of as good spirits or angels."[66] In fact, such cosmic dualism has been so apparent that the history of theology has had to weather the incessant complaint that it is uncritically and unabashedly Platonistic.[67] While on the subject of Platonism, I should note that this has (at least partly) motivated philosophers since William of Ockham to abandon any third reality consisting of not-quite-material-and-not-quite-spiritual objects, for it would complicate matters by positing a special world of hybrids. Such a world would be awkwardly situated as a tertiary, quasi-material world. It seems to me that unless there are some convincing reasons for such a hybrid world, the simplest explanation apart from any such speculation would be to see the world of the *pneumata* ("spirits") in the most robust and simplest way, namely that it just is the world of *immaterial spirits*–a state of utter otherworldly existence where the invisible, intangible God himself resides.[68] And this leads to–barring any irreconcilable problems–the inference that we should prefer a purely immaterial status for those intermediary beings also said to share in God's abode. This sets the stage for thinking that the ontologies of those beings inhabiting the same realm should be expected to be essentially uniform. Thus, in the absence of any evidence requiring anything other than a cosmic dualism, it is evident that the expected nature of demons, as creatures not of this world, should be seen as members of the world God inhabits. And if the world God inhabits is utterly otherworldly (viz., purely immaterial), then demons should be considered purely immaterial as well.

At this point we need to return to the specific notion of anthropological dualism in the Bible and fill out an argument in favor of it since the mere appearance of such dualism is itself not enough. We need to do this mostly because it would increase the elegance of the explanation that dualism offers but also partly because an upcoming discussion of human soul-soul commerce presumes such dualism and constitutes a part of my case for the uniformity of cognitive interaction involving spiritual beings.[69] If the New Testament *prima facie* suggests an anthropological dualism, then I submit that we have one more reason to affirm a cosmic dualism.[70] And if human beings

---

66. Dunn, *The Christ and the Spirit*, 5.

67. See the critical discussion by Travis, "Psychology," 986. For a thorough critique of the idea that the New Testament writers uncritically intimated Greek thought in this way, see Ferguson, *Backgrounds of Early Christianity*.

68. For some medieval philosophers, they would argue that the Great Chain of Being requires an intermediate ontology between anthropological duality and divinity. But such a view seems untenable since one must assume in advance that God *must* only create an optimal universe where all gradations are realized. But if that is so, it seems to me that *somewhere* along the Great Chain of Being would be incorporeal beings that are thoroughly immaterial but not divine. And how do we know that *these* aren't the intermediary beings described in the Bible? For a traditional response, see Adler, *The Angels and Us*, 59–63.

69. See chapter 8.

70. Other contemporary philosophers see anthropological dualism taught in the Bible. For

are composites of two substances, of which one is purely immaterial, then we have independent confirmation of two fundamentally different kinds of substances. Let us now turn to a brief (theological) defense of anthropological dualism.

John W. Cooper, a notable proponent of anthropological dualism being taught in Scripture, cautions readers of the New Testament that its usage of "[p]articular words such as *sarx*, *sōma*, *psychē*, *pneuma*, and *kardia* have a variety of meanings which can vary from one New Testament book to another" and so if such a case is based solely on this terminology, "the case for dualism is pretty slim."[71] Cooper explains that biblical writers did not write from a Platonistic standpoint and, so, merely finding words like "body" and "soul" in reference to human beings does not *prima facie* entail such dualism. To avoid Cooper's just criticism, I shall advance my case based on passages that do not rely on the mere presence of the words "body" and "soul." In each of the following select passages, there are terms being used specifically of the human body which imply the notion of *occupancy* or *inhabitation* by a subject or ego:

"Temple" (1 Cor 3.16–17; 6.19)

"Vessel" (1 Pet 3.7)

"Tent" (2 Cor 5.1–4)

"Cloth[ing]" (2 Cor 5.4)

With respect to the latter two references, Cooper is clear to say that they endorse anthropological dualism.[72] Since the *pneuma* of God and angels is described as having otherworldly attributes (being invisible, intangible, etc.[73]) and that the body is likened to a corporeal exterior to the inner subject, it is difficult to not see the overall insinuation of an anthropological dualism.[74] It is even more difficult when one considers also the previous evidence that there seems to be a cosmic dualism, too. And if demons should share the ontology of God and angels (beings that are purely immaterial) in a bifurcated reality so described, then it is likely that demons are uniformly immaterial along with God and angels.

Thus dualism, both cosmic and anthropological, seems to be promoted in the Bible. And if the demons's nature should be the same as the other spiritual agencies, then we have a stronger argument for their being immaterial. This leads us to the next evidential claim under discussion, namely, that the ontological substance of demons (and angels) is indeed the same as the ontological substance of God.

---

example, see Goetz, "Human Persons are Material and Immaterial"; Goetz and Taliaferro, *A Brief History of the Soul*, 30–32; Moreland and Habermas, *Beyond Death*.

71. Cooper, *Body, Soul and Life Everlasting*, 96 and 99.

72. See Cooper, *Body, Soul and Life Everlasting*, 141–49.

73. E.g., Luke 24.39; Rom 1.20; Col 1.15–16; 1 Tim 1.17.

74. For a more extensive defense of a biblical anthropological dualism, I refer readers to the entirety of Cooper's *Body, Soul, and Life Everlasting*.

PART III: ONTOLOGICAL MATTERS

Evidence #2: The description of the ontology of angels and demons (as rûaḥ and pneuma) is the same as that of God[75]

The Bible contains *explicit* descriptions of the demons's (and Satan's) ontology even if such descriptions turn out to be ambiguous or variegated. In particular, I want to discuss how demons (and angels) are described with the same terminology used of God, viz., "spirit," and that such terminology is unqualified, that is, is used univocally in each case. If such terminology designates God as purely immaterial then, *ceteris paribus*, we should think of demons the same way. However, some have suggested that there are other passages in which it is implied that the demons are in fact material or quasi-material. I shall simply say up front that no such passages exist and that any putative references thought to imply the materiality of demons do not do so.[76]

Concerning the positive data (or evidence), I turn to the Old and New Testaments which use the phrases "evil spirit" and "unclean spirit" in describing demonic beings.[77] Both the Hebrew phrase (*rā rûaḥ*) and the Greek ones (*pneuma poneron* for "evil spirit" and *akatharton pneuma* for "unclean spirit") represent the English translation of "evil spirit"/"unclean spirit" which are meant to account for and describe the incorporeality and spirituality of such beings, for, as Cyril of Jerusalem had explained, "everything that does not have a solid body is generally called spirit [and since] the devils do not have such bodies they are called spirit."[78] *Rûaḥ* itself, though engendering a variety of usages throughout the Hebrew Bible, consistently refers to (when applied to personal beings) an imperceptible facet of one's nature. For example, it is the same noun as used in the designation "Spirit of God" where it seems to connote or imply some immaterial and intangible aspect of God's nature (Ps 51.11).[79] "Spirit"

---

75. In the analysis that follows, I have left out any discussion regarding *nephesh* and *psuchê* (the Hebrew and Greek terms, respectively, for "soul") since these terms are very much ambiguous in just about every occurrence within the Bible. Though I find it fair to equate "soul" with "spirit" in English for simplicity's sake, we do not have any indisputable indication that this is the case of the Bible's various uses. "Soul" may just refer to a person as in 1 Pet 3.20 which mentions the "eight souls" who were rescued in Noah's Flood. This would mean that a passage like "the soul who sins shall die" (Ezek 18.20) could be taken to refer to the entire composite unity of the embodied person or it could refer to the judgment of the psychical aspect (or neither perhaps). And some biblical verses seem to speak of "soul" and "spirit" as if referring to two separate things *within* the same person (cf., Job 7.11; 1 Thess 5.23; Heb 4.12).

76. I shall address these in chapters 10 and 11. That demons are purely immaterial is a dominant view that is held by most conservative Christian scholars today. For example, see Kreeft, *Angels and Demons*, 95; Sluhovsky, *Believe Not Every Spirit*, 10; Dickason, *Angels*, 124 and 174; Unger, *Biblical Demonology*, 63; Koch, *Demonology Past and Present*, 27.

77. See Judg 9.23; Luke 7.21; 8.2; Acts 19.12–16. We cannot say the same for the Old Testament's use of "familiar spirit" (*'ōwḇ*) since such an expression appears to refer to deceased persons and not demons even if it should turn out that familiar spirits are in fact demons.

78. Cyril of Jerusalem, *Catechesis*, I.XVI.15: 85. For Cyril, "spirit" is understood to be the contrastive expression to "body" when used of personal agents. Origen used the reference to *pneuma* in describing what God is as his evidence for the incorporeality of God. See his *De Principiis*, I.1.

79. For some examples of "spirit" in general application to God, see Gen 1.2; Exod 31.3; Num 24.2; 1 Sam 10.10; Isa 61.1; Ezek 39.29.

is also used to distinguish some inner (non-public) aspect of the human person (Zech 12.1). However, it is also worth mentioning that, etymologically, *rûaḥ* can sometimes take on the quite ordinary connotations of "wind" and "breath."[80] But it seems to me that the Hebrew term's association with such things really does underscore the *insensible* and *imperceptible* aspects of God and does not intend to literally describe God as having atmospheric or vaporous attributes (viz., attributes that are really physical but just elusive to an outside observer's five senses).

However, it is no small point that the "aerial" designation for demons does not seem to be necessarily ruled out simply on the basis of the etymology of these Hebrew nouns since *pneuma* was believed by many ancient Greeks to refer to a quasi-material ontology.[81] Yet it should also be pointed out that when "wind" is to be the preferred, literal connotation, the Septuagint uses the Greek term *anemos* and not *pneuma* to translate the Hebrew *rûaḥ*. This is stronger indication that *pneuma* is the distinctive term normally associated with an immaterialist ontology.[82] Given *rûaḥ*'s overt application to God's nature, it is difficult to think that this term should pertain to an aerial or quasi-material ontology since God's nature is supposed to be the instantiation of maximal being.[83] Thus, *pneuma* should be understood in a full Hellenistic-Jewish context and not a context that indiscriminately appeals to its bald usage in unrelated pagan (viz., Greek) sources. In other words, there is more to interpreting a term than merely its conventional usage outside of its local context. We have already seen this phenomenon with the New Testament's employment of *daimon* being distinct from the ancient (pagan) Greek conception of it.[84]

One might then argue (as Hobbes did) that "Spirit of God" is in fact intended to be understood metaphorically,[85] as are "spirit of whoredom"[86] and "spirit of divination,"[87] where such designations refer to exhibited patterns of behavior embod-

---

80. The abutting connection of "breath" with "spirit" is very apparent in passages like Gen 2.7 and Job 27.3.

81. I.e., Anaximenes, a pre-Socratic, believed that the soul was composed of air (Burnet, *Early Greek Philosophy*, 77). In the post-Socratic world, Plato uses *pneuma* to refer to a vaporous substance (*Timaeus*, 49c; 78A, B; 84D, E). On the ancient Greek usage of *pneuma* as "wind" or "air," see Paige, "Who Believes in 'Spirit'?" Incidentally, such a historical intertwining of "spirit" and "wind" has an ancestry beyond ancient Greece in most parts of the world. See Parkin, "Wafting on the Wind," S40–S42.

82. See the classical contribution by Schoemaker, "The Use of 'Ruah' in the Old Testament," 36. Sometimes *psyche* is used by the LXX translators in place of *rûaḥ* if a vague general principle of inner vitality is envisaged. See Lys, "The Israelite Soul According to the LXX," 213f.

83. One may thus continue to agree with P. A. Nordell's insistence that "in each advance in meaning the underlying conception of the word [*rûaḥ*] is still that of an invisible, immaterial force, cognizable through its effects. Such . . . is the Hebrew usage of the word" ("The Old Testament Doctrine of the Spirit of God," 434).

84. See chapter 3.

85. Hobbes writes: "Spirit [is] either properly a reall substance, or Metaphorically, some extraordinary ability or affection of the Mind, or of the Body" (*Leviathan*, III.34: 433).

86. Hosea 5.4.

87. Acts 16.16.

ied in those who practice such things, noting that they are not designating something called "whoredom" to be an immaterial existent. However, something like "whoredom" and "divination" are not themselves persons at all, they are *tendencies*. Contrast this with Haggai 1.14 which uses "spirit of Zerubbabel," "spirit of Joshua," and "spirit of all the remnant of the people" where such designations are not meant to refer to behavioral dispositions but to the *inward natures of these men* (however that might be understood); thus, the passage says that "the LORD stirred up" the core natures of these men, which is to say that their consciences and desires were aroused within them. Consequently, when "spirit" is predicatively applied to "God" (or any *person*), it almost always seems to emphasize the non-terrestrial and otherworldly nature of that being and does not simply promote the personification of an abstract attribute or behavior.

The New Testament appears to offer up the same understanding of "spirit." In fact, its designation of demons as *pneuma(ta)* seems to be a *prima facie* indication of their having an incorporeal nature (given that "a spirit does not have flesh and bones"[88]) and likely one that hints at a full-blown immaterialist ontology given the contrastive spirit-flesh couplets one finds in passages like the following:[89]

> "Watch and pray that you may not enter into temptation. The *spirit* indeed is willing, but the *flesh* is weak" (Matt 26.41)

> "[Y]ou are to deliver this man to Satan for the destruction of the *flesh*, so that his *spirit* may be saved in the day of the Lord" (1 Cor 5.5)

> "For the desires of the *flesh* are against the *Spirit*, and the desires of the *Spirit* are against the *flesh*, for these are opposed to each other, to keep you from doing the things you want to do" (Gal 5.17)

It is *prima facie* apparent that the ontic contrary of *flesh* is *spirit* and that each is an extremity fundamentally distinct from the other. When we turn to the Johannine account of Jesus's own incarnation, we read that, as the pre-existing *logos* of God, this personage takes on the additional nature of *flesh* for the purpose of being "in the world" and to "dwell among us."[90] It is not surprising, then, that *pneuma* might be unequivocally used to describe God, angels, departed human beings, and demons. This would be an effective way to enunciate each's non-physical status. The understanding of "spirit" as describing something non-physical, as it pertains to demons

---

88. Luke 24:39.

89. See Schoemaker, "The Use of 'Ruah' in the Old Testament," 66. David Paulsen, himself a quasi-materialist even of God's ontology, acknowledges that the early Christian church in their fight against those who (in some quarters) proffered the corporeality of God (after early deliberation on the subject) believed that the Bible advocated the incorporeality of God. See Paulsen, "Early Christian Belief in a Corporeal Deity." Jacobs draws on a similar sentiment in his "Are Created Spirits Composed of Matter and Form?"

90. John 1.10, 14.

in particular, becomes all the more evident in Paul's contrast of the authorities of the physical world with the "spiritual [*pneumatika*] forces of evil in the heavenly places" (Eph 6.12c). Paul's use of "in the heavenly places" (*tois epouraniois*) seems to indicate the celestial province of these spirits that exist apart from the terrestrial–something to be expected if *pneuma* is indeed a reference to something immaterial.[91] And such a pneumatology may have interesting implications for systematic theologians who want to find solidarity between these conclusions and the conclusions about reality offered up in non-biblical disciplines like astrophysics.[92]

We have seen the positive data pertaining to the biblical terms *rûaḥ* and *pneuma* and how the data appear to support a pure immaterialist framework,[93] namely, that throughout the canon the self-same term "spirit" (*rûaḥ; pneuma*) is consistently applied to God, angel, and demon alike. This is not to say that *rûaḥ* or *pneuma* might not have multifaceted meanings, but only that there are no positive reasons to suppose that.

In the case of demonic ontology, I have shown how pure immaterialism not only accommodates the canon but, in some cases, is actually more compatible with

91. Paul uses *tois epouraniois* in describing the otherworldly "location" of the post-resurrected Christ in Eph 1.20. I suppose one could appeal to Paul's correspondence in Eph 2.2 (that Satan is the "prince of the power of the air") for some internal, direct biblical support of the aerial nature of demons that does not merely rely on the etymology of *pneuma* (this point is advanced by Augustine in his *De Agone Christiano* III). However, it seems to me that such an appeal is dubious simply because it puts a lot of stock in the use of the genitive preposition "of the power of the air" (*tes exousias tou aeros*). At best this preposition suggests merely the *jurisdiction and extent of authority* and does not in and of itself invoke any metaphysical commitment based on that jurisdiction. To see this, consider parallel prepositions connoting some form of provincial authority, as in Ps 104.21's use of "ruler over all his possessions" (*archonta pases tes kteseos autou*, LXX) and Dan 11.22's use of "prince of the covenant" (*egoumenos diathekes*, LXX). Surely neither the "ruler" nor the "prince" in these passages is meant to be metaphysically composed of "possessions" or "covenants."

92. If one is doing systematic theology (and so including other disciplines outside of immediate biblical hermeneutics), one may consider that the standard Big Bang theory within contemporary cosmology envisages *all matter and energy* as having emerged from the universe's birth some 13.77 billion years ago. Or, it could be that matter and energy emerged from the birth of a multiverse if one indeed precedes our present universe. And, in such a case, there are good reasons to think that the multiverse itself would be the *terminus* of all matter, energy, and space such that no physical particles would precede or reside outside of its boundaries anyway. On either theory, God precedes materiality and so this is the sort of ontology of spiritual beings we would expect to find if God and other spiritual agencies should precede the universe. See the discussion by Craig and Sinclair in their "The *Kalam* Cosmological Argument," 136ff.

93. I have deliberately left out of my survey references to *dis*embodied persons, namely deceased saints, due to concerns similarly echoed by Corcoran (see chapters 5 and 6 of his *Rethinking Human Nature*). Corcoran believes that the only reason one comes to believe that the deceased saints are purely immaterial is due to an unconscious imposition of Platonism on one's exegesis of such passages (23ff). Any time a deceased saint communicates with persons in the spatio-physical world, they are inevitably described in anti-Cartesian terms, viz., they can, *inter alia*, be seen and heard. But as I have previously noted about the angels, this phenomena is not surprising given that it is God who supernaturally makes this possible per occasion for the benefit of physical observers (cf., Num 22.31; 2 Kgs 6.17). But since offering this alternative to those anti-Cartesian descriptions is merely to blunt a materialist interpretation, neither does it suggest that those deceased saints are best seen via an immaterialist interpretation. Such data, one might say, is just too ambiguous for consideration.

it (being used consistently of God and demons without the ambiguity of a quasi-materialism). This point should not be understated. If the Bible described a villain, say Pontius Pilate, as "human" (*anthropos*) knowing that the non-Roman Israelites were also "human" (and likewise designated *anthropos*), we obviously would not imagine that the *anthropos* of Pilate was ontologically different from the *anthropos* of the Israelites–particularly since they live in the same world. That the villainous demons are "spirit" should not be understood any differently from the angels and God being "spirit" if we are going to be consistent in our exegesis. Merrill Unger thus speaks very strongly against the many attempts by Judeo-Christian philosophers at making the demons ontological "half-spirits": "scriptural truth . . . at once disposes of the notion of 'half-spirits,' and with it the greater part of rabbinic and ethnic demonology, where the essential characteristic of spirit is violated."[94]

This assessment gives rise to a curious implication: if demons are indeed purely immaterial spirits and they are not aided by God in their activities, then they should not be expected to physically manifest in the material world. This is to say that demons would not genuinely have any physical properties allowing them to naturally interact with the world. It is, of course, possible that demons have certain powers that allow them to manifest at will. But if demons are never reported to manifest or interact with this world in a matter conducive to having a (quasi-)material nature, then the absence of any such reports would constitute evidence for their being purely immaterial after all. Instead, demons would, at most, only be capable of something like a visionary encounter with a percipient (something comparable to having a vision of God or Christ). This prediction gives rise to another datum we can consider in finalizing all of the relevant data to be considered: the absence of any occurrences of extramental, physical manifestations by Satan and/or his demons implies that they are probably not purely immaterial. We turn to this point now.

Evidence #3: There is a disproportionate set of manifestation stories in that angels manifest frequently to observers but demons never do

God is evidently behind the deployment and empowering of his angelic emissaries in their having commerce with human beings (Num 22.31; 2 Kgs 6.17; Rev 7.2). As such, it is of no surprise that they should be resourced by God in his equipping them with temporary visibility or corporeality or power or whatever. This is, after all, the fundamental prerogative of God as creator. Consequently, we should not be surprised if there are (numerous) occurrences of manifestations of angels. As it turns out, the Bible is filled with examples of angelic manifestations that occur outside of the context of a visionary encounter. Here is but a partial list exemplifying this phenomenon:

> Two angels appear to Abraham and they rest and dine with him (Gen 19.1–3).

---

94. Unger, *Biblical Demonology*, 65.

On the Spiritual Nature of Demons

An angel blocks Balaam from passage (Num 22.22–35).

An angel speaks to the nation of Israel (Judg 2.4).

An angel sits down and appears to men (Judg 6.11–12).

An angel touches the tip of the staff (Judg 6.21).

An angel appears and ministers to Manoah and his wife (Judg 13.2–21).

An angel is located by a threshing floor (2 Samuel 24.16).

An angel touches a man (1 Kgs 19.7).

An angel is seen by Ornan (1 Chron 21.20).

An angel is seen dawning a sword (1 Chron 21.30).

An angel is seen by myrtle trees (Zech 1.11).

An angel appeared, moved a large stone, and spoke to women visiting the tomb of Jesus (Matt 28.2–5).

An angel appears on the right side of an altar (Luke 1.11–12).

An angel appears to Jesus (Luke 22.43).

An angel opens prison doors and speaks (Acts 5.19–20).

Angelic faces apparently can have physical characteristics (Acts 6.15).

An angel appears in a house (Acts 11.13).

Angels can apparently blend in with ordinary human beings in everyday life (Heb 13.2).

The list could perhaps continue, but I have highlighted some of the clearest references to angelic manifestations that cannot be explained away as mere visions or cases of mistaken identity (just in case the episodes described therein are not to be interpreted in a non-literal sense). The only substantial exception would perhaps be whether the designation "angel of the Lord" (*Yahweh mal'ak̲*) refers to *God himself* manifesting (viz., a *theophany*) or an angelic ambassador of sorts (viz., an *angelophany*).[95] Even if this is the case, there are many remaining passages above that do not hinge on the *Yahweh mal'ak̲* being a reference to theophany. But now contrast this list with how many *demonic* apparitions or physical manifestations are said to occur. As it turns out, *there are no such passages at all* (at least there are no *uncontested* passages).[96] As theologian B. J. Oropeza observes, "there is no biblical reference to demons' manifesting

---

95. The former view (theophany) is the position, for example, of the Old Testament scholar Mark Rooker. See his "Theophany," particularly subsection 9.

96. See chapters 10–11.

themselves physically."[97] This radical disparity between angels and demons is significant since angels and demons are overwhelmingly considered by most to have the same ontology as each other with only their moral character differentiating their natures. If angels and demons share a material or quasi-material nature, then why do they not visibly or tangibly manifest outside of possession cases (i.e., cases where they do not independently manifest but utilize the minds of other sentient beings)? If this is right, and both angels and demons are purely immaterial, then God would have to creatively aid any of the angels in their visible or corporeal manifestations since they would presumably (without presuming some ancillary power) be unable to do so on their own. I assume that this is already what we think when it comes to *human* souls said to visibly appear to others in the Bible, viz., that God is the one who has made it possible if it in fact happens in an extramental way. By contrast, demons, being unaided by God's power, would be ill-equipped to appear or manifest physically in any way. This would lead to an expected absence of any references in the Bible to demonic manifestations or apparitions of this sort. As it turns out, this is what we find. When we consider the ramifications of pure immaterialism, what we have in the canon (the Bible) is exactly what one would expect.

Altogether, we have three intriguing pieces of evidence that, when taken individually, constitute independent reasons for suspecting that demons are purely immaterial. But it also appears to be the case that when the claims are taken together, we seem to have an elegant narrative of mutual support for the overall hypothesis that demons are purely immaterial. In the next section, I want to consider how the conjoining of these three lines of evidence together serves to strengthen the case for the pure immaterialism of the demons. In so doing, I shall be incorporating some of the salient virtues of what makes a good explanation and showing how pure immaterialism best explains the aforementioned evidence. And, in rounding out the chapter, I shall formulate the overall inductive argument for that pure immaterialism.

A Cumulative Case

Having discussed what I find to be relevant, individual pieces of evidence for thinking that demons are immaterial, I now want to incorporate these evidences in a cumulative argument that entitle us to an inference to pure immaterialism as the best explanation of the demons's ontology. I shall do this by first showing how pure immaterialism is more parsimonious than (quasi-)materialism. Secondly, I shall show how pure immaterialism enjoys consilience with both theological and philosophical expectations. These factors in concert with the evidence provide, I submit, a good cumulative case for demonic pure immateriality. Let us first take a look at the contribution of parsimony.

---

97. Oropeza, *99 Answers*, 74.

Pure Immaterialism is More Parsimonious than (Quasi-)Materialism

I have argued that we should believe that there are two different kinds of substances in Scripture: material and immaterial. This leads us to consider simplifying and disambiguating our interpretive framework in the usages of *rûaḥ* and *pneuma*. This point should not be overlooked since it reduces ambiguity over what these terms refer to when used to describe an otherworldly being's ontology. It also simplifies matters by reducing a bloated number of realms that exist (only two as opposed to three). To use the appropriate jargon, the pure immaterialism of angels and demons enjoys more qualitative parsimony over (quasi-)materialism.

However, one may push back here and suggest that the contribution of a qualitative simplicity is not prohibitive when other factors are considered. If demons are in fact purely immaterial beings, how would they be able to cause the sorts of physical mischief attributed to them? The (quasi-)materialist can assert that their ontology permits them the necessary means for explaining any material interactions spirits may have with the material world and with the sense perceptions of human beings. But that explanation only goes so far. If demons possess physical bodies (and, hence, have mass and physical boundaries), it remains a mystery how demons otherwise might tempt or communicate with the souls (or minds) of human beings that are beings of a rather different nature. No doubt this problem goes away once we adopt the traditional stipulation that demons have special powers that allow them to transgress the limitations of ordinary, finite beings—material or otherwise. For those unwilling to be universal materialists of a sort, demons are assigned powers that allow them these privileges. But if one is already ceding that demons have special powers, then the pure immaterialist can employ *that* as the basis for any alleged matter-interacting effects ascribed to them. There is no longer a need for insisting on adding a material constitution in the ontology of demons to account for the full scope of the data so construed.

There is another suggestion on offer that does not punt to "special powers"—one that derives from the early medieval period, specifically Augustine. Augustine suggested that demons have the ability to "stir up" the inner fluids of the human body—which makes sense if they are composed of a finer material (aerial) substance such as Augustine thought.[98] Since our physical, sensuous temptations are due exclusively to our bodies, any will to sin being rooted in our spirits, entities that interrelate to our bodies already, would be brought on by the body's preexisting causal relation to that spirit. This scenario nicely resolves the problem for the (quasi-)materialist. However, it can no longer accommodate other kinds of phenomena. For example, it does not explain how a demon, construed as material or quasi-material, can incite his victim to false doctrine (1 Tim 4.1). Neither does it explain how demons can co-inhabit a human being in great numbers without tumefying or inflating the victim (Mark 5.8–9). Would not a legion of demons possessing a singular man cause him to

---

98. Augustine, *De Divinatione Daemonum*, IX.

become bloated? In fact, not even a singular demon could enter into a physical body, for not even air can penetrate the skin. I suppose one could adopt a view offered by some church Fathers wherein a victim might inhale a demon into one's lungs or that it might find its way into one's stomach. Would not the victim's respiratory and digestive systems somehow absorb or break down the invading material substance? Moreover, would we not feel the inner stirrings of our fluids as we do when we consume caffeine (particularly if such demonic stirring actually *changes* something in us)? And, finally, what about their interactions in the realm of God? How can a quasi-material demon reside or commerce in a province that is the very abode of God who himself is purely immaterial (Job 1.6)?

In positing (quasi-)materialism, one is clearly robbing Peter to pay Paul. For it does not take much to see that one must posit a more complex system of demonic activity that forces one to end up adding special powers, to which we now add the power to resist digestion and the power to not be absorbed. Of course if one is willing to grant any special powers to demons in order to account for these difficulties and oddities, then so can the pure immaterialist when it comes to temptations and such. This push-back by an objector at worst only collapses into *which* mystery one prefers, not *whether* a mystery obtains altogether.

Pure immaterialism actually does not have to suffer this dilemma, for it need not invoke any kind of special power after all. If, as I have argued, demons have the same kind of spiritual nature as God and angels, then they probably can mentally communicate with other minds.[99] Accordingly, they can accomplish all of their temptations and interactions in that way. They simply would communicate false doctrines or temptations with the spirits of their subjects. And temptation need not be the bestowing of an ability not already present in a human creature. That human beings are already predisposed to carnal desires would require only making such desires more conscious to (and more justified in the eyes of) the subject. Moreover, invading immaterial spirits would not face digestion or absorption or compression in the bodies of their victims, for they would not physically occupy any points in space-time much less occupy the same points of space-time in great numbers.

In considering all of these factors, being immaterial can accommodate the fullest range of data about the demons and their putative activities. Of course we have yet to industriously delve into whether the Bible teaches that demons interact with the physical world at all.[100] (Such a possibility will, nevertheless, play a role in the next explanatory virtue under consideration below.) Aside from that, I conclude that pure immaterialism is the simpler hypothesis, and that it suffers from none of or fewer than the aforementioned problems about how demons are able to interact with human beings. Let us now turn to another explanatory virtue in seeing how pure immaterialism emerges better across multiple disciplines, viz., philosophy and theology.

99. This notion shall be defended in chapter 8.
100. This notion shall be discussed at length in chapters 8 and 9.

Pure Immaterialism Fosters Consilience with Philosophical and Theological Expectations

Philosophers of mind consistently work from the presupposition that under anthropological dualism, spirits are not in space and as such it is not clear how they would be capable of interacting with other souls much less with their own physical bodies. This has led many to reject dualism, and often this is because of the apparent lack of a sufficient explanation as to how such soul-body pairing/causality can obtain.[101] As the Bible makes apparent, demons, when they tempt or communicate with human beings, never have location apart from the accident of being located here or there in virtue of the *host's* or *victim's* location. No biblical passage suggests that demons are literally located in this province or that one. While the Bible does speak of demons (or Satan himself) being *affiliated* with certain locales (as being the "prince of Persia"[102] or that "Babylon [is] a dwelling place for demons"[103]), these are just conventional expressions similar to one's referring to "the Prime Minister of Saudi Arabia" or to metaphorical idioms of geography like "the devil's playground." The former expression represents agential *control* and *sovereignty* over such a province, not that the agent is necessarily *located* there.[104] In the latter expression, that Babylon would be the "dwelling place for demons" is perhaps meant to designate the Babylonian people as being in such solidarity with demonic principles that it is as if ran by demons directly, or that they are governed indirectly as a people who are under the dominant influence of demonic (cognitive) communication.[105]

Needless to say, human beings as embodied minds have location. And the demons's location is only known insofar as they manifest through their cognitive interaction with those humans. As such, the expectations of philosophical metaphysics and theological demonology accord quite well together in that the expectations of both revealed theology and philosophy regarding notions of pure immateriality (i.e., whether the *res cogitans* of Cartesianism or the subsisting form of Thomism) never

---

101. Even Thomistic dualists note that it is the material corpus that affords spatiality to an individually subsisting soul (something not peculiar to Cartesians). Moreland and Rae, themselves Thomists, say: "The soul occupies the body, but it is not spatially located within it.... When we say that the soul occupies the body we mean at least that (1) it has *direct, immediate* conscious awareness throughout the body, though not necessarily of each and every part of the body, and (2) it can *directly* and *immediately* will to move the various parts of the body.... While it is true that you 'occupy' your body, you (your soul) are not a spatially extended thing that is located within the geometrical boundaries of your body" (Moreland and Rae, *Body and Soul*, 202–3).

102. Dan 10.13.

103. Rev 18.2.

104. There is a similar point I made earlier in the misuse of the Pauline reference "the prince of the power of the air" in Eph 2.2 as evidence for the demons's aerial ontology. See n. 92.

105. Parallels of this expression can be seen elsewhere where, literally, authors are not addressing the location of Satan or the demons. I.e., Smyrna is called the "synagogue of Satan" (Rev 2.9) and Pergamum is "where Satan dwells" (v. 13). Obviously Satan, who is not omnipresent, cannot be located in both Smyrna and Pergamum!

locate the spirits in any place apart from a bodily union. But if no physical properties emerge for demons, and so no materialist interpretation is required by the Bible, then so much for the need for materialism. And that just means that, on the basis of the Bible, we see that Satan and his cohorts are not said to be spatially located anywhere and are not said to interact directly with physical objects. *Inter alia*, these are the very expectations pure immaterialism preserves.

Therefore, it would appear that what philosophy makes clear–that immaterial spirits would not be located in any place–is implied by (or accords with) the biblical testimony about the abode of the demons. Demons are never located in this or that location, something we would expect to see in harmony with theology if we are to insist that both circles of study are aimed at representing reality. If we consolidate all of our findings so far–that is, if we accept all of the distinct points I argued for about pure immaterialism here and above–then we have a powerful, cumulative argument for the pure immateriality of demons. This is the culminating focus of the next section in its drawing together all of the distinct arguments raised thus far.

The Best Explanation of the Evidence is that Demons are Purely Immaterial Beings

Given that one has no *a priori* reason to favor the hypothesis that demons are purely immaterial over its rivals (i.e., that such a notion is neither logically nor metaphysically impossible), I have subsequently advanced a series of arguments based on *a posteriori* considerations. Once we combine the posterior evidence with the previously established possibility of pure immaterialism, we can see that the overall probability of pure immaterialism is increased. This is to say that the specific evidence of the Scriptures is made more reasonable (and more expected) than rival hypotheses simply given the hypothesis of pure immaterialism. But we cannot reasonably say the same thing for (quasi-)materialist views of demons since the evidence is less probable (or less expected) if (quasi-)materialism is true of those beings. The specific evidence is actually less expected and so *lowers* the probability of any (quasi-)materialism than it would without such evidence.

The inclusion of the posterior evidence shows two things on behalf of the pure immaterialist's model: (i) the probability of the hypothesis of pure immaterialism is a coherent and viable option in a Judeo-Christian framework as an apt description of the ontology of demons; and (ii) the specific data of the Bible increases the likelihood of the hypothesis of pure immaterialism as the preferred explanation for that ontology. In arguing for (ii) in this chapter, we see that not only are the individual considerations confirmatory (to some degree) of pure immaterialism but that, when taken together, constitute a powerful, cumulative case for pure immaterialism. To put the matter succinctly, it is a simpler hypothesis and it harmonizes philosophy and theology better than its rivals. As long as the evidence is not incomplete then, in simple terms, pure immaterialism is the better justified explanation based on a combination of philosophically-informed background information and the specific evidence of the scriptural data.

Conclusion

We have seen that pure immaterialism is not itself an objectionable doctrine. It is neither logically nor metaphysically impossible. In fact we have seen how, quite to the contrary, pure immaterialism seems rather probable as an accurate description of the demons's ontology. In this chapter we examined three pieces of evidence based on data from Scripture that seem to support the notion that the demons's ontology is one of pure immaterialism. I argued that, *prima facie*, the Bible seems to imply cosmic and anthropological dualism, that the description of the ontology of angels and demons (as *rûaḥ* and *pneuma*) is the same as that of God, and that there is a disproportionate set of manifestation stories in that angels manifest frequently to observers but demons never do. I then formulated a cumulative case by pointing out that once we take the biblical data and apply it to some of the principles that make a good explanation, pure immaterialism comes out ahead of its materialist rivals. It seems to me that, apart from any mitigating counter-considerations, the weight of the evidence is on the side of demonic pure immaterialism.

Given that the notion of demonic power has reared its head numerous times already, we shall now segue into considering the nature and extent of the abilities and powers of Satan and his demons. According to tradition, demons are capable of interacting with human souls. This much is relatively uncontroversial among demonic realists. But it is also thought that demons are endowed with a matter-interacting power to manifest. In fact, they are thought to have a great deal of matter-interacting power–a power so extraordinary that it nearly rivals those of the miracle-working apostles. Accordingly, they are thought to traffic in quasi-miraculous activities and other fantastic interactions with the material world beyond apparitions and manifestations. This traditional portrait of demonic power is a view that has been shared by the vast majority of demonic realists. Thus, in the next chapter we shall explore these putative abilities and consider reasons as to how much of this traditional portrait is accurate or not.

8

On the (Delimited) Powers of Demons (I)
Cognitive Interaction and Psychokinesis

IN THE PREVIOUS CHAPTER, I advocated that pure immaterialism is likely the most accurate ontological description of Satan and his demons by having shown it to be (a) a coherent metaphysical theory, and (b) a more plausible alternative to the convoluted (quasi-)immaterialist theories offered by Christian philosophers since the second century. I ultimately argued that the concept of a purely immaterial mind or self is neither logically nor metaphysically impossible and that there are good reasons for thinking the demons to be immaterial. But a comprehensive metaphysical theory of the demons's ontology does not end there. As I noted in the last chapter, demons are considered by a number of demonic realists to be able to interact with other souls as well as the physical world. This raises the issue as to what powers the demons have, for it is curious how a purely immaterial spirit might interact with other beings and things apart from a physical medium. And it is even more curious if we suppose that a demon can interact with a completely different kind of substance totally distinct from its own like the physical world. Essentially, we want to know what kind of *other*-interacting powers they have (for we presume that if demons exist, then it is uncontroversial to suppose that they have certain self-contained *internal* powers such as thinking and emoting). Regarding their capacity to interact with things outside of themselves, however, there is an important consequence of defining the demons's constitution as purely immaterial: If demons are devoid of any kind of spatial or physical properties, how can it be that they causally interact with other minds in their non-spatial realm and with physical objects in the material world? Or, do they even interact with the physical world at all?

Their putative interaction with other minds is often considered less controversial to those who already believe in the community of spirits. However, the traditionally adjoining view that demons can interact with and manipulate physical systems is very controversial. For, on the one hand, any interactivity between demons and this physical universe would *prima facie* require (in some way or other) some kind of physical medium or vehicle (a proxy that is already, at least in part, "in" this world and interacting with it) as a sort of conduit or translator for demons in order that they may have some kind of self-disclosure and influence in that universe (much like how voice recognition software allows one kind of thing, i.e., sound, to interact with another kind of thing, i.e., digital text). On the other hand, as Richard Swinburne imagines, spirits (*qua* poltergeists) may have the power to directly manipulate physical objects apart from such a medium.[1] Such a power would be like a human soul's interacting with its own body or something like God's causal interaction with the universe. But that would seem to be true *only if* we could meaningfully justify that the immaterial spirit in question could directly interact with physical objects. This is not hard to imagine if one thinks about the substantial ontology of God. God, as an immaterial divine spirit himself, is essentially omnipotent on most views of classical theism (not the least of which is Christianity). Omnipotence *at least* entails that one can do anything that is logically possible for that agent to do. It is, therefore, understandable that an omnipotent being would be able to create or move objects through resources intrinsic to his nature since it is logically possible for one to have such a power. But why think that the less divine spirits can and do the same thing since the inference to God's power to interact with matter derives not from his ontological spirituality but from his omnipotence?

Such matter-interacting power cannot be essential to the nature of a *finite* spirit (one whose spiritual essence would not in any way entail his omnipotence). Accordingly, any attributed potency of this sort to semi-divine spirits like the gods of this world would be extrinsic to those spirits, which would therefore only possess it contingently. Since such spirits are not omnipotent, we could not infer from their ontology alone the nature and extent of their power much less the power to interact with matter.[2] That such spirits would have the ability to interact with matter would have to be an accidental power which would make it possible to explain such a causal relation between spirits and the physical world. Now, there is no reason to think that this scenario is not remotely possible. But any move to rationally accept that this is a feasible solution will require justification apart from such mere possibility.

Perhaps demons acquired their special matter-interacting abilities from God during their initial tenure as good angels. A number of traditional demonic realists maintain that the good angels are given such a power at their creation.[3] While this is possible, why think that this is in fact so? It is no doubt because Scripture reports that

---

1. "It is possible that we might find certain otherwise inexplicable phenomena that could be explained by the action of a non-embodied agent, such as a ghost or a poltergeist" (Swinburne, *The Existence of God*, 63).

2. As Jaegwon Kim has pointed out, purely immaterial spirits (being non-spatial) may lack any sort of causal power and thus be "lonely souls." In fact, this is his expectation about unembodied spirits. See Kim, "Lonely Souls," 36.

3. I.e., Meyers, "Angel," 63; Adler, *The Angels and Us*, 129; Dickason, *Angels*, chapter 2.

angels often do manifest in the phenomenal world.[4] But why think the *angel himself* is responsible for the manifestation? This is not how we read the apparition stories of disembodied *human* spirits, after all. Case in point: Samuel's spirit is reported to have become visible and interacted with Saul and the sorceress of Endor in 1 Sam 28.11–20, but we no doubt imagine that it was God who made this possible and that Samuel himself lacked any special spirit-matter interactive power in his disembodied state. But on his own, he would not have been capable of the apparition Saul and the sorceress experienced. This leads us to now ask: If demons are indeed incapable of interacting with matter, how else can they move human beings and afflict them with illnesses? Are these not indisputable occurrences that obtain in Scripture?

I propose that angels, and so demons, have the ability to cognitively interact with other souls and that this constitutes the maximal extent of their ability to interact with others. I take it that if God created all spirits, it is possible that he has not created them in utter communicative isolation from each other. Based on Scripture's portrait of angels communicating with God and other spirits, this notion appears to be an uncontroversial theological datum.[5] And when it comes to demons, the ability to communicate appears to also not be in dispute,[6] though we shall consider arguments as to whether this is truly the case or not. Consequently, one might consider spirit-spirit interaction to be a basic power of angels and demons.[7] But such spirit-spirit interaction can mean a lot more than simple communication from one unembodied spirit to another. This is to say that if such interaction obtained between an unembodied spirit and an *embodied* spirit, the spirit of the embodied being could serve as a proxy for the interacting unembodied spirit by and through which to affect changes in the physical world. The embodied person's spirit would be something of a medium for demonic spirits in that they may influence the thoughts of human recipients thereby leading them (the human host) to perform acts with their bodies as objects already in the physical world. I shall thus refer to the notion of spirit-spirit commerce as *cognitive interaction* in order to distinguish it from other potential forms of interaction. I shall discuss and argue in more detail for the probability that demons have this communicative power in this chapter.

By contrast, the evidence for spirit-*matter* interaction (or, as I shall refer to it, *psychokinesis*) of the demons is less than convincing. For it is believed that demons are reported to move upon the physical world in such remarkable ways that their feats may potentially be indistinguishable from divine miracles. It is also assumed that this is the only way to understand how demons can cause human sicknesses and other physical ailments reported of demons in Scripture. We shall begin to address this in

---

4. See Matt 4.11 and Heb 13.2.

5. We shall consider the legitimacy of this notion below.

6. In addition to Jude 9, see 1 Chron 21.1–2, Luke 22.3–4 (paralleled in John 13.2, 27), and Acts 5.3. I shall have more to say about these passages later on.

7. So Swinburne, *The Existence of God*, 130.

this chapter but carry it over into the next in showing why demonic realists are not justified in drawing this conclusion. This is to say that the overall case to be made shall show that demons, while possessing the power of cognitive interaction, do not have a separate psychokinetic power. And the power to cognitively interact with embodied souls can provide an adequate explanation for the interactions we see in Scripture between demons and humans.

Beginning in this chapter, then, we shall examine a more detailed discussion and defense of the powers the demons likely have and do not have. We shall begin by elucidating the two putative powers: cognitive interaction and psychokinesis. For these are both alleged by traditionalists to be powers had by Satan and his cohorts.

Cognitive Interaction

A *cognitive* interaction, as I am employing the phrase, is an interaction due to the conscious intellectual activity bound up in the *res cogitans* (the thing that thinks) of a given subject. Thinking/mentation is presumably a natural power for any mind of a person or higher consciousness, and so I take *cognitive* to be understood in the usual manner as volitional, autonomous intellectual activity. That such activity should involve other spirits or minds is what makes this a cognitive *interaction*. I thus define cognitive interaction in the following way:

> (CI) Person S_1 is cognitively interacting with person S_2 if and only if S_1 is communicating with S_2 through the mental transmission of thoughts and S_1 is not communicating with S_2 through any other means of verbal or non-verbal communication.

This definition for CI is meant to permit the correlative interaction of souls on a cognitive level such that S_1 and S_2 might both be thoroughly immaterial, both embodied souls, or both disparate entities where one soul is embodied and the other soul not. This is to say that a soul's intellectual activity can affect the intellectual activity of another soul regardless of what other properties or accidents the soul may possess.

If demons can cognitively interact with other minds, then those demons are bounded by that person's volition–i.e., what that person wills and desires to will. This volitional will can be affected by an alien spirit, like a demon, in bringing about changes in the victim's behavior. Such demonic manipulation might occur in degrees, everything from being *seductive* to being *coercive*. In the former case, the person is somehow convinced (either emotionally or intellectually) to relinquish a certain amount of control (or utter control) to the alien spirit. In the latter case, it is possible that the alien spirit might overcome and even hijack the person's mind for its own complete governing of that person toward some particular task (or of the person altogether).

Part III: Ontological Matters

Consider an analogy in thinking about the degrees of influence one might have on another along these lines. Think of a terrorist hijacker that can, to varying degrees, influence the pilot of a commercial airplane. While the pilot may directly work the controls in the cockpit, there would be no doubt who was *really* in control of the airplane in the presence of such a hijacker. The implication of this analogy is that the more a soul's intellect can be governed by the alien soul's prompting, the more likely there would be an increase in the alien soul's *control* over that mind. Now, this seems to suggest that a certain amount of resistance is possible even if strained (after all, even a hijacking victim can flout the orders barked by her captor if she cares not for her life or the lives of those on board). I think this is correct and well within the parameters set forth above that such control occurs in degrees. Whether the hijacker coerces the pilot or seduces her into courses of action she would not have otherwise done, the demon can accomplish some end result at its behest. To what extent can the demon control its victim? Presumably to the point of possession, viz., total control. Some historical cases of alleged demonic possession give the impression that the demon's cognitive interaction with the victim can potentially be extremely dramatic and quite violent.[8] It may even lead to the victim becoming completely overwhelmed against her will, thus giving rise to total control as envisaged in some demon-possession cases.

But the demon's interaction with the host's mind would not only be bounded by the host's mentation, it would also be bounded by the host's physical constraints. While a demon could incite (from seduction to coercion) the host mind to do things human persons can already do, it could not have a human person do things she has no power to perform. For example, the alien spirit could not manipulate a person to have her suddenly flap her arms and fly to the next city. The only way a demon could manipulate its victim in this non-natural way would be for it to possess preternatural powers that would supplement its ability to cognitively interact with other souls. But we are not yet ready to entertain that possibility just yet.

The overall point here is that though some, like theologians, may have no qualms about soul-soul communicative interaction so understood, not all philosophers are so easily convinced that this is possible. Let us look at some reasons to think that soul-soul interaction of any sort is possible and, so, the possibility of CI.

On the Possibility of Cognitive Interaction

If CI is true of demons, it means that such souls can act on other souls in some way. On the one hand, it is readily conceivable that substances can affect similar substances. In fact, for many, there is an expectation that this to be a necessary condition for such interaction, which is why according to many philosophers of mind anthropological dualism is no longer a majority position. That similar substances can affect or provide

---

8. I refer readers to the fascinating but tragic case of Anneliese Michel. See Goodman, *The Exorcism of Anneliese Michel*.

the means of knowing similar substances has a long ancestry dating back to the ancient Pre-Socratic doctrine of *homoion-homoioi* ("like for like"). This doctrine finds an original expression in Empedocles:

> For 'tis through Earth that Earth we do behold,
> Through Ether, divine Ether luminous,
> Through Water, Water, through Fire, devouring Fire,
> And Love through Love, and Hate through doleful Hate.[9]

As Aristotle summarily puts it, "like . . . is known by like."[10] And Aristotle's view of this has influenced medieval philosophers like Aquinas to conceive of angelic CI in a similar way.[11] Being the same kind of substance was, and for many still is, a necessary condition for any natural interactions between separate objects.

If demons are indeed purely immaterial spirits, then not only is their interaction with other souls causal but it is a causal relation that would obtain in a wholly nonspatial and nonphysical environment. So understood, Jaegwon Kim wonders how it would be possible, in the absence of a spatial relation, to have "causality within a purely mental world."[12] In other words, since purely immaterial souls (as in the anthropological case of so-called Cartesian egos) necessarily lack spatiality then there must be some alternative to space that helps makes sense of the causal CI-relation between subjects. As Kim insists, "we seem to be in need of a certain kind of 'space'" in order for a mental subject (soul A) to distinguish or "pick out" another mental subject (soul B) from among other mental subjects (soul C, soul D, etc.).[13] Simply acknowledging a nonphysical "mental space" might seem to save the concept, but Kim quickly dismisses its plausibility as he does not have "the foggiest idea what such a framework might look like."[14] Thus if one follows Kim in holding that causality between objects requires a spatial relation, then any sort of soul-soul causation or interaction would be metaphysically impossible (not the least of which any soul-*body* interaction would be dismissed *a fortiori*). This leads Kim to offer an obviously tongue-in-cheek implication for the inter-commerce of things like immaterial persons:

> A purely Cartesian world seems like a pretty lonely place, inhabited by immaterial souls each of which is an island unto itself, totally isolated from all other souls. . . . [If] we are immaterial souls, [it] would be a lonely place for us.[15]

---

9. Empedocles, *Fragments*, 109: 50.
10. Aristotle, *De Anima*, I.2.404b18: 645.
11. Aquinas, *Summa Theologiae*, I.89.
12. Kim, "Lonely Souls," 36.
13. Kim, "Lonely Souls," 37.
14. Kim, "Lonely Souls," 37.
15. Kim, "Lonely Souls," 39. This is repeated again in his more recent *Physicalism, or Something Near Enough*, 84.

Part III: Ontological Matters

If Kim is right and the very concept of a causally efficacious immaterial subject is incoherent, then, apart from being causally *isolated*, an uncomfortable dilemma arises. Either one must suppose that demons would not be immaterial things after all, or suppose that demons would just be, *mutatis mutandis*, causally effete (and we default to either relegating the ability of souls to interact as a mere mystery or we give up the notion altogether). Either way, CI would be impaled on the horns of this dilemma, for either we sacrifice an understanding of the demons's *ontology* or we sacrifice the notion that they can communicate with other souls. So the challenge here is whether the pure immaterialist can surmount the problem of soul-soul causality as posed by Kim. I think that she can, and that Kim's own sentiment on the subject is not as averse to this as one might think.

First, it is not at all clear how causality *prima facie* entails or (at least) requires some kind of spatiality.[16] Kim argues that the absence of a spatial matrix makes tracing a causal pathway obscure since we ordinarily trace effects to their causes in terms of spatial contiguity. This much can be granted. But it does not entail that because we are *ignorant* of such a pathway that, therefore, there is no way to justify mental causation. Kim is not entitled to this conclusion. The problem centers on wanting to make sense of such causation apart from a spatial context: "It is the problem of showing how mental causation is possible, not *whether* it is possible."[17] But if we can say as much–that such a "mental space" is metaphysically *possible* though explanatorily obfuscated–then it is unclear how wondering "How?" is itself grounds for an automatic rejection.

Consider David Hume who in his own way complained about the "how" of justifying causality between ordinary, *physical* objects–objects that are even contiguous with each other in a spatio-temporal way.[18] For Hume, even such ordinary causal occurrences seemingly envisage, in his words, a "secret power" of their own perhaps every bit as mysterious as, say, a "mental space" in which two mental subjects might interact. Hume's justification for the causal relation seems to have been grounded in the habitual experience (viz., an inductive generalization) of such repeated cause-effect pairings and not in whether the causal relationship could be mechanistically clarified. As J. P. Moreland observes,

> the absence of a complete analysis of such [mental causal] contact afflicts physical causality, and this fact weakens the force of Kim's claim that in the

---

16. Enough critics have challenged Kim on this score that it is not necessary to rehearse all of the objections here. For a sampling, see Bailey, Rasmussen, and Horn, "No Pairing Problem"; Madell, "The Road to Substance Dualism"; Jehle, "Kim Against Dualism"; Moreland, "If You Can't Reduce, You Must Eliminate." Also worthy of note is E. J. Lowe's reflection on David Hume's attitude about formulating *a priori* notions about such requisites of causality in noting that, for Hume, "there are simply no *a priori* constraints on what kinds of states or events can enter into causal relationships with one another. As Hume himself puts it at one point: 'to consider the matter a priori, any thing may produce any thing'" (*An Introduction to the Philosophy of Mind*, 23).

17. Kim, "Mental Causation," 128.

18. See Hume, *An Enquiry Concerning Human Understanding*, IV.I–V.1.

absence of such an analysis regarding Cartesian souls, we are not justified in believing in their existence or causal power.[19]

Thus, one is not reasonably forbidden from inferring soul-soul causation as long as there is somehow a way to trace the causal trajectories of immaterial subjects. What it takes to show *that* there is a causal relation is unaffected by our inability to show *how* that causal relation obtains. Even so, Kim would only caution that one should not make the mistake of conflating the establishing of causal sufficiency with the establishing of causation itself.[20] But even if epistemically opaque, any alternative to "mental space" as defining a determinate causal relationship will still, in Kim's own words, "enable us to make sense of causal relations between non-spatial mental entities."[21]

Timothy O'Connor, himself no Cartesian dualist, insists that one can conceivably use spatial terms as a useful metaphor. How so? Because it would allow one "to characterize the ordering that structures the interaction of souls in a space-less world. This should not in itself be objectionable, however."[22] This, he continues, would permit one to eschew "external relations within an array in favor of a primitive sort of intrinsic informational state had by each soul, such that it knows 'where' it is 'in relation to' all the others."[23] As such, it would make "all causal interactions . . . a function entirely of intrinsic properties." Mental subjects, upon communicating with or acting upon another, could commerce with each other as long as the subject had some conventional way to differentiate its relation from one to another (whatever that might be). Even if this rough schema does not work to rescue the anthropological dualist's case of soul-*body* pairing (as O'Connor is quick to mention) it would have no negative bearing at all on my view of intermediary beings engaging in soul-*soul* commerce. But then, what kind of "intrinsic informational state" exists to make sense, even metaphorically, of soul-soul interaction?

For those medieval thinkers who conceived of demons as quasi-material, the solution was easy. Augustine, as we noted earlier, seems to have suggested that demons have a semi-physical sense perception and transmission mechanism that can pick up

---

19. Moreland, "If You Can't Reduce, You Must Eliminate," 469.

20. Kim levels this charge against John Foster's use of the nomological theory in justifying causal pairings between mental and physical events. See Kim, "Causation," 230.

21. Kim, "Lonely Souls," 37. Kim goes on to speak of a second possibility whereby one can affirm soul-soul interaction without the arbitrary metaphysic of a recondite "mental space" (see 37–38). In this case one can circumvent the need for some undisclosed kind of spatial proxy altogether by positing a causal relation that is predicated on a non-spatial causal chain. But Kim finds this maneuver problematic for he wants to know what it means to have an "in between" link (that there exists something that mediates between soul A and soul B) in a strictly mental universe. This, Kim fears, must be a failed salvage operation since it attempts to solve a causal connection problem by multiplying the amount of causal connections. I am inclined to agree.

22. O'Connor, "Causality, Mind, and Free Will," 107.

23. O'Connor, "Causality, Mind, and Free Will," 108.

and manipulate the bodily traces of human thoughts.[24] It is through this medium that demons are able to read, communicate thoughts, and stir the passions within their victims. And Augustine, in one of his correspondences with Nebridius, proffers the notion that such internal agitations in human beings are (possibly) demonic movements of fluids inside the body (viz., "bile") affecting the mind.[25] But this potential solution will not do since it assumes that demons are (quasi-)material. For the pure immaterialist, any correspondence between two souls apart from a physical universe must be divested of any appeal to a physical medium. After all, the point is to avoid treating soul-soul communication as though it were the spatial transmission of an audio signal from one agent to another.

The resolution to this problem may not be so difficult to find. We need not think of soul-soul communication as a form of physical correspondence that has transitory velocity and moves through a spatial medium. Instead, such communicability would be direct and non-physical as a conscious agent's intentional juxtaposition of ideas in one's mind. Such mental ideas have no external relations and can be "picked out" simply by mentally differentiating them individually as "to my left" and "to my right" as we often do of distinct images in our minds. Also, persons (each bearing a unique identity) would not need to be differentiated spatially as long as an outsider can still pick out, say, the angel Gabriel from Michael with whom to interact. If I use Dissociative Identity Disorder as an analogy, a patient's psyche may fragment into seemingly independent personalities. It is possible for an outsider to address one personality and not the other *even though the multiple personalities are non-spatially related to each other in the self-same host*. This is only an analogy, but if offers us a possible framework as to how different persons may be differentiated from each other apart from considerations of space. Indeed, other things can be differentiated from each other without having to appeal to the relative locations of the different objects. For example, we can distinguish between the musical notes F-sharp and C-minor. And distinguishing these notes from each other is not a matter of location but of pitch. Therefore, space is not a necessary condition for differentiating similarly composed things from each other.

CI may very well be an exemplification of the alleged phenomenon of *telepathy*, which, given its familiar connotation in the literature, serves as a useful frame of reference. Telepathy, whether or not it is a precise way to describe this view, at least offers us an intelligible way of understanding the notion of non-verbal communication that is not based on any physical factors whatsoever. As with descriptions of telepathy, the communication is purely mental and can function in two ways, viz., each soul could

---

24. Augustine, *De Divinatione Daemonum*, IX.3; Also see O'Daly, *Augustine's Philosophy of Mind*, 122–24.

25. Augustine, *De Divinatione Daemonum*, IX.3.

be both a transmitter and a receiver of each other's thoughts. For those who believe in demons, such a mechanism is already granted and easily imagined.[26]

Skeptics about such a mechanism will complain that telepathy (of the nonphysical sort mentioned) adds nothing to the explanatory work needed to account for soul-soul communication. Antony Flew, in objecting to the use of telepathy as an explanatory vehicle for occult mediums in séances, complains:

> "Telepathy" is not the name of a means of communication; whereas the mention of radio telephony does explain how certain results are achieved, by indicating the mechanisms involved. Telepathy is no more an explanation of the paranormal element in séance performances than memory is an explanation of our capacity to give our names and addresses.[27]

Flew seems to be concerned that "telepathy" is an unenlightening description–a mere label–of the very phenomenon one seeks to explain and so it does not itself serve to add anything to our understanding of the *how*.

While the *how* of telepathy is surely unavailable in this reductionist sense, this is not necessarily an objection to it as being an explanation in another sense (perhaps something like what "folk psychology" has been, for better or worse, in the philosophy of mind[28]). An advocate of telepathy has (at least) a *meaningful* vehicle for communication even though it may not be a complete *elucidation* of a contiguous, supernatural contraption of some sort reducible to fields and waves (or particles) in motion such as we have in radio telephony. To insist on such would seem to sneak in the imposition that all explanatory mechanisms, whether physical or not, must offer the same level or species of explanation. But there are countless counterexamples to this in comparing, say, *social* mechanisms with electronic mechanisms. The former will lack the causal specifics exhibited in the latter. It is no *less* an explanation even though it lacks the niceties of a reductive physical science. Even physical mechanisms serve to be meaningful though may still be lacking in the how. For example, quantum mechanisms like "quantum tunneling" (the mysterious ability of a particle to pass through a physical barrier) and "the observer effect" (that consciousness somehow affects the objects of observation) both refer to interactions between objects that seem to lack the reductionist virtues of radio and telephony. But Flew's criticism is actually problematic even for his own paradigm examples, namely that radio and telephony are appropriate levels

---

26. For example, Merrill F. Unger explicitly "finds in telepathy a rational basis of corroboration" for angelic and demonic communicability with embodied persons (*Biblical Demonology*, 78).

27. Flew, *A New Approach to Psychical Research*, 69.

28. "Folk Psychology" is a "commonsense" or "everyday" explanation of cognitive processes that is perhaps based on "core propositional attitudes, beliefs and desires, alone." See Radcliffe and Hutto, "Introduction," 1–2. Opponents believe that folk psychology is "hopelessly primitive" and that cognition ought to be explained in terms of "the framework of a matured neuroscience." This is because it promises to offer an understanding of *how* such processes transpire. Accordingly, folk psychology is a "higher-level explanation" whereas neuroscience is a "lower-level explanation," and it is highly debatable whether instances of the former are reducible to the latter (Churchland, *Matter and Consciousness*, 77).

on which mechanistic explanations ought to reside seems problematic. "Radio" is just a higher referent for invisible electromagnetic radiation which is to say that "radio" is not itself irreducible. And is not invisible electromagnetic radiation itself reducible to waves and fields? The need to keep reducing to the lower levels is only necessary if the current level does not adequately explain the *explananda*. That I stopped at an intersection in my car because I depressed the brake pedal explains sufficiently how I stopped. I do not have to reduce this explanation to the material make-up of the brake pedal and its connected parts in order to make sense of my stopping. Suppose I know *nothing* about how brakes even work. Perhaps braking systems reduce to the phantom operations of "ectoplasmic radiation." Nothing about this level of reduction is necessary for explaining how I stopped at the intersection. It is, therefore, no objection to me that I not explain soul-soul commerce in more reductionist terms.

We might now anticipate an additional challenge: if we are to understand souls as having the power to interact in such a way, how is it a specific soul cannot interact at will with any other soul? After all, embodied human souls appear not to be able to cognitively interact at will with other embodied human souls. So, what makes a soul's delimited causal transmission so discriminating as to await, say, separation from its body in order to communicate with a fellow soul? A reasonable answer is that it is most likely the case that our paired bodies (if *sui generis*) simply *prevent* such soul-soul interaction. And, once a soul is separated from its body, it may be free or less encumbered to engage in such commerce. Perhaps it is analogous to the Socratic notion of anamnesis in that being embodied (viz., incarnated) hinders one's mental powers such that one is unable to recall past knowledge from a previous state of existence.[29] But there is another reasonable answer, perhaps more so, in that God might be the one to prevent such soul-soul communication until the departed are in company with each other. Luke 16 (whether parabolic, folk, or otherwise) implies that God can indeed impose certain restrictions (in this case proximity) between souls in certain contexts: "[B]etween us and you a great chasm has been fixed, in order that those who would pass from here to you may not be able, and none may cross from there to us."[30] But this shows *at best* that soul-soul interaction *qua* soul-soul communication is deliberately hampered between *un*embodied souls. What of being embodied? It is interesting that in Scripture the misbehavior of living (embodied) men with their (obviously embodied) wives may actually hinder the husbands's prayerful communication to God:

> Likewise, husbands, live with your wives in an understanding way, showing honor to the woman as the weaker vessel, since they are heirs with you of the grace of life, so that your prayers may not be hindered (1 Pet 3.7).

---

29. Plato, *Phaedo*, 66–67c; Plato, *Meno*, 85d–86c.

30. Luke 16.26. During the correspondence of the rich man and Abraham, Lazarus never participates.

The prayers (and so communication) to God are "hindered" (*egkoptesthai*), not by God in merely refusing to listen, but by the husband's disrespecting of his wife. According to Timothy Friberg, Barbara Friberg, and Neva F. Miller, *egkoptesthai* means "*impediment, blockage*" in the same sense as used in 1 Cor 9.12: "we endure anything rather than put an obstacle [*egkopēn*] in the way of the gospel of Christ."[31] It is probable, then, that a deliberate interruption in soul-soul communication occurs. This, I think, along with Luke 16, offer some general precedent as to how (at least occasionally or circumstantially) souls can be delimited in their interaction (particularly in their communication) with other souls regardless of whether any of those souls is embodied.

But there is something to be said about my own awareness that my soul does not directly interact with someone else's (as far as I know!). Perhaps being mutually embodied is among one of the circumstances imposed by God in which my embodied soul's ability to commerce with another embodied soul is cut off. This could be why the Bible contains such strong prohibitions against necromancy.[32] It might also explain Paul's statement in 2 Cor 5.6 which states that "while we are at home in the body we are away from the Lord." Though this is obviously speculation, it is reasonable to posit that the deliberate hampering of soul-soul communication at least bears some type of evidential precedent. And the lack of any first-hand awareness of such communication (viz., participating in telepathy with another embodied human while being embodied myself) is consonant with the entire biblical paradigm of soul-soul commerce.

So far, we have looked at how soul-soul communication is to be understood in terms of CI. We have also explored a number of potential challenges to the notion that telepathy is an appropriate framework by which to comprehend the basis of its mechanism. Let us now move on to consider evidence for soul-soul interaction in Scripture.

On the Probability of Cognitive Interaction

I submit that there are a number of passages in Scripture indicating that souls in general and demons in particular cognitively interact with other souls. As such, the occurrences of cognitive (or soul-soul) interaction are variegated. Sometimes the immaterial soul of one cognitively interacts with another immaterial soul. Sometimes the immaterial soul of one cognitively interacts with an embodied soul. Sometimes it is the embodied soul that cognitively interacts with an immaterial soul. And these souls range from human souls (as instances of embodied souls) to angelic souls to God himself (both as instances of unembodied souls). Demons are also in the mix of unembodied souls.

---

31. Friberg, Friberg, and Miller, *Analytical Lexicon of the Greek New Testament*, 127.
32. Leviticus 20.27; Deut 18.10–11; 1 Chron 10.13; Isa 8.19.

Part III: Ontological Matters

First of all, there are a few explicit occurrences in the Bible where we find an unembodied soul communicating with another unembodied soul. Let us survey just three of them: Job 1.7–12, Jude 9, and Rev 6.9–10. Job 1.7–12 reads:

> The LORD said to Satan, "From where have you come?" Satan answered the LORD and said, "From going to and fro on the earth, and from walking up and down on it." And the LORD said to Satan, "Have you considered my servant Job, that there is none like him on the earth, a blameless and upright man, who fears God and turns away from evil?" Then Satan answered the LORD and said, "Does Job fear God for no reason? Have you not put a hedge around him and his house and all that he has, on every side? You have blessed the work of his hands, and his possessions have increased in the land. But stretch out your hand and touch all that he has, and he will curse you to your face." And the LORD said to Satan, "Behold, all that he has is in your hand. Only against him do not stretch out your hand." So Satan went out from the presence of the LORD.

Jude 9 reads:

> But when the archangel Michael, contending with the devil, was disputing about the body of Moses, he did not presume to pronounce a blasphemous judgment, but said, "The Lord rebuke you."

And Rev 6.9–10 reads:

> When he opened the fifth seal, I saw under the altar the souls of those who had been slain for the word of God and for the witness they had borne. They cried out with a loud voice, "O Sovereign Lord, holy and true, how long before you will judge and avenge our blood on those who dwell on the earth?"

The souls in two of the cases (Job 1.7–12 and Jude 9) explicitly involve Satan. In Job 1, we have Satan in a direct conversation with God.[33] Satan challenges Job's fidelity to God by arguing that that relationship is contingent on the many blessings he receives from God, thus showing Job's faith to be based on his lack of hardship as God's servant. It is Satan's challenge as communicated directly to God that spurs him on to demonstrate Job's faithfulness despite extreme adversity. And, so, we have here an episode of an unembodied soul communicating with another unembodied soul.

In turning to the New Testament, Jude 9 mentions a "dispute" over the body of Moses that occurs between Michael the archangel and Satan. The final reprimand issued by Michael–"the Lord rebuke you!"–is specifically directed to Satan. In the remaining account, Rev 6.9–10, there is a situation noted by its author whose visionary account of heaven depicts the souls of martyred saints ("the souls of those

---

33. I recognize that some commentators find *haśśāṭān* ("the Satan") of Job to be a reference to a good angel acting the role of adversary for the sake of the dialog. Even so, it remains as a case of soul-soul interaction *qua* CI.

beheaded"[34]) enjoined together in pleading to God for judgment and retribution by asking, "O Sovereign Lord, holy and true, how long before you will judge and avenge our blood on those who dwell on the earth?" Hence, these episodes exemplify two (or more) unembodied souls in communication.

There are also examples of communication between an unembodied soul and a soul that is embodied. One can turn to passages like Neh 2.12 ("... I told no one what my God had put into my heart to do for Jerusalem ...") and John 16.13 ("... whatever [the Spirit] hears he will speak, and he will declare to you the things that are to come"), though we must acknowledge that these instances involve God himself as the unembodied spirit. As such, these passages may not figure as fair illustrations of what a created, finite spirit may normally be capable of. But in 1 Sam 28.7–20, we do indeed have a created, finite spirit in such a position. In the passage therein, there is a deceased person, Samuel, who is reported to be conjured up by a sorceress (or "medium") under the direction of the living Saul. Once Saul makes contact, Samuel communicates directly with him.[35] It is true that Samuel is not directly identified as an unembodied "spirit" or "soul" here, but that he would have been an unembodied spirit or soul is implied by Saul's utilizing the services of a "medium at Endor" (v. 7) who divines "by a spirit" a way to conjure up the late Samuel (v. 8). According to John H. Walton, Victor H. Matthews, and Mark W. Chavalas, Canaanite mediums were commonly understood to be "conjurers of ancestral spirits who could speak of the future."[36] Since Samuel was dead, readers are probably expected, given the backdrop of mediums in the Mesopotamian culture of the time, to suppose that the medium was indeed conjuring a spirit.[37] Barring any good reason to think otherwise, this episode is quite supportive of commerce between an unembodied (finite) soul and an embodied soul.

---

34. See Bauckham, "Revelation," 1294. It is possible Rev 19.4 is also an instance of human souls (viz., the "twenty-four elders") cognitively communicating with (by singing to) God. Craig Keener says that the "twenty-four elders" are the "faithful dead [being] portrayed as priests offering worship to God" (*The IVP Bible Background Commentary*, 776). But this is disputable in light of its use of angelic typology in Isa 24.23 and Dan 7.9 (cf., Bauckham, "Revelation," 1293).

35. Some interpreters, beginning with Tertullian, believe that Samuel is a demonic apparition (see Murphy, *1 Samuel*, 263). Given that "Samuel" speaks on behalf of "the LORD" and speaks of events of the past (v. 17) and of the future (v. 18) with accuracy, and also condemns Saul for not going directly to the Lord, it is doubtful that these would be the righteous utterances of a demonic spirit. Even if it were the case that it was a demon, it would not change this as an instance of an unembodied soul in communication with an embodied soul.

36. Walton, Matthews, and Chavalas, *The IVP Bible Background Commentary*, 318.

37. Walton, Matthews, and Chavalas also add that the "spirits who emerged were in human form and generally were able to communicate directly with the client" (*The IVP Bible Background Commentary*, 318.). Verse 14 does offer a physical description of Samuel's appearance as an old man wearing a robe and this might suggest a physical manifestation. But this was more likely a visionary representation put into the mind of the medium. This is likely because if it was an extramental physical manifestation, then it would not be the case that only the medium sees the apparition and Saul does not.

Part III: Ontological Matters

If we suppose that CI captures what immaterial persons generally do, and we impose a sort of metaphysical principle of uniformity (specifically, that all immaterial persons of the same type would likely have the same fundamental capabilities), we should then expect that immaterial persons like angels and demons would also be capable of the same.[38] As it turns out, there are examples taken from episodes involving specifically *demonic* soul-soul interaction (apart from Job 1 and Jude 9) that involve their interaction with embodied human beings. I have in mind 1 Chron 21.1–2, Luke 22.3–4 (paralleled in John 13.2, 27), and Acts 5.3. First Chronicles offers a rather straightforward depiction of King David being inclined by Satan to some action:

> Then Satan stood against Israel and incited David to number Israel. So David said to Joab and the commanders of the army, "Go, number Israel, from Beer-sheba to Dan, and bring me a report, that I may know their number.

As noted in chapter 2, it is unclear whether the "Satan" here is the chief of demons. But if it is, then we have an early non-Christian, though canonical, account of Satan internally inciting a human being. In Luke 22.3–4, it is implied there that Satan commerces with Jesus's betrayer, Judas Iscariot, by having "entered" (*eisēlthen*) into him in order to precipitate his betrayal of Jesus with the chief priests and officers. Even though this might be more accurately a demonic possession case, I submit that demonic possession (or demonization) is just a rather aggressive form of soul-soul interaction. For that matter, I should point to *all* of the demonic possession passages for similar support.

In Acts 5.3, Luke reports Peter's accusation that Satan has directly "filled [Ananias's] heart to lie to the Holy Spirit." This is interesting in connection with an aforementioned passage, Neh 2.12, where it is God's natural privilege to direct one's "heart" one way or another. Acts 5.3 would thus suggest that this mechanism of interaction is available also to Satan. 1 Thess 3.5 reads, "For this reason, when I could bear it no longer, I sent to learn about your faith, for fear that somehow the tempter had tempted you and our labor would be in vain." It seems to imply that Satan (or a demon), if he is the "tempter" envisioned here, can directly lure people away from faith.[39] Second Tim 2.26 ("and they may come to their senses and escape from the snare of the devil, after being captured by him to do his will") likewise implies Satanic CI whereby living saints can have their wills ensnared by the devil.

---

38. Science adopts a principle of uniformity that pertains to the idea that the regularities and laws of nature that are perceived to exist in the observable universe likely exist everywhere else in the (unobserved) universe. In a correspondence with Sophie Charlotte (cir. 1704), G. W. Leibniz acknowledges this as a metaphysical principle and applies it to his particular metaphysics. And so, in commenting on the ontologies of God, angels, and human souls, he says that "the principle of uniformity holds that nature is always the same in its fundamentals, although it makes use of a great variety in its ways . . . among the angels and among the animals as among us, among the dead as among the living" (*Leibniz and the Two Sophies*, 319). I am indebted to Lloyd Strickland for pointing this out to me.

39. Recall "The Edenic Serpent" in chapter 2.

The results are quite telling. First, we have CI explicitly occurring between unembodied souls. This alone suggests that there may be a "natural" power available to such souls. Second, we have CI explicitly occurring between demons (or, at least, Satan) and both embodied and unembodied souls. Third, we have explicit mention of Satan participating in the phenomenon in question. As long as one is willing to grant that Satan is a typical representative of what demons can do, the conclusion here strongly indicates that cognitive interaction is not only feasible for demons, but actual. And this conclusion is further bolstered by the fact that the demonic possession cases of the New Testament supply interaction between demons other than Satan and human beings.[40]

Having established both the possibility and the probability of CI for finite spirits in general and for demons in particular, in the next section we shall consider whether demons might have another form of causal interaction, namely psychokinesis.

Psychokinesis

The previous power, CI, entails that demons have a specific kind of causal relation with other immaterial souls. However, CI cannot account for any other kinds of interaction, especially interaction with things that are material. This leads us to now consider what else Christians have traditionally supposed about the demons's powers. As chronicled in chapter 3, demons (as purely immaterial spirits) are said to be able to directly interact with the physical world. According to this position, demons are not only capable of cognitively interacting with other souls but they also have a special power that enables them to interact directly with material things like rocks, tables, animals, and human bodies. Such interactive abilities can be used to the extent of manipulating matter such that they can produce seemingly miraculous events. One might consider such an ability to be indistinguishable from what we might call magic–an occultic ability to defy physical laws and natural powers of ordinary persons and objects.

It is interesting that the traditional view amongst Christians affirmed such a power for the demons despite their commitments about the ontology of demons. A number of early Greek Christians and some later Franciscans asserted quasi-materialism and yet did not hesitate to imagine that demons have a psychokinetic power. Let us consider in more detail here what I mean by demons having the power of psychokinesis. In a more formal codification of this idea, Stephen E. Braude has offered up a more precise definition of psychokinesis that is worth incorporating:

---

40. We could also add John 8.38 to the mix, for therein Jesus accuses the Jews of having "heard" (*ēkousate*) from their father who is identified as "the devil" (v. 44). It is apparent in this chapter that Satan has prompted these particular Jews toward their aversion to Jesus and his teachings.

> Psychokinesis (PK) = the causal influence of a person (organism) on a physical system *s* without any known sort (or scientifically recognized) physical interaction between the person's (organism's) body and *s*.[41]

Such a definition seems nearly ideal but leaves open the epistemic possibility that a *physical* mechanism may yet be discovered by which the process of an agent's influence on *s* may eventually be explained in scientific terms. Any real supernatural power manifesting as a psychokinetic ability, particularly when applied to God's interactive ability with nature, will never be known or "scientifically recognized." Psychokinesis should be fundamentally incapable of being scientifically recognized since it is considered a purely supernatural phenomenon. As Braude himself acknowledges, the above definition can only be offered "in terms of ignorance of the processes involved" thereby threatening to make the definition of PK obsolete.[42] But for things like angels and demons, PK should never be found out to be scientific or physical for beings that are *ex hypothesi* supernatural and falling outside the purview of science.

Furthermore, I think it is too restrictive to say that such commerce is one that may occur between a person's *body* and *s*. While it gives the uncontroversial impression that PK is possibly independent of conscious awareness (which remains reasonably possible even for demons), it is predicated on the misleading notion of one's having a "body" (whatever this might mean). For a PK ability that is possessed by someone like God, it should not intrinsically connote having a body. In order to avoid these problems in the present context in talking specifically about (incorporeal) demons, I propose a modification that broadly includes divine and semi-divine beings (which are part of a larger order of supernatural beings). As a concomitant of my purposes here, it is also necessary to drop the use of "organism" from the definition. Thus, I propose the following, less restrictive definition for the purpose of framing a more traditional view of demonic interaction:

> (PK*) The direct causal influence of a person on a physical system *s* apart from any mundane physical (or material) interaction between the person and *s*.

In PK*, there are no ontological commitments being assumed. We just simply want to say that there is a possible means for a person to manipulate a physical system apart from any of the usual physical means (if applicable to those agents). The only metaphysical commitment is that any interaction of the PK* sort will be, frankly, *super*natural.

So understood, PK* and not PK is indeed a better codification of the traditional view of the demons's mechanism for interacting with the physical world. It suggests in a rather straightforward manner that demons, as purely immaterial creatures, can and do interact directly with physical systems. And such a notion typically goes beyond

---

41. Braude, *ESP and Psychokinesis*, 27; Also see Braude, *The Limits of Influence*, 220.
42. Braude, *ESP and Psychokinesis*, 27.

the mere *moving* of objects to the extent of *transforming* them into different kinds of objects (e.g., from manipulating the senses of perceivers to causing diseases and natural disasters). Apart from demons having PK*, CI seems inadequate on its own to explain how demons can have any direct interaction with physical systems whatsoever. In fact, CI does not imply *any* direct interaction between a soul and anything that has a different ontology from that soul. But an initial challenge facing the attributing of PK* to demons is that there is no reason to do so other than on the presumption that CI cannot otherwise account for all of their actions. For there is nothing about being an immaterial spirit that, in itself, accounts for its ability to interact with substances quite distinct from its own. In the case of God, his PK*-interaction with this world is due, not to his cognition or his being a spirit, but to his omnipotence. This same appeal cannot be made about any of the gods of this world. One must simply assert PK* as a feature of these beings if and only if there is no simpler explanation for their alleged intra-worldly behavior and the less extraordinary alternatives are exhausted.

The final point to consider is *to what extent* Satan and his demons can psychokinetically interact with the physical world. It is conceivable that demons might possess a supernatural PK* power in which to enact φ-occurrences, viz., the manipulation of physical objects, laws, and the physical sense receptors of human and animal perceivers. But if that is possible, what would be the extent of that power? Might demons have interacted with biological and cosmic things that have ultimately given shape to our physical reality? Michael Murray asks,

> Could these beings . . . have exercised control over which natural laws obtain in our physical cosmos, over the quantity of matter the universe contains, over the speed with which habitable planets came into being, over the course of natural selection, over the genotype of various physical organisms or genotypic variation over evolutionary history? Could these beings be to blame for the fact that human beings often have bad backs, myopia, liability to cancer and heart disease?[43]

As Murray implies, there may be no obvious limit as to how far demons may go in manipulating objects within the universe or in the formation of the universe. But what is normally considered evidence for PK* is often those passages that envisage Satan and his cohorts doing extraordinary things. Thus, it is difficult if not impossible to disentangle a more benign PK* with an extraordinary one. To have PK* is just to have the ability to perform extraordinary, non-natural feats.

Now, I take it that the extent of this extraordinary power the demons have is not a settled opinion amongst all Christian thinkers. As such, we shall meticulously and carefully explore this subject in the remaining chapters that follow. For now, let us briefly consider what positive evidence there is for demonic PK* *simpliciter* if any at all.

---

43. Murray, *Nature Red in Tooth and Claw*, 103.

Part III: Ontological Matters
On the Probability of Psychokinesis

The reader should know that the next chapter, along with other chapters later in this book, are indeed mostly devoted to filling out a cumulative case against the idea that demons likely have PK*. In the next chapter in particular, I shall offer a positive, cumulative case for the notion that demons, in terms of other-interactive powers, only have the power of CI. Moreover, in further chapters, I shall in part be defending their exclusively having CI against any real or would-be objections based on Scripture and philosophical reflection. Here, I shall only mention some things by way of anticipation.

Now, it is no secret that Scripture in both the Old and New Testaments appears to report demons causing certain events in nature. For example, one kind of event that is sometimes attributed to demons is the deliberate onset of certain kinds of human illnesses. In Job 2.7, for example, we are told that Satan inflicted Job with skin lesions. If Satan did indeed cause such lesions, it is supposed that those lesions could have only come about by a matter-interacting ability that justifies how an immaterial being is able to directly manipulate Job's biochemistry. We are also told in Luke 13.11 that an unspecified demonic spirit caused a woman to be "bent double" for eighteen years. It would appear, based on this passage, that demons can apparently cause morphological changes in human beings. Thus, it has become commonplace to imagine that demons can psychokinetically interact with the physical materials of nature in order to wreak all manner of biological havoc. This is all part of the traditional PK* hypothesis–that a spirit is thought to directly interact with the physical world in creative ways wholly apart from any mental proxy (that is, beyond the reach of their CI).

Since there are a wide variety of passages enlisted to support demonic PK*, some of which can double as support some form of ontological (quasi-)materialism, I shall defer the reader to Part IV which treats Job 2, Luke 13, and the lot with some detail in showing there to be no positive scriptural reasons to think that demons cause such events psychokinetically. By way of summary of what is to come, I shall argue that either the events reported in those respective passages are misunderstood or that, when properly understood, they are (better?) accounted for in other ways–ways that do not appeal to powers outside of CI. I shall also interact with a series of would-be philosophical objections to my case against demonic PK* in chapter 12. For it may yet be that, despite Scripture, PK* is still a necessary power to assign to demons. But I shall establish that those objections do not lead one to assert a demonic PK* power. Thus, as a sort of promissory note being placed here, I am suggesting that neither Scripture nor philosophical reflection support the notion that demons have PK*. The immediate next chapter shall focus on a more positive case for why we should think that demons only have CI and do not have any ancillary PK* power with which to interact with this world.

So far we have surveyed reasons to think that demons might have two other-interacting powers: cognitive interaction (CI) and psychokinesis (PK*). We have explored support for CI which, for Christians in particular, is not a controversial notion. But the evidence for PK* is not as forthcoming as we shall see, for it is a subject that requires a considerable amount of meticulous attention.

Conclusion

It is one thing to establish the immateriality of a certain kind of person–in this case of *demons*–it is by far another thing to establish how they may interact with things and beings (especially other souls) embedded in this world. What makes this exploration challenging for both CI and PK* is the obvious metaphysical notion that their interactions cannot be based on a physical environment or a spatial trajectory indicative of common causal pathways. Spirits on their own just do not operate through space. Due to this challenge, some philosophers (like Jaegwon Kim) object to the metaphysical possibility that unembodied souls can even interact with each other much less with any objects substantively distinct from their own kind. I have argued that it is quite coherent to imagine how unembodied souls like demons could interact if such causal contact is had through the vehicle of cognitive interaction with other souls–souls that are of the same kind of substance. I then argued for the prior probability that demons would likely be expected to have this communicative power given that other souls like God, angels, and disembodied human beings commerce with each other according to a variety of biblical passages (a prior that is predicated on one's acceptance of scriptural testimony, of course). I also pointed out that there is scriptural support for the notion that specifically demons can commune with other souls whether these souls be embodied or not. This increases the overall probability that demons have CI given the addition of this posterior evidence.

I further discussed the traditional portrait of the demons's powers that are thought to extend beyond mere CI. According to the traditional view, demons are also capable of directly interacting with distinct material substances via the power of PK*. But as for the probability of demons having PK*, we have deferred this controversial issue to the next chapter and beyond. Hence, in the next chapter I shall present a positive cumulative argument showing that demons likely do not have a PK* ability. Though I do not have a principled objection to the possibility of demons having PK*, we shall see why we may expect that CI is, nonetheless, the *de facto* exclusive mechanism had by the purely immaterial demons. I shall then argue in Part IV that there is no reason to think demons have PK* since CI alone is actually sufficient to account for all of the biblical data on intra-worldly demonic interaction. We shall also see that no would-be philosophical objections lead us to think otherwise.

9

On the (Delimited) Powers of Demons (II)
The Exclusivity of Cognitive Interaction

The Argument for the Exclusivity of Cognitive Interaction in Demons

IN THIS CHAPTER, I shall build a case that demons do not likely have the ability to directly interact with or manipulate physical laws and objects. That is to say, it is here that I shall argue that the demons likely do not have the ancillary power of PK* even though, as we have seen, they do have the ability to cognitively interact with other souls (whether those souls are embodied or not). Accordingly, I shall present and defend the following argument that CI is the only other-interacting power that demons have:

1. That immaterial things can causally act on material things is initially improbable.
2. It is highly likely that one of the demons's powers is CI.
3. The good angels, from whom the demons derive, lack a PK* ability.
4. Therefore, the canonical data are what we should expect to find if CI is the exclusive power of demons.
5. In addition, the prospect of a creative power to generate diseases and perform miracles inappropriately attributes divine powers to demons.
6. Therefore, it is probably true that the only power demons have is CI.

This is a serial argument in that statements (1), (2), and (3) inductively lead to (4). And (4) is meant to be combined with a somewhat independent premise (5) which then converge on the overall conclusion (6). Let us now consider a defense of each statement.

On the (Delimited) Powers of Demons (II)

(1) The notion that immaterial things can causally act on material things has a low prior probability

It is customary for Christian thinkers in particular to consider soul-matter interaction to be a rather pervasive phenomenon in God's creation. For many posit not only that humans are instances of soul-matter interaction but that some animals, angels, and God himself are all spiritual beings that interact either with their own bodies (as in the case of humans and animals) or with something else that is physical (as in the case of angels and God). However, none of these thinkers believe that such interaction is due in any part to the substantial makeup of a spirit. For immaterial spirits and material objects have disparate and incommensurate natures. It is no wonder that early Christian philosophers and theologians insisted on demons being quasi-material. As for God's interacting with a physical world, recall what I had said in the introduction to chapter 8. There I pointed out that God's ability to interact with matter are not due to his being *spiritual*, rather they are due to his being *omnipotent*–an attribute no *created* spirit possesses. As for angels having an ability to interact with material objects, this will be addressed in premise (3) below. For there I argue that God is the only causal agent who manifests the angels in their various ways for all of their intra-worldly deeds and that they, therefore, do not interact with the world on their own accord.

Accordingly, a pure spirit's ability to interact with something physical is just not due to its being immaterial, for that would be counterintuitive. Instead, a pure spirit's ability to interact with something physical is better understood to be an endowed though native power in one's spirit as given by God. We have been identifying this all along as PK*. But a closer examination calls this addendum into question. For if human beings and (some) animals have spirits that interact with bodies, having PK* as a power native to spirits should entail that those spirits be able to interact with chunks of matter that are not just associated with that spirit's body. I am quite sure that I cannot move someone else's arm so as to be extended in the air or cause someone else's body to pirouette on demand. Neither can I move lamps, bend spoons, or levitate rocks with my spirit.[1] Perhaps we can import an explanation as given by parapsychologists, namely that PK* must be a *learned* power–one that is activated only after careful study and mastery. But this amounts to an attempted explanation as to why there is a particular absence of evidence for PK*. We are only entitled to consider the extent and further mechanics of PK* once we acquire any evidence *for* a soul's having PK*. As to its being a learned power, it is unclear why it is that one must have training in order to so much as activate this kind of mental activity. No other act of mentation requires this. For example, I do not need lessons on how to activate the

---

1. At this point, one may be tempted to consider the numerous claims of parapsychologists that (some) people have the power of psychokinesis and/or telekinesis. The legitimacy of those claims aside, a number of supporters of this phenomenon think such power is "special" or a "gift" and not something intrinsic to everyone's spirit. Stephen E. Braude thinks the research is insufficient to draw any conclusions either way. See his *ESP and Psychokinesis*, 5–6.

ability to move my right arm or how to emote. The operations of internal thought are immediate to me–judging, willing, believing, etc.–and do not need activation as such. Though the objects of those operations–ideas–may not be innate themselves, the operations surely are, even in the case of *involuntary* operations (like having a doxastic attitude about how conclusive some piece of evidence is). While acts of mentation can be sharpened or enhanced via education, it is odd to think that any native act of mentation can only be inaugurated by it.

Perhaps instead one might insist that though the power may indeed be activated at a spirit's creation, one's spirit nevertheless has *boundaries* or *limitations* on her PK* power. That is to say that one's spirit may only interact with one's own body and no one else's because one's body constitutes an essential part of one's identity. We can see such limitations in the analogous case of substance dualism. But this is still just another attempt at explaining away an absence of evidence when we are still attempting to determine if there is any reason to think PK* exists in souls at all. Never mind that. For if my spirit is limited in its power to act on only those bodies that are mine, then already we can see that substance dualism is not homogeneous with demonic PK* since in demonic PK* demons are not putatively interacting with bodies or things that are *theirs* (and, so, parts of the demons's identities). (I shall have more to say about the equating of demonic PK* with substance dualism in chapter 12.) Hence, it seems that the notion of an immaterial spirit having a PK* power finds no clear precedent in any would-be analogues. And that my spirit cannot act on just any chunk of matter is not only unsurprising, it is what we would expect if PK* is not native to immaterial spirits. That there is no direct relation between one's own spirit and any other object in the physical universe is firsthand evidence for oneself that spirits cannot naturally interact in that way. And that one would need to posit a PK* power at all with curious limitations puts the cart before the horse in assuming in advance that demons can directly interact with the physical world. But the verdict is still out on that, for we have yet to see any evidence that *any* immaterial spirit, much less a demon, can interact with physical objects on their own (at the exclusion of God, of course, who is omnipotent).

Let us now take a look at how our metaphysical intuitions in certain philosophical subdisciplines consistently bear this out, namely that we naturally expect that purely immaterial things do not, *ceteris paribus*, interact with material things.

In the philosophy of mind, one of the mainstay criticisms of particularly Cartesian-type models of anthropological substance dualism pertains to what is called the "pairing problem." In brief, one wonders just how it is that if a human person is in some sense a mind or spirit inhabiting a body, then it is a mystery how that mind or spirit interacts with and controls that body. Such concerns have fueled alternative models of substance dualism ranging from Aristotelian hylomorphism to Thomistic dualism to emergent dualism. Others have abandoned the prospect of a dualism altogether by opting for physicalist models of the human person. Why? Because it is inexplicable how an immaterial mind or spirit can interact with its body–a specific body and not any other body. This suggests that the hypothesis that a mind interacts with a body is not only not self-evident, it requires a burden of proof to justify how such a relation is feasible. *That* it happens is only a good answer if and only if some version of substance dualism is likely true. But it would undoubtedly be *sui generis*.

Consider an example from the philosophy of science. A number of scientists have at least a passing familiarity with the "weirdness" that is quantum mechanics. It is somewhat a rival model of the mechanics of the universe itself, or of the microcosm underlying the universe, to those of Newton and Einstein. Discoveries about how fundamental particles, or waves, can be in "superposition" (i.e., that the position and momentum of a particle is in all possible states or positions at once) give rise to speculations that either we know very little about the properties of fundamental particles or that reality consists of true uncertainties. The notion that particles can be in, say, two positions at once or in neither strikes us as absurd, for obviously no object of observation is in fact in two positions at once or in neither. Everyone seems to agree that neither of these competing quantum interpretations, nor those in between, ultimately satisfy our quest for how it is reality appears to be fixed and definite. This brings us to one novel attempt at explaining such a reality: the von Neumann model that consciousness creates reality.[2] The mathematician John von Neumann (1903 to 1957) offered a solution to the metaphysical problem of superposition by suggesting that a conscious observer is ultimately what "realizes" things or their dynamic attributes. The position of a particle is merely in potentiality but is given reality if and only if there is a conscious observer–a mind wholly distinct from any physical measuring apparatus–who "sees" the particle or object where it is. The details of von Neumann's model need not be elucidated here. It is only relevant to note that his model amounts to the notion that consciousness indeed gives rise to reality. The main criticism of his model is perhaps to be expected: that similar to that of the pairing problem, it is metaphysically abhorrent how something immaterial can affect anything material. Nick Herbert suggests that von Neumann's model of explaining reality in this way is an instance of assigning "magical properties to a mysterious and elusive event," viz., consciousness affecting reality.[3] Herbert's reaction is no doubt predicated on the metaphysical predilection (an *a priori* notion?) that we have been insisting on, namely that immaterial things do not naturally interact with material things without appealing to what Herbert could only call "magic."

Next, let us consider an example in the philosophy of metaphysics. Perhaps the most obvious example of a metaphysical problem from the ancient world is how Platonic forms *qua* universals can in any way interact with the particulars said to

2. This is a far more drastic model than that of the so-called Copenhagen interpretation wherein it is the presence of a measuring device that itself interacts with particles so as to "realize" its position and momentum (i.e., to collapse its wave-function). Von Neumann's model locates this "realization" or collapse to pure consciousness, for the measuring devices themselves are nothing special apart from the things they measure.

3. Herbert, *Quantum Reality*, 148.

participate in those universals. If some transcendent form called "chairness," for example, is what gives rise to there being individual chairs (or, that a chair is an instance of "chairness"), it is quite perplexing just how this is accomplished. That forms can act on or inform matter will require that there be an efficient cause–one not explained by the forms themselves, especially since not all forms have a material instantiation. Saying that some chunk of matter "participates" in a particular form is no more demystifying. Again, it is a challenge to Platonism, and certain other metaphysical theories to boot, how an immaterial thing can affect anything material without appealing to an efficient cause (like God or a Demiurge).

Thus, on the basis that one's own spirit does not interact with just any material objects at will, it is likely that purely immaterial things are naturally unable to interact with material things. The radically disparate natures of materiality and immateriality alone lead us to intuit this. Having granted that, one might then suppose that immaterial spirits have a native PK* power. But why think this other than as an *ad hoc* solution to the specific problem as to how demons can interact with the physical world? For it seems thus far that demons do not directly interact with the physical world. I grant that such a phenomenon is *possible*, for it is in the case of substance dualism, but it nevertheless has a low intrinsic probability in the unrelated cases of spirits interacting with physical objects that are not their own bodies.

Having given an *a priori* reason as setting the stage of the argument here, we now move on to the next premise (2) which reaffirms a conclusion that was already reached in the last chapter.

(2) It is highly likely that one of the demons' powers is CI

I must preface that by "powers" here I am delimiting such a reference to other-interacting powers, viz., the ability and extent of one causally interacting with something outside of oneself. Now, in our discussion in the previous chapter on the probability of CI, we looked at a list of biblical passages that entail that this kind of other-interacting powers exists. In those passages we looked specifically at how at least one of the soul-to-soul communicating parties is unembodied. These passages include 1 Sam 28.7–20, 1 Chron 21.1–2, Job 1.7–12, Neh 2.12, Luke 22.3–4 (cf., John 13.2, 27), John 16.13, Acts 5.3, Jude 9, and Rev 6.9–10. Some of these (1 Chron 21.1–2, Job 1.7–12, Acts 5.3, and Jude 9) involve demonic (viz., Satanic) spirits in particular, thus strengthening the case that demons *qua* immaterial spirits can cognitively interact with other souls whether those receiving souls are unembodied or not. It is unlikely that their mode of communication is verbal for two reasons. First, they are purely immaterial spirits and, so, if we do not assume in advance that they have certain psychokinetic powers, they would lack a natural power to cause auditory vibrations in our atmosphere (for the material and the immaterial are radically disparate, incommensurable natures). Second, the mode of communication in Acts 5.3 ("... why has Satan filled [*eplērōsen*] your heart ...") seems to pattern that of the Holy Spirit as seen in, e.g., Acts 4.31 ("... filled with [*eplēsthēsan*] the Holy Spirit..."). There may also be a possible connection to one of God's modes of communication as seen in Neh 2.12 ("... my God had put into my heart...") though the phrasing is certainly different from the ones in Acts and John 13.2.[4] However, the communication with one's heart, so to speak, is an interesting common thread in all of these references to such internal interaction.

Now, one may wonder, do not the angels implement apparitions and other manifestations for human percipients? Do they not interact with human beings in overtly physical ways? For these phenomena would entail PK* for the good angels. And if the angels do these things, and the demons derive from the angels, should we not expect that demons, too, would have such power? This naturally leads us to the next premise under consideration: that the good angels themselves likely lack such an ability.

(3) The good angels, from whom the demons derive, probably lack a PK* ability

It is commonplace to see the good angels as the archetypes for how one is to understand demons. I happen to think that this notion is a mistake since we cannot guarantee that God is not resourcing the angels with certain temporary provisions with which to carry out their various intra-worldly tasks.[5] And this impediment is in addition to our already limited ability to draw conclusions about the angelic nature. Yet we are not left to merely speculate about whether God leaves the angel to manifest in the world himself or whether God intervenes to manifest the angel on his behalf, since the Bible has a number of passages that explicitly credit God for such manifestations. For one, we have the account of Balaam's riding of his donkey and being blocked by an angelic presence in Num 22.26–31. Far from seeing angels enacting extraordinary acts potentially rivaling divine miracles, Numbers 22 tells us that it is God's interaction that made the simple task of being visible to percipients possible for the angel in question:

> ... the angel of the LORD went further, and stood in a narrow place where there was no way to turn to the right hand or the left. When the donkey saw the angel of the LORD, she lay down under Balaam; so Balaam was angry and struck the donkey with his stick. And the LORD opened the mouth of the donkey, and she said to Balaam, "What have I done to you, that you have struck me these three times?" Then Balaam said to the donkey, "Because you have made a mockery of me! If there had been a sword in my hand, I would

---

4. John 13.2 has *beblēkotos eis tēn kardian* ("[having] put into the heart") whereas Nehemiah (LXX) has *didōsin eis kardian mou* ("[had] put/given into my heart").

5. We do not know what angels could theoretically do apart from God's influence because, as David Keck aptly notes, "it is impossible to see an angel in its natural condition or to observe an angel's cognitive processes at work" (*Angels and Angelology*, 75).

have killed you by now." And the donkey said to Balaam, "Am I not your donkey on which you have ridden all your life to this day? Have I ever been accustomed to do so to you?" And he said, "No." *Then the LORD opened the eyes of Balaam, and he saw the angel of the LORD standing in the way with his drawn sword in his hand*; and he bowed all the way to the ground.[6]

The author of this account surely credits the Lord as the sole cause of Balaam's seeing of the angelic presence impeding his journey.[7] In another passage, one from the New Testament, the author of Revelation gives the following account to his readers regarding a specific occasion where four apocalyptic angels of judgment are instructed by a fifth angel to inflict global disaster:

> Then I saw another angel ascending from the rising of the sun, with the seal of the living God, and he called with a loud voice to the four *angels who had been given power to harm earth and sea*, saying, "Do not harm the earth or the sea or the trees, until we have sealed the servants of our God on their foreheads."[8]

Observable activities of the angels–in this case their interaction with the material world–are also caused by God as the occasion demands. Since angels are consistently declared to be dispatched and resourced by God,[9] few conclusions can be drawn about what angels can do on their own.

---

6. Emphasis mine. Many Old Testament scholars challenge this story as merely incorporating the device of fable as seen in Egyptian and Assyrian writings around the same time. Given the obvious linguistic ties to the phrase "the LORD opened the eyes of Balaam" of verse 31 as it mirrors verse 28's "the LORD opened the mouth of the donkey"—where the latter is the sort of thing we might find in the genre of fable–one might conclude that the account is anything but historical. I am not interested in entering into that dispute here, but suffice it to say that our concern is merely with the well-established fact that the account credits God as the sole and singular cause of both the donkey's speech and the angelic manifestation. This is enough to support my present concern.

7. Another biblical account seems to offer up a similar example of God's making visible some aggregate of invisible beings:
> When the servant of the man of God rose early in the morning and went out, behold, an army with horses and chariots was all around the city. And the servant said, "Alas, my master! What shall we do?" He said, "Do not be afraid, for those who are with us are more than those who are with them." Then Elisha prayed and said, "O LORD, please open his eyes that he may see." So the LORD opened the eyes of the young man, and he saw, and behold, the mountain was full of horses and chariots of fire all around Elisha (2 Kgs 6.15–17).

It is unclear whether the "horses and chariots" that Elisha requested to be made visible are, in fact, *angelic* manifestations, but nonetheless the account serves to independently confirm an additional *explicit* reference to God's making some person see what is otherwise imperceptible. Most biblical apparition stories of one sort or another lack any such qualifier.

8. Rev 7.2–3; emphasis mine. Blount writes of this episode that the angelic power "was not something the angels acquired on their own; it was given (*edothē*) to them by God" (Blount, *Revelation*, 141).

9. See Ps 91.11 (cf., Matt 4.6; Luke 4.10); Matt 13.41; 24.30–31; 26.53; 2 Thess 1.7; 1 Tim 5.21; Heb 1.7; 1 Pet 3.21–22; Rev 16.1.

On the (Delimited) Powers of Demons (II)

Additionally, how the angelic community *communicates* to human intelligences (whether through a mere visionary encounter[10] or a direct, corporeal visitation[11]) will also fall under the same difficulty (after all, as was pointed out in the previous piece of evidence, it is the case that the Bible often reports angel-human interaction). We are also told in Numbers 22 that the same Lord who "opened the eyes of Balaam" to see the angel also "opened the mouth of the donkey" (v. 28) to speak. It seems to me that God has causally but temporarily manifested the angelic beings on their behalf–as the present cases suggest–so that they should be visible to and interactive with residents of this world. This would mean that any angelic manifestations in and with the physical world are divinely resourced, presumably in order that they may carry out their ministerial functions on behalf of God.

Thus, if angels must rely on God's power for manifesting, then this implies that they lack any such intrinsic power of their own. What is now evidently true of the angels–that they owe their manifestability to God's direct interaction and not to some power intrinsic to their nature–is *a fortiori* true of the demons. It would be an awkward leg to stand on to affirm that demons are intrinsically endowed with PK* but the angels are devoid of such power. It is simpler to affirm that demons, as with the angels, have no ability to manifest on their own.

This assessment of the scriptural data reveals that there is no explanatory need thus far to attribute to a created spirit–albeit angel or demon–a PK* ability.[12] But if spirits in general were to engage in behavior thought impossible for immaterial spirits unless aided by God, we should just think that God has made it possible for such behavior and not that such a spirit possesses that gifted ability itself. If one already acknowledges that God exists in the way classical theism portrays, it is *easier* to attribute such extraordinary behavior to the hand of God. To illustrate the force of this point, consider how the Bible occasionally affirms that human beings are capable of certain extraordinary feats like miracles.[13] If we were unaware of any specific passages that stipulated that God grants such powers to human beings (e.g., Acts 14.3), I highly doubt that one might conclude that healing powers, miracles, and such were actually the standalone results of the intrinsic powers of first-century human beings themselves. We would naturally opt for such acts to be the products of the agency of God because of who he is. And positing special, unique powers intrinsic to humanity during, but only during, this time would be exceedingly unnecessary. Thus Occam's Razor shaves off, so to speak, the unnecessary hypothesis that a finite creature can

---

10. Some clear examples of visionary encounters with angels are reported in Luke 24.23 and Acts 10.3. I discussed both visionary encounters and corporeal visitations in the last chapter.

11. Some clear examples of corporeal visitations of angels appear in Gen 19.1–3 and Heb 13.2.

12. I remind the reader that we have yet to explore whether there may still be passages unaddressed that betray a PK* power in the case of demons in particular, and this I will do in the upcoming Section IV. Here, I merely submit that no passages imply such a power.

13. I.e., Mark 16.17–18; Acts 2.1–4; 3.1–10; 5.16; 8.7; 28.8–9; James 5.16;

perform an action that is impossible for it given the nature it has. Even today, given the relevant theological backdrop of a believer in today's world, one might be quicker to affirm some supernatural occurrence as an act of *God's* doing rather than as the result of a special, this-worldly PK* force. If a deceased man suddenly burst from his grave and began singing, I am quite sure we would not think that this person was particularly gifted with a PK* power to cause such a self-animated revivification. We would more likely think God, or some outside force, had performed that miracle before our eyes (and ears). And when we consider how disembodied human persons are reported in the Bible to appear and interact with living persons,[14] I submit that we would be inclined to think that God is responsible for such intra-worldly activity and that disembodied persons are not specially endowed with the power to make themselves manifest.

It is true that reports of hauntings and poltergeists throughout history have left people imagining that immaterial spirits have some sort of intrinsic PK* ability to affect the senses of others and to move physical objects (as well as make sounds and manipulate environmental conditions) apart from divine intervention–particularly if those spirits are thought to be demons. But interpreters of such manifestations, if they genuinely occur at all, may just be guilty of wild speculation similar to interpreters of *biblical* demonology.[15] Such counterexamples uncritically assume that the data are, at the outset, unquestionably real. Even so, such occurrences would only mean that believers in hauntings would need to reconsider their *interpretation* of such things (perhaps as naturally induced hallucinations or divine acts of God) and not the occurrences of the haunting experiences themselves.[16] If our natural disposition is to attribute all acts of extraordinary ability to God and that, additionally, we were to lack any data (whether dubious or probable) that cannot already be accounted for by the uncontested use of some other already-granted power, then why should we posit any sort of extraneous PK* ability? This cannot be seen as anything but an *ad hoc* maneuver. We just lack sufficient data that would require us to have to look beyond CI for answers. Thus the simpler view is that demons only have the ability to cognitively interact with others. And this is supported here by the fact that it is God who acts on the good angels's behalf in order to manifest them in the ways Scripture indicates.

---

14. I.e., 1 Sam 28.11–19; Matt 17.3–8.

15. Uncritically pushing for a special power in order to account for putative demonological behavior strikes me as something of a *deus ex machina* plot device often found in ancient Greek tragedy plays. Nobody wants to say that it *cannot* happen, but it is explanatorily *ad hoc* to suppose that it *did* happen.

16. I dealt with this point at length in a slightly different context in chapter 12.

On the (Delimited) Powers of Demons (II)

(4) Therefore, the canonical data are what we should expect to find if CI is the exclusive power of demons

C. S. Peirce suggested that what makes a preferred explanation for some specific, relevant evidence is the fact that if the hypothesis were true, we would not be surprised to find such evidence than we would otherwise be without it.[17] As part of a greater dialectic against demonic PK*, the canon we have (viz., the specific evidence of the biblical record regarding Satan and the demons and also of the good angels) is exactly what we would expect to find if demons had the ability to cognitively interact with other souls (embodied or not) and *lack* a PK* power. That Satan and the demons are consistently said to interact cognitively, that any physiological disturbances in victims of maladies are consonant with psychologically-based etiologies, and that demons never interact with this world except through living human proxies, all strike me as the kinds of data one would expect if CI is the exclusive means through which demons commerce with the world. But if Satan and the demons were to have a PK* power, then the hypothesis would be most conducive to any facts that entailed that Satan and the demons frequently manifest themselves, create multiple organisms, and bring about various physical disturbances (viz., the kinds of events that would be inexplicable by mere appeal to CI). The apparitions and corporeal visitations of humans, angels, and God are sometimes described in Scripture even if symbolically (e.g., 1 Sam 28.14, Ezek 10.8–14, and 43.2, respectively). But I submit that no such descriptions, symbolic or otherwise, appear in reference to Satan or any other demon. We might even expect to find certain common expressions used to refer to audible expressions of Satan and the demons as we do with God, angels, and human beings (i.e., "hear the voice of," "he spoke unto them," and "the sound of"). Yet none exist. In order to save the PK* theory from the awkwardness of such silence, one must insist that the demons have either been largely restrained by God from manifesting or have chosen to restrain themselves. Traditional demonic realists are likely to account for this by supposing that God has so restrained the demons's causal activity that this is why we have scant occurrences of intra-worldly activity apart from CI. In the Bible, God explicitly delimits the activity of Satan as seen in Job 1.10, 2.6, Matt 12.27–29 (Mark 3.26–27), Mark 1.34, and Revelation 20.2 despite his penchant for predatory behavior.[18] If there were even just a few references to scenarios that were best defined as acts of PK* manipulation, then accepting the hypothesis of demonic PK* would make sense. However, I say, it is not that we have just a *few* references best explained by appeal to a PK* power, it is that we have *no references whatsoever* to which to make such an appeal.

Could my contention just be an argument from silence (viz., an appeal to an absence of evidence)? In other words, am I merely making my case based on the idea

---

17. Peirce, "Pragmatism as the Logic of Abduction," 231.
18. 1 Pet 5.8.

that there is a lack of evidence for any of the alleged manifestations attributed to Satan and the demons? While it is true that I cannot say that demons do not have a PK* power *simply because* we lack the specific scriptural facts noted above if they did, it is but one part of the larger case against demonic PK* that I am offering. Otherwise, what is to prevent us from positing *any* power that demons might have only to complain that any lack of specific evidence of certain phenomena hardly counts as a refutation? Suppose that we allege that demons can burn down houses, freeze lakes, manufacture land masses, form galaxies, or fashion new universes. It seems reasonable to suppose that there would be reports of some demons being responsible for burned houses, frozen lakes, etc., on which to help support such powers. If we were to not take the silence of the Bible seriously wherein these reports do not exist, that the Bible were to be silent on such matters would end up being strangely unimportant.[19] It seems reasonable that in order to have warrant for supposing that demons have any kind of power, we should always have positive reasons to do so. And since there appears to be no such reason to do so, with an absence of particular evidence as added confirmation of that, then there is no reason to stipulate an *ad hoc* supposition that demons do have a PK* power but are, say, being restricted by God or by their own wills from actually using it. That they simply do not have such abilities is much simpler to affirm. And that the Bible lacks any reports of any extramental manifestations of the sorts mentioned because demons cannot do so seems a more natural conclusion.

Thus, that one might expect there to be some biblical reports of manifestations if demons have a PK* ability suggests that any absence of such evidence makes the hypothesis less probable. Therefore, the claim that CI is the exclusive vehicle of demonic commerce with this world is more in keeping with the content of the scriptural canon.

(5) In addition, the prospect of a creative power to generate diseases and perform miracles inappropriately attributes divine powers to demons

There is one thing that all scholars of demonology operating within the Christian tradition will affirm, namely, that one should avoid taking attributes that belong solely to God and applying them to God's archenemies, the demons. This may have been one of the motivating reasons for Augustine's post-conversion resistance to Manichaeism.[20]

---

19. One could perhaps offer up an *ad hoc* explanation here and surmise that God merely has forbidden such activities from taking place; thus, it is not unexpected that there be no reports of such demonic activities. But the implications here are too costly. As Yonatan Fishman explains: "it is possible to devise ad hoc explanations for the absence of evidence or the disconfirming of the supernatural that would render supernatural claims immune to falsification. However, if such a strategy is permissible, then mundane claims involving natural phenomena are not falsifiable either, as one can always invent an ad hoc hypothesis to explain away any observation or the outcome of any experimental test" ("Can Science Test Supernatural Worldviews?," 178).

20. According to Inta Ivanovska, Augustine himself, while in Cassiciacum, "tried to 'demythologize' what might be considered the miraculous aspects of demonic activity in order to safeguard against their claim to divine power and divine knowledge" ("The Demonology of St. Augustine of Hippo," 64).

On the (Delimited) Powers of Demons (II)

When we consider the kinds of PK* powers thought to be had by demons, it is almost unanimous that such powers involve the extraordinary. That is to say, the reason why PK* is invoked as a power had by the demons is due to the biblical reports that demons can and do generate or stimulate diseases in people, manufacture bodies (or body parts) for the purposes of facilitating apparitions and manifestations, and generally performing "signs and wonders." It is clear that the PK* of demons is not merely the ability to move upon objects. By supposing that demons can do these things obviously implies their ability to interact with the physical world but in even more extraordinary ways. As noted in the previous chapter, it is difficult if not impossible to disentangle a PK* *simpliciter* from this level of PK*, for it is instances of the latter that constitute much of the evidence for PK* in demons at all (a point that will be supported below).

But this seems to tread dangerously on creative prerogatives that are thought to be exclusive to God. In order to generate anything from a tumor to a hominid, it would appear that the demon would not only possess a PK* gift that enables them to interact with matter but a gift capable of *creating newly functioning* things that not even embodied persons can accomplish. Demons would not just be manipulating raw materials, but they would be (instantaneously?) converting raw material into flourishing organisms (i.e., viruses, bacteria, and parasites) or into full-blown organic hominids (i.e., tangible apparitions). In short, if such putative phenomena are legitimate occurrences in nature, it would appear that demons can act as supernatural creators. This would seem to contravene King David's declaration: "There is none like you among the gods, O Lord, nor are there any works like yours" (Psalm 86.8). And despite much of the past consisting of these putative creations by demons, Paul assures the Colossians that "by [God through Jesus] all things were created, in heaven and on earth, visible and invisible, whether thrones or dominions or rulers or authorities--all things were created through him and for him" (Col 1.16). Though God himself is supposed to be, according to orthodoxy, the ultimate creator (either directly or indirectly) of every concrete thing,[21] traditionalists in demonology may quickly blunt this concern by emphasizing that God is a creator *ex nihilo* ("out of nothing") whereas demons are merely *craftsmen* with sufficient power to manipulate pre-existing matter and energy, viz., creators *ex materia* ("out of [pre-existing] material").[22] Thomas Aquinas explains that

> by [the demons'] natural power they can produce as art produces things, those effects only that result from the natural forces contained in bodies, which obey them in respect of local movement; and thus they can employ them in producing an effect in a very short time. Now by means of these powers it is possible for bodies to undergo real transformation: inasmuch as in the natural course one thing is generated from another. . . . Accordingly demons can

---

21. Jer 10.10–11; 1 Cor 8.5–6.

22. For a thorough discussion as to the distinction between these two kinds of creators (as well as a philosophico-theological defense of God as one who creates *ex nihilo*), see Craig and Copan, *Creation out of Nothing* and Craig and Copan, "Craftsman or Creator?"

work wonders in us in two ways first by means of real bodily transformation: secondly by disturbing the imagination so as to delude the senses. But neither of these works is miraculous but is like the work of a craftsman.[23]

How much different a disease in the body or an apparition in the air? Could these not be the results of a craftsman of the kind envisioned?

Surely demons would not be creators *ex nihilo*, but there is something yet unsettling about the demons's supposed ability to engage in "real bodily transformation" if they can craft fully functioning organisms like diseases or talking serpents. Traditional demonic realists infer specific abilities of Satan according to passages like Exodus 7 where Satan is thought to empower Pharaoh's high priests to cause the turning of staffs into snakes, the generating of frogs upon the land, and the converting of rivers into blood. These would not only be extraordinary acts of abiogenesis, they would be extravagant acts (at least in some cases) of creating *fully realized* organisms. And if poor Job (Job 2.7) were stricken with leprosy (a condition brought on by the introduction of a specific bacterium), any dermatological symptoms would have to have been accelerated beyond normal physical mechanisms.[24] But even more troubling is the changing of a staff into a snake and the saturation of the Nile with blood, both which would involve a miraculous transformation of inorganic matter into organic matter–even to the extent of creating a living organism (assuming, of course, that all such events are not acts of mere trickery). And if these feats are achievable, one wonders why Satan could not resurrect a body or create human life altogether. At the very least, Satan *could* do these things even if he were forbidden by God from doing so. And such an ability would appear to be virtually indistinguishable from the heresy of Manichaeism. Thus the proponent of demonic craftsmanship is saddled with the burden of explaining why God would have empowered demons with or has permitted them the ability to perform such extraordinary PK* feats if the powers are essentially indistinguishable from divine miracles (that is, distinguishable apart from the motives of the miracle-working agent).

Aquinas once argued that "if the demons whose whole will is diverted to evil, were to receive the power to work miracles, God would vouch for their falsehood, which is repugnant to his goodness."[25] Centuries later, William Fleetwood argued in a different way by pointing to the concern that it would confound the very concept of miracle. He made his point by challenging those who believe that Satan can do such extraordinary feats to

---

23. Aquinas, *De Potentia Dei*, VI.5: 185.

24. Leprosy has "a long incubation period (2–11 years)" (Lockwood and Reid, "The Diagnosis of Leprosy is Delayed in the United Kingdom," 207). While it is not impossible to suppose that Job had a two-year break before any skin eruptions obtained, it contravenes the immediate succession of Satan's departure from his conversation with God to the visible manifestation of the skin lesions which obtain as if the events occur seamlessly one after another (cf., Job 2.7).

25. Aquinas, *De Potentia Dei*, VI.5: 185.

> shew me what difference there is betwixt God and the Devil, in respect to Miracles: and how I shall know which of them acts; or if this cannot be shewn, (as I doubt it much) then we must be to seek of what Use Miracles can be; and I think you will find them to be of none at all.[26]

If the purpose of miracles is to confirm God's revealed truth in a given situation, then, as Fleetwood cautions, the epistemic indistinguishability of divine miracles from diabolical ones from without will have forced the miracle to lose its evidential impact. In other words, the very purpose of employing a miracle gets compromised.

There were two responses that were offered by contemporaries of Fleetwood. First, in a letter responding to Fleetwood directly, Benjamin Hoadly (1676 to 1761) argued that "there may be so plain and evident a *distinction* made" between divine and diabolical miracles "if there be *greater*, and *more, Miracles* on one side than the other."[27] Hoadly presses the point that there is a qualitative distinction, for "some *Miracles* are *greater* than others." Second, Samuel Clarke (1675 to 1729) argued that a distinction could be made on the basis of doctrinal infidelity. He writes: "If the doctrine attested by miracles be in itself *impious*, or manifestly *tending to promote vice*, then, without all question, the miracles, how great soever they may appear to us, are neither worked by God himself, nor by his commission."[28] However, in the event that this cannot be determined, Clarke defaults back to the aforementioned means of distinguishing:

> *If* the Doctrine attested by Miracles, be in itself indifferent, that is, such as cannot by the Light of Nature and right Reason alone, be certainly known whether it be true or false; and at the same time, in opposition to it, and in proof of the direct contrary Doctrine, there be worked other Miracles, more and greater than the former, or at least attended with such Circumstances, as evidently show the Power by which these latter are worked, to be superiour to the Power that worked the former; then That Doctrine which is attested by the *Superiour Power*, must necessarily be believed to be Divine.[29]

I submit that neither of these responses are very satisfactory. Let us consider the first posed criterion for determining an authentic miracle: the contradistinction between two or more miracles. Such a criterion predicates the identity of a miracle as divine or diabolical solely on the basis of an outside observer's ability to discern the superior power. This puts that outside observer in an awkward position. For the boundaries in which a miracle is deemed diabolical or divine are set, not by any static standard of measurement, but by its always being weighed against a different miracle. While certainly not impossible to do in some circumstances, it would clearly be problematic unless the two (or more) miracles in question squared off with each on the

---

26. Fleetwood, *An Essay Upon Miracles*, 91.
27. Hoadly, *A Letter to the Reverend Mr. Fleetwood*, 8.
28. Clarke, *A Discourse Concerning the Being and Attributes of God*, 382.
29. Clarke, *A Discourse Concerning the Being and Attributes of God*, 382.

same occasion or in temporal proximity. To wit, the miracles must obtain somewhat concurrently and in direct competition with each other–sort of like a Wild-West-style duel that determines which miracle one can attribute to God. (The faceoff between Moses and the Pharaoh's magicians in Exod 7.7–12 springs to mind.) Even so, two properly *divine* miracles could easily be contrasted with each other (e.g., Is not Jesus's resurrection far more impressive than Elijah's calling fire down from heaven?). But the awe-inspiring gravity of one over the other hardly implies that one is diabolical and the other not.

Moreover, such a criterion is predicated on the limited epistemic domain of a particular outside observer. For example, consider a diabolical act that could have been executed so ingeniously so as to give rise to an event that parallels the most impressive divine miracle. Suppose Satan, in a minor act of PK*, simply infused a false prophet with a particular substance (tetrodotoxin?) that perhaps can, let us suppose, mimic the symptoms of death for a number of days. Upon the person's "post-mortem" burial and a subsequent revival, the false prophet could proclaim a resurrection. Just how is an outside observer supposed to know on the sole basis of contradistinction with "lesser" miracles that this act was diabolical? Would this diabolical "resurrection" not appear to be superior to Jesus's turning water into wine? Imagine that this false prophet performed this feat at the wedding feast of Cana–on the occasion of Jesus's turning water into wine (cf. John 2.1–11). Surely the false prophet's "resurrection" would easily be construed by outsiders as outperforming Jesus's luxury miracle which could be used to demonize Jesus in front of his family and friends. How ironic! It is no wonder that preternatural outperformance is never employed biblically as a means of miracle identification.[30]

The second criterion–doctrinal fidelity–would not suffer from these challenges, for no competing miracles need obtain in adjudicating a true miracle.[31] Any would-be miracle could be assessed purely by observing the miracle-wielder's teachings that ac-

---

30. The "showdown" at Mount Carmel in 1 Kgs 18.15–39 is not a counterexample, for the prophets of Baal do not manage any kind of miracle despite their best efforts (vv. 26 and 29). God's miracle of burning up the sacrifice drenched in water is not contrasted with any counter-miracle. It is contrasted with there being no action by the gods of this world whatsoever.

31. It has been suggested that doctrinal fidelity is an established criterion in Torah for determining which miracles are God's or not in its test of a false prophet:
> If a prophet or a dreamer of dreams arises among you and gives you a sign or a wonder, and the sign or wonder that he tells you comes to pass, and if he says, 'Let us go after other gods,' which you have not known, 'and let us serve them,' you shall not listen to the words of that prophet or that dreamer of dreams" (Deut 13.1–3; cf., Mark 13.21–22).

But the "sign or a wonder" envisaged here is not a PK*-based preternatural act but, rather, a *prophecy that has failed to come true* ("the sign or wonder *that he tells you* comes to pass"). That prophetic failure and not the preternatural manipulation of nature is in view seems right when compared with a similar warning that appears five chapters later: "[W]hen a prophet speaks in the name of the LORD, *if the word does not come to pass or come true*, that is a word that the LORD has not spoken; the prophet has spoken it presumptuously" (18.22; emphasis mine). And this kind of binary test is certainly a sensible one.

company it. However, there remain undue demands on the observer in that she must have access to all of the available theological canons by which to expose doctrinal vice and heresy. Consider that it was on the very grounds of doctrinal deviance that the Jews made their case that Jesus was operating by the power of Satan (e.g., Matt 12.2, 22–24). This illustrates that the outside observer must also be keen to discern between deviant, conflicting revelation and legitimate, progressive revelation that only *appears* to conflict with previously established doctrines. In fact, citing doctrine to validate the miracle has things quite backwards. In the case of Jesus, it was actually his miracles that authenticated his message, not the reverse (John 4.48; 10.37–38; Acts 2.22). If doctrinal deviance becomes a test for sorting out diabolical miracles from divine ones, then the circle becomes unacceptably vicious: miracles provide the validation of the doctrine, but it is the doctrine that provides the validation of the miracle. By punting to doctrinal fidelity as the test for a miracle, then what remains the use of the miracle? The nineteenth-century philosopher Robert William Mackay reveals the awkwardness latent here:

> A certain doctrine is offered for acceptance; a miracle wrought to prove its truth. But we are now told that the miracle is no satisfactory proof at all; it may be a diabolical miracle . . . ; only when I am already convinced of the soundness of the doctrine can I admit the genuineness of the miracle. But then what is the use of the miracle? We are answered that it is for the purpose of determining the character of the performer as a divine messenger. But then why should God employ a mode of attestation confessedly liable to so awful a mistake? especially when the only use of so attesting the nature of the performer is to guarantee the authenticity of a message already accredited and guaranteed before these precarious credentials are presented.[32]

Moreover, can we really say that some–indeed *most*–alleged diabolical miracles are accompanied by doctrinal deviance at all? If, as a number of Christians surmise, demons are responsible for menial things like ghostly apparitions, poltergeist behavior, transmutations, and other magical feats all unaccompanied by doctrinal pronouncements or dogmatic commitments, then these could not in principle be determined to be diabolical. That demons sometimes profess things that are *true* (e.g., "[Jesus is] Son of the Most High God"; Mark 5.7) is further reason to think little of this criterion. In fact, if it served the diabolical spirit well, why not perform the miracle with the accompaniment of a true saying first and then, after time has passed and he has won the trust of his flock, proceed to spoon-feed them with heresy? That an evil spirit should articulate an overtly and discernibly false doctrine in the wake of a diabolical miracle seems rather cretinous for a being that is supposed to be endowed with a higher level of intelligence.

---

32. Mackay, *The Tübingen School and Its Antecedents*, 385.

The Gospel of John gives a different impression that is worth noting. It implies in various dialogues that *only* God's chosen can enact miracles. For example, when Nicodemus confronts Jesus one night, he confesses that "we know that you are a teacher come from God, for *no one can do these signs that you do unless God is with him*" (John 3.2; emphasis mine). In 9.16, while some Pharisees repudiate Jesus for his doctrinal deviance, others nonetheless query about his miracles: "How can a man who is a sinner do such signs?" Such a question implies that wrong-doers *cannot do these kinds of things*, and, so, it explains why some inevitably demur from their fellow Pharisees. As such, the confession being backed by Jesus's signs implies that he is no sinner. However, if miracles serve exclusively as divine endorsements because only God can perform them, then the vicious circle is broken and miracles serve their intended purpose.[33]

Therefore, given the *de facto* evidence that only God acts in this way along with Aquinas's contention that God would not be an accomplice to the demons's physical shenanigans, it seems more likely that a PK* ability to interact with matter to the extent of creating fully functioning diseases, animals, and the lot on demand is the sole preserve of God. Moreover, the problems of distinguishing divine from diabolical miracles add acute epistemic problems regarding the identification of miracles, which flies in the face of what miracles are supposed to do in serving as "signs." Thus, any expectation that demons would have this kind of PK* power–one that implies an extraordinary power to boot–is significantly lowered if not completely squashed.

Therefore, (1)–(5) ultimately support (6) which, as the conclusion, states that it is probable that the only power demons have is CI. Though this is an inductive argument and one that does not deliver a necessarily true conclusion, one cannot avoid force of the preponderance of evidence that mitigates against the notion that demons have PK*.

Conclusion

I argued that while demons have the other-interacting (communicative) ability of CI, they do not have a PK* ability. I supported this conclusion by defending a six-step argument based on our metaphysical intuitions along with three key pieces of evidence. These evidences include the following: (i) that the Bible offers *a posteriori* support for CI; (ii) that the good angels's (from whence the demons derive) apparent creative powers are likely the result of God's direct intervention, not as the result of a PK* power inherent to them; and (iii) that the prospect of a creative power to generate diseases and perform miracles inappropriately attributes divine powers to demons.

33. There was a third response offered by Hoadly, but his comments pertain only to Fleetwood's apparent acknowledgment that the good angels indeed have such a power: "That these [evil] Spirits had an *inherent Power*, before their Fall, of doing some *Works*, which you your self acknowledge to be truly *Miracles*, to me is past doubt: And I'm sure I may say, no one can prove that their *inherent Power*, or *Knowledge*, is dimish'd since their Fall" (*A Letter to the Reverend Mr. Fleetwood*, 6). As my support for premise 3 above demonstrates, this is not a problem for me since, as I argue, neither do the good angels have such "inherent Power."

I argued that Occam's Razor eliminates the addition of an inherent PK* power in demons and that the canonical texts are what we should expect to find if CI is the exclusive mechanism demons utilize for their activity in the world. As such, when it comes to other-interacting powers, the demons only have the causal power of CI because it is the simpler explanation and one that accords better with the totality of scriptural evidence and philosophical reflection.

Now, I remind the reader that there are scriptural passages and some philosophical would-be objections pending that might yet controvert this conclusion. It is something that the previous chapter also anticipated as a possibility. Without disputing the notion that demons interact with this world *simpliciter*, we need a satisfactory account of how Satan and his demons can be said to cause the things attributed to them as reported in Scripture. For example, we know that demons are reported to sometimes cause certain maladies in people. But how does a proponent of the CI-only view of the demons's other-interacting abilities accommodate and/or explain such data? Since there is much territory to cover both in Scripture and in any would-be philosophical push-back, I have devoted the next Part to dealing with both kinds of objections in turn.

Part IV

Objections

"[O]bjections built on popular notions and prejudices, are easily conveyed to the mind in few words; and so conveyed, make strong impressions: but whoever answers the objections, must encounter all the notions to which they are allied, and to which they owe their strength; and it is well with many words he can find admittance."

—Thomas Sherlock, *The Trial of the Witnesses of the Resurrection of Jesus* (1800)

10

Objections Based on Passages in the Old Testament

THE ARGUMENTS OF THE previous Part focused on building a case for how to understand the metaphysics of Satan and his demons. I first offered a strong cumulative case for the pure immateriality of demons as the best explanation of their ontology. I then argued that their power to affect others is exclusively through the vehicle of cognitive interaction (or ECI). Consequently, demons do not have an ancillary power like psychokinesis (or PK*). However, despite this positive case, (quasi-)materialism and/or PK* may yet prevail in ways other than what has been addressed. We turn to those remaining ways by focusing on a variety of specific objections in the current section. Over the course of the next few chapters, we shall explore and assess two primary categories of objections that are or can be levelled against either the pure immateriality of the demons or the truth of ECI. The first two chapters (10 and 11) shall consist of theological objections–objections from Scripture that allegedly imply either a (quasi-)material nature or a PK* ability. The third chapter that follows (12) shall consist of principled philosophical objections and push-back that do or could arise in attempts to undermine the conclusions for which I have argued.

Let us set the stage by briefly observing how contemporaries envision the kinds of abilities Satan and his cohorts can and do facilitate in this world apart from CI. C. Samuel Storms opines that "demons can appear to us in various forms, both spiritual and physical."[1] Sometimes such apparitions are even considered graphic. C. Fred Dickason, for example, specifies that when "Scripture records their appearance, they assume hideous and fearsome forms like animals" and that this is due to their having a "supernatural power."[2] But if demons do have or can manifest tangible properties of any sort, then such apparitions or manifestations would seem to support, at least initially, either a (quasi-)material constitution (for matter is a sensible and tangible substance) or, as Dickason hints at, a PK* power sufficient to create such

1. Storms, *Tough Topics*, 157.
2. Dickason, *Angels*, 176–77.

a constitution on demand. Therefore, I take it that such scriptural data that include references to anything like demonic appearances, embodied incarnations, or physical manifestations of any other sort, constitute reasonable counterexamples–no matter how strong or weak–to the views I have defended.

In this chapter, we shall consider key passages only in the Old Testament that appear to imply either apparitions or manifestations of a sort that would give credence to the notions of (quasi-)materialism or a PK* ability. We shall further explore passages in the New Testament in the chapter that follows.

The Serpent's Tempting of Eve in the Garden of Eden in Gen 3.1–6 Is Likely an Instance of an Apparition of Satan

In Gen 3.1–6, the author(s) communicate the initial conditions under which sin originally entered the world.[3] The account begins with the appearance of a serpent in the Garden of Eden which then beguiles Eve into eating the forbidden fruit. The passage reads in context:

> Now the serpent was more crafty than any beast of the field which the LORD God had made. And he said to the woman, "Indeed, has God said, 'You shall not eat from any tree of the garden'?" And the woman said to the serpent, "From the fruit of the trees of the garden we may eat; but from the fruit of the tree which is in the middle of the garden, God has said, 'You shall not eat from it or touch it, lest you die.'" And the serpent said to the woman, "You surely shall not die! "For God knows that in the day you eat from it your eyes will be opened, and you will be like God, knowing good and evil." When the woman saw that the tree was good for food, and that it was a delight to the eyes, and that the tree was desirable to make *one* wise, she took from its fruit and ate; and she gave also to her husband with her, and he ate.

Marvin E. Tate reports (based on this familiar narrative about the temptation of Eve by "the serpent" and the subsequent Rabbinic thoughts that had developed) that it is "not surprising that a long line of Christian explanation takes the serpent as Satan in disguise."[4] Indeed, Genesis 3 might serve as an interesting example of how demons (if indeed "the serpent" represents either a demon or Satan himself) manifest in a tangible, visible, and even audible way. But just how is one to understand this dramatic portrayal of a bizarre dialogue involving a (presumably literal) talking serpent? One

---

3. It is in vogue amongst Old Testament scholars to assert what is called the Documentary Hypothesis in that Genesis (and the rest of the Pentateuch) was authored by a community of Israelites over time (commonly differentiated by the Jahwist, Elohist, Priestly, and Deuteronomic traditions). For a thorough treatment of the background and development of the hypothesis (along with some critical remarks), see Roland Kenneth Harrison's impressive and thorough contribution in his *Introduction to the Old Testament*, 3–82, 501–41.

4. Tate, "Satan in the Old Testament," 467.

obvious response would be to find the account merely allegorical. But this reply will not suffice for those conservative interpreters who prefer a semi-literal realism here. Assuming the narrative is at least literal in regard to some proto-human in a primeval geographical province that is being tempted by a being called a "serpent," what metaphysical conclusion are we entitled to draw from such an encounter?

The implications here for any demonic pure immaterialism or ECI are obvious given a traditional interpretation of this account as an extramental encounter. What we would have, at face value, is a clear physical manifestation of Satan or a demon who has adopted an animal form that could, for all intents and purposes, be captured visually with a polymodal recording instrument such as a camcorder.

From what I can tell, there are four conservative interpretations on the table in understanding the Genesis 3 narrative of the temptation.[5] Most of these views assume either a literal or semi-literal interpretation that embraces the idea that Satan, a demon, or some other oppressive villain has, in some way, openly manifested himself to Eve. These views are as follows:[6]

i. The serpent could be an actual, talking animal (a reptilian creature or ophidian of sorts) that is cognitively possessed and controlled by Satan (or a demonic villain) himself (Augustine; Francis Schaeffer; Franz Delitzsch).[7]

---

5. Here we are not considering liberal views. By *liberal* I am referring to what Williams broadly identifies as pertaining to "the movement in modern Protestantism which during the nineteenth century tried to bring Christian thought into organic unity with the evolutionary world view" (Williams, *God's Grace and Man's Hope*, 22). Philo was among the first to consider the serpent story to be more of an allegory of human nature and its internal conflicts (Philo, *On the Creation of the Cosmos According to Moses*, LVI). For examples of contemporary views, see Pagels, *The Origin of Satan*. In chapter 2 of Pagels's book, she argues that Satan is but an evolved epithet for Israel's own internal conflict and enmity (49). See Carr, "The Politics of Textual Subversion." For Carr, the account is a personified polemic against wisdom. See Joines, *Serpent Symbolism in the Old Testament*. For Joines, the serpent represents youthfulness, wisdom, and chaos. Also see Ricoeur, *The Symbolism of Evil*, 232ff. Given that liberal views amount to denying that the story is a historical occurrence at all, such a notion, if true, would render Genesis 3 (and any other passages) irrelevant to an interlocutor. I thus presume a more conservative (read: literal) understanding in my responses. For additional exposition about the serpent, see "The Edenic Serpent" in chapter 2 of this book.

6. I am delimiting the views here to *conservative* interpretations, viz., interpretations that take the narrative as indicative of some sort of real malevolent presence in the Garden.

7. See Augustine, *De Genesi Ad Litteram*, XXVIII.35. Francis Schaeffer was a more recent yet notable conservative philosopher to hold this view. See his *Genesis in Space and Time*, 75–80. The Bible is (elsewhere) completely silent on such things as animal possession by demons which would make this instance a standalone event. A possible exception occurs in the exorcism of the Gadarene demoniacs in Matt 8.28–33 (also reported in Mark 5 and Luke 8) where the demons possessing the two men implore Jesus to "send us into the herd of swine" (v. 31). When Jesus dispatches them to the nearby swine, Matt notes that "the whole herd rushed down the steep bank into the sea and perished in the waters." But I am not sure this is the result of the demons's own powers since the demons do not seem to have entered the swine on their own accord ("If You are going to cast us out, [*you*] send us into the herd of swine," Matt. 8.31). Thus, any appeal to animal possession as the justification for Satan's manifestation in the Garden would be based on controversial speculation. Also see Delitzsch, *A New Commentary on Genesis*, 146–49.

Part IV: Objections

ii. The serpent could be an apparitional or corporeal realization of Satan in the Garden (much like a ghostly apparition) (Michael Heiser).[8]

iii. The serpent could be a gifted, self-conscious animal that has no affiliation with any otherworldly demon (Josephus).[9]

iv. "The serpent" could be an iconographic term meant to designate the *character* of a spiritual being (perhaps Satan) in the Garden who communicates *internally* and whose presence does not involve either a serpentine apparition or the literal embodiment of an ophidian animal (M. M. Kalisch; John Walton).[10]

Now, it seems to me that out of these four options, only (ii) would require either an overtly (quasi-)materialist view of Satan or a view that sees him employing special powers with which to manifest. Interpretation (i) leaves the pure immaterialism of demons alone but would still envisage a special power had by "the serpent" that would account for this kind of self-disclosure. As for (iii), I have deep reservations about which ophidian species might at one time have been capable of intellectual autonomy and the ability to vocalize. Though such is baldly conceivable in an age permissive of the miraculous, it comes across as an anomaly when we consider the wider biblical landscape of animals apart from this Edenic episode (especially animals under the taxonomy of squamata). And those motivated to remove the superstitious elements from Genesis's primeval history will likely find such an interpretation unsatisfying. I have lodged my specific complaints about this view in chapter 2. But never mind. For (iii) has no bearing whatsoever on demonology and may be adopted as a possible interpretation of Genesis 3. As for the remaining interpretation (iv), I also argue in chapter 2 that it is quite plausible. If we do not already assume that Satan has a magical PK* ability to create an animal's vocal chords, then this interpretation better preserves both a conservative reading of Genesis 3 and the fuller ontological portrait I have defended in the last section.[11] As an equally viable interpretation of the serpent, Genesis 3 cannot be blindly appealed to as clear refutation of that portrait.

Therefore, an appeal to Genesis 3 as a counterexample to either pure immaterialism or ECI falls flat since other interpretations, such as (iv), are possible and yet

---

8. E.g., Heiser, "The Nachash (הַנָּחָשׁ) and His Seed."

9. E.g., Josephus, *Antiquities of the Jews*, I.4. Support for this is the fact that the serpent is simply classified along with the other animals ("[being] more crafty than any other beast of the field," Gen 3.1) and made specially deserving of the divine curse that is described in vivid, physical detail later on. Also see Davidson, Stibbs, and Kevan, *The New Bible Commentary*, 79. This is view is the most popular one amongst conservative academics.

10. E.g., Kalisch, *A Historical and Critical Commentary on the Old Testament*, 79–81; Walton, *The Lost World of Adam and Eve*, 128–39.

11. Incidentally, needing to invoke PK* is one of the reasons the classic commentator Adam Clarke rejected the idea that this could have been a snake. See his *The Holy Bible with a Commentary and Critical Notes*, 50–51. Clarke's preferred alternative, an ape, is no doubt susceptible to the same criticism.

preserve a conservative view. Based on my arguments in chapter 2, interpretation (iv) actually strikes me as a plausible one. But the possibility of (iv) or even (iii) is enough to consider Gen 3.1–6 as offering no grounds for arguing that the ontological constitution of Satan and the demons is (quasi-)material or that they have a PK* power to create such a bodily form.

The "Sons of God" of Gen 6.1–4 Are Fallen Angels and They Copulate with the "Daughters of Men"

As a datum for ancient Jewish and Christian source material in determining the metaphysics of demons, no passage is cited more frequently by Christian philosophers and theologians alike than Gen 6.1–4:[12]

> When man began to multiply on the face of the land and daughters were born to them, the sons of God saw that the daughters of man were attractive. And they took as their wives any they chose. Then the LORD said, "My Spirit shall not abide in man forever, for he is flesh: his days shall be 120 years." The Nephilim were on the earth in those days, and also afterward, when the sons of God came in to the daughters of man and they bore children to them. These were the mighty men who were of old, the men of renown.

Many equate the "sons of God" here with the "watchers" of the Pseudepigraphal I Enoch.[13] Contained in I Enoch's narrative is an unconcealed description about fallen angels copulating with human women and producing a progeny of sinister giants. If the "sons of God" are in fact fallen angels, it is difficult to see how they could either be purely immaterial creatures or incapable of manufacturing a human body since such beings would be sensually driven to their "crime" on the basis of finding the "daughters of man ... attractive" to begin with. While 1 Enoch appears to be an attempted commentary *inter alia* of Genesis 6, the fundamental issue we must primarily resolve is whether the "sons of God" likely describe fallen angels or not.

There are some reasons to think that they do. First, given the entire narrative of I Enoch, it is quite obvious that 1 Enoch means to commentate on Genesis 6, and in that sense there is a deliberate connection. And second, as far as we know, the fallen angels view is the oldest interpretation of Gen 6.1–4 by rabbinic Jews. But these points are not interesting enough, for, as a non-canonical work, the commentary could simply be mistaken despite its being old and original. That there appears to be an implicit endorsement of I and II Enoch's content at the hands of Peter and Jude (2 Pet 2.4;

---

12. E.g., Justin Martyr, *The Second Apology of Justin*, V; Athenagoras, *A Plea for Christians*, XXV. For modern appeals, see, e.g., Routledge, "'My Spirit' in Genesis 6:1–4"; Boyd, *Satan and the Problem of Evil*, 314; Newman, "The Ancient Exegesis of Genesis 6:2, 4."

13. See 1 Enoch 6.1–6; 15.8–16.2; Cf., 2 Enoch 18; 29.4f. There are also suggested parallels to the Book of Jubilees, Damascus Document, Wisdom of Solomon, III Maccabees, and III Baruch (among other fragments of Qumran).

Jude 14) is far more interesting. If there is such an endorsement, then its descriptions should be taken seriously. Third, the expression "sons of God" (*hāĕlōhîm bənê*) is used elsewhere as an explicit reference to angels in Job 1.6, 2.1, and 38.7. Thus, the Enochian connection is not unwarranted. Fourth, if the "sons of God" are merely human beings, how would such a union be able to produce physical giants? Such an origins story accounts for a rogue aggregate of disenfranchised spirits who seek revenge on God and his creation. Thus we have at least one can account for how these combative spirits *qua* demons arise on earth, for they are the departed spirits of deceased angel-human hybrids–viz., the Nephilim. There is much here to commend the view; however, these reasons do not seem compelling. Let us consider three responses in detail.

First, it is true that the earliest rabbinic interpretation of Genesis 6 was the fallen angels view. And the fallen angels view is explicitly captured in I Enoch–a book that is not only a commentary on Genesis 6 but also putatively an extended revelation of it. But this alone is not traction enough, especially considering by comparison that the earliest rabbinic views of the "serpent" of Genesis 3 did not connect it with Satan–a notion that has been largely abandoned by a number of Old Testament scholars. However, that 1 Enoch has exegetical weight is supported by the fact that Jude cites the book approvingly. It is further alleged that Jude goes so far as to identify the sin of the fallen angels as sexual sin:

> And the angels who did not stay within their own position of authority, but left their proper dwelling, he has kept in eternal chains under gloomy darkness until the judgment of the great day–just as Sodom and Gomorrah and the surrounding cities, which *likewise indulged in sexual immorality and pursued unnatural desire*, serve as an example by undergoing a punishment of eternal fire (Jude 6–7).

This passage appears to secure Jude's wholehearted endorsement of the relevant *particulars* of the physicality of the fallen angels. Here, the sins of the angels who "did not stay within their own position of authority" are thought to have committed sins similar ("likewise") to those of Sodom and Gomorrah, namely "sexual" ones. But this is a misreading of the passage. The "likewise" connects, not the angels, but "the surrounding cities" with Sodom and Gomorrah. That is, the surrounding cities, like Sodom and Gomorrah, indulged in sexual immorality. The only connection with the angels here, as far as Jude's argument is concerned, is that *nobody* evades punishment–not even God's angels!

As for the undue attention given to I Enoch, I have three things to say. First, it is odd for an *evangelical Protestant* to cite the centuries-later 1 Enoch for exegetical support (this criticism obviously would not apply to non-Protestants). Those that side with the Reformed tradition of *sola Scriptura* are under no compunction to prefer doctrines advocated by extra-canonical works, especially if those works come centuries later. Otherwise, what would prevent a wag from using the Zohar of Kabbalah to interpret the Torah? That 1 Enoch interprets the "sons of God" of Genesis 6 as fallen angels may be every bit as good a reason for *rejecting* it as for accepting it. What prevents one from taking the metaphysical awkwardness of that interpretation as evidence against its likelihood? Second, as for whether merely citing a source work is sufficient grounds for canonizing it,[14] one must consider the obvious counterexamples that occur in the New Testament. For example, when the Apostle Paul is preaching to an Areopagus council in Athens, he cites approvingly the *pagan* Greek "poet," Epimenides of Crete (Acts 17.28; perhaps also in Titus 1.12). But his inclusion is surely not to endorse Epimenides's beliefs about God as Zeus and the nature of his divine offspring. Thus, an honorable mention of a Pseudepigraphal work by a prophet is not evidence that that prophet considered the entirety of the work's contents to be inspired. Third, and more importantly, 1 Enoch advocates certain things about the angelic episode that make it an unacceptable interpretation of Genesis 6. For example, 1 Enoch 15 locates the domicile of the departed spirits (viz., the demons) on the earth (vv. 8–10). Ephesians 6.12 contravenes this and locates the home of evil spirits "in the heavenly places." Also, the place where the fallen angels are punished is patterned uncritically after the Tartarus of the Homeric epics (being explicitly so in 1 Enoch 20.3).[15] The place of their punishment is, thus, in a subterranean cavity in the earth (1 Enoch 22; cf., *Jubilees* 5.6). Incidentally, 1 Enoch 10.4–7 supposes the strange notion that spirts *can be contained by earthly enclosures*. Aside from its importing of pagan material in explicating the destination of fallen angels, the metaphysics is all wrong here (not to say anything of the curious *physics* of 1 Enoch).[16]

Let us now move on to the second overall reason why the fallen angels view is questionable, namely that the expression "sons of God" does not always, or even *usually*, connote angels. Of particular note is that within the local Pentateuch itself the various iterations of the phrase is *always* used in reference to human beings. For example, Exod 4.22 has, "Thus says the LORD, Israel is my firstborn son" (*yiśrā'ēl bəkōrî bənî*). Since it is God speaking, Israel is declared to be the collective son of God. Deut 14.1 makes this more explicit wherein Moses, on behalf of God, pronounces to the Israelites, "You are the sons of the LORD your God" (*'ĕlōhêkem Yahweh 'attem bānîm*). The same can be said about the Greco-Jewish understanding of Deut 32.8. In the Masoretic version of the Hebrew Bible, the passage simply makes a reference to the "sons of Israel" (*bənê . . . yiśrā'ēl*). But, as with the more reliable Qumran version,[17] the subsequent Greek Septuagint does not have "of Israel" (*yiśrā'ēl*) but instead "of

---

14. Also see my brief comments under "Biblical Demonology" in chapter 2.

15. On Jude 6 and 2 Pet 2.4's connection to Tartarus, see my comments in chapter 2 n. 26.

16. I suppose one may be able to negotiate some of the tension by insisting on its being a literary apocalypse. But I have singled out the more problematic points in the context that cannot all be easily dismissed by such appeals. Moreover, the central objection loses its force, for, on such a reading, one could see the fallen angels as the agents positioned *behind* the "sons of God" and not *as* the "sons of God."

17. See Heiser, "Does Deuteronomy 32.17 Assume or Deny the Reality of other Gods?," 140 n. 7.

God" (*theou*), which shows that some ancient Jews understood the sons of God in Deuteronomy to be the sons of Israel–something already established to some extent by Exodus 4 and Deuteronomy 14. Why preference is given to the remote book of Job over the local books of Exodus and Deuteronomy strikes me as problematic, particularly if the same author(s) responsible for the local books is also responsible for Genesis.

Third, the presence of Nephilim in Gen 6.4 as the putative offspring of the "sons of God" demands explanation. And, in fact, there is a less offensive way to understand them–one that is not motivated by any preconceived agenda. The proponents of the fallen angels view tout that this explains where demons, as the spirits of the deceased Nephilim, came from and why they roam the earth. But the Hebrew *nəp̄îlîm* is used in conjunction with *gibbôrîm* ("men of old/renown") which likely suggests that the *nəp̄îlîm*, whatever this means, refers, not to being *physically* extraordinary in height (which might imply a supernatural parent), but to the *positional magnitude* of their heroic stature;[18] hence, there is no reason not to think that the *nəp̄îlîm* are just ordinary human men but of a high (or "giant") caliber, i.e., *men of renown*. Exegetical support for the fact that being a *gibbôr* connects to being a warrior and not to a monster can be found in the warrior descriptions of Nimrod just four chapters later in Gen 10.8–9. In the twenty-first century, we are no strangers to this kind of talk. For when the U.N. President of the General Assembly, Nassir Abdulaziz Al-Nasser, recently called the late Nelson Mandela a "giant of history,"[19] no one thought that Mandela's physical height was the focus of his laudatory remarks.

Consequently, none of the reasons offered in support of the fallen angels view seem compelling. I shall now offer up some positive reasons to think the fallen angels view to be dubious if not outright incorrect. And even the mere presence of doubt

---

18. Birney, "An Exegetical Study of Genesis 6:1–4," 50–52; Kaiser et al., *Hard Sayings of the Bible*, 108. Some have offered up arguments outside of Genesis 6 to support the view that the *nəp̄îlîm* are physical giants. They cite Num 13.33 which says, "And there we saw the Nephilim (the sons of Anak, who come from the Nephilim), and we seemed to ourselves like grasshoppers, and so we seemed to them." Would this not be an admission of visual perspective, viz., that the Israelites, when physically compared to the Anakim, seem to be as visibly small as grasshoppers? Not necessarily. There is a similar construction in Isa 40.22 ("It is he who sits above the circle of the earth, and its inhabitants are like grasshoppers; who stretches out the heavens like a curtain, and spreads them like a tent to dwell in"). At first glance, this *could* seem like a reference to the perspectival size of the "inhabitants." However, the context concerns itself with the exalted wisdom and power of God, not his size or relative distance from the earth. It seems to me that "like grasshoppers" refers to a diminution of the wisdom and power of the people, which is why the passage ends with one of the most celebrated promises in the Old Testament: "they who wait for the LORD shall renew their *strength*; they shall mount up with wings like eagles; they shall run and *not be weary*; they shall walk and *not faint*" (v. 31; emphases mine). If being *nəp̄îlîm* amounts to being an aggregate of people who are mighty and heroic, as I have argued, the "like grasshoppers" of Num 13.33 could also be seen as a mere metaphorical contrast to power and might. Cf., Judg 6.5; 7.12. Even if "like grasshoppers" did refer to a contrast of physical statures, I would imagine a larger-than-average height would be quite conducive to one's being a heroic warrior.

19. Al-Nasser, "General Assembly President's Remarks."

Objections Based on Passages in the Old Testament

cast on the fallen angels view constitutes a successful deflection of Genesis 6 as an objection to my overall case.

First, there are alternative interpretations (not unlike Genesis 3) that come from *sympathizers* of the general view that demons are quasi-material and/or can physically manifest and interact with human beings at will. Nevertheless, these sympathizers do not see the "sons of God" as fallen angels in Genesis 6. I shall mention two alternative views here that are on offer. First, some early philosophers and theologians have claimed that the "sons of God" are to be understood as referring to the Godly lineage of Seth.[20] Coming on the heels of Genesis 5's specific noting of the lineage of Seth, such an interpretation is possible. Even if such a view lacked clear exegetical support, as I think it does, it should still be preferable to an exotic interpretation that stresses our metaphysics. Second, others note that the "sons of God" was a common expression in the Ancient Near East that kings and nobles would use of themselves.[21] Hence, the "sons of God" were men occupying positions of governmental authority who perhaps thought more of their power than they ought to have. This view has some exegetical support by Gen 6.1–4's being similarly ordered with the events of 4.19–24. In this latter passage, there is a tyrant, Lamech, who takes multiple wives and produces a dynasty. When one also takes into account that the plural term "gods" (*ĕlōhîm*) sometimes refers to judges and magistrates (i.e., Exod 21.6; 22.8; *possibly* Ps 82.1, 6), a regal view of the *hāĕlōhîm bǝnê* in Genesis 6 becomes more likely. The point is not to *endorse* this or that interpretation, only that there have been dissident views posed by those who have no agenda in opposing the pure immateriality of demons or ECI.

Second, there are some contextual considerations that make the fallen angels view too problematic. Consider that divine judgment in the form of a deluge is unleashed upon *all mankind*. The extent of such retribution is rather peculiar if not wholly unjust if the "sons of God" are residents of the heavenly realms and, so, unrepresentative of the human race on earth. It is no wonder that *Jubilees* 5.3–4 makes sure to attribute the sole reason for the deluge to the sins of human beings. Moreover, the "sons of God" do more than have sexual intercourse with their human exploits, they *marry* them. However, the angelic order in some sense lacks the practice of marriage (cf., Mark 12.25; Matt 22.30), to say nothing about a power to procreate new life. For, as *The Jerome Biblical Commentary* points out, the "example of angels [in Matt 22.30] refers to a life in which sex plays no part."[22]

Moreover, these liaisons must have occurred not only once but *twice*, for Gen 6.3 says that the *nǝpîlîm* were not only "on the earth in those days," but "also afterward!" Given that, after the deluge of Noah, only "a few, that is, eight persons, were brought

---

20. E.g., Julius Africanus, *Chronographia*; Augustine, *De Civitate Dei*, XV.22.

21. E.g., Birney, "An Exegetical Study of Genesis 6:1–4," 43–52; Kaiser et al., *Hard Sayings of the Bible*, 106–8.

22. Brown, Fitzmyer, and Murphy, *The Jerome Biblical Commentary*, 101.

safely through water" (1 Pet 3.20), there must have been another angelic romp with the women–yet another fall, as it were. It is increasingly hard to square this with the fact that this is why God flooded the land to begin with. If these considerations were not prohibitive enough, consider that a procreative encounter would require a certain kind of libido angels do not already have. Accordingly, one must imagine a rather awkward backstory to the episode in Genesis, namely that the angels consciously decide to create a libido that would serve no other purpose than to do that which they already knew was wrong for them to do. And that does not seem defensible.

Michael S. Heiser offers an alternative reading–one that is not predicated on there being a literal sexual means of fathering. He writes that it is possible that "the language of cohabitation is used to convey the idea that divine beings ... are responsible for producing the Nephilim," but that such language is "euphemistic, not literal" in the same way one would understand the notion that "Yahweh 'fathered' Israel" through Abraham and Sarah.[23] Even so, in order to make sense of the fallen angels's active involvement as the progenitors of the nəpîlîm, they still must have utilized some kind of PK* power (i.e., "divine intervention of some sort was necessary"[24]). Likewise, the nəpîlîm "existed because of some sort of *supernatural intervention* of rival gods."[25] Regardless of the nuance, one would have to insist that the gods *qua* angels are capable of manipulating human nature in order to bring forth progeny of a sort. Accordingly, all views–Heiser's included–suppose that there is a way that they can be *creators of a new kind of life*. This is striking, for God is otherwise said to be the sole creator of every kind of life given that "by him all things were created, in heaven and on earth, visible and invisible, whether thrones or dominions or rulers or authorities–all things were created through him and for him" (Col 1.16). Put another way, (fallen) angels are assumed to create–an attribute that is solely the preserve of God. Furthermore, these "sons of God" do not just supernaturally father their offspring, however that is supposed to be understood, they are, as discussed above, *attracted to* and *marry* the mothers-to-be (Gen 6.2). Heiser's position does not advert the reader away from this insurmountable awkwardness. Even if Heiser's interpretation is the best way to salvage the notion that angels caused the nəpîlîm to come into being, the cost for preferring it is also prohibitive.

Given the various challenges pro and con, we have no reason to prefer the view that Gen 6.1–4 refers to fallen angels being sexually interactive and procreative with human women regardless of whether that capability derives from their intrinsic nature or through an *ad hoc* PK* power. Despite serious attempts to learn about the metaphysics of demons on the basis of this interpretation of Genesis 6 that sees demons as having abused their angelic status by copulating with terrestrial women, such a view is dubious at best. And since the Bible elsewhere seems to suggest that pride (*tuphóo*)

---

23. Heiser, *The Unseen Realm*, 187–88.
24. Heiser, *The Unseen Realm*, 188.
25. Heiser, *The Unseen Realm*, 188; emphasis mine.

According to Job 1–2, Satan Causes Atmospheric Disturbances and Smites Job with Skin Lesions

The account of Job in the book bearing his name could be seen as evidence that demons can and do interact with the physical world.[27] The story of Job–a literary work that is by no means incontrovertibly historical[28]–is known to feature *haśśāṭān* (the Hebrew term for "the satan" or "Satan") as one exhibiting supernatural power over the material world surrounding Job, in order to perturb his spiritual fidelity.[29] The author of Job chronicles the hardship wrought on Job by beginning with the destruction of some of Job's servants at the hands of the Sabeans where, following this, "[t]he fire of God fell from heaven and burned up the sheep and the servants and consumed them" (1.16). This incident is immediately followed by another tragedy: "The Chaldeans formed three groups and made a raid on the camels and took them and struck down the servants with the edge of the sword" (v. 17). In the next few verses we learn of another atmospheric tragedy, namely, that "a great wind came across the wilderness and struck the four corners of the house, and it fell upon the young people, and they are dead" (v. 19). It is then in the next chapter that the author reports a direct physical assault by Satan on Job's flesh:

> Then Satan went out from the presence of the LORD, and smote Job with sore boils from the sole of his foot to the crown of his head (2.7).

The problem, specifically for anyone defending ECI, is that if Satan can produce a "fire . . . from heaven," "a great wind," and "sore boils" then there exist phenomena that require some ability beyond mere mental communicability. In assuming the traditional view that *haśśāṭān* is indeed Satan proper, the following are some reasons from the narrative itself to question the notion that Satan directly manipulates matter/energy. I submit that either Satan is actually not the vehicle of the reported disasters at all or that these occurrences are explicable by CI and are consistent with ECI, understood weakly.

---

26. E.g., 1 Tim 3.6. On Isa 14.12–19 and Ezek 28.13–16, see "Biblical Demonology" in chapter 2.

27. I.e., Storms, *Tough Topics*, 147 and 149; Boyd, *God at War*, 144–49, 165–67; Unger, *Biblical Demonology*, 189; Habel, *The Book of Job*, 88–96.

28. For examples, see the diversity of opinions offered by Walton, Matthews, and Chavalas, *The IVP Bible Background Commentary*, 491–94; Harrison, *Introduction to the Old Testament*, 1022–27; and Habel, *The Book of Job*, 1–12. The Book of Job belongs to a category of Jewish writings called "Wisdom Literature" and if it contains any historical contribution, it is nonetheless highly poetic and unascertainable save a slight biographical parallel with another historical figure, Elkanah, in 1 Samuel 1 (compare with Job 1). But this is not conclusive and is nonetheless irrelevant to the more salient point, namely, that the *śāṭān* in Job is *believed* by many to be the devil of the New Testament.

29. For more on the *haśśāṭān* of Job, see "(The) Satan" in chapter 2.

Part IV: Objections

First, Job 1 does not seem to suggest that Satan is actually the *direct* cause or the *sole* cause of the calamities noted therein (viz., the attack of the Sabeans, the "fire ... from heaven," the Chaldean raid, and the "great wind"). The "fire ... from heaven" itself, according to verse 16, is said to be the fire *of God*. Satan's challenge is actually laid at God's feet:

> "But put forth Thy hand now and touch all that he has; he will surely curse Thee to Thy face." Then the LORD said to Satan, "Behold, all that he has is in your power, only do not put forth your hand on him." So Satan departed from the presence of the LORD (vv. 11–12).

The divine limitation to "not put forth your hand on him" may actually suggest that these are *God's* direct handiwork in that he would "put forth [His] hand" and "touch all that [Job] has"–all of this after God's own removing of a "hedge about him" (v. 10). This is directly in line with Job's lament in verse 21 ("the *LORD* has taken away"; emphasis mine) and his familial consolation in 42.11 ("Then all his brothers, and all his sisters ... consoled him and comforted him for all the evil that *the LORD* had brought on him"; emphasis mine). By extension, it has solidarity with Isaiah, who quotes God as saying, "I ... create calamity; I am the LORD who does all these things" (Isa 45.7; cf., Deut 29.22) and with James in the New Testament, who commentates on Job's steadfastness as the "outcome of *the Lord's* dealings" (James 5.11; emphasis mine). This is not to say that only God was involved. Perhaps it was a *cooperative* series of events with Satan as co-conspirator. In this case it may be that Satan's role was to weakly actualize the events by (cognitively) directing Job's servants to the appropriate locales by which God unleashes the various phenomena responsible for Job's loss of servants and property.[30]

Thus, it seems plausible that Satan is actually not the vehicle of the reported disasters after all. But, secondly, it may also be that these occurrences are explicable by and consistent with ECI if understood weakly. Regarding Job 2.7's mentioning of the infliction of "sore boils" on Job's skin, it explicitly says that Satan "struck" Job with this affliction. Curiously enough, even the use of the indicative verb "struck" does not necessarily mean that the subject (in this case Satan) actually inflicted the ailment by his own hand. In 2 Samuel, to cite a parallel, Nathan accuses King David of directly having "struck down Uriah the Hittite with the sword" (12.9). But we know from chapter 11 that Uriah was simply deployed by David (through Joab) to a military post that was inevitably going to lead to his death. Perhaps the same meaning attends Satan's involvement in Job 2.6–7. It seems as if this reflects the consistent storytelling

---

30. In this sense, Satan would weakly actualize (as opposed to *strongly* actualizing) the various tragedies unleashed on Job's servants in that it is the sort of thing "in which a person can arrange it that some state of affairs obtains by inducing someone else to cause it to happen" (Wierenga, *The Nature of God*, 22). In this case, Satan can arrange for the servants and family members to behave in such a way that they end up putting themselves in harm's way. And so Satan can rightly be said to "arrange it that some state of affairs obtains without *causing* it to obtain" (21).

device that puts the instrument of affliction (or killing) into the hands of the one morally responsible for the end result even though the very medium of affliction (or "smiting" in this case) was indirect.[31]

This view might be defensible only if we have a viable interpretation of Satan's activity in 2.6–7 in accord with ECI. Such an interpretation is indeed available and accords well with ECI given the notion that Satan could incite Job to produce the lesions psychosomatically. I should begin by noting that the word expressed as "sore boils" in some translations (e.g., the KJV and NASV) is *shehîn* in Hebrew (*elkos* in the Greek LXX) which refers to some unspecified kind of skin lesions. In the Pentateuch, such a condition has been understood by some scholars and commentators to be a form of leprosy (specifically *elephantiasis*)[32] sometimes said to be brought on through divine judgment.[33] But any specific diagnosis or pathology remains elusive in principle and in fact. Principally, it may be difficult if not impossible to formulate any kind of retrospective diagnosis of any historical symptoms from a modern vantage point given that diseases are perspectival interpretations of certain phenomena.[34] At the very least, there are situational and textual obstacles (the meaning of key words used in describing the symptoms, the ignoring of additional key pieces of data, etc.) that make any diagnostic task less than straightforward. In fact, even if a clear set of symptoms could be reasonably ascertained in some historical description, we may be ignoring the possibility of an unknown cause or even of multiple causes of the noted symptoms. Biological anthropologist Piers Mitchell cautions:

> Sometimes the list of symptoms given may not seem to match up with any single modern disease. Alternatively, the symptoms may be compatible with a number of conditions. It is not always clear which symptoms are most important in helping us come to a diagnosis.[35]

As it pertains to the present case, what are we to do with Job 2.8's mentioning of Job using broken pottery fragments to scratch his skin lesions? It is unclear whether Job

---

31. Consider also how the Pentateuch declares that "the LORD hardened Pharaoh's heart" (Exod 9.12). But given that we are also told that "Pharaoh hardened his [own] heart" (8.32) then we might imagine that the divine hardening was a complex and indirect result of the plagues.

32. See Hagin, *The Book of Job*, 19; Davidson, Stibbs, and Kevan, *The New Bible Commentary*, 389; Brown, Fitzmyer, and Murphy, *The Jerome Biblical Commentary*, 515; Evangelatou, "From Word into Image," 23; Wilson, "Leprosy In Ancient Mesopotamia," 56f.

33. Cf., Exod 9.9 and Deut 28.27.

34. Andrew Cunningham believes that any "disease" is mostly a social convention apart from any biological considerations, and so "there is no 'real' disease, with an identity separate from its sufferers at any given time, which can be separated out as a timeless entity for us to give our modern labels to, years —centuries— after the events" ("Identifying Disease in the Past," 20). This is not to deny that victims lack their self-described symptoms, only that different societies (past and present, domestic and abroad) will have a different "array of diseases" from which to diagnose those symptoms.

35. Mitchell, "Retrospective Diagnosis," 84. Mitchell himself offers six criteria that augment the reliability of any retrospective diagnoses through historical texts (85), citing a chronicle of William of Tyre as a paradigm example.

uses those fragments to scratch the lesions for relief or out of some symbolic gesture.[36] Apart from this interpretive difficulty, the use of *shehîn* evinces some kind of sudden erythema which seems to be a description *inconsistent* with the typical onset of elephantiasis.[37]

One possible alternative conducive to such a sudden onset is the condition of having "hives" or, more formally, *urticaria*. Urticaria is acknowledged to sometimes be derived from "[psychological] factors [that] seem to play a considerable part in approximately one-third of chronic urticaria cases."[38] Such has been specifically categorized as *cholinergic urticaria*, which refers to the eruption of hives as a result of emotional stress.[39] Though urticaria is not always the result of psychological causes, the fact that it is a body-wide set of skin lesions accompanied by itching and erupts as a result of emotional stress make it a justified possibility. Job's immediate reaction associated with its possible itching condition (2.8) and the fact that these eruptions occur in the wake of what would be considered by all lights to be one of the most emotionally stressful occurrences anyone could suffer–the loss of one's children, friends, and possessions–make cholinergic urticaria a more reasonable diagnosis (if one can be given). My objective here is not to actually diagnose this condition but to suggest that a condition of urticaria bearing such symptoms in the context of Job's loss is every bit as possible a diagnosis as some non-psychologically derived skin condition. As Norman C. Habel correctly notes: "The sickness with which Job is afflicted is probably not to be identified with a specific disease."[40] If Satan is a thoroughly immaterial being who interacts only cognitively, this would not be a medical episode inconsistent with what one might expect of someone like Job under extreme mental duress.

Accordingly, Satan might have exacerbated the problem by mentally communicating to Job that *You have been unfairly judged by God* (Job 19.6–7; 27.1–2) and that *God deliberately refuses to hear your cries* (30.20–31). These thoughts would result not only in emotional trauma (a sort of crisis of faith) but an expectation that God might continue to be arbitrarily torturing such an upright man as Job himself. What we can say is that if Satan is truly culpable for having "smote" Job with skin lesions in some way, at least the duress of abandonment from God, the removal of his protection, and the willful infliction of suffering are surely traumatic enough so as to produce some of the most dramatic psychosomatic physical conditions consonant with the

---

36. See Walton, Matthews, and Chavalas, *The IVP Bible Background Commentary*, 496.

37. "Elephantiasis develops slowly, and often lasts for years before death ensues; but the narrative almost certainly intends us to understand that Job was immediately smitten with intensely painful and loathsome symptoms . . ." (Driver and Gray, *A Critical and Exegetical Commentary on the Book of Job*, 24).

38. Grahame, "Management of Chronic Urticaria," 382.

39. See Wedi, "Urticaria," 314. Also see "Urticaria"; Greaves, "Chronic Urticaria," 667; Davis and Kennard, "Urticaria."

40. Habel, *The Book of Job*, 95.

phenomenon of cholinergic urticaria.[41] And this understanding is perfectly consistent with, if not suggested by, the mechanism of CI alone.

Therefore, the book of Job, even if taken at face value, does not offer readers any support for demonic PK*.

Conclusion

So far, we have explore certain key passages in the Old Testament that putatively imply that Satan and his cohorts are either (quasi-)material or have some kind of PK* power with which to creatively interact with the physical world. In our exploration, we examined Genesis 3, Genesis 6, and Job 1–2. But, without having to assume anything less than a literal reading, in each case we were able to see how these passages are not successful challenges to either the pure immateriality of demons or ECI. If the alternative readings I have offered are at least equipossible, then such passages do not constitute a mitigating threat to my previous arguments.

In the next chapter, we shall turn our attention to passages in the New Testament that are appealed to as implying either the demons's materiality or their ability to directly interact with the physical world via PK*.

---

41. Another example of a physical condition resulting from extreme stress is recorded in Luke 22.44 where Jesus is said to be anticipating his own death and this agonizing results in his sweating drops "like great drops of blood."

11

Objections Based on Passages in the New Testament

UNLIKE THE OLD TESTAMENT, the New Testament's dossier on Satan and his cohorts does not seem to be ambiguous about the identity of the diabolical. As we saw in the last chapter, the Old Testament's talk of Genesis's serpent, the "sons of God," and Job's Satan have been interpreted by a number of scholars as referring to things other than as gods of this world. My approach was more of a mixed bag. To wit, I aired my misgivings about the identity of the "sons of God" as not referring to fallen angels. But in cases where the diabolical is clearly in mind, as I think it is in Genesis 3 and Job 1–2, I argued that we, nevertheless, lack any credible reasons to think that demons are either (quasi-)material or have a PK* ability. As such, a persistent disputant might prefer instead the more definitive passages of the New Testament that speak with such clarity about evil spiritual agents. Perhaps it is there that one might find support for demons being (quasi-)material and/or their having PK*. For, as we shall see, prevalent are the intra-worldly, physical harassments of Satan and his cohorts all throughout the Gospel and Epistolary books.

This chapter, then, is devoted to looking at the particular passages in the New Testament that seem settled on the identity of the diabolical and yet imply either the corporeality of demons or their ability to act psychokinetically upon this world. As the following discussions shall reveal, it turns out that any aversions to pure immaterialism or ECI on the basis of the New Testament are, like those of the Old Testament, unwarranted.

According to Mark 1.12–13, Matt 4.1–11, and Luke 4.1–13, Satan Physically Appears to Jesus and Tempts Him During His Forty-Day Wilderness Trek

The Synoptic accounts of Jesus all agree that the launching of Jesus's ministry after his public baptism began with his 40-day fast in his wandering in the wilderness (an apparent connection with the Israelites's iconic exodus out of Egypt). I shall use Matthew's more developed presentation as representative of the event in question:

Objections Based on Passages in the New Testament

> Then Jesus was led up by the Spirit into the wilderness to be tempted by the devil. And after fasting forty days and forty nights, he was hungry. And the tempter came and said to him, "If you are the Son of God, command these stones to become loaves of bread." But he answered, "It is written, "'Man shall not live by bread alone, but by every word that comes from the mouth of God.'" Then the devil took him to the holy city and set him on the pinnacle of the temple and said to him, "If you are the Son of God, throw yourself down, for it is written, "'He will command his angels concerning you', and "'On their hands they will bear you up, lest you strike your foot against a stone.'" Jesus said to him, "Again it is written, 'You shall not put the Lord your God to the test.'" Again, the devil took him to a very high mountain and showed him all the kingdoms of the world and their glory. And he said to him, "All these I will give you, if you will fall down and worship me." Then Jesus said to him, "Be gone, Satan! For it is written, "'You shall worship the Lord your God and him only shall you serve.'" Then the devil left him, and behold, angels came and were ministering to him (Matt 4.1–11).

The significant detail of the story is that Jesus has a deliberate confrontation with Satan in the form of three distinct but overlapping temptations that feature Satan's luring of Jesus to different geographical landmarks. Some who believe in demons are quick to press the point that Satan, then, must be capable of apparitional manifestations as implied by these temptation narratives.[1] To cite a contemporary example, Merrill F. Unger does not hesitate to call Matthew's temptation account a "personal appearance of Satan" which is typical of many Christians who believe in the existence of demons.[2]

Upon careful inspection, however, what we find is that there is *no* visible apparition by Satan that occurs in any of the temptation narratives. Each of the Synoptic accounts begins with the straightforward fact that "Jesus was led up by the Spirit" or "The Spirit immediately drove him out" and that, subsequently, "the tempter . . . came to him" or that "he was . . . being tempted by Satan/the devil."[3] The identification of the tempter as Satan is not in question by demonic realists and neither do I dispute it. However, some interpreters (e.g., Pierre Benoit and Kenneth Waters) are more cautious about the temptation narrative being in any sense a genuine manifestation event since it is couched in apocalyptic visionary language.[4] Missing from these accounts is any explicit apparitional *language* in the passages since they do not say anything like "Satan appeared" (*ho satanas ephano*) or "Satan manifested" (*ho satanas ephanerothe*). The Synoptic usage of "came to him" (*prosēlthon . . . auto*) in reference to Satan/the

---

1. I credit Book II of John Milton's *Paradise Regained* as a major influential factor in the seeing of Satan's temptation of Jesus as an extramental apparitional event.
2. Unger, *Biblical Demonology*, 68.
3. Matt 4.1, 3; Mark 1.12–13; Luke 4.1–2. The Synoptics pose variations of the selfsame event.
4. See Benoit, *The Passion and Resurrection of Jesus Christ*, 204; Also see Kenneth Waters's relevant remarks over Matthew 4's peculiar use of "holy city" in his "Matthew 27:52–53 as Apocalyptic Apostrophe."

tempter no more carries an apparitional connotation than the temptation's postscript of Matthew regarding the ministering angels when they "came" (*proselthon*) to Jesus to minister to him.[5] We should not think that the *proselthon* of the demons in any way entails a metaphysical (much less physical) component any more than the phenomenal arrival of a thought might "come" to me in the middle of the night. In this manner, it is feasible that Satan merely tempts Jesus through his ordinary means of cognitive interaction between minds.

As for Jesus's being led to different geographical locales by Satan, either Jesus was prompted mentally to move to this or that location or Satan imposed a visionary experience on Jesus such that he was imagining that Satan "took him" to the Temple, a high mountain, and the "kingdoms of the world."[6] And this latter suggestion has already been posed by New Testament scholars that are not motivated by any agenda to affirm one kind of metaphysics of demons over another.[7] Thus, if interpreters are not committed to seeing this passage as a genuine manifestation account, then no information whatsoever about the ontological make-up of demons or their alleged PK* power can be teased out of this temptation narrative as is.

Satan Makes a Human Being "Blind and Mute" in Matt 12.22–28

The central text here concerns an exorcism given by Jesus on the Sabbath day–an event that provokes criticism from his Jewish interlocutors. In the specific account as told in Matthew 12, Satan is reported to have made someone blind and mute:

> Then there was brought to [Jesus] a demon-possessed man who was blind and dumb, and He healed him, so that the dumb man spoke and saw. And all the multitudes were amazed, and began to say, "This man cannot be the Son of David, can he?" But when the Pharisees heard it, they said, "This man casts

---

5. Matt 4.11; cf., Mark 1.13. Many New Testament commentators point out that the angelic ministry in the temptation was corporeal and "impl[ies] the provision of food" to the starving Jesus. Twelftree, "Temptation of Jesus," 825. But this is not a commentary on *proselthon* ("[they] came") itself but with its contextual usage of *diekonoun* ("[they] were ministering"). The root term *diakoneo* is variably used to connote either a figurative form of servitude (e.g., Matt 10.45; Acts 19.22) or a literal waiting on someone as if at a dinner table (e.g., Luke 12.37; 22.26f). The latter is only suggested given the antecedent Old Testament account of an angelic ministry of food service in 1 Kgs 19.5–8. And even if this corporeal visitation was the preferred connotation of the angelic ministry to Jesus, this could easily be accommodated as being the result of God's power and not that of the angels. It thus begs the question to suppose that Satan came (*proselthon*) to Jesus in a corporeal way.

6. The language of bringing someone somewhere is not unusual in visionary encounters as can be seen in other passages that are clearly visionary, e.g., Ezek 8.3 ("He put out the form of a hand and took me by a lock of my head, and the Spirit lifted me up between earth and heaven and brought me in visions of God to Jerusalem, to the entrance of the gateway of the inner court that faces north . . .") and Rev 4.1c ("Come up here, and I will show you what must take place after this").

7. See Schiavo, "The Temptation Of Jesus." Schiavo lays out three categories of interpretations of which the visionary account is but one.

out demons only by Beelzebul the ruler of the demons." And knowing their thoughts He said to them, "Any kingdom divided against itself is laid waste; and any city or house divided against itself shall not stand. And if Satan casts out Satan, he is divided against himself; how then shall his kingdom stand? And if I by Beelzebul cast out demons, by whom do your sons cast them out? Consequently they shall be your judges. But if I cast out demons by the Spirit of God, then the kingdom of God has come upon you" (Matt 12.22–28).

The implication is obvious: If Satan made a man "blind and mute," then he must have the power to directly affect one's biology. However, there are three possible interpretations of this episode that have a bearing on this implication one way or the other: (i) The man was not actually demon-possessed but simply had an ailment that was associated with a demon on the grounds that illnesses and diseases were often attributed to such spirits; (ii) The demonic possession is merely coincidental with the man's otherwise naturally derived illnesses, a situation in which the man is subsequently freed from both; and (iii) the demonic possession is the direct cause of the man's being blind and mute. I take this last interpretation to be the most common position,[8] and one that would appear to be in support of demonic PK*, and therefore potentially threatening to ECI.

But in seeking an adequate explanation of the man's condition, it seems to me one can affirm (iii) while also denying that it threatens ECI after all. I first remind readers of the difficulties of engaging in a firm retrospective diagnosis as it may be difficult or impossible to do.[9] More specifically, the passage only indicates that the man has the symptoms of being "blind and mute" with no other decisive indicators, not to mention how those symptoms came to be. As it turns out, there is another cause that can yield these symptoms—a cause not necessarily rooted in a *biological* malady. Of course if we *knew* that the ailments are defined in such a way as to suggest some sort of creative power (say, the sudden appearance of cancerous tumors) there would be a need to invoke a psychokinetic power to explain that. But since the passage speaks merely of the man displaying the symptoms "blind and mute," one would need to rule out the possibility of something like a cognitive malfunction that could be to blame in order for this passage to count as a sufficient counterexample to ECI.[10]

As it turns out, there is a known cognitive malfunction—a documented mental disorder—that relegates the conjoined symptoms of deafmuteness to a singular cognitive cause. This condition is referred to as *functional neurological symptom disorder* (or "conversion disorder") which is to say that sensory or mobility functions (such as limb

---

8. See Broadus, *Commentary on Matthew*, 267; also see Brown, Fitzmyer, and Murphy, *The Jerome Biblical Commentary*, 85.

9. Recall my discussion on Job 1–2 in chapter 10.

10. We should think also about how sin is said to affect our cognitive abilities (cf., Gen 3.6–11; 4.6–7; Rom 3.10–18; Heb 3.13; 1 John 2.9, 11). A similar association (viz., "transworld depravity" and its ability to adversely affect good choices) appears in Plantinga, *God, Freedom, and Evil*, 48–53.

mobility or the ability to see, hear, or speak) are disabled but are not the result of any bodily maladies. Conversion disorder is identified by the most recent *Diagnostic and Statistical Manual of Mental Disorders* (V) as a mental disorder "characterized by neurological symptoms that are inconsistent with neurological pathophysiology."[11] Psychologist John Kihlstrom explains some of the interesting symptoms of conversion disorders:

> The conversion disorders, for their part, include psychogenic deafness, blindness, and other impairments of sensory-perceptual function, either general (i.e., affecting the entire modality) or selective (i.e., affecting the perception of only certain categories of objects and events), as well as paralysis, aphonia, and other impairments of voluntary motor function (these, too, may be general or specific). Again, these are functional disorders of perception and action (Kihlstrom, Barnhardt, & Tataryn, 1991), mimicking neurological disease, but occurring in the absence of organic damage. . . . [Dr. Pierre] Janet's patients said that they could not see, hear, or feel; yet at the same time, their behavior was obviously responsive to visual, auditory, or tactile events. . . . Since the appearance of Janet's treatises, a number of formal experiments have confirmed his essential observations.[12]

Kihlstrom later invokes Dr. E. R. Hilgard who asks us to

> [i]magine a circumstance in which the subsystem responsible for visual perception is cut off from the executive ego, but remains able to communicate laterally with other subordinate systems. A person in this situation will be denied the experience of seeing; yet because the visual subsystem continues to process inputs, execute outputs, and pass information to (and receive information from) other subsystems, the person may still be able to respond adaptively to visual events–a common observation in cases of functional blindness.[13]

Thus, blindness in this sense is simply "mimicking neurological disease" in that the patient is being "denied the experience of seeing" that is not reducible to any "organic damage."

Furthermore, research in neuropsychology is already reporting numerous accounts of how one can be paralyzed so as to be unable to speak (among other cognitive disorders) that is induced by the occurrence of psychological trauma.[14] If these conditions lack any known physical cause and mental events can be directly responsible for things like "functional blindness" and "aphonia," then the ability to cognitively induce such occurrences would not be beyond the power of a purely immaterial being like a demon. For, it is possible that psychosomatic perturbations in a human being can be

---

11. American Psychiatric Association, *DSM-V*, 326.
12. Kihlstrom, "Dissociative and Conversion Disorders," 248.
13. Kihlstrom, "Dissociative and Conversion Disorders," 263.
14. For example, see Weber and Reynolds, "Clinical Perspectives on Neurobiological Effects of Psychological Trauma."

induced by the demon's interaction with the host spirit (viz., CI). Again, this is not to diagnose the Matthean case of demonic possession as a definitive case of "conversion disorder," only to point out that the event is consistent with the man's condition being caused purely psychologically. A demon, thus, can cognitively interact with a person in such a way as to make the person seem "blind and dumb," in which case the demon counts as being part of the psychogenic origin. Since conversion disorders are typically treated with stress-relief practices, one might consider the removal of a demon to be anti-stress therapy *par excellence* as surely the jettisoning of a demonic presence would inaugurate the healing process.

But are there any clear *morphological* maladies by demons reported in the Gospels that would appear to be inexplicable by similar means? Next up we shall explore the occurrence of a woman being "bent double" by Satan, something that would seem to necessarily imply a PK* ability.

Luke 13.11–16 Reports that Jesus Healed a Woman Physically "Bent Double" by Satan

According to this particular incident in Luke, there is a woman who is said to be "bent double" (*sugkúptousa*) in which case we would have a physical effect resulting from a non-physical "spirit" (and so demonic PK*):

> And there was a woman who had had a disabling spirit for eighteen years. She was bent over and could not fully straighten herself. When Jesus saw her, he called her over and said to her, "Woman, you are freed from your disability." And he laid his hands on her, and immediately she was made straight, and she glorified God. But the ruler of the synagogue, indignant because Jesus had healed on the Sabbath, said to the people, "There are six days in which work ought to be done. Come on those days and be healed, and not on the Sabbath day." Then the Lord answered him, "You hypocrites! Does not each of you on the Sabbath untie his ox or his donkey from the manger and lead it away to water it? And ought not this woman, a daughter of Abraham whom Satan bound for eighteen years, be loosed from this bond on the Sabbath day?" (Luke 13.11–16).[15]

The word translated as "disabling" is *astheneia* and refers to "a state of incapacity" which could be due to any number of possible causes.[16] It seems rather clear in context

---

15. There are other Lukan passages (like Luke 9.42 and Acts 19.15–16) that speak of demons doing things like "throwing" and "overpowering" physical persons. But the contexts make apparent that these are possession cases, and possession cases are not instances of demonic souls acting directly on physical bodies.

16. Friberg, Friberg, and Miller, *Analytical Lexicon of the Greek New Testament*, 78. Graham H. Twelftree interprets "disabling spirit" as "a spirit of sickness . . . or infirmity" (*In the Name of Jesus*, 86). *Astheneia* can be due to anything from less severe ailments to diseases. If understood figuratively, the disability may be one of moral incapacity, such as character weakness or lack of insight.

that her being "bent double" is this disability and so we should not think of the disability as somehow distinct from her physical condition. But verse 11 does make clear that the condition is not naturally derived but is caused by "a spirit" (*pneuma*). The very last verse (v. 16) removes any ambiguity as to which "spirit" is said to be responsible for this physical malady, namely "Satan." Thus, any attempt to disassociate Satan from the woman's condition in order to avoid any negative implications for ECI would fail.[17] Hence, on the basis of this passage, theologians like Merrill Unger are quick to say that demons have "amazing strength" and that they "have power over the human body to cause . . . physical defects and deformities (Luke 13:11–17)."[18] But is this the best conclusion to draw?

It is not beyond imagination that a malevolent mind could incite the woman to simply will herself into being bent over (as if by hypnotic suggestion) and, subsequently, develop a malformed spine (as in inflicting upon oneself a form of scoliosis). This would be another instance of Satan weakly actualizing some affliction which in this case is the indirect causing of the woman being "bent double."[19] And since the woman is said to be bent *over* ("bent over" is the primary translation of *sugkúptousa*)[20] rather than, say, bent *sideways* (something indicative of scoliosis), perhaps a physiological comparison can be made in what is medically identified as a species of *kyphosis*.[21] Kyphosis (or "hunchback") is defined as an

> abnormal degree of backward curvature of the part of the spine between the neck and the lumbar regions. Backward curvature is normal in this region and kyphosis is an exaggeration of the normal curve. It is commonly the result of bad postural habits in adolescence or of osteoporosis.[22]

Despite its being common among adolescents (usually as a mild condition resulting from slouching), if such a condition, as noted here, can be the result of "bad postural habits" (and so officially referred to as *postural kyphosis*), then it might be something that could be exaggerated even more so in order to lead to a dramatic

---

17. Luke's opening remarks about the victim having a "sickness caused by a spirit" (verse 11) seems conclusive. However, Luke, in his commentary on the situation in the same verse, might simply be attaching an unwarranted theological context to the woman's malady. And given that the passage repeatedly refers to this as a "sickness" (one that lasted 18 years no less!) and that it is not ultimately handled as an exorcism proper, the likelihood of this being a demonic possession case is small. The crux, then, lies in Jesus's response in verse 16 where he says that "Satan has bound [her] for eighteen long years." That Satan is said to be the direct agent of her "binding" (*desmou*—from the same root word used of Jesus who "binds (*dēsē*) the strong man," Matt. 12.29) surely evinces a diabolical bringing about of the woman's physical back problem.

18. Unger, *Biblical Demonology*, 67.

19. See chapter 10 n. 30.

20. Friberg, Friberg, and Miller, *Analytical Lexicon of the Greek New Testament*, 360.

21. I remind the reader once again of the difficulties of retrospective diagnoses as discussed in chapter 10.

22. Youngson, "Kyphosis." I am not insinuating that the woman herself was an adolescent. The study only shows that such conditions are *common* in adolescents, not exclusive to them.

curvature of the spine. Perhaps during a large portion of the woman's 18 years she was mentally coerced into her ongoing acts of extreme bad posturing. If the woman were "trained" into this position for multiple years, perhaps she had fallen prey to some exaggerated form of kyphosis (or something like it) which then was subsequently healed by Jesus some 18 years henceforth. In short, what began as a "willed" contortion of the spine ended up as a more permanent malformation long after the Satanic influence. Such an act is consistent with the apparent absence of any explicit exorcism taking place in the woman's healing despite the 18-year condition as being the ongoing PK* product of a spirit.

Suffice it to say, one need not appeal to any mysterious auxiliary power like PK* in order to account for the demonic affliction when it seems perfectly within a medical context to adduce a behavioral habit to explain the woman's malady (a habit that could be imposed or communicated through an ongoing cognitive suggestion by an evil spirit).

According to 2 Cor 11.14, Satan Can (Occasionally) Masquerade as an Angel of Light

In chapter 11 of Paul's second letter to the Corinthians, he attempts to rehabilitate the Greek community of Corinth (a province west of Athens) which he believes has been seduced into sin by Satan through the cunning wisdom of counterfeit apostles. Paul expresses his lack of surprise that there are such alleged fellow apostles capable of deceiving their listeners into a false gospel. And why not be surprised? Because "even Satan disguises himself as an angel of light" (11.14). It is taken by some readers of 2 Corinthians (e.g., Peter R. Schemm Jr., John Phillips, David E. Garland, Linda L. Belleville, Merrill F. Unger, Robert Morey, Grant McColly, and William Caldwell) that Satan's deceiving capabilities apparently include the ability to appear in a way that a normal onlooker would easily confuse with an angelic manifestation, thus making Satan a virtual master of disguise.[23]

The confusion, so we assume, is due to the fabricated similarity of *appearances* between both demon and angel and, thus, one could be made manifest to look like the other. By extension, the eminent John Warwick Montgomery goes so far as to utilize 11.14 as a proof-text for the notion that Satan can even appear as a human being: "If Satan can transform himself into an angel of light . . ., he can certainly disguise himself as a dead saint."[24] Moreover, there are two first-century (AD) passages within the Jewish tradition that offer a description of Satan as one who appears in the visible form of a beautiful angel (*Life of Adam and Eve* 9.1; *Apocalypse of Moses*

---

23. Schemm, "The Agents of God," 305; Phillips, *Exploring 2 Corinthians*, 251–54; Garland, *2 Corinthians*, 485; Belleville, *2 Corinthians*, 282–83; Unger, *Biblical Demonology*, 64; Morey, *Satan's Devices*, 30–31; McColly, "Paradise Lost," 192; Caldwell, "The Doctrine of Satan," 169.

24. Montgomery, *Principalities and Powers*, 142.

17.1–2). Lee Martin McDonald remarks: "Whether Paul knew these documents is uncertain, but the tradition that lies behind them is also assumed by Paul."[25] Consequently, 2 Cor 11.14 may be support for the idea that Satan can physically appear as an angel.

The force of this interpretation is significant since we tend to see visibility as entailing physicality of some sort (as I think one should, at least apart from God's direct intervention or any additional reason to think otherwise). If Satan can indeed appear as a sort of wolf in sheep's clothing, then this phenomenon would point to Satan's bearing properties that would make him visible. And if Paul does have the tradition that underlies the *Life of Adam and Eve* and the *Apocalypse of Moses* in mind, then it is perhaps difficult to think that Paul did not accept the ability of Satan to visibly manifest.

By way of response, Paul's use of "disguise" (*metaschēmatizetai*) is unlikely to be referring to a physically visible occurrence (though it *can* have this connotation as it does in other Pauline passages[26]). It is important to note that the root word used here is also used in its immediate context in verse 13 where the false teachers are also said to be "disguising" (*metaschēmatizetai*) themselves, but in their case as counterfeit apostles; and verse 15 further adds that "his servants also disguised (*metaschēmatizetai*) themselves as workers of righteousness." Does this suggest that the false apostles and their followers could *physically* and *visibly* disguise themselves–as if to say that the false apostles were adept at costuming? And just what would "righteousness" look like anyway? Surely this "disguise" has to do with *the illusion of doctrinal purity and moral virtue* and not with the cosmetic issues of *physicality* or *appearance*. As such, Paul is not surprised that there would be false apostles and teachers since doctrinal and ideological deception is a game played by the worst of God's creatures, Satan. As tradition reports, even God's supreme enemy can appear to be an "angel of light" despite his true identity as an "angel of darkness" (1 Thess 5.5).[27] And this is a well-established interpretation of Paul's admonition in 2 Corinthians, having been offered by a number of other New Testament scholars and commentators (e.g., Robert H. Gundry, Murray J. Harris, Charles Hodge, and R. C. H. Lenski).[28]

---

25. McDonald, "2 Corinthians," 442.

26. Philippians 3.21 uses *metaschematisei* as a deliberate reference to "the [physical] body" (*to soma*). See Phillips, *Exploring 2 Corinthians*, 251–52. However, as commentator Paul Barnett observes, despite multiple occurrences of *metaschematisei*, "none of which references gives a clear idea of the meaning" of the Apostle Paul's usage in 2 Corinthians 11. See Barnett, *The Second Epistle to the Corinthians*, 523 n. 3.

27. Also compare with Acts 26.18; Rom 13.12; 2 Cor 6.14; Eph 5.8; 1 Pet 2.9; 1 John 1.5–6; 2.8–9.

28. See Gundry, *Commentary on the New Testament*, 721–22; Harris, *The New International Greek Testament Commentary*, 771–75; Hodge, *2 Corinthians*, 204; Lenski, *The Interpretation of II Corinthians*, 1256–58.

Objections Based on Passages in the New Testament

To better ground this interpretation, it needs to be noted that being an "angel of light" does not entail that the "light" (*phōs*) so described be a reference to a bright, visible manifestation of wavelengths or quanta. Rather, it is more likely to be understood in accord with Paul's normal usage throughout his correspondence with the Corinthians:

> "the Lord comes who will both bring to light [*phōtisei*] the things hidden in the darkness and disclose the motives of men's hearts" (1 Cor 4.5).

> "the god of this world has blinded the minds of the unbelieving, that they might not see the light [*phōtismon*] of the gospel of the glory of Christ" (2 Cor 4.4).

> "For God, who said, 'Light [*phōs*] shall shine out of darkness', is the One who has shone in our hearts to give the light [*phōtismon*] of the knowledge of the glory of God in the face of Christ" (2 Cor 4.6).

This local context of 2 Corinthians 11 is quite telling. "Light" is better understood, not as a visible form of radiation, but rather as a metaphor for contrasting the good with depravity and deception (viz., "darkness"). Even though "angel of light" seems to reflect those passages from the *Life of Adam and Eve* and the *Apocalypse of Moses* where Satan's physical transmutation is clearly in view, Murray J. Harris explains that the expression

> could be a Pauline coinage, prompted on the one hand by the common association of Satan with darkness (6:14–15) and deception (4:4) and of God or Christ with light and illumination (4:6; Rom. 13:12,14; Eph. 5:11–14), and on the other hand by his own experience and observation of Satan's various stratagems (2:11).[29]

The same Greek term, in its being used symbolically in other ancient contexts, is famously employed in Plato's dialogue regarding his much-celebrated Allegory of the Cave where "light" is taken to refer figuratively to intellectual illumination.[30] The use of "light" is more akin to the popular saying, "I have seen the light!" and "I have been enlightened!" in light's association with *comprehensibility*, *truth*, and *purity*.[31] As such, the possible allusion by Paul to Satan's transfiguring himself as a shining angel in *Adam and Eve* and the *Apocalypse of Moses* are not necessarily being remembered in 2 Corinthians for the *how* of Satan's deception, rather they may be remembered only for the *fact* of such deception and nothing more. And this is consistent with, if not better understood by, a reading that sees "angel of light" as a metaphorical reference to virtuous teaching.

---

29. Harris, *The New International Greek Testament Commentary*, 774–75.

30. Plato, *Republic*, VII.514a.

31. Paul elsewhere parallels this sentiment and meaning of 2 Cor 11.14 in his later letter to Timothy: "The Spirit clearly says that in later times some will abandon the faith and follow deceiving spirits and things taught by demons" (1 Tim 4.1).

PART IV: OBJECTIONS

Therefore, the apparitional interpretation of "angel of light" as evidence for Satan being either a (quasi-)material being or having the PK* power to manifest is predicated on weak exegesis. The only information we have about Satan, according to 2 Corinthians 11, is that he is a villainous manipulator of doctrine as are the false apostles. A demonstration of the demons's ontology is not in view here, and so we, once again, do not have a viable objection.

Second Thessalonians 2.8–9 Reports that Satan Can Perform "Signs and Lying Wonders"

God, as the creator of the universe, is well-understood to have the divine power to create and manipulate the universe under his control. We are wholly accustomed to the declarations that God's ongoing interventions in history are miraculous acts or, to use the biblical terminology, "signs and wonders."[32] However, the New Testament also comments on Satan's apparently similar ability to perform "signs and wonders" according to Paul's Second Letter to the Thessalonians, where he writes:

> And then that lawless one will be revealed whom the Lord will slay with the breath of His mouth and bring to an end by the appearance of His coming; that is, the one whose coming is in accord with the activity of Satan, with all power and signs and false wonders.[33]

The "lawless one" (whose identity is undefined) is "in accord with the activity of Satan" and will engineer all "power and signs and false wonders." Naturally, such a description invokes the language of the kinds of miracles of the Hebrew Exodus under Moses, the miracles of Jesus, and the miracles of Jesus's post-ascension disciples. Each of these display clear physical acts of creation or manipulation of earthly elements. It would be natural to suppose that since the "lawless one" is said to parrot such activity in a "lying" manner, then the power of Satan (and, subsequently, a demon) to physically interact with the world would appear to have canonical support.[34]

However, it is not clear that "the activity of Satan" is necessarily parallel to the grand "signs and false wonders" variously affected by God. Even Thomas Aquinas considers such a comparison "repugnant."[35] Just to contextualize this passage, the medium

---

32. See Deut 6.22; 7.19; 26.8; 29.3; 34.11; Neh 9.10; Ps 135.9; Jer 32.20; Dan 4.2–3; 6.27; Acts 2.19, 22, 43; 4.30; 5.12; 6.8; 7.36; 14.3; Rom 15.19; 2 Cor 12.12; Heb 2.4.

33. There is little doubt that this sentiment reflects the Old Testament's similar prohibition of following a "prophet" or "dreamer" that can perform "a sign or a wonder" (Deut 13.1–3).

34. Unger is quite sure that the Satanic "signs and wonders" of 2 Thess 2 entail a "full and startling display of diabolic miracle" (*Biblical Demonology*, 208) since the pervasiveness of cultural superstition of the past and present would make denying such power to Satan "difficult to account for" otherwise (66).

35. Thomas Aquinas, *De Potentia Dei*, VI.5: 185. The full context of his point is: "God does not give [demons] the power to do things that surpass the faculty of their nature, because seeing that a miraculous work is a divine witness to God's power and truth, if the demons whose whole will is diverted

Objections Based on Passages in the New Testament

intellect here–said to be the agent of such action–is this anonymous "lawless one." Some theologians suppose that this refers to an eschatological antichrist figure (a geo-political magistrate) said to be instantiated prior to the divine Parousia (the second coming of Jesus).[36] In this case it is likely to be understood as a human agent (minimally a non-spiritual, physical entity) who is bringing about these "signs and false wonders." But never mind that. If Satan is the agent behind such power, just what *is* the nature of this power that enables him to perform "signs and wonders"? On this, I note that the phrase "signs and wonders" does not *ipso facto* refer exclusively and necessarily to *miraculous* or *supernatural* occurrences of a psychokinetic nature and that to treat "signs" or "wonders" as synonyms for "miracles" is generally mistaken.

Samuel Meier, Professor of Hebrew at the University of Ohio, notes how "signs" (used predominantly of the Mosaic "ten plagues of Egypt" event of the Exodus) sometimes connotes events that are not actually supernatural (or directly miraculous). For example, some scholars recognize that it is likely that in the Old Testament, Pharaoh's magicians (Exod 7–8) imitated some of the various "signs" through simple trickery or sleight of hand as exemplified in the changing of the staff into a serpent (7.10–12).[37] Acts of illusion might dazzle an ancient Egyptian audience

---

to evil, were to receive the power to work miracles, God would vouch for their falsehood, which is repugnant to his goodness. Hence at times they perform by God's permission only such works as seem miraculous to men, and which are within the limits of their natural power."

36. The performance of such "signs and wonders" immediately brings to mind Jesus's warnings in Matt 24.24 in his discourse about "false Christs and false prophets"; John would later make the direct connection with the antichrist figure in Rev 19.20 (presumably the false prophet refers to the same figure as John's descriptions in 1 John 2.18 and 4.3). Contextually, the "antichrist" refers to (or typologically invokes) at least one of the persecuting Roman emperors of the day (most likely Nero). Though the antichrist clearly comes in the power and mantel of Satan, he is (likely) a human and not Satan himself. This would accord with Jesus's description of the "abomination of desolation" (Matt 24.15) who will iconoclastically persecute the followers of Christ. Other interpretations of "antichrist" also fail to be associated with unembodied spirits (e.g., McGinn, *Antichrist*).

37. See Scott, *The Existence of Evil Spirits Proved*, 213ff; Murison, "The Serpent in the Old Testament," 122 n. 23; Davidson, Stibbs, and Kevan, *The New Bible Commentary*, 112. The notion of trickery is not a recent suggestion in an attempt at responding to worries about demonological sorcery being a cause of the magicians's power, but is a suggestion dating back to Josephus (*Antiquities of the Jews*, II.13.3) who makes no such connection between the magicians and demonology. In the response to Moses by Pharaoh's magicians, they first imitate the staff-to-serpent miracle. That this event deflates the Mosaic display is rather evident, and it may have to do with the fact that some cobras, when held appropriately at the neck, will straighten and remain still (and would appear staff-like). This would account for the illusion of the magician's staff seemingly turning into a serpent without the aid of any supernatural psychokinetic power. But, as some have pointed out, the details of the story are not generally consistent with the ancient occurrences of snake charming (e.g., Jacob, *The Second Book of the Bible*, 254; Walton, Matthews, and Chavalas, *The IVP Bible Background Commentary*, 82). It is no insignificant point if one interprets the magicians's activities to be supernatural since it is generally assumed that such counterfeit miracles would surely be the work of demons as evidenced by the "witch craze" of the early modern period. As Dónal P. O'Mathúna writes, "Divination and magic are dangerous because they bring people into contact with evil spiritual beings and forces" and that the magicians's activities, among others, exemplify "that these powers can be harnessed" ("Divination, Magic," 196).

Part IV: Objections

entrenched in folklore, but such acts would lack any actual supernatural origin. Thus, Meier says that "sign"

> need not be extraordinary, and indeed it can be a predictable phenomenon that one expects with regularity.... [T]hese [miraculous] instances [of "wonder"] indicate that this is not its only or even primary focus. Instead, a "wonder" (*môpēt*) remains primarily an unusual portent accompanying the disruption of the status quo.[38]

Canonical support for this can be found in Isa 8.18's declaration that Isaiah himself and his children serve as "signs" in themselves: "Behold, I and the children whom the LORD has given me are *for signs and wonders* in Israel from the LORD of hosts, who dwells on Mount Zion."[39] Surely no supernatural element is intended here. Equally benign, King Nebuchadnezzar personally reflects on the "signs and wonders" God has done for him through the prophet Daniel when he proclaims:

> It has seemed good to me to declare *the signs and wonders* which the Most High God has done for me. How great are His signs, And how mighty are His wonders! His kingdom is an everlasting kingdom, And His dominion is from generation to generation.[40]

But, one might protest, some translations (like the New International Version) in 2 Thess 2.9 add "miracles" alongside of "signs and wonders." This gives the impression that even after analyzing the bald usage of "signs and wonders" as something not necessarily supernatural, the fact that "miracles" is deliberately added might make the supernatural dimension of this power all the more evident. But the Greek word translated "miracles" in the New International Version here is *dunamei* which just simply means *ability* or *power*.[41] It is a term that is already more accurately reflected in the other translations in its being phrased as "power and signs and false wonders" and is not necessarily a miracle proper. The interpretation here in 2 Thessalonians, it seems to me, is best understood as a flagrant and direct play on the miracles of Moses and Jesus. But just as the magicians of Pharaoh's court (as well as the actions of antichrist noted in Matthew 24) are not necessarily conjuring truly supernatural counter-miracles, neither are we obliged to think that Paul had in mind supernatural psychokinesis in 2 Thess 2.8–9. I should add that the very description of such wonders as "false" (*pseudous*) perhaps is meant to underscore the very *lack* of any supernatural dimension one might affix to the miracles of the "lawless one," to wit, that they are anything other than supernatural. As Mortimer Adler aptly summarizes of the good angels, "they cannot produce miracles. Only God can do that."[42] How much less the demons?

38. Meier, "Signs and Wonders," 757.
39. Emphasis mine.
40. Dan 4.2–3; emphasis mine.
41. Friberg, Friberg, and Miller, *Analytical Lexicon of the Greek New Testament*, 121.
42. Adler, *The Angels and Us*, 74.

Objections Based on Passages in the New Testament

It could be pointed out that the additional "signs and wonders" subsequently produced by the magicians in counterfeiting Yahweh's power through Moses may not be so easily broad-brushed as clever acts of chicanery. We are told in Exod 7.20–8.7 that the magicians also counterfeited the turning of the Nile into blood and the bringing of frogs onto the land of Egypt. If these events are indeed to be construed as supernatural events, I do not believe we are committed to thinking that these are acts of Satan or his demons. According to Scott Noegel, the magicians's acts may be an extension of *God's* doing.[43] It could be, he says, that the magicians imitate the Mosaic plagues and so unwittingly "conjure more bloody water and more frogs, and thus, assist Moses in his plight."[44] But lest the magicians be seen as equally endorsed by God, the miracles of God end up embarrassing the magicians and eventually the miracles performed by Moses precipitate an act of (temporary) repentance by Pharaoh. The magicians just unwittingly become the instruments of God's will for increasing such calamity and get humiliated in the process–a double-edged sword if ever there was one!

It is, therefore, unjustified to think that 2 Thessalonians 2 is a datum of Satan's abilities to manipulate physical objects in creation considering the elusive nature of what "signs and wonders" are and that there is no unambiguous precedent in the Bible. And if it is inconclusive to say that 2 Thessalonians 2 shows such interaction, then we have even less reason to think that Satan and the demons utilize PK*.

Satan and His Cohorts Have Certain Powers Over the Air (Eph 2.2), the Cosmos (6.12), and Death Itself (Heb 2.14)

The New Testament does appear to attribute to Satan and his demons a certain amount of undisclosed superhuman power. This is to say that demons are not described in the same way as disembodied saints, which can do nothing special or unique. Instead, demons are described as being virtual superpowers that can do things beyond the normal abilities of other creatures. The Bible explicitly refers to demons as "cosmic powers" (Eph 6.12). This is not surprising since the good angels are said to be "greater in might and power" over human beings (2 Pet 2.11). Satan himself, however, has "all power" (2 Thess 2.9) to the extent that the "whole world lies in the power of the evil one" which includes "the power of the air" (Eph 2.2) and even the "power over death" (Heb 2.14). There is little doubt that "power" (when translated from *dunamis*) refers to *force* and *deed* and not to mere *authority* (as in having the "power" or "right" to marry or to adjudicate–something that is better captured by the use of *exousia* as we see in John 1.12). Are we not obliged to see these as indicative of demonic PK*?

---

43. Noegel, "Moses and Magic," 48–49. Noegel evidently follows William Fleetwood here. Cf., Fleetwood, *An Essay Upon Miracles*.

44. Noegel, "Moses and Magic," 49.

Part IV: Objections

Not at all. It seems to me that one need not exaggerate the sort of power had by Satan and the demons in order to consider them *operationally* superior to human beings, because even if one assumes of them ECI, the exercise of CI could give rise to significant consequences. By analogy, consider how the New Testament speaks of human beings as doing "greater works" than Jesus Christ himself (John 14.12). This is not meant to suggest that the works of believers will be more miraculous or extravagant than Jesus's own ministerial works (i.e., the resuscitation of corpses or healings from diseases). Rather, the context suggests that the "greater works" refers to the evangelistic means to reach more individuals globally and to the ability to bring, in terms of sheer quantity, more people into the fellowship of God.[45]

If, instead, the powers of Satan and the demons refer to their *level of influence* then there is no reason, as with the "works" of John 14.12, to suppose that the *dunamis* is a miraculous or supernatural PK* power.[46] The term *dunamis* itself need not entail a supernatural connotation since it generically refers "to the inherent or derived ability to perform an action."[47] That Satan has the ability to perform acts of chicanery (2 Thess 2.9) or that angels have undisclosed abilities beyond human beings (2 Pet 2.11) is no direct challenge to ECI. That demons can successfully disseminate a wide range of deceitful doctrines[48] and temptations[49] makes their power, in this cognitive sense, far more dangerous than any PK* ability, for it commands *the free will* of victims which is the pinnacle of control. Cognitive ascendancy is, after all, how one is able to make sense of clichés like "the pen is mightier than the sword." It is a far more terrible power that one could make another *want* to be evil.

We can also infer from the Johannine report of Satan and his demons losing a battle against Michael and the good angels that the demons's power is not as strong as that of the good angels.[50] The other terms used to describe the "power" of Satan (*exousia* and *kratos*) refer to one's merely having *authority* or *jurisdiction*. The reference to Satan having the "power (*kratos*) of death" does not mean that Satan simply can inflict physical death on demand but, according to the noted commentator William L. Lane, he is attributed with such power because he introduced death by having initially "seduced humankind to rebel against God."[51] In this sense it is similar to a governmental ruler "bear[ing] the sword" (cf., Rom 13.3–4) which does not itself entail that one personally wields the instrument of destruction. Moreover, as Luke Timothy Johnson

---

45. See Brown, Fitzmyer, and Murphy, *The Jerome Biblical Commentary*, 453.

46. As it turns out, *dunamis* is only used of Satan and angels in 2 Thess 2.9 and 2 Pet 2.11, respectively.

47. Arnold, "Power," 938. *Dunamis* surely has no supernatural connotation when used in places like 1 Cor 15.56 where Paul writes, ". . . the power of sin is the law."

48. 1 Thess 4.1; 1 John 4.1.

49. Matt 4.3; 6.13; 1 Cor 7.5; 1 Thess 3.5.

50. Rev 12.7–8.

51. Lane, *Hebrews 1–8*, 61; Lane, *Hebrews*, 50.

and Jennifer K. Cox point out,[52] it is more of an expression of apocalyptic imagery–that Jesus's conquering of death is one of cosmic proportions. Thus, Satan's "power over death" expresses his territorial *authority* and *dominion* and not some PK* ability over another's body with which to directly end one's life.

Therefore, the powers of Satan and his demons to influence doctrine and human behavior are best seen as reflections of their widespread ability to cognitively interact with other minds. This is perfectly in keeping with the scriptural assertion that angels and demons possess a power beyond human ability, and so there is no reason to hypothesize that Satan and/or his angels possess any PK* powers.

Conclusion

I have proposed and responded to several passages thought by some to oppose either the pure immateriality of demons or ECI. In the previous chapter, we looked to Old Testament passages and found that they do not imply that demons are either (quasi-)material or have an auxiliary PK* power. In the current chapter, we specifically looked at passages in the New Testament with its clear references to Satan and/or his demons. But, like those of the Old, we still lack any good reasons or counterexamples to abandon the conclusions drawn thus far. However, this is not the end of any actual or would-be objections. For, though from the theological point of view nothing is available to call my arguments into question, we have yet to explore philosophical push-back that may yet do just that.

In the next and final chapter of this section, we shall survey some philosophical objections that could be raised against the twofold hypothesis about the metaphysics of demons I have been defending. I will show that none of those objections are successful either.

---

52. "Since Hebrews makes no further mention of the devil (*ho diabolos*), of Satan, or of any other demonic powers, it is safe to suppose that this formulation emerges from the apocalyptic framework widely shared by ancient Jews and Christians, in which the devil stands for the cosmic forces opposed to the righteous (see Matt 4:1; 25:41; Luke 8:12; John 6:70; 13:2; Acts 10:38; Eph 4:27; 6:11; 1 Tim 3:6; 2 Tim 2:26; Jas 4:7; 1 Pet 5:8; 1 John 3:8; Rev 12:9; 20:2), and over whom the Messiah will triumph.... Because the devil, in turn, can be associated intimately with death (see above all Wis 2:24), victory over him can be expressed in terms of a victory over death (see Hos 13:14; 1 Cor 15:26, 55; 2 Tim 1:10; Rev 20:14; 26:4)" (Johnson and Cox, *Hebrews*, 100).

12

Philosophical Objections

THE LAST TWO CHAPTERS contained a series of biblical references thought to imply either that demons are (quasi-)material beings or that they should be seen to have a PK* ability with which to interact with the physical world. However, it turns out that none of them offer such implications for the sundry reasons expressed therein. But this is not enough for the philosopher, for she is not merely committed to the deliverances of special revelation in filling out her metaphysical worldview. Metaphysical reasoning *sans* Scripture can often provide insight as to what might probably be the case. For example, in the philosophy of mind, one might reflect on the disparity between mental states and their correlative physical states and infer that the two are fundamentally separate–even separate substances. Such a conclusion can obtain wholly apart from any conclusions drawn from biblical examination. Or, perhaps there are further philosophical reflections about the nature of God not settled merely by scriptural appeal. For example, the theologian may infer God's timelessness solely on the basis of his aseity; or, she may draw a different conclusion in that nothing about God's aseity vis-à-vis the nature of time can imply the timelessness of God.

Similar grounds for push-back can be offered against the cases that I have made both for the pure immateriality of demons and for ECI. In this chapter, we shall explore some would-be objections that need to be assessed in finalizing whether the metaphysical arguments of the demons's nature in this book are ultimately justified. We shall parse out these objections below by considering, first, those against pure immaterialism and, second, those against ECI.

Contra Pure Immaterialism

The counter-arguments in this section consist of both principled and factual disputes to the claim that demons are purely immaterial. I consider the objections raised below to be the most paramount but also widely representative of the kinds of philosophical objections that may be raised. But since my argument is a preliminary strike against materialist and quasi-materialist views of demonology, these objections do not belong to any known interlocutor and so are merely anticipatory. But they are informed by years of personal interaction with a number of scholars, ministers, and even the laity. Let us look to each in turn.

Objection #1: That a spirit would be invisible and incorporeal in no way mitigates against a spirit's being composed of an aerial substance as evident in the ancient Greek view of the daimon

In this objection, we are to imagine the possibility of an object's being composed of a set of particulate matter arranged in such a way (or placed in such a state) that outside observers would not see the object with the naked eye. If this is metaphysically possible, as indeed it is considering that there are such "insensible" things as helium, oxygen, nitrogen, and water vapor, there is nothing about the Bible's description of spirits as "invisible" and "incorporeal" that in any way diminishes the hypothesis that demons are composed of a fine, insensible material. This ontology would certainly be consistent, more or less, with one's being incorporeal (viz., without any "gross matter") and invisible (unable to be seen by the naked eye). It also would enjoy terminological harmony with ancient Greek conceptions of "spirit" for they had conceived of spirits as quasi-material.[1] Such a description of demons implies that they are compositions of particulate bits of matter that could be made invisible to perceivers when arranged "demonwise."[2] Of course this is possible just as visible particles like sand, when chemically arranged "glasswise," can be made relatively invisible to perceivers. However, even though such a scenario may be *consistent* with the biblical descriptions of invisibility and incorporeality, why think it is the *better* explanation?

One problem with this is that we would have a mereology of demonic composition which would multiply the existence of concrete objects (perhaps numbering in the trillions or some such grand number) far beyond what is necessary in order to account for the demons's invisibility and incorporeality. If we are opting for a metaphysics that is quantitatively simpler, this would be headed in the wrong direction. Worse, if we must entertain the idea that to be a spirit means to be composed of some sort of individual spirit particles, we must be prepared to suppose that God is composed of these discrete particles, too. This would undoubtedly upset orthodoxy's insistence that God has no parts. Rather, one should think that the demon would be an utterly immaterial object devoid of composition since one should rightly resist such a composition for God–a being also described as "spirit" (e.g., John 4.24). The closer we envisage a consistent, simpler ontology consonant with being invisible and incorporeal, the less

---

1. Recall "Early Greek Views of (Apparent) Demonic Realism" in chapter 3.
2. I am borrowing from Peter van Inwagen's familiar way of speaking of things composed of material simples. See van Inwagen, *Material Beings*, 109f.

we are entitled to the more complicated and heterodox ontological structures that would implicitly compromise the ontology of God.

Now, if we ignore these difficulties for one willing to accept such a mereological composition for God, one might further complain that such a notion lacks qualitative parsimony. For the history of the universe has far more *frequent kinds* of finer material objects that are invisible and incorporeal than objects that are as abstract as a purely immaterial spirit bearing those properties. For example, there are many different kinds of things we know about that are invisible and yet composed of material simples (like helium, air, water vapor, methane, carbon monoxide, Higgs field, black holes, dark matter, etc.). Contrast this to how few kinds there are of invisible things affirmed in mainstream Christianity that are not composed of material simples: God, angels, and *maybe* human souls. Given such (frequency) probabilistic expectations about what would likely be an imperceptible ontology of demons, one might reasonably conclude that such an ontology would be of a finer material so described.

However, if we accept a frequency probability here, aerial natures are not the sorts of things that are most frequent, even less so when we imagine *persons* that are supposed to be aerial. In the history of the universe, we should be quite sure that *no* persons are incorporeal and invisible if we do not assume in advance that spirits or ghosts already are. But just what are these things anyway? We cannot assert up front that they are aerial for that would obviously be begging the question. Hence, we cannot defer to a frequency probability of kinds of persons here for the simple reason that we lack any such precedent. The properties of incorporeality and invisibility are being assigned to persons, and that has no non-question-begging antecedents. Anyway, it is more reasonable to abandon a frequency probability view and opt for an explanatory probability based on the available evidence. And that evidence, when taken in its totality, implies pure immaterialism.

Perhaps the most egregious problem with this objection is its core assumption that terms like "invisible" and "incorporeal" are merely *perspectival*. For example, the Bible speaks of God as being "invisible" in a variety of New Testament passages (Rom 1.20; Col 1.15–16; 1 Tim 1.17; Heb 11.27). The term "invisible" (*aoratō*) is sometimes translated as "unseen" which could imply, not an ontological invisibility, but merely being in a relation to an observer such that one is not, *from the observer's perspective*, visible.[3] However, at least in 1 Tim 1.17, this is not likely the right interpretation here. This passage reads in full: "Now to the King eternal, immortal, invisible, the only God, be honor and glory forever and ever." Being eternal and being immortal are both ascribed to God in the same thought; and such ascriptions appear to be utilized apart from the perspective of any would-be observers.[4] It would seem that just as the

---

3. Friberg, Friberg, and Miller, *Analytical Lexicon of the Greek New Testament*, 60.

4. Note how "immortal" (*aoratō*) is a negative term and is translated as "undecaying" which could also be construed as being merely observer-dependent (e.g., an epistemic observation that something appears to be lacking decay over time). But this is not the preferred understanding. Clearly

property of being eternal is not dependent upon an observational perspective, neither should invisibility, *ceteris paribus*, be understood this way. And if so, the simplest understanding of "spirit" is to imagine it as an indivisible substance being *intrinsically* incorporeal and invisible.

Therefore, the objection to the pure immaterialism of demons on the grounds that the biblical data employ "invisible" and "incorporeal" as mere perspectival designations fails to take seriously the threat of diminishing God's spiritual nature, the self-defeating implications if taken on grounds based on a frequency probability view, and an unwarranted exegetical analysis of 1 Tim 1.17. Instead, the simplest explanation–one free of these problems–is that beings described as invisible and incorporeal should be understood to be purely immaterial in being and not merely in perspective.

Objection #2: Some personal testimonies, including testimonies to demonic materiality or quasi-materiality, ought to be considered as part of the data in determining the best explanation of the demons's ontology

A number of Christian philosophers and theologians have suggested (or implied) that personal testimony has evidential weight when it comes to demonology.[5] We also explored the possible positive contribution of various diabolical experiences in this book.[6] It is something that can and perhaps should be taken into account in a larger apologetic for demonic realism. But it does not follow that though some testimony is good that, therefore, all such testimony must be considered good. Never mind that. For the objection is carefully worded as to the legitimacy of only *some* testimonies of people who have had first-hand experiences with demons as perceptible objects. The implication, of course, is that something that is a perceptible object in these experiences would either not be a purely immaterial spirit after all or would have an ancillary power of PK* with which to be sensible. The objector will also insist that one cannot respond by then dismissing personal testimony wholesale on grounds that any eyewitness testimony is, *ex hypothesi*, inherently unreliable, for this would be to dismiss *all* testimonies *on all matters* of the same sort. This would mean that eyewitnesses could never give evidence in a court of law or that one's having been in pain could be mistaken when recalled. But these seem like incredible consequences if we dismiss testimony altogether. Surely at least some testimony is reliable. And if so, this would probably include many personal testimonies related

---

the property of not being mortal is an intrinsic and inherent property of God despite observational affirmation. Given the conjunction of similar descriptors, we should be confident that God has the property of being *aoratō* in the sense that it is his ontology that is intrinsically invisible.

5. For example, see Prince, *They Shall Expel Demons*, part 2; Dickason, *Angels*, 176; Koch, *Demonology*, 53–74. Even secular philosophers are warming up to the bald idea that one *could* have a personal experience of a demon that would count as knowledge. See McCraw, "Reformed Demonology?"

6. Recall "The Argument from (Diabolical) Experience" in chapter 5.

to demonic materiality. One might delimit her criticism of eyewitness testimony, then, to only testaments to supernatural entities. But now one must universally disavow all testimony to the divine, including religious experiences. Despite being an acceptable consequence to some, it presumes that the rich philosophical discussions over the doxastic virtues of such experiences have all been settled in the negative.

However, one need not cede such a skeptical conclusion in order to interact with the posed objection. One can affirm that testimony, even of the supernatural, *can* indeed be a reliable means of acquiring knowledge. But, insofar as it is applied to demonic encounters, I submit that not all such experiential encounters should automatically be considered as straightforward evidence because many experiences are overlaid with an interpretive framework that introduces elements not evident in the encounter itself.[7] For example, someone may observe near a production studio in Hollywood, California what appears to them as a green tree. But someone else, receiving the same experiential data, may think that they are experiencing a movie prop that only looks like a green tree. To call such an experience evidence of there being a green tree would be to impose an interpretation of that experience which would be justifiable if, *inter alia*, the movie prop hypothesis was not a better interpretation of the same experience. This is not to say that neither one is correct, but rather that one is not justified in drawing a particular metaphysical conclusion when an alternative hypothesis that is just as likely to be true in the given circumstances might also accommodate the same data. That one is being appeared to green-treely is not in dispute. But whether it is an actual tree or a manufactured fake is not settled in the experience itself. And so it would be with any putative demonic perception.

This much may be granted by most. What concerns the hypothetical objector here is that the few reliable eyewitnesses (or *ear*witnesses or whatever) of demonic encounters *do* testify to a material or quasi-material ontology of demons in the absence of a better explanation of the specific experiential data in question. The percipient may get the precise interpretation wrong, but surely they cannot be wrong about the physical attributes they are beholding. Often, paranormal things like apparitions and voice phenomena are experienced in *this* or *that* location. For someone not committed to a certain metaphysical idealism, these cannot be dismissed as being merely part of an interpretive framework any more than my experiencing pain *in my right leg* can. An outsider could dismiss such testimonies as lies, but then one would be using pure

---

7. E.g., Kuhn, *The Structures of Scientific Revolutions*, 16–17, 52–53; Cartwright, "How We Relate Theory to Observation"; Baergen, "The Influence of Cognition upon Perception"; Papineau, *Theory and Meaning*. I certainly do not think that because testimony is prone to interpretive ambiguity that it, therefore, is utterly unreliable. Instead, one should follow something like the criteria of testimonial reliability laid out by Robert Audi: "First, we might say that at least normally, a belief based on testimony is thereby justified (that is, justified based on testimony) provided the believer has overall justification for taking the attester to be credible regarding the proposition in question. Second, we might say that at least normally, a belief based on testimony thereby constitutes knowledge provided that the attester knows the proposition in question and the believer has no reason to doubt either the proposition or the attester's credibility regarding it" (*Epistemology*, 123–28).

immaterialism as an *a priori* test for what constitutes a lie or not–a criterion that obviously begs the question. So the problem of how to handle the testimony of a delimited few whose credible testimonies are, by all lights, based on legitimate experiences of the relevant sort does not go away by merely forbidding such potential evidences from being part of the *explananda*. To do so would be to beg the question as to what constitutes admissible evidence.

The epistemically safest thing to do is perhaps to insist that each experience should be taken on a case-by-case basis and evaluated accordingly. In so doing, one may discover that each testimony is refutable. But that is too quick. We cannot simply say in advance that no putative testimony will ever challenge the pure immaterialist hypothesis. How could we possibly know that? But rather than insisting on a hypothetical notion that any testimony in the future may be discredited, there is actually a way to embrace every putative experience of a demon–of both sight and sound–without thinking the pure immaterialist thesis to be incorrect. The consequence would be, not to dismiss individual testimonies, but to neutralize their effectiveness in constituting evidence against pure immaterialism. If it turns out that *at least one* testimony is sufficiently credible, then, one might argue, this would imply the falsity of pure immaterialism. But, in assuming the credibility of the experience, if there exists an alternative explanation for that experience, then the objection based on testimony would itself fail to refute pure immaterialism.[8] For the alternative explanation can account for the data of the *explananda*.

It turns out that there is indeed an alternative interpretation found in antiquity. In his *De Civitate Dei*, Augustine seeks to appease his pagan readers by tacitly accepting the eyewitness testimonies of those who believe in the supernatural power of *transmutation*.[9] He probably conceded the testimonies so that the audience of his evangelistic efforts, those same pagans, would not dismiss his evangelism outright.[10] But it is *how* he accommodates their alleged eyewitness testimonies that deserves attention here. I cite him at length:

> I cannot ... believe that even the body, much less the mind, can really be changed into bestial forms and lineaments by any reason, art, or power of the demons; but the phantasm of a man which even in thought or dreams goes through innumerable changes, may, when the man's senses are laid asleep or overpowered, be presented to the senses of others in a corporeal form, in some

---

8. One could assert a counterexample such as the following: Assuming that demons are purely immaterial, perhaps they manifest, not by virtue of their ontology, but by virtue of having magical powers. While this reply would serve to adequately deflect the objection, it would then become an objection to ECI.

9. Augustine is particularly invoking the transformation of Ulysses's companions into beasts and the morphing of the Arcadians into wolves. See his *De Civitate Dei*, XVIII.17.

10. G. R. Evans says that "there is good authority for the view that magicians can sometimes really perform the marvels credited to them ... It is no good his simply dismissing these evidences ... if he wants to convince his pagan readers of the soundness of the Christian view" (*Augustine on Evil*, 108).

indescribable way unknown to me, so that men's bodies themselves may lie somewhere, alive, indeed, yet with their senses locked up much more heavily and firmly than by sleep, while that phantasm, as it were embodied in the shape of some animal, may appear to the senses of others and may even seem to the man himself to be changed, just as he may seem to himself in sleep to be so changed, and to bear burdens; and these burdens, if they are real substances, are borne by the demons, that men may be deceived by beholding at the same time the real substance of the burdens and the simulated bodies of the beasts of burden.[11]

It is not that the bodies of certain people suddenly transform; rather, the phenomenon is likely due, says Augustine, to the demons's ability to produce a phantasy of the transmutation exclusively in the minds of the percipients (whether it beone who perceives their own transmutation or an outside eyewitness of another's transmutation). Gillian R. Evans explains that

> a phantasy of a man's mind . . . could perhaps take on the form of a body by some kind of projection, and be somehow presented to the perceptions of others. It may even seem to the man himself that he is changed. . . . We are dealing, not with real change, but with deceiving appearances, and those, as we know, are well within the capacity of demons.[12]

Demons, then, traffic in the art of illusion through the manipulation of the human imagination. And where more than one person is involved, the *phantasma* (a fabricated but illusory mental projection) could be coordinated in some way to affect any and all persons "observing" that *phantasma*. It would be something analogous to, or identical with, a visual hallucination. This is perhaps why pagan reports of groups of people transforming into wolves and back again seem authentic not only to the agents themselves but also to external eyewitnesses.

Such a notion is not expressed only by ancient speculation. In 1766, Immanuel Kant saw fit to publish a defense of the right of someone–Emanuel Swedenborg–to believe in immaterial spirits on the basis of his own alleged apparitional encounters even if it was possible that he was in fact deluded. (The work was apparently intended as a tongue-in-cheek disparagement of the inadequacies of "speculative metaphysics.") In that short work, Kant seems to find no way for the metaphysician to successfully object to the notion that a spirit, as an entity devoid of any positive, material properties, might cause an internal mental projection giving rise to what appears to be an externally caused sensory phenomenon:

---

11. Augustine, *De Civitate Dei* XVIII.18: 466–67.
12. Evans, *Augustine on Evil*, 108. Inta Ivanovska insists that, for Augustine, "it is the capacity of demonic or angelic *bodies* that allow them to perform such stunts" ("The Demonology of Saint Augustine of Hippo," 14; emphasis in the original). For my purposes here, I shall take this phenomenon to be, *contra* Ivanovska, a mental power of sorts conducive to mere cognitive interaction.

> Departed souls and pure spirits can indeed never be present to our external senses, nor communicate with matter in any other way than by acting upon the spirit of man, who belongs with them to one great republic. The spirits must act in such a way that the ideas which they call up in man's mind clothe themselves in corresponding pictures according to the law of imagination, thus causing any objects which fit into the picture to appear as if they were outside of him. This deception can affect any one of the senses, and, however mixed it may be with incongruous fancies, it should not keep one from supposing spiritual influences in it.[13]

It appears that what Augustine calls *phantasma* Kant here calls "corresponding pictures," and they are internal phenomena precipitated purely by spirit-to-spirit interaction. Let us refer to this hypothetical phenomenon wherein spirits, such as demons *per* our present concern, can incite this kind of "deception" of representation as a *psycho-projection*–a phenomenon that could be any kind of hallucination whether visual, aural, or tactile if we accept, as Kant suggests, that such a "deception can affect any one of the senses."

Psycho-projection is a workable theory that provides an alternative explanation of any experiences that appear to evince a (quasi-)material constitution of demons. It could be that the perceived demon is somehow triggering a hallucinatory projection of a beastly form or sound (or whatever is being experienced). From the percipient's standpoint, the demon would appear to have visible form but in reality it would be a mental projection–a *psycho*-projection–caused by the unknown cognitive influence of that demon. It would be analogous to how certain hypnotic suggestions have been known to make it appear to a percipient that there is something happening "out there" when in fact there isn't.[14] If a demon could act as a sort of hypnotist and could influence a human mind to project a false image, then the percipient may come to believe that what she sees is a real encounter with a (quasi-)material demon. Psycho-projection, then, is consonant with all of the data one might have in an alleged perception of a demon. Moreover, it would have the added benefit of being equally accommodating of all of the evidence we have for the demons being purely immaterial spirits.

Hence, despite the rote possibility of dismissing all or some testimonials to (quasi-)material demons on grounds that they are all overlaid with faulty interpretive frameworks, the pure immaterialist is able to accommodate the same experiential data by offering a competing hypothesis consistent with her pure immaterialism, namely psycho-projection. If this is possible, then any credible testimony affirming demonic (quasi-)materialism would be successfully neutralized as putative counter-evidence.

---

13. Kant, *Dreams of a Spirit-Seer*, 72.

14. Psychologists refer to this phenomenon as *hypnotic hallucination*. See Bryant and Mallard, "Seeing Is Believing"; Barber and Calverley, "An Experimental Study of 'Hypnotic' (Auditory and Visual) Hallucinations."

Part IV: Objections

Having addressed some potential (and actual) philosophical push-back against the notion of demonic pure immaterialism, and to some extent perhaps even ECI, we now turn to those objections one might pose exclusively against the notion of ECI.

Contra ECI

In this section we shall consider a number of philosophical objections to ECI. These objections tend to center around whether affirming ECI is explanatory overreach in my philosophical and theological approach to demonology.

Objection #1: When dealing with supernatural beings, which lie beyond our experience, it is impossible to ascertain either the extent of their powers or the limits thereof

Some may think that there is something that smacks of presumptuousness when a finite, temporal, spatially-restricted human being (me) proceeds to say what a race of super-beings can or cannot do. And if it is presumptuous to limit the powers of super-beings, then we are in no position to say that demons do not have any PK* ability. In reply, I do think that this is a misplaced concern, and a concern that ultimately misunderstands the program I am defending. First of all, we do impose boundaries and restrictions on the supernatural in a variety of other contexts. For example, some classical theists are content to say that the omnipotence of God in some way excludes being able to lie, steal, or murder even though these are mundane acts that can be performed by finite human persons.[15] They correctly support such an exclusion on the basis that God not only possesses maximal power but also maximal virtue. And to suppose that God is able to perform acts of vice fails to take into consideration that such acts are prevented by God's maximal virtue. This means that either God is incapable of such acts due to his moral nature or that he is prevented from such acts because he always wills not to do them. Either way, God never performs vices because they are either prevented by his nature or his will. Likewise, angels are thought not to be omniscient or omnipresent since these are attributes exclusive to God. For in the case of omniscience, no finite being, such as an angel, can sequentially amass discrete segments of knowledge (viz., propositions) such that they can add up to the infinite set of knowing all things.[16] This is so since one can never arrive at an unbounded value like infinity one member at a time (for one can always add to it).[17] Hence, angels *qua* finite beings are prevented from being infinitely knowledgeable (viz., omniscient).

---

15. See, for example, Gellman, "Omnipotence and Impeccability," 21–37.

16. See Beckwith and Parrish, *See the Gods Fall*, 111–16.

17. This would not preclude God from being omniscient, for he would not have acquired his knowledge one proposition at a time. Instead, his omniscience would be had all at once.

Consider demons in particular. They are thought to be unable to fully demonize individuals who have freely acquired the salvation of God since two mutually exclusive ultramundane beings cannot simultaneously rule over their physical hosts.[18] The point is not how good these reasons are for thinking that such beings have limitations, rather it is the fact that a number of thinkers do not think it presumptuous to conclude that some supernatural entities have limitations. Therefore, the problem is not whether one is permitted any principled objections to the notion of supernatural beings having limitations, but in whether there are any reasons to suggest that there are any such limitations. And I have advanced some reasons to think that demons, as fellow supernatural beings, do have such limitations.

Furthermore, those who believe that demons have PK* *themselves* often impose different kinds of limitations on Satan and the demons. For example, C. Fred Dickason speaks generally of Satan's "creaturely limitations" and that he is "limited by God in his power and activity."[19] Merrill F. Unger also speaks of Satan's limitations as one who can "create nothing, nor can he perpetrate any evil, physical or moral, without Jehovah's sanction."[20] C. Samuel Storms even contrasts the powers of demons with those of the good angels when he writes that "Michael and his elect angels are more powerful than Satan and his demonic hosts."[21] Each of these theologians proceeds to address in their respective works how the serious Christian practitioner, though not immune to the influences of demons, can overcome their dominative influence and power. But this is enough to establish that one is indeed permitted to delimit the powers of demons. The task before the supporter of demonic PK*, then, is not to object to ECI on the basis of any *a priori* forbiddance of our ability to discern a delimited demonic power, but on the basis of reasons given by which to infer those delimitations.

Finally, it is important to recall the distinction between what is metaphysically *possible* and what is *plausible*. The former is an acknowledgment of what *could feasibly* obtain. The latter is an acknowledgment of what *probably did* obtain given what is known of the relevant history of the actual world. I have acknowledged already that it is metaphysically possible that demons utilize PK*. But its metaphysical possibility is not sufficient to establish whether demons actually utilize such a mechanism. Likewise, ECI is a metaphysical possibility and, so, cannot be rendered impossible, particularly on grounds that it is presumptuous. I have already noted that it is not only not presumptuous, but that traditional supporters of demonic PK* themselves imply that limitations on the powers of demons can, in fact, be made. Since I have given reasons for thinking that the demons's interactions with this world are limited to CI, then any objections to my conclusion will have to interact with those reasons.

---

18. Full demonization typifies complete ownership, and, so, multiple agents cannot both be the complete owner of the same thing.
19. Dickason, *Angels*, 181 and 235.
20. Unger, *Biblical Demonology*, 26.
21. Storms, *Tough Topics*, 163.

Part IV: Objections

I shall turn now to consider the objection that if a PK* ability is probabilistically ruled out as a basic power of (at least some) created spirits, then this would have implications for human souls thought to be PK*-related to their bodies on substance dualism.

Objection #2: If it is unacceptable that demons psychokinetically interact with matter for the reasons given in chapter 9, then this means that it would be unacceptable for human souls (per substance dualism) to interact with matter, namely their own bodies, for similar reasons

There might be a concern amongst anthropological dualists in thinking that PK* is not a known mechanism of created souls in general and of human souls in particular. Indeed, it would seem that anthropological dualism *qua* substance dualism entails some kind of PK* in that human souls interact with their physical bodies. Gregory Boyd explains what he sees as a connection between anthropological PK* and demonic PK*:

> The mystery of how spirit affects the physical world is hardly unique . . .; it is manifested in every free action humans perform. For example, one might analyze the neurological processes of the brain that precede all of my actions to understand the mechanics of how my brain affects my body. But scientific analysis is unable to explain how *I* affect these neurological processes or even define what *I* am. In every explanation other than a strictly materialistic one, *I* transcend the physical processes of the brain. *I* make free decisions that *somehow* activate all this neurological activity. But the inherent limitations of our empirical methodologies are such that this "somehow" remains a mystery. We see, then, that the claim that evil spirits can adversely affect our physical environment should in principle be no more controversial to the nonmaterialist than the claim that . . . I can affect my environment.[22]

Naturally, some may wonder whether the case against demonic PK* in chapter 9 would constitute objections to anthropological PK* (viz. soul-body interaction) given Boyd's implied notion that both kinds of PK* are actually the same kind of activity and, so, equally uncontroversial for the "nonmaterialist." If it is right to draw this comparison, then it implies that PK* is not a unique power assigned to demons but is something that also obtains in human spirits. And if PK* does not likely occur in one kind of created spirit, neither might it occur in another kind of created spirit–especially if the power in question is sufficiently analogous. I want to respond to this objection by arguing that comparing demonic PK* to anthropological PK* is actually unwarranted since they are actually substantially dissimilar; hence, one kind of PK* does not act as precedent for the other.

Consider, first, the usual approach offered by Cartesians vis-à-vis substance dualism in that the human spirit is *paired* (by God) with its body so that there just

---

22. Boyd, *Satan and the Problem of Evil*, 304–5.

is an undisclosed causal connection (or a fixed nomological association) between a spirit and its material body.[23] But if this serves to elucidate how demons interact with physical objects, the dissimilarities are immediately apparent: unlike Cartesian dualism, the "pairings" of demons with objects are ephemeral and pertain to a variety of different, successive objects diachronically. Cartesian-style pairing in human composites consists of lifelong pairings for as long as the human person exists with her body. And that body is the only object the soul will ever be paired with. However, one might point out that since the body naturally changes over time (particularly since individual cells die out and get replaced by new ones) then the enduring body is actually a series of new objects as well. But surely the substance dualist is referring to the body as a *kind* such that there can be changes–gradual changes to the point of every cell being replaced–that do not break such pairing. It would be analogous to how a remote control is paired with a certain device. Surely that device could undergo all sorts of changes and never break that pairing. But those changes would only be permitted to a certain extent. If crucial changes *in kind* obtained (say, that the remote was transformed into a smartphone), then no doubt the pairing would be broken. Of course a succession of kinds is not occurring in the case of growing and aging human bodies.

If Cartesian dualism is the right context for understanding demonic PK*, then demons would be engaging in serial (viz., diachronic) pairing with various objects. In other words, demons would not pair with only one object during its lifetime, but it would pair with multiple objects one after another. It seems obvious to me that the gradual changes of the human body that retain the pairing relationship are nothing like the changes of objects to which demons would be similarly paired. Furthermore, Cartesian pairing is not a *voluntary* action on the part of the subject of that pairing. It is as much an involuntary action in human beings as the brain's processing of a pain signal from a pin prick. Demonic pairings, if the comparison holds, would presumably be *willful* and *on demand* by the subject thus making the acts of pairing completely voluntary. It is increasingly apparent, then, that the Cartesian notion of anthropological PK*, if that is what we want to call it, is just not the right comparison with demonic PK*. Thus, the former does not pave the way for the latter.

If the Cartesian version of substance dualism is not what the objector has in mind, then perhaps Thomistic dualism may draw the appropriate comparison. For Thomistic dualists, following Aristotle, they posit that the spirit *informs* its body (its *hylas*) and is an essential part of the person's whole metaphysical nature.[24] There is a sense that the form, or the soul (its *morphē*), essentially *belongs* with/in its body

---

23. E.g., Foster, *The Immaterial Self*, 163ff. That human spirits are paired with certain chunks of matter is a feature angels lack. Angels, after all, were not created as indigenous inhabitants of this world whereas human beings are.

24. E.g., Moreland and Rae, *Body and Soul*, 202–3; Feser, *Philosophy of Mind*, chapter 8.

Part IV: Objections

while it is alive and then is unnaturally separated from it when the body perishes. It is now starting to look like Thomistic anthropology is also unhelpful as a comparison with or as a precedent for demonic PK*. No demon could be the substantial form (or soul) of any physical object for the same reasons that discharge a Cartesian association: the interactions are ephemeral, with multiple, successive objects, and are voluntary. Perhaps the Thomist will consider comparing the hylomorphism of a demon and an object with the doctrine of the Incarnation of Christ. This would avoid any speculation as to whether the demon provides the sole *esse* to any particular object. But another problem arises in the comparison. For Aquinas, the Incarnation entails a singular, unifying individual (*hypostasis*) bearing two natures.[25] When one refers to "Christ" she is referring to the compositum that includes both his divine nature and his human nature in a whole subject. The same should be said of the demonic hylomorphism if understood this way, viz., that we have a new compositum through incarnation on our hands. The demon-object becomes a whole subject. On this reading, the relationship between demon and object implies an awkward result, namely, the object is a nature sustained by the demon. It becomes part of the nature of the demon.

Let us imagine that some demon, call it Azazel, incarnates a chair at t. Thus, if Azazel is referred to by another demon, then "Azazel" refers to the soul *and the chair it incarnates*. Azazel, during his union with the chair has, at t, a chair nature. The chair is, at t, the body of Azazel. While this scenario is possible in elucidating how a demon temporarily informs some object or other, the result remains too awkward in that the object is also forever part of the subject. Once Azazel departs the chair at $t+1$ then the chair is the former body or *corpse* of Azazel. The chair will always be identified with Azazel just as the body of Moses will always be his. Accordingly, I do not think even Aquinas would construe demonic PK* as an instance of either an incarnation or a hylomorphic composition. Given the disparity, anthropological PK* cannot be compared to demonic PK* on Thomistic grounds.[26]

I have one final critique of the objection raised in this section that does not depend on which notion of anthropological dualism one adopts. That souls would be united with bodies at all is declared to be the prerogative of God (e.g., Gen 2.7;

---

25. Aquinas, *Compendium Theologiae*, I.211–212.

26. I will make quick mention of one more possibility, namely that of emergent dualism. Emergent dualism is the view that the human soul emerges out of the development of the human organism once certain, relevant conditions are met. Once the soul emerges, it can interact with its body. Now, it seems rather self-evident to me that emergent dualism cannot be the right theory since the corporeal body to which the soul belongs must begin to exist *prior* to the emergence of its interactive soul (see Hasker, *The Emergent Self*). The soul emerges only after the body from which it comes physiologically develops in some relevant way. But this cannot be enlightening at all for understanding demonic PK*. Demons obviously do not emerge from the development of certain objects by which to interact with those object, nor is it even generally correct to say that they have their genesis in the material world at all. But even if they did, some of the same objections to Cartesianism and Thomism as analogies to demonic PK* also apply here (e.g., being an ephemeral and voluntary connection).

Zech 12.1) and so any attribution to demons of being united with physical objects, along with its other difficulties, would be an encroachment upon the prerogative of God as this kind of special creator. Consequently, the PK* power of demons cannot be compared to the PK* power human souls have. The demons's alleged PK* power, in addition to its being ephemeral, voluntary, and diachronically affective of multiple objects, seems to be a power exclusively relegated to God. This makes it an extremely controversial comparison. These considerations, then, seem lethal to any hope of associating demonic PK* to the divine prerogative of anthropological pairings. Therefore, the comparison of anthropological PK* with demonic PK* is inappropriate for the reasons given. If the comparison is inappropriate, as I have argued, then the objections to demonic PK* do not function as objections or challenges to anthropological PK*.[27]

In the last of the philosophical objections, I shall review and consider the objection based on the apparent widespread reports of demonic PK* phenomena.

Objection #3: If demonic PK* is false, then it would be difficult if not impossible to account for rampant worldwide reports of apparitions and poltergeists from the past to the present

Reports of first-hand experiences of sinister spirits interacting with human beings and nature seem to be universally cross-cultural.[28] None of the reported episodes is restricted to a certain social class, time period, or province. Unger argues:

> Denying all possibility of diabolic miracle as an underlying cause and dynamic, it seems difficult to account for the perpetuation of such a vast mass of superstition and fanaticism from the very dawn of historical times to the present. Where there is a great deal of smoke, there is likely to be a fire somewhere.[29]

However, there are other potential causes that can account for the "perpetuation of such a vast mass of superstition and fanaticism" that are not predicated on the actual occurrence of "diabolical miracle."

---

27. I remind the reader that the project of defending ECI in chapter 9 was to show, not that demonic PK* is somehow metaphysically *impossible*, but only that such a power for demons is *unlikely*. That anything should have any kind of PK* ability is bound to be mystifying, but I do not think it to be an impossibility. And it is an obvious error of extrapolation to insist that the unlikelihood of PK* for one kind of being is to affirm the unlikelihood of PK* for all kinds of beings. My project has been, to frame it in the negative, to offer a de facto case against positing PK* as a power had by the demons in order to fully explain how they interact with this world. And this will not entail that no other kind of being (i.e., angels) does not or cannot have this power.

28. See Keener, *Miracles*, 2:769–856. Though Keener's primary focus in his documentation of demonic activity both past and present is demonic possession, he also chronicles recurrent episodes of demonic PK* abilities (e.g., demons causing illnesses).

29. Unger, *Biblical Demonology*, 66.

Part IV: Objections

For one possibility, perhaps the reports of demonic PK* activity are (unfairly?) Westernized interpretations of cross-cultural spiritual phenomena. Christopher Partridge argues that there is a pervasive spiritual awakening that can be felt in the West that has been obtaining, and may continue to obtain, despite the decline of traditional religious systems.[30] As indicated by Partridge, they tend to be taking their interpretive cues of various spiritual phenomena from Eastern thought. But, he adds, one "turns . . . West for its demonology." Why? Because it is due, at least in part, to

> its familiarity and accessibility. In other words, while there are, of course, demonologies within the Indian religious tradition that could be used in Western alternative spiritualities, these are complex, not well known, and are not prominent within the reservoir of Western occulture. Christian demonology, on the other hand, is familiar and, perhaps largely because of popular culture, plausible. We should not be surprised therefore that . . . it is Christian demonology that is pre-eminent and dominant in the Western psyche.[31]

What I do *not* want to imply is that the overlay of Christian demonology in interpreting alleged demonic activity on a worldwide basis is somehow inappropriate, only that the "familiar" framework that is privileged as "Christian demonology" already contains the controversial tenet of demonic PK*–the very matter under dispute. In other words, perhaps the belief in "diabolical miracle" is derived simply from the sociological fact that it is a *familiar explanation* and not because it is directly observed. I remind the reader that observations are often (if not always) overlaid with interpretations that tend to go beyond the immediate warrant of the evidence. Perhaps the *explananda* that is the "vast mass of superstition" is one that is merely met with a *mis*interpretation. Even someone like Derek Prince, himself a champion of demonic PK*, is quick to caution that "[p]ersonal experience by itself is never a sufficient basis for establishing biblical doctrine."[32]

What could be a rival interpretation to the one offered by traditionalists like Unger? The Augustinian-Kantian interpretation I offered in chapter 12 (second objection) could be applied here. That is to say that perhaps many first-hand experiences of alleged physical manifestations of demons are really internalized psycho-projections of phenomena that only *appear* to be of extramental realities (something like a vision or hallucination). If psycho-projection is at least as good an explanation as Unger's "diabolical miracle" hypothesis, then perhaps the cross-cultural experiences shared by those past and present are simply further evidences of the *extent* to which psycho-projection obtains.

But what of situations where there is material evidence (say, that there are physical injuries, changes in temperature, or relocated objects said to be caused

---

30. Partridge, *The Re-Enchantment of the West*.
31. Partridge, *The Re-Enchantment of the West*, 278.
32. Prince, *They Shall Expel Demons*, 27.

by demonic activity)? Perhaps these are not caused by demons at all. Instead, the demons in the psycho-projections merely lead one to *think* that they caused them. In those cases, there may be perfectly ordinary explanations that explain the material evidence.[33] But given the concurrence of the demonic encounter, the victim is duped into thinking that a demon indeed caused it. For example, there was a recent report in Pennsylvania of a demon alleged to scratch the hand of a photojournalist who visited a house thought to be inhabited by demons. It was reported that the photojournalist "felt his hand burning and saw a scratch on his wrist."[34] Supposing that the encounter were unquestionably demonic (let us suppose that a ghastly apparition gestured to the photojournalist's hand and said, "See what I did!"), and the experience was not a deliberate hoax, the scratch could have been caused by some ordinary object prior to the photojournalist's arrival into the home. Bear in mind that some scratches can occur unnoticeably. Once in the home, perhaps the man begins to sweat with fear. The salt in the sweat then burns the pre-existing scratch on the hand of the photojournalist who, upon being prompted by the apparition, makes the obvious connection.

The point is that psycho-projection can accommodate indubitable experiences of the demonic even in situations where material evidence is present. If the notion of psycho-projection can accommodate these reports, even in cases where material evidence is present where one cannot rule out the concurrence of an ordinary cause, then psycho-projection is preserved. And if psycho-projection is preserved, then such reports do not automatically constitute refutations of ECI. Therefore, we are under no obligation to affirm demonic PK* merely on the basis that there are such worldwide reports.

Conclusion

We have explored a series of would-be objections and push-back to the conclusions I have drawn about the metaphysics of demons, namely demonic pure immaterialism and ECI. After having concluded that none of these objections offer any serious challenge to either pure immaterialism or ECI, we must consider the positive case for these notions made primarily in chapters 7–9 of this book to be more firmly established. This is not to say that no further counter-arguments cannot or will not be offered. Quite the contrary, my hope is that this book serves as the groundwork by which to stimulate further thinking on these matters even if that entails new and interesting arguments that call my conclusions into question.

In the concluding chapter that follows this one, we shall draw an end to our comprehensive discussion about a realist view of Christian demonology. Therein I shall string the various threads of discussion in this book together in summary form.

33. See Houran and Lange, *Hauntings and Poltergeists*, Section II.
34. See Loreno, "Ghost Attacks Photographer in PA House 'Haunted' with Demons, Spirits."

Part IV: Objections

Following that, I shall formulate an overall picture of the model I think best represents the metaphysics of Satan and his cohorts as evil spiritual beings–to wit, as gods of this world. I will then offer up some concluding thoughts about the implications of this book's conclusions and the future prospects it may have for additional work both in philosophy and theology.

Part V

Conclusion

"Light, true light, in the mind is, or can be nothing else but the evidence of the truth of any proposition; and if it be not a self-evident proposition, all the light it has, or can have, is from the cleanness and validity of those proofs, upon which it is received. To talk of any other light in the understanding is to put ourselves in the dark, or in the power of the Prince of darkness, and by our own consent to give ourselves up to delusion to believe a lie."

—JOHN LOCKE, *AN ESSAY CONCERNING HUMAN UNDERSTANDING* (1690)

13

Gods of this World

THE HISTORY OF PHILOSOPHY has not settled on the issue of whether the *daimonion* exist. And ever since the Enlightenment, few have even bothered to revisit this question. For the intelligentsia have ruled that, like minotaurs and Titans, demons are not the sorts of things that exist. One primary aim of this book has been to offer up a philosophically informed case for the existence of such beings in opposition to the anti-realist views of the academic masses. I began by assessing the case for demonic anti-realism (see chapter 4) and found arguments in support of it to be flawed. I then visited some arguments for demonic realism (see chapters 5 and 6) and found them to be somewhat inconclusive for the most part, save for one–the historical argument. The historical argument for the existence of demons, one predicated on the New Testament as a source for its historical data, does offer good reasons to believe in demons. And when some of the earlier arguments are consolidated with the historical case, it is increasingly evident that the gods of this world really do exist.

But the journey did not end there. For the history of Christian philosophy (surveyed in chapter 3) has been riddled with diverse and conflicting views about the nature of Satan and the demons. From its earliest stages in the first century, Christian philosophers (like Justin Martyr, Origen, Tertullian, and Augustine) had incorporated antecedent Greek views about the *daimon* in which such beings are said to be "spiritual" and "incorporeal" but, at the same time, "aerial" or "ethereal." When cashed out, the early Patristic and medieval understanding of "spirit" in reference to demons pertained to their having a quasi-material nature that is composed of an imperceptible though material kind of substance. Other Christian philosophers later in history (i.e., Pseudo-Dionysius, *probably* Thomas Aquinas, Mortimer J. Adler, Peter Kreeft, and Peter Williams) have opted for a pure immaterialism–that Satan and the demons are purely immaterial every bit as much as God and the angels are. If the conflicting opinions about the demons's ontology were not problematic enough, how Satan and the demons interact with the physical world has also been a pervasive mystery. The history of Christian demonology amongst philosophers spanning the last two-thousand

Part V: Conclusion

years often included the notion of a special psychokinetic power (PK*) to the demons's repertoire, such that demons would be able to directly interact with the world to the extent of enacting "diabolical miracles."

No matter what views one takes on demons, there are challenges to be met–challenges not adequately handled by demonic realists. Quasi-materialism, for example, seems to deviate from the usual biblical (and more uniform) sense of "spirit" by making it heterogeneous. It adds to the notion of a spirit a secondary, hybrid meaning that forces "immaterial" to be concurrently "material" at the same time. As such, it makes little sense in elucidating what it means to be a spirit at all. For those repulsed by this apparent incoherence, one may be driven instead to the niceties of pure immaterialism. But here, one struggles to explain how created immaterial agents can interact with a physical world. Such a view presumably requires that a PK* power be added to the demons's other-interacting capabilities after all. However, such a hypothesis seems uncomfortably *ad hoc* since it mysteriously affixes an additional power to the demons without any careful thought as to whether or not demons even directly interact with the world and how this might be accomplished apart from God's intervention. That demons would appear to be causally effective in both the material and immaterial worlds is what makes the sundry (quasi-)materialisms attractive. And what makes the notion of "spirit" more uniform in its understanding vis-à-vis God is the appeal of pure immaterialism. We are thus saddled with needing a lovely framework that offers a satisfactory ontology of demons along with a less metaphysically bloated understanding of their power.

I have offered a theory that is free of any of these challenges by arguing for an immaterialist view with some important modifications (see chapter 7). That is, I posited the view that demons are purely immaterial, a view which avoids any unnecessary ambiguity over "spirit" and conforms to a *prima facie* reading of the biblical descriptions of the demons. I argued for this by showing how such an ontology is *possible* and has no conceptual disadvantages over rival theories. I then argued in favor of the theory by providing and defending specific evidences for it and indicating why it is the best explanation of all of those evidences over materialist and quasi-materialist alternatives.[1]

I then proposed that any activity of Satan and the demons in the world can be adequately explained by their basic power of cognitive interaction (CI), a claim elucidated in chapter 8, and not by any PK* power. I then argued that demons *exclusively* act in this world via their cognitive interaction with embodied minds, viz., human beings (this I call ECI) (see chapter 9). Such activity, I explained, only obtains by their utilizing human cognition to manipulate the bodies of those humans and the environment of which they are a part. I argued for the coherence of this notion and that there is no reason to think that souls cannot be causally related to other souls,

---

1. For an abridged version of some of the central arguments I raised, see Guthrie, "Christian Demonology."

whether those other souls be embodied or not. I then argued that there are reasons and particular pieces of evidence that, especially when taken together as a cumulative argument, imply ECI. I then followed those discussions by addressing a series of theological and philosophical objections that could be raised against either demonic pure immaterialism or ECI and found them unconvincing (see chapters 10–12).

Therefore, by assessing all of the available evidences regarding the gods of this world, I concluded that they exist as purely immaterial beings and have the delimited power of ECI when it comes to their other-interacting abilities. But more should be said in filling out our understanding. In what follows, we shall explore what a complete model of the conclusions arrived at in this book looks like in thinking further about demonic realism.

Psychodynamic Immaterialism

When I first undertook research on the metaphysics of demons as the focus of my doctoral work at Manchester Metropolitan University in England, I consolidated the notions of pure immaterialism and ECI together under the umbrella term *psychodynamic immaterialism*.[2] The second term, "immaterialism," speaks for itself. It refers to the previously established notion that the good and evil angels are purely immaterial. "Psychodynamic," on the other hand, is meant as a more nuanced reference to the mechanism of CI–one where a demon's cognitive involvement is more dynamic than one might think. The term itself is actually a specialized term of psychology and psychiatry and has been closely associated with Sigmund Freud's concept of psychoanalysis. More importantly it is a term utilized more broadly to express how external psychological forces can (though usually subconsciously) influence human behavior, personality, and emotion. Despite its specialized usages in the literature, I am using the language of psychodynamics in a more generic (and perhaps heterodox) way but not wholly unrelated. By "psychodynamic" I mean the ability of a person's mind to actively and consciously or subconsciously influence the mind of an embodied other (via CI) in such a way that there are resulting physical and environmental consequences brought about by that other. They are physical in terms of ultimate control over the other's body (whether in its movements or its psychosomatic effects) and environmental in terms of using the other's body to cause changes in the wider physical world within the natural reach of that individual.

Here is what this might look like in demon-persons. In terms of the psychodynamics of CI, the other-interacting dynamics of a demon's mentation is such that a demon's mind (M_1) can use the mind of another (human) (M_2) to control her physical body (B_2), or some element therein, within her physical environment (E). Suppose M_1 wanted to change something in E. M_1 could not do this directly since M_1 is an

---

2. See Guthrie, "A New Metaphysics for Christian Demonology."

immaterial spirit and would *ceteris paribus* be incapable of such a feat. But M1 could influence M2 (via CI) to use B2 in order to bring about the change in E. Put another way, M1 psychodynamically brings about a change to E. In no case would M1 directly interact with B2 in circumventing the natural sovereignty of M2 over her body, for demons cannot directly interact with bodies. But M1 can act on M2 if M1 wanted to attempt some level of ascendancy over that person.

This is to say that the psychodynamic spirit (or soul) of a demon would not circumvent the mind of the receiving spirit but would be operative directly with and through it. As such, the psychodynamic spirit can communicate not just information content but illustrative (imagery) content like visions or hallucinations (of course these may not be phenomenally distinct). M1 could use M2 in some way to affect psychosomatic changes in B2. It is already clear that M2 can effect changes in her own B2. For example, she could mentally ponder a tragedy thereby inducing depression and so incite her own body to be lethargic,[3] or she could become mentally stressed to the extent that she increases her body's blood pressure. If M1 wanted B2's blood pressure to increase, M1 could psychodynamically make that happen. In this case, the manipulative spirit does not exercise a special material-interacting power but, rather, that soul would simply *communicate* the stressful situation through the same "ordinary" means of informational soul-soul communication (viz., CI). M1 can communicate the reality that M2 is without a family, abandoned by her friends, and living in isolation. This thought would be reflected upon by M2 thereby leading her body to physiologically react such that lethargy sets in. Though M2's depressing thoughts partially explain her lethargy M1 also serves as a partial explanation of her lethargy since without the communicated thoughts of M1, M2 may not have ever become depressed. Suppose that M1 wanted B2 to be paralyzed without the use of injury or trauma. M1 could impart (also through CI) a thought provoking extreme fear. This extreme fear would psychosomatically induce B2 to become (at least temporarily) paralyzed. If M1 wanted B2 to be permanently *and physically* paralyzed, M1 may impart the influential thought of having M2 engage in behavior that would lead M2 to injure her B2 (perhaps by influencing M2 to recklessly drive a motorcycle that would predictably lead to a spinal injury). In either case, M1 would be psychodynamically related to B2 as well as, as mentioned earlier, E. And in no case would a special interactive spirit-matter power have to be invoked just in case we are seeking the simplest explanation by not adding powers beyond necessity.

Let us consider an analogy with which to elucidate better: the back-seat driver. The back-seat driver is thought to be a person riding in a vehicle she is unable to physically control directly but attempts to do so remotely. As such, she cannot directly

---

3. There are different forms of depression. *Clinical*, or *major*, depression can result from a chemical imbalance in the person's body not precipitated by any thought of tragedy or loss. Ordinary depression tends to result in some people for no *physical* reason but for reasons associated with thinking about tragedy or loss. My reference to a self-induced form of depression has this latter, ordinary form of depression in mind.

control the vehicle's destination. Suppose further that she is equally unable in principle to *physically* interact with the driver. Let us say that these occupants are in a limousine separated by a glass shield but have a two-way transmitter with which to communicate. The back-seat driver, being literally in the back seat, can communicate to the driver her wishes and desires for the driver to change lanes in order for a more efficient commute. This may be enough to influence the driver in reconfiguring her route. But if the actual driver is stubborn, the back-seat driver will have to consider other means at her disposal. Perhaps she can threaten the driver and scare her into a lane change. Perhaps she can exploit the driver's sense of compassion by insisting that remaining in the present lane is similar to a tragic past event in the driver's childhood (that her careless father would always veer into the same lane just prior to violently wrecking the car). And if that failed to work, perhaps she can cleverly and convincingly form sounds with her mouth emulating the sound of a flat tire so that a lane change, being inevitable if it is necessary in order to pull over and stop, would obtain.

What may be true of the back-seat driver might be true of demonic spirits. Though their means of communication would be psychical and not oral, they may be able to cognitively suggest course changes in our lives or even invoke an experiential illusion or two in getting us to behave accordingly. There are purely psychological conditions that can incite a person to hallucinate (perhaps by entering into a trance state or by meditating). I see no reason why an external mind could not psychodynamically cause a hallucination by influencing the mind of some host. Either way, we may remain ignorant (particularly if it is subconscious) as to whether such communication is demonic, self-derived, or otherwise. We may imagine the back-seat driver to be anonymous or a schizophrenic (audible) hallucination of the driver herself and it would not change the driver's response to each communicative attempt. None of this is to say that demons *do* act this way, only to illustrate what they would likely accomplish if they did.

Therefore, since demons are realities that are reported in Scripture to interact with members of this world, and perhaps implied by a number of claims to personal experience in various human civilizations, psychodynamic immaterialism provides us a conciliatory and defensible model of what that might look like.

The Future of Research in the Philosophy of Demonology

The notions of demonic realism and psychodynamic immaterialism directly impact other areas of study. It seems to me that the way in which philosophical discussions about God have precipitated sundry discussions in the philosophy of religion is bound to be repeated in future developments in the philosophy of demonology that also begins with a discussion about demons. Let us take a brief tour of the potential areas of impact in developing a philosophy of demonology informed by psychodynamic immaterialism.

PART V: CONCLUSION
Diabolical Theodicies

If it should turn out that the demons are purely immaterial and that they are incapable of interacting with the world directly, then there are implications for certain theodicies and defenses of God's existence against evil that are posited. For example, some philosophers have followed Augustine in offering up a defense of God's existence that shifts the blame for natural evils (evils that are thought to be independent of human activity such as atmospheric and earthly disturbances, physical maladies, illnesses, and animal suffering) from God to human beings. The Augustinian solution roots the blame for natural evil specifically in Adam and Eve's disobedience to God in the Garden of Eden which, then, prompted God's curse of creation. But this solution is increasingly difficult to defend thanks to the paleontological evidence for death, disease, and decay in the animal kingdom prior to the arrival of human beings.

As a result, philosophers have turned to a possible pre-Adamic circumstance that would explain the existence of such evils that clearly arose prior to the arrival of human beings. Since the Adam and Eve story contains at least one pre-existing malevolent intelligence prior to the Fall (viz., Satan), it is natural for Christian philosophers to appeal to Satan and his demons as likely candidates for natural evil's origin.[4] But this notion will require that demons (or at least Satan) have some ability to interact with the physical universe, an ability with which they can disrupt the tranquility and harmony of God's creation. If it should turn out that demons are incapable of such feats, any theodicy that utilizes demons in this way would be undermined.[5] As such, psychodynamic immaterialism would essentially make diabolical theodicies implausible.[6]

In the next section, I shall consider a sensitive issue in the philosophy of the cognitive sciences: the notion of demonic possession.

---

4. See Murray, *Nature Red in Tooth and Claw*, 103–6; Boyd, *Satan and the Problem of Evil*, 293–318; Kelly, "The Problem of Evil and the Satan Hypothesis"; Penelhum, *Religion and Rationality*, 246; Lewis, *The Problem of Pain*, chapter 9; Mascall, *Christian Theology and Natural Science*, 301–2; Trethowan, *An Essay in Christian Philosophy*, 128.

5. Such a view would be undermined *even if* the demons were originally embodied creatures who resided in a pre-Edenic landscape that was later destroyed, leaving the demons in a permanently disembodied state (this pre-Edenic view is defended by Boyd; see his *Satan and the Problem of Evil*, 310–17). Being material or corporeal does not guarantee the ability to perform physically impossible or supernatural feats of wonder. The demonic realist, if he is going to affirm this theodicy, cannot afford to disavow the demons's ability to directly interact with the physical world in this special way.

6. See Guthrie, "A New Challenge to a Warfare Theodicy."

Psychiatry, Demonic Possession, and Philosophy of the Cognitive Sciences

As discussed in a previous chapter,[7] the phenomenon of demonic possession is considered by many to be a prescientific (mis)understanding of mental disorders. Accordingly, demons should never be entertained as genuine etiological causes of human maladies–especially when it comes to assessing one's psychology. In some geographical pockets in human history, such as the infamous Salem Village in Massachusetts of colonial North America during the seventeenth century, superstition had given rise to brutality.[8] Such concerns about brutality and primitiveness obviously carry over into the clinical practices of the contemporary world of the cognitive sciences. As such, despite much press given to the notion of demonic possessions, clinical psychologists and psychiatrists seem averse to entertaining the prospect of demonic realism in the healing process of the afflicted.

However, if so-called possession cases are not fully and universally explicated by appeals to known mental disorders, then the rejection of demonic possession as a viable option in at least some cases smacks of rank prejudice against the supernatural. Yet if demons do exist and psychodynamic immaterialism is a fact of their existence, we really should have another look at possession cases through this framework. For one, we should not expect that demons can be detected lurking in the temporal lobe or hypothalamus somewhere, for demons would not have spatial properties. Nor would their control over the host be obvious since they act, in many cases, subliminally. And yet the occurrences of demonic CI in the Bible do not always make it clear to the victim who is responsible. For example, if we revisit the episode of Job, it is apparent that Job thought *God* was solely responsible for his maladies![9] The Apostle Peter had no idea his passion to protect Jesus from suffering *was motivated by Satan!*[10] As such, there is no reason or theological expectation to think that the demonic etiology of any genuine possession case could be empirically identified.

Moreover, the superstitious elements of magic and spells would never again be confused with patients suspected of possession since, on this theory, demons would be incapable of disturbing the natural order or performing any extraordinary feats like levitation, curses, or any other kind of extramental magical extravagance. Thus, any pretense to magical behavior such as that found in the lore of witchcraft would be quashed *ex hypothesi*.

It turns out that we may have been looking at this all wrong. Why suppose that a diagnosis is to be predicated on *either* some natural pathology or some spiritual one? If a patient was inflicted with urticaria (i.e., the formation of hives on the skin), it

---

7. Chapter 4.
8. See Gross, *The Salem Witch Trials*.
9. Job 12.9; 16.7–9; 23.16; 27.2; 30.11, 19–23.
10. Matt 16.21–23.

would be "urticaria" sure enough. In some cases of urticaria, the condition is known to be caused by emotional stress. But this does not mean that there is no supernatural etiology. Regardless of whether or not that stress were induced by a supernatural agent is obviously not to say that the condition is *not* urticaria, only that its being urticaria has an immediate cause. I suspect whether there was a known supernatural etiology behind the stress or not an afflicted patient would still engage in some form of stress management. But this treatment does not amount to either a denial of the presence of stress or a supernatural cause. Instances of Dissociative Identity Disorder and demonic possession obtaining together strike me as fulfilling the same analogous pattern in terms of potential symptom treatment; but then, this is not to look at one's condition as an *either-or* but rather as a *both-and*.

And this leads to one final point. The remedy for some particular possession case may or may not be handled with an exorcism. There is more harmony than division when it comes to treating all possession cases with concomitant symptoms. Regardless of whether one is suffering from tonsillitis or streptococcus, the initial onset of symptoms (i.e., having a sore throat) will likely be handled with hot tea, chicken broth, and plenty of water. Despite its etiology, one may successfully overcome the condition by waiting it out without ever having to expel the cause directly. The same might be said of demonic possession understood as a dramatic exemplification of the CI-relation. One could treat the symptoms through conventional means if it culminates in finding relief. This would not be to deny a demonic presence. For if it works, it matters not whether the cause was diabolical or natural. As philosopher and religious studies professor L. Stafford Betty comments:

> [I]t is not at all ludicrous to consider the possibility that drugs and ECT [electroconvulsive therapy] might inhibit spirit oppression or possession. Is it really so preposterous that a spirit utilizing in some mysterious way a person's body, more particularly [the] brain, should be disturbed or even uprooted when that body with its brain is subjected to a shock as violent as ECT?[11]

On psychodynamic immaterialism, this is certainly a possibility. And this would lead both psychiatrist and priest to consider more conventional steps with which to begin only to be followed by, if necessary, the expulsion tactics of exorcists. It would be no different than initially staving off the impact of depression by means of anti-depressants before dealing with the root of the matter. Sometimes remedy comes in phases, but any initial act is not necessarily an attempt at a final amelioration. Should it be that the symptoms are unmanageable, attacking the cause would be a natural follow-up. All in all, considering all options on the table affords us a more holistic approach devoid of unnecessary prejudice and bias that allows us to be compassionate enough to expand our means to heal. And it is one that takes a conservative approach that considers first and foremost the possibility that the affliction just is natural.

---

11. Betty, "The Growing Evidence for 'Demonic Possession,'" 21.

In the next section, I shall consider another area of thought how a philosophy of demonology, particularly the one I have defended, can inform our understanding of the popular notion of so-called paranormal phenomena.

The Metaphysics of Demons and Paranormal Phenomena

Paranormal activity refers to a set of phenomenal (perceptible) experiences resulting from the manifestations of disembodied spirits in the physical world.[12] Such manifestations can be visual (apparitions), audible (voice phenomena), tactile (scratches and chills), or some combination thereof. Such phenomena could be as dramatic as a UFO visitation which is thought by some to be a category of demonic manifestations.[13] The naturalist obviously proposes that any supernatural interpretation of alleged paranormal activity is altogether wrong-headed or outright incorrect. As with demonic possession cases, it is also a mainstay in our post-Enlightenment culture to have principled, *a priori* resistance to favoring explanations rooted in the supernatural. Since these skeptics have an aversion to *any* supernaturally-based hypothesis, their survey of the evidence of such phenomena is vitiated.

Yet many in the Judeo-Christian tradition hold that paranormal activity is in fact due to the mischievous and deceptive behavior of Satan and/or the demons.[14] While one could always defend the naturalist's contention that such activity is not paranormal at all, one may integrate psychodynamic immaterialism in the way I did in accounting for alleged extramental manifestations (see chapter 12, objection #2). I echoed a view I called *psycho-projection* which holds that demons truly do facilitate such paranormal phenomena but not as an extramental reality. Instead, they somehow induce the human mind to project or hallucinate an apparition or some phenomenal experience, giving the false impression that the source of the phenomenon is external to the percipient. It is, incidentally, a version of a hypothesis offered up elsewhere in the literature on paranormal activity.[15]

Such a view would have quite an impact in legitimizing the testimony of some who experience such phenomena while denying that demons have any powers to interact directly with the physical world. If ECI is true, then there is no reason to suppose that the experience is a fabrication or misunderstanding of the phenomenal evidence. Instead, one may suppose the experience to be real but defined in such a way that is consistent with a demonology that affirms the demons's ability to deceive

---

12. Some activity deemed to be paranormal may have nothing to do with things like disembodied spirits but could be due to natural causes that are undetectable through ordinary, scientific means.

13. See Partridge, "Alien Demonology."

14. This is a view that was primarily, though not exclusively, espoused by the early Protestant Reformers of Christianity. See Russell, *The Prince of Darkness*, 167–85; Russell, *Mephistopheles*, 25–76.

15. See Evans, "The Ghost Experience in a Wider Context," 58–59; Lund, *Death and Consciousness*, chapter 10.

in such ways. This alternative interpretation offers us a different way to appreciate the legitimacy of the experiential data without dismissing the contribution of a demonic cause. For demons should not, per psychodynamic immaterialism, leave behind any physical evidence when their acts of deception are carried out exclusively in the minds of their victims. Needless to say, much more could be said about this.

Let us now take a look at how a philosophy of demonology can also help the Christian theologian who seeks to engage in systematic theology.

Philosophical Theology

Psychodynamic immaterialism will aid the theologian in her craft, too. If we understand that there are no exegetical reasons to prefer any one interpretation over another when it comes to passages that speak of demonic interaction, perhaps by re-looking at those passages under the assumption that PK* is not present in demons may lead to a more elegant understanding of those passages in question. For example, if the serpent in the Garden of Eden with Eve was not a physical manifestation of Satan, one wonders what the serpent was. It is interesting that John H. Walton, in concluding his theological analysis that the serpent was, in some sense, Satan, adds that such a "discussion quickly becomes very esoteric and is both out of my area of expertise and out of the range of this book." However, the theologian could revisit this question with the psychodynamic immaterialist framework in mind. Perhaps Eve was tempted by a spirit that did not appear to her at all. Instead, perhaps the tempter engaged in a private dialogue that was *internal* to Eve (much like how we understand *anyone* to be tempted). After all, Adam is said to have been "with her" (Gen 3.6) and yet does not protest, question, or push back against Eve's subsequent beckoning of him to partake of the forbidden fruit. And neither of them seem particularly bothered at the idea that *this* being talks.

Accordingly, if one wants to maintain a conservative interpretation of the events depicted therein, the conservative theologian could develop a hypothesis that makes elegant all of the data mined from Genesis 3 in attempting to fill out the "esoteric" discussion about the serpent. For we want to know how a genuinely immaterial spirit can incite one to fall from grace and, yet, be described in animalistic terms. Given psychodynamic immaterialism, one may be led to consider seriously the idea that the author(s) of Genesis 3 are using "serpent" as a way to describe the *disposition* of the villain rather than its ontology. Perhaps it is rhetoric that patterns modern expressions such as one's being "wise/crafty as a serpent" or of one "slithering" out of a situation. This would be in solidarity with modern designations of adversaries caricatured by familiar animal expressions such as "John is a real snake for swindling me like that!" and "I can't believe you dated that rat!" Such idioms invoking snakes and rats are meant to describe the behavioral traits of the person, not their ontology. This would allow the theologian to see differently verse 3's mentioning that "the serpent was more crafty than any other beast of the field" because it would not be a reference to the serpent *as* a beast of the field but that his *characteristics* are those of this beast of the field. And given that a serpent *already* traverses "on [its] belly" forces the theologian to find a better interpretation of God's punitive curse than a morphological change in the serpent that is really no change at all. In short, the account can be a literal one overlaid with verbal symbolism at the same time. Literal with respect to there being a real villain tempting Eve and symbolic with respect to how the villain is described. It would play to the strengths of both a theologically liberal and conservative outlook without abandoning the notion that Satan literally tempted Eve in the Garden at the onset of humanity's primeval history.[16]

Now, this is just one way that psychodynamic immaterialism may allow us to see familiar passages in a different light. It may be that the intent of the author(s) of Genesis has been mired in unnecessary controversy over the fantastic portrait of a talking snake. And, at the same time, one is not forced to think of Genesis as echoing some kind of fable with its talking serpent. But I can only leave it to the theologian to improve upon this suggestion–a suggestion that becomes more palpable on a reading of the passage through the eyes of psychodynamic immaterialism.

Systematic theology is not the only theological benefit of the kind of philosophy of demonology I have championed. Practitioners of Christian theology can also find practical applications of such a theory. Let us take a look now at such a possibility.

Practical Theology

Practitioners of the Christian faith are obliged to interact with and even combat the nuisances of demons in a way that respects God's prescribed solutions. This kind of interaction with demons is often described as the Christian's call to *spiritual warfare*. While the means of spiritual warfare are delineated in various passages of the New Testament, clarity of such prescriptions are often muddled by misconceptions about what demons putatively can and cannot do. It is the case that a deep, exegetical analysis can be a benefit in elucidating such prescriptions, but any exegesis of the relevant passages will require an interpretive framework by which to make the best sense of their practice. To see why, consider an analogy in the commandment that "you shall not commit adultery" (Exod 20.14). In order to understand the command, one must obviously have a working knowledge of the necessary and sufficient conditions for what constitutes adultery. Concerning the prescriptions of spiritual warfare offered to Christian believers, readers are told to "[r]esist the devil, and he will flee" (James 4.7), to "not be outwitted by Satan" (2 Cor 2.22), and to "stand against the schemes of the devil" (Eph 6.11). Unfortunately, even knowing what "resist," "not be outwitted," and "stand" mean, the reader is left with a rather vague notion of defense against

---

16. For a preliminary discussion about the serpent, recall "The Edenic Serpent" in chapter 2.

the diabolical. How does one practice these prescriptions in light of psychodynamic immaterialism?

A philosophy of demonology, such as the one I have defended, can allow both the theologian and layperson to understand more specifically what these could mean in practice. Let us just take the example of "resist" as a paradigm case study. Would resisting the devil be like resisting an assault by another human being (cf., Matt 5.39), viz., as a sort of physical parry? As a matter of historical import, some ancient texts on magic instructed the demonically harassed to utilize incantations with which to make demons flee.[17] So, why *not* think that this is one of chasing away the devil with a clever use of verbal magic given such a general cultural context? If a philosophy of demonology as the one I have championed is adopted, it makes the prescription more illuminating and insightful. After all, if demons are purely immaterial creatures, then they simply cannot *hear* an incantation for they would lack ear drums. Pure immaterialism positions the reader to consider an alternative meaning, perhaps one that ends up being more faithful to the context of the fourth chapter of James itself (viz., that it is incumbent upon the Christian to change her ways). Psychodynamic immaterialism underscores Craig Keener's explanation, for example, that in James's context, "the idea here is moral, not magical. One must choose between the values of God and those of the world."[18] Resistance is, therefore, best understood as a *refusal*–a refusal to give in to the devil's temptations. We can now feel more confident in preferring a less mysterious notion like a magical parry and prefer a more acceptable solution such as the verse being a call for a virtuous submission to God in resisting the vicious (cognitive) entrapment of Satan. Given the surrounding verses, it is clear that this is a far more coherent fit for the chapter not to mention our metaphysical predilections. And given psychodynamic immaterialism, it is no surprise that a proper interpretation centers on the contrast between virtue and vice as opposed to magic. Accordingly, psychodynamic immaterialism serves to help Christians to demythologize their orthopraxy against the superstitions of the ancient world.

There are many verses in the New Testament that could be made more insightful and shown to make the most sense of the entire corpus of spiritual warfare passages in light of psychodynamic immaterialism. But that will have to be a project for another day. We now have come to the end of a research program that has much to its credit, not only in terms of its philosophical attraction but in terms of its widespread application. As such, psychodynamic immaterialism not only accounts for the metaphysics of demons but also, by extension, promotes much-needed further guarded thinking in our everyday Christian demonology.

---

17. See Keener, *The IVP Bible Background*, 699.
18. Keener, *The IVP Bible Background*, 699.

Conclusion

The evidence suggests that the gods of this world are real. Believing that there is a Satan and an accompanying band of cohorts should not be any more intellectually offensive than belief in ISIS terrorists or corrupt politicians seeking to do the average (innocent) person harm. And having surveyed the history of demonic realism amongst Christian philosophers in order to codify a consistent message of the metaphysics of demons, such a survey has brought to light more problems and challenges that have gone unaddressed . . . until now. As a problem bequeathed to the present-day philosopher of demonology, I have sought to posit and defend a codification that best explains all of the data on the demons. I have argued that psychodynamic immaterialism accomplishes this and much more thus leaving the demonic realist in an intellectual position so as to no longer be, as the saying goes, caught between the devil and the deep blue sea.

Bibliography

Adler, Mortimer J. *The Angels and Us*. New York: MacMillan, 1982.

Africanus, Julius. *Chronographia*. In *The Sacred Writings of Julius Africanus*. Translated by Stewart Dingwall Fordyce Salmond. Altenmünster: Jazzybee Verlag Jürgen Beck, 2012.

Alden, Robert L. "Lucifer, Who or What?" *Bulletin of the Evangelical Theological Society* 11 (1968) 35–39.

"Alister Hardy RERC Archive Database." http://www.uwtsd.ac.uk/library/alister-hardy-religious-experience-research-centre/online-archive/.

Allen, Kenneth W. "The Rebuilding and Destruction of Babylon." *Bibliotheca Sacra* 133 (1976) 19–27.

Allestree, Richard. *The New Whole Duty of Man, Containing the Faith as well as Practice of a Christian*. 29th ed. London: W. Bent, 1810.

Almond, Philip C. *The Devil: A New Biography*. London: Taurus, 2014.

Al-Nasser, Nassir Abdulaziz. "General Assembly President's Remarks." July 18, 2012. http://www.un.org/en/events/mandeladay/2012/ga-message.shtml.

Alston, William P. *Perceiving God: The Epistemology of Religious Experience*. Ithaca: Cornell University Press, 1991.

Alter, Robert. *The Wisdom Books, Job, Proverbs, and Ecclesiastes: A Translation and Commentary*. New York: Norton, 2010.

American Psychiatric Association. *Diagnostic And Statistical Manual of Mental Disorders: DSM-5*. Arlington, VA: American Psychiatric Association, 2013.

Anselm. *De Casu Diaboli*. In *Complete Philosophical and Theological Treatises of Anselm of Canterbury*, translated by Jasper Hopkins and Herbert Richardson, 214–61. Minneapolis: Banning, 2000.

Aquinas, Thomas. *Compendium Theologiae*. Translated by Richard J. Regan. New York: Oxford University Press, 2009.

———. *De Malo*. Edited by Brian Davies. Translated by Richard Regan. New York: Oxford University Press, 2003.

———. *De Potentia Dei*. Translated by Lawrence Shapcote. London: Burns, Oates & Washbourne, 1933.

———. *De Spiritualibus Creaturis*. Edited and translated by Mary FitzPatrick. Milwaukee: Marquette University Press, 1949.

———. *Summa Theologiae*. In *Thomas Aquinas: Selected Writings*. Translated by Ralph McInerny. London: Penguin, 1998.

Aristotle. *De Anima*. In *Complete Works of Aristotle, Volume 1: The Revised Oxford Translation*, edited by Jonathan Barnes, 641–92. Princeton: Princeton University Press, 1984.

———. *Meteorologica*. In *Complete Works of Aristotle, Volume 1: The Revised Oxford Translation*, edited by Jonathan Barnes, 555–625. Princeton: Princeton University Press, 1984.

Armstrong, D. A. *A Materialist Theory of Mind*. London: Routledge and Kegan Paul, 1968.

Arnold, Clinton E. "Power." In *Dictionary of the Later New Testament*, edited by Ralph P. Martin and Peter H. Davids, 938–41. Downers Grove, IL: InterVarsity, 1997.

Athenagoras. *A Plea for the Christians*. In *Justin Martyr and Athenagoras*, edited by Alexander Roberts and James Donaldson, 375–422. Translated by Marcus Dodds et al. Ante-Nicene Christian Library 2. Edinburgh: T. & T. Clark, 1879.

Audi, Robert. *Epistemology*. New York: Routledge, 1998.

Augustine. *Adnotationes in Iob*. Edited by Joseph Zycha. Vienna: F. Tempsky, 1895.

———. *The Confessions of Saint Augustine*. Translated by E. M. Blaiklock. London: Hodder & Stoughton, 2010.

———. *De Anima et eius Origine*. In *Saint Augusti: Anti-Pelagian Writings*, edited by Philip Schaff, 310–73. Translated by Peter Holmes and Robert Ernest Wallis. Nicene and Post-Nicene Fathers First Series 5. Buffalo: Christian Literature, 1887.

———. *De Beata Vita*. In *Augustine of Hippo: Selected Writings*, edited by Mary T. Clark, 163–93. Mahwah, NJ: Paulist, 1984.

———. *De Civitate Dei*. Translated by Marcus Dods. Peabody, MA: Hendrickson, 2009.

———. *De Correptione et Gratia*. In *Saint Augustine: Christian Instruction; Admonition and Grace; the Christian Combat; Faith, Hope and Charity*, translated by John Courtney Murray, 245–308. Washington, DC: The Catholic University of America, 1947.

———. *De Diversis Quaestionibus*. In *Augustine: Earlier Writings*, edited by J. H. S. Burleigh, 376–406. London: SCM, 1953.

———. *De Divinatione Daemonum*. In *Saint Augustine: Treatises on Marriage and Other Subjects*, edited by Roy J. Defarrari, 415–40. Translated by Ruth Wentworth Brown. Washington, DC: The Catholic University of America, 1955.

———. *De Genesi ad Litteram*. Vol. 1. Edited by Johannes Quasten et al. Mahwah, NJ: Paulist, 1982.

———. *De Ordine*. In *Divine Providence and the Problem of Evil: A Translation of St. Augustine's De Ordine*. Translated by Robert P. Russell. New York: Cosmopolitan Science & Art Services, 1942.

———. *Enarrationes in Psalmos*. Translated by Boniface Ramsey. Vol. 5. New York: New York City Press, 2003.

———. *The Enchiridion*. Translated by Thomas Hibbs. Washington, DC: Regnery, 1996.

———. *Epistula*. Edited by John E. Rotelle. Translated by Roland Teske. Hyde Park: New City Press, 2001.

Bacon, Francis. *The Advancement of Learning*. In *The Works of Francis Bacon, Baron of Verulam, Viscount St. Alban, and Lord High Chancellor of England*, 1:2–109. London: A. Millar, 1753.

Baergen, Ralph. "The Influence of Cognition upon Perception: The Empirical Story." *Australian Journal of Philosophy* 71 (1993) 13–23.

Bailey, Andrew, Joshua Rasmussen, and Luke Horn. "No Pairing Problem." *Philosophical Studies* 154 (2011) 349–60.

Bailey, Michael D. "A Late-Medieval Crisis of Superstition?" *Speculum* 84 (2009) 633–61.

Baker, Lynne Rudder. *Persons and Bodies: A Constitution View*. New York: Cambridge University Press, 2000.

Bibliography

Bamberger, Bernard J. *Fallen Angels: Soldiers of Satan's Realm*. Philadelphia: Jewish Publication Society, 1952.

Barber, Theodore Xenophone, and David Smith Calverley. "An Experimental Study of 'Hypnotic' (Auditory and Visual) Hallucinations." *The Journal of Abnormal and Social Psychology* 68 (1964) 13–20.

Barnard, Leslie William. *Justin Martyr: His Life and Thought*. Cambridge: Cambridge University Press, 1967.

Barnett, Paul. *The Second Epistle to the Corinthians*. Grand Rapids: Eerdmans, 1997.

Bauckham, Richard. *Climax of Prophecy*. Edinburgh: T. & T. Clark, 1993.

———. *Jesus and the Eyewitnesses: The Gospels as Eyewitness Testimony*. Grand Rapids: Eerdmans, 2006.

———. "Revelation." In *Oxford Bible Commentary*, edited by John Barton and John Muddiman, 1287–1305. Oxford: Oxford University Press, 2001.

Beckwith, Francis J., and Stephen E. Parrish. *See the Gods Fall: Four Rivals to Christianity*. Joplin: College Press, 1997.

Bekker, Balthasar. *The World Bewitch'd, or, An examination of the common opinions concerning spirits: their nature, power, administration and operations, as also the effects men are able to produce by their communication: divided into IV parts / by Balthazar Bekker . . . ; vol. I translated from a French copy, approved of and subscribed by the author's own hand*. London: Printed for R. Baldwin in Warwick-Lane, 1695.

Belleville, Linda L. *2 Corinthians*. IVP New Testament Commentary. Downers Grove, IL: InterVarsity, 1996.

Benoit, Pierre. *The Passion and Resurrection of Jesus Christ*. Translated by Benet Weatherhead. London: Darton, Longman & Todd, 1969.

Betty, L. Stafford. "The Growing Evidence for "Demonic Possession": What Should Psychiatry's Response Be?" *Journal of Religion and Health* 44 (2005) 13–30.

Birney, Leroy. "An Exegetical Study of Genesis 6:1–4." *Journal of the Evangelical Theological Society* 13 (1970) 43–52.

Blomberg, Craig. *The Historical Reliability of the New Testament*. Nashville: B&H Academic, 2016.

Blount, Brian K. *Revelation*. Louisville: Presbyterian, 2009.

Blunt, John James. *Undesigned Coincidences in the Writings Both of the Old and New Testaments: An Argument of Their Veracity. With an Appendix Containing Undesigned Coincidences Between the Gospels and Acts, and Josephus*. New York: Robert Carter, 1857.

Boa, Kenneth D., and Robert M. Bowman Jr. *Sense and Nonsense about Angels and Demons*. Grand Rapids: Zondervan, 2007.

Bonaventure. *Commentaria in Quatuor Libros Sententiarum*. Translated by a Franciscan Brother. Mansfield: The Franciscan Archive. https://franciscan-archive.org/bonaventura/sent.html.

Boring, M. Eugene. *Mark: A Commentary*. Louisville: Presbyterian, 2006.

Boureau, Alain. *Satan the Heretic: The Birth of Demonology in the Medieval West*. Translated by Teresa Lavender Fagan. Chicago: University of Chicago Press, 2006.

Bourget, David, and David J. Chalmers. "What Do Philosophers Believe?" *Philosophical Studies* 170 (2014) 465–500.

Boyd, Gregory A. *God at War*. Downers Grove, IL: InterVarsity, 1997.

———. *Satan and the Problem of Evil: Constructing a Trinitarian Warfare Theodicy*. Downers Grove, IL: InterVarsity, 2001.

Braude, Stephen E. *ESP and Psychokinesis: A Philosophical Examination*. Philadelphia: Temple University Press, 1979.

———. *The Gold Leaf Lady and Other Parapsychological Investigations*. Chicago: The University of Chicago Press, 2007.

———. *The Limits of Influence: Psychokinesis and the Philosophy of Science*. Lanham, MD: Routledge & Kegan Paul, 1986.

———. "Personal Identity and Postmortem Survival." *Social Philosophy and Policy* 22 (2005) 226–49.

Broadus, John Albert. *Commentary on Matthew*. Grand Rapids: Kregel, 1989.

Brown, Christopher M. "Making the Best Even Better: Modifying Pawl and Timpe's Solution to the Problem of Heavenly Freedom." *Faith and Philosophy* 32 (2015) 63–80.

Brown, Raymond E., Joseph A. Fitzmyer, and Roland E. Murphy, eds. *The Jerome Biblical Commentary*. Upper Saddle River, NJ: Prentice-Hall, 1968.

Bryant, Richard A., and David Mallard. "Seeing Is Believing: The Reality Of Hypnotic Hallucinations." *Consciousness And Cognition: An International Journal* 12 (2003) 219–30.

Bultmann, Rudolf. *History of the Synoptic Tradition*. Rev. ed. Translated by John Marsh. New York: Harper and Row, 1963.

Burkill, T. A. "The Historical Development of the Story of the Syrophoenician Woman (Mark VII: 24–31)." *Novum Testamentum* 9 (1967) 161–77.

Burnet, Josh. *Early Greek Philosophy*. London: Adam and Charles Black, 1892.

Caldwell, William. "The Doctrine of Satan: III. In the New Testament." *The Biblical World* 41 (1913) 167–72.

Campbell, Keith. "Swimming Against the Tide." *Inquiry* 36 (1993) 161–77.

Carr, David. "The Politics of Textual Subversion: A Diachronic Perspective on the Garden of Eden Story." *Journal of Biblical Literature* 112 (1993) 577–98.

Cartwright, Nancy. "How We Relate Theory to Observation." In *World Changes: Thomas Kuhn and the Nature of Science*, edited by Paul Horwich, 259–74. Cambridge, MA: MIT Press, 1994.

Cavin, Robert Greg. "Is There Sufficient Evidence to Establish the Historicity of the Resurrection of Jesus?" *Faith and Philosophy* 12 (1995) 361–79.

Chalmers, David J. *The Conscious Mind: In Search of a Fundamental Theory*. New York: Oxford University Press, 1996.

Charles, J. Daryl. "The Angels under Reserve in 2 Peter and Jude." *Bulletin for Biblical Research* 15 (2005) 39–48.

Charles, R. H. *The Book of Enoch; Or, 1 Enoch*. Oxford: Clarendon, 1912.

Chilton, Bruce. "An Exorcism of History: Mark 1:21-28." In *Authenticating the Activities of Jesus*, edited by Bruce Chilton and Craig A. Evans, 215–46. Boston: Brill, 2002.

Churchland, Paul M. *Matter and Consciousness: A Contemporary Introduction to the Philosophy of Mind*. 3rd ed. Cambridge, MA: MIT Press, 2013.

Churchland, Paul M., and Patricia S. Churchland. *On the Contrary: Critical Essays, 1987–1997*. Cambridge, MA: MIT Press, 1998.

Cicero. *Tusculanae Disputationes*. Translated by Andrew P. Peabody. Boston: Little and Brown, 1886.

Clarke, Adam. *The Holy Bible with a Commentary and Critical Notes, Volume I: Genesis to Deuteronomy*. London: Thomas Tegg and Son, 1836.

Bibliography

Clarke, Samuel. *A Discourse Concerning the Unchangeable Obligations of Natural Religion and the Truth and Certainty of the Christian Revelation*. In *The Works of Samuel Clarke*, edited by Benjamin Hoadly. Facsimile ed. London: Thoemmes Continuum, 2002.

Coder, S. Maxwell. *Jude–Everyman's Bible Commentary: Acts of the Apostates*. Chicago: Moody, 1986.

Coleridge, Samuel Taylor. *The Poetical and Dramatic Works of Samuel Taylor Coleridge*. London: Basil Montagu Pickering, 1877.

Colishrcia, L. *Peter Lombard*. Vol. 1. Leiden: Brill, 1994.

Collins, John J. "The Son of Man and the Saints of the Most High in the Book of Daniel." *Journal of Biblical Literature* 93 (1974) 50–66.

Collins, Raymond F. *I and II Timothy and Titus: A Commentary*. Louisville: Westminster John Knox, 2002.

Conybeare, F. C. "The Demonology of the New Testament I." *The Jewish Quarterly Review* 8 (1896) 576–608.

Cooper, John W. *Body, Soul and Life Everlasting: Biblical Anthropology and the Monism-Dualism Debate*. Grand Rapids: Eerdmans, 1989.

Cooper, Rachel. "What's Special About Mental Health and Disorder?" In *Arguing About Human Nature*, edited by Stephen M. Downes and Edouard Machery, 487–500. New York: Routledge, 2013.

Copleston, Frederick. *A History of Philosophy*. 2 vols. New York: Doubleday, 1993.

Corcoran, Kevin. "Human Persons Are Material Only." In *Debating Christian Theism*, edited by J. P. Moreland, Chad Meister, and Khaldoun A. Sweis, 270–82. New York: Oxford University Press, 2013.

———. *Rethinking Human Nature: A Christian Materialist Alternative to the Soul*. Grand Rapids: Baker Academic, 2006.

Cowan, Steven B. "Compatibilism and the Sinlessness of the Redeemed in Heaven." *Faith and Philosophy* 28 (2011) 416–31.

Craig, William Lane. "The Doctrine of Creation." http://www.reasonablefaith.org/defenders-2-podcast/s8.

———. *God Over All: Divine Aseity and the Challenge of Platonism*. Oxford: Oxford University Press, 2016.

———. *The Kalām Cosmological Argument*. Eugene, OR: Wipf & Stock, 2000.

———. *Reasonable Faith*. 3rd ed. Wheaton, IL: Crossway, 2008.

Craig, William Lane, and Paul Copan. "Craftsman or Creator?" In *The New Mormon Challenge*, edited by Francis J. Beckwith, Carl Mosser, and Paul Owen, 95–152. Grand Rapids: Zondervan, 2002.

———. *Creation Out of Nothing: A Biblical, Philosophical, and Scientific Exploration*. Grand Rapids: Baker Academic, 2004.

Craig, William Lane, and James D. Sinclair. "The Kalam Cosmological Argument." In *The Blackwell Companion to Natural Theology*, edited by William Lane Craig and J. P. Moreland, 101–201. Oxford: Wiley-Blackwell, 2009.

Crockett, William V. "The Metaphorical View." In *Four Views on Hell*, edited by William Crockett, 43–76. Grand Rapids, Zondervan, 1996.

Cunningham, Andrew. "Identifying Disease in the Past: Cutting the Gordian Knot." *Asclepio* 54 (2002) 13–34.

Cupitt, Don. "Four Arguments against the Devil." *Theology* 64 (1961) 413–15.

Bibliography

Cyril of Jerusalem. *Catechesis*. In *The Works of Saint Cyril of Jerusalem*, translated by Leo P. McCauley and Anthony A. Stephenson, 2:4–206. The Fathers of the Church 64. Baltimore: Catholic University of America Press, 2010.

Davidson, Francis, A. M. Stibbs, and E. F. Kevan. *The New Bible Commentary*. Grand Rapids: Eerdmans, 1965.

Davis, D. Russell, and D. W. Kennard. "Urticaria." *Journal of Psychosomatic Research* 8 (1964) 203–6.

Davis, John Jefferson. "How Personal Agents Are Located in Space." *Philosophia Christi* 13 (2011) 437–44.

Dawkins, Richard. *The God Delusion*. London: Bantam, 2006.

Day, Elizabeth. "God Told Us to Exorcise My Daughter's Demons. I Don't Regret Her Death." *The Telegraph*, November 27, 2005. http://www.telegraph.co.uk/news/worldnews/northamerica/usa/1504158/God-told-us-to-exorcise-my-daughters-demons.-I-dont-regret-her-death.html.

De La Torre, Miguel A., and Albert Hernández. *The Quest for the Historical Satan*. Minneapolis: Fortress, 2011.

Delitzsch, Franz. *A New Commentary on Genesis 1*. Edinburgh: T. & T. Clark, 1888.

Descartes, René. "Meditation I." In *Discourse on Method and Meditations on First Philosophy*, translated by Donald A. Cress, 59–62. 4th ed. Indianapolis: Hackett, 1998.

Dickason, C. Fred. *Angels: Elect and Evil*. Chicago: Moody, 1975.

"Does God Exist? William Lane Craig vs. Christopher Hitchens." http://www.reasonablefaith.org/does-god-exist-craig-vs-hitchens-apr-2009.

Donelson, Lewis R. *I and II Peter and Jude*. Louisville: Presbyterian, 2010.

Driver, Samuel Rolles, and George Buchanan Gray. *A Critical and Exegetical Commentary on the Book of Job*. Vol. 1. New York: Scribner's, 1921.

Dunn, James D. G. *The Christ and the Spirit, Volume II: Pneumatology*. Grand Rapids: Eerdmans, 1998.

Eccles, John, and Karl Popper. *The Self and Its Brain: An Argument for Interactionism*. Berlin: Springer, 1997.

Empedocles. *Fragments*. In *The Fragments of Empedocles*, translated by William Ellery Leonard. Chicago: The Open Court, 1908.

Epicurus. *Letter to Herodotus*. In *Letters and Sayings of Epicurus*, translated by Odysseus Makridis, 1–28. New York: Barnes & Noble, 2005.

Euripides. *Hippolytus*. In *The Hippolytus of Euripides*, translated by Gilbert Murray. London: George Allen, 1904.

Evangelatou, Maria. "From Word into Image: The Visualization of Ulcer in Byzantine Illustrated Manuscripts of the Book of Job." *Gesta* 48 (2009) 19–36.

Evans, G. R. *Augustine on Evil*. New York: Cambridge University Press, 1991.

Evans, Hilary. "The Ghost Experience in a Wider Context." In *Hauntings and Poltergeists: Multidisciplinary Perspectives*, edited by James Houran and Rense Lange, 41–61. Jefferson, NC: McFarland, 2001.

Farris, Joshua R. *The Soul of Theological Anthropology: A Cartesian Exploration*. London: Routledge, 2017.

Ferguson, Everett. *Backgrounds of Early Christianity*. 3rd ed. Grand Rapids: Eerdmans, 2003.

Feser, Edward. *Aquinas*. London: Oneworld, 2015.

———. *Five Proofs of the Existence of God*. San Francisco: Ignatius, 2017.

———. *Philosophy of Mind: A Beginner's Guide*. London: Oneworld, 2006.

Bibliography

Fishman, Yonatan. "Can Science Test Supernatural Worldviews?" In *Science, Worldviews and Education*, edited by Michael R. Matthews, 165–90. Sydney: Springer Science and Business Media, 2009.

Fleetwood, William. *An Essay Upon Miracles: In Two Discourses*. London: np, 1702.

Flew, Antony. *A New Approach to Psychical Research*. London: Watts, 1953.

Forsyth, Neil. *The Old Enemy*. Princeton: Princeton University Press, 1987.

Foster, John. *The Immaterial Self: A Defence of the Cartesian Dualist Conception of the Mind*. London: Routledge, 1991.

Fowl, Stephen E. *Ephesians*. Louisville: Westminster John Knox, 2012.

Friberg, Timothy, Barbara Friberg, and Neva F. Miller. *Analytical Lexicon of the Greek New Testament*. Grand Rapids: Baker, 2000.

Friedkin, William. "The Devil and Father Amorth: Witnessing 'the Vatican Exorcist' at Work." *Vanity Fair*, December 2016. https://www.vanityfair.com/hollywood/2016/10/father-amorth-the-vatican-exorcist.

Fudge, Edward. *The Fire That Consumes*. 3rd ed. Eugene, OR: Wipf & Stock, 2011.

Gale, Richard. "A Note on Personal Identity and Bodily Continuity." *Analysis* 29 (1969) 193–95.

Gallagher, Richard. "As a Psychiatrist, I Diagnose Mental Illness. Also, I Help Spot Demonic Possession: How a Scientist Learned to Work with Exorcists." *Washington Post*, July 1, 2016. https://www.washingtonpost.com/posteverything/wp/2016/07/01/as-a-psychiatrist-i-diagnose-mental-illness-and-sometimes-demonic-possession/?tid=sm_fb&utm_term=.5b494bc9ad71.

Garland, David E. *2 Corinthians: An Exegetical and Theological Exposition of Holy Scripture*. New American Commentary. Nashville: B&H, 1999.

Garson, Justin. *The Biological Mind*. London: Routledge, 2015.

Gellman, Jerome. "Omnipotence and Impeccability." *The New Scholasticism* 51 (1977) 21–37.

Gilson, Étienne. *The Philosophy of St. Bonaventure*. Translated by Dom Illtyd Trethowan and Frank J. Sheed. Paterson, NJ: St. Anthony Guild, 1965.

Goetz, Stewart. "Dualism, Causation, and Supervenience." *Faith and Philosophy* 11 (1994) 92–108.

———. "Human Persons Are Material and Immaterial (Body and Soul)." In *Debating Christian Theism*, edited by J. P. Moreland, Chad Meister, and Khaldoun A. Sweis, 261–69. New York: Oxford University Press, 2013.

Goetz, Stewart, and Charles Taliaferro. *A Brief History of the Soul*. Oxford: Wiley-Blackwell, 2011.

Goodman, Felicitas D. *The Exorcism of Anneliese Michel*. Eugene, OR: Resource, 1981.

Grahame, Anne. "Management of Chronic Urticaria." *Canadian Family Physician* 33 (1987) 378–84.

Graham, George. *The Disordered Mind: An Introduction to Philosophy of Mind and Mental Illness*. 2nd ed. London: Routledge, 2013.

Greaves, Malcolm. "Chronic Urticaria." *The Journal of Allergy and Clinical Immunology* 105 (2000) 664–72.

Greenhut, Z. "The 'Caiaphas' Tomb in North Talpiyot, Jerusalem." *'Atiqot* 21 (1992) 63–71.

Gross, K. David. *The Salem Witch Trials*. Westport, CT: Greenwood, 2008.

Guiley, Rosemary. *Encyclopedia of Demons and Demonology*. New York: Visionary Living, 2009.

Gundry, Robert H. *Commentary on the New Testament*. Peabody, MA: Hendrickson, 2010.

Guthrie, Shandon L. "Christian Demonology: A New Philosophical Perspective." In *Philosophical Approaches to Demonology*, edited by Benjamin W. McCraw and Robert Arp, 59–74. London: Routledge, 2017.

———. "A New Challenge to a Warfare Theodicy." *International Journal of Philosophy and Theology* 5 (2017) 35–43.

———. "A New Metaphysics for Christian Demonology: Psychodynamic Immaterialism." PhD diss., Manchester Metropolitan University, 2015.

Habel, Norman C. *The Book of Job: A Commentary*. Philadelphia: Westminster, 1985.

Habermas, Gary R., and Michael R. Licona. *The Case for the Resurrection of Jesus*. Grand Rapids: Kregel, 2004.

Haight, David. "What Have We Learned from Ontological Devil-Arguments?" *International Philosophical Quarterly* 34 (1994) 301–6.

Haight, David, and Marjorie Haight. "An Ontological Argument for the Devil." *Monist* 54 (1970) 218–20.

Harris, Murray J. *New International Greek Testament Commentary: The Second Epistle to the Corinthians*. Grand Rapids: Eerdmans, 2005.

Harrison, Roland Kenneth. *Introduction to the Old Testament*. Grand Rapids: Eerdmans, 1969.

Hasker, William. *The Emergent Self*. Ithaca: Cornell University Press, 1999.

Hawking, Stephen, and Leonard Mlodinow. *The Grand Design*. New York: Bantam, 2011.

Heiser, Michael S. "Does Deuteronomy 32.17 Assume or Deny the Reality of Other Gods?" *The Bible Translator* 59 (2008) 137–45.

———. "Monotheism, Polytheism, Monolatry Henotheism? Toward an Assessment of Divine Plurality in the Hebrew Bible." *Bulletin for Biblical Research* 18 (2008) 1–30.

———. "The Nachash (הַנָּחָשׁ) and His Seed: Some Explanatory Notes on Why the Serpent in Genesis 3 Wasn't a Serpent." http://www.scribd.com/doc/68024391/Serpent-Seed-Dr-Michael-S-Heiser.

———. "Should אלהים ('ĔLŌHÎM) with Plural Predication Be Translated 'Gods'?" *The Bible Translator* 61 (2010) 123–36.

———. *The Unseen Realm*. Bellingham, WA: Lexham, 2015.

Henderson, James. "Exorcism and Possession in Psychotherapy Practice." *The Canadian Journal of Psychiatry* 27 (1982) 129–34.

Herbert, Nick. *Quantum Reality: Beyond the New Physics*. New York: Anchor, 1985.

Hesiod. *Theogony*. In *Works and Days, Theogony and The Shield of Heracles*, translated by Hugh G. Evelyn-White, 27–56. Mineola, NY: Dover, 2006.

———. *Works and Days*. In *Works and Days, Theogony and The Shield of Heracles*, translated by Hugh G. Evelyn-White, 1–26. Mineola, NY: Dover, 2006.

Hick, John. *Philosophy of Religion*. 4th ed. Upper Saddle River, NJ: Prentice Hall, 1990.

Hitchens, Christopher. "Cross Examination." http://www.reasonablefaith.org/does-god-exist-craig-vs-hitchens-apr-2009#section_6.

———. *God Is Not Great: How Religion Poisons Everything*. New York: Twelve, 2007.

———. "Opening Speech." http://www.reasonablefaith.org/does-god-exist-craig-vs-hitchens-apr-2009#section_3.

Hoadly, Benjamin. *A Letter to the Reverend Mr. Fleetwood, Occasion'd by his Essay on Miracles*. In *The Works of Benjamin Hoadly, D.D.*, edited by John Hoadly, 1:5–18. London: W. Bowyer and J. Nichols, 1773.

Hobbes, Thomas. *Leviathan*. Edited by C. B. MacPherson. London: Penguin, 1985.

BIBLIOGRAPHY

———. *The Elements of Law, Natural and Politic.* Whitefish. MT: Kessinger, 2004.

Hodge, Alexander. *Outlines of Theology.* New York: Robert Carter, 1860.

Hodge, Charles. *2 Corinthians.* The Crossway Classic Commentaries. Wheaton, IL: Crossway, 1995.

Hoehner, Harold W. *Ephesians: An Exegetical Commentary.* Grand Rapids: Baker Academic, 2002.

Hoffman, Joshua, and Gary Rosenkrantz. *The Divine Attributes.* Oxford: Blackwell, 2002.

Holmes, Ronald M., and James E. DeBurger. "Profiles in Terror: The Serial Murderer." *Federal Probation* 49 (1985) 29–34.

Hopkin, Charles Edward. "The Share of Thomas Aquinas in the Growth of the Witchcraft Delusion." PhD diss., University of Pennsylvania, 1941.

Houran, James, and Rense Lange, eds. *Hauntings and Poltergeists: Multidisciplinary Perspectives.* Jefferson, NC: McFarland, 2001.

Hume, David. *An Enquiry Concerning Human Understanding.* Edited by Peter Millican. New York: Oxford University Press, 2007.

Insel, T., et al. "Research Domain Criteria (RDoC): Toward a New Classification Framework for Research on Mental Disorders." *The American Journal Of Psychiatry* 167 (2010) 748–51.

Ivanovska, Inta. "The Demonology of Saint Augustine of Hippo." PhD diss., Saint Louis University, 2011.

Jacob, Benno. *The Second Book of the Bible: Exodus.* Edited by Walter Jacob. Translated by Yaakov Elman. Jersey City: KTAV, 1992.

Jacobs, Nathan A. "Are Created Spirits Composed of Matter and Form? A Defense of Pneumatic Hylomorphism." *Philosophia Christi* 14 (2012) 79–108.

Jehle, David. "Kim Against Dualism." *Philosophical Studies* 130 (2006) 565–78.

Johnson, David Kyle. "Justified Belief in the Existence of Demons Is Impossible." In *Philosophical Approaches to Demonology*, edited by Robert Arp and Benjamin McCraw, 175–91. London: Routledge, 2017.

———. "Justified Belief in Miracles Is Impossible." *Science, Religion and Culture* 2 (2015) 61–74.

Johnson, Luke Timothy, and Jennifer K. Cox. *Hebrews: A Commentary.* Louisville: John Knox, 2006.

Joines, Karen R. *Serpent Symbolism in the Old Testament.* Haddonfield, NJ: Haddonfield, 1974.

Jones, Scott C. "Lions, Serpents, and Lion-Serpents in Job 28:8." *Journal of Biblical Literature* 130 (2011) 663–86.

Josephus, Flavius. *Antiquities of the Jews.* Translated by William Whiston. Nashville: Thomas Nelson, 1998.

Joshi, Purushottam. "Mental Health in a Historical Perspective." *Annales Médico-Psychologiques* 1 (1971) 185–214.

Kaiser, Walter, Jr., et al., eds. *Hard Sayings of the Bible.* Downers Grove, IL: InterVarsity, 1996.

Kalisch, M. M. *A Historical and Critical Commentary on the Old Testament, with a New Translation: Genesis.* London: Longman, Brown, Green, Longmans, and Roberts, 1858.

Kandel, E. R. "A New Intellectual Framework for Psychiatry." *American Journal of Psychiatry* 155 (1998) 457–69.

Kant, Immanuel. *Dreams of a Spirit-Seer—Illustrated by Dreams of Metaphysics.* Edited by Frank Sewall. Translated by Emanuel F. Goerwitz. London: Swan Sonnenschein, 1900.

Kay, William K., and Robin Parry, eds. *Exorcism and Deliverance: Multi-Disciplinary Studies.* London: Paternoster, 2011.

Keating, Daniel A. *First and Second Peter, Jude.* Catholic Commentary on Sacred Scripture. Grand Rapids: Baker Academic, 2011.

Keck, David. *Angels and Angelology in the Middle Ages.* New York: Oxford University Press, 1998.

Keener, Craig S. *The IVP Bible Background Commentary: New Testament.* Downers Grove, IL: InterVarsity, 1993.

———. *Miracles.* 2 vols. Grand Rapids: Baker Academic, 2011.

Kelly, Henry Ansgar. *The Devil, Demonology, and Witchcraft: The Development of Christian Beliefs in Evil Spirits.* Eugene, OR: Wipf & Stock, 2004.

———. "The Devil in the Desert." *Catholic Biblical Quarterly* 26 (1964) 190–220.

———. "Review: The Devil at Large." *The Journal of Religion* 67 (1987) 521–23.

———. *Satan: A Biography.* New York: Cambridge University Press, 2006.

Kelly, Stewart E. "The Problem of Evil and the Satan Hypothesis." *Sophia* 36 (1997) 29–42.

Kihlstrom, John F. "Dissociative and Conversion Disorders." In *Cognitive Science and Clinical Disorders*, edited by Dan Stein and Jeffrey Young, 248–71. London: Academic, 1992.

Kim, Jaegwon. "Causation, Nomic Subsumption, and the Concept of Event." *The Journal of Philosophy* 70 (1973) 217–36.

———. "Lonely Souls: Causality and Substance Dualism." In *Soul, Body, and Survival: Essays on the Metaphysics of Human Persons*, edited by Kevin Corcoran, 30–43. Ithaca: Cornell University Press, 2001.

———. "Mental Causation: What? Me Worry?" *Philosophical Issues* 6 (1995) 123–51.

———. *Physicalism, or Something Near Enough.* Princeton: Princeton University Press, 2007.

Koch, Kurt E. *Demonology Past and Present: Identifying and Overcoming Demonic Strongholds.* Grand Rapids: Kregel, 1973.

Kreeft, Peter. *Angels and Demons: What Do We Really Know About Them?* San Francisco: Ignatius, 1995.

Kretzmann, Norman. *The Metaphysics of Theism: Aquinas's Natural Theology in* Summa Contra Gentiles I. Oxford: Clarendon, 1997.

Kuhn, Thomas. *The Structures of Scientific Revolutions.* 2nd ed. Chicago: University of Chicago Press, 1970.

Lactantius. *The Divine Institutes.* In *Fathers of the Third and Fourth Century*, edited and translated by Alexander Roberts, James Donaldson, and Arthur Cleveland Coxe, 9–223. The Ante-Nicene Fathers 7. New York: Scribner's, 1886.

Lane, William L. *Hebrews: A Call to Commitment.* Vancouver, BC: Regent College, 2004.

———. *Hebrews 1–8.* World Biblical Commentary 47b. Dallas: Word, 1991.

Langton, Edward. *Essentials of Demonology.* London: Epworth, 1949.

Larmer, Robert. "Is There Anything Wrong with 'God of the Gaps' Reasoning?" *International Journal for Philosophy of Religion* 52 (2002) 129–42.

Latourette, Kenneth Scott. *A History of Christianity.* Vol. 1. New York: Harper & Row, 1975.

Law, Stephen. "Evil God and Mirror Theodicies." *Free inquiry* 36 (2016) 18–21.

———. "The Evil-God Challenge." *Religious Studies* 46 (2010) 353–73.

Leftow, Brian. *God and Necessity.* Oxford: Oxford University Press, 2012.

Leibniz, G. W. *Leibniz and the Two Sophies: The Philosophical Correspondence.* Edited and translated by Lloyd Strickland. Toronto: CRRS, 2011.

Bibliography

———. *Monadology*. In *Leibniz's Monadology: A New Translation and Guide*. Translated by Lloyd Strickland. Edinburgh: Edinburgh University Press, 2014.

———. *Philosophical Selections*. Translated by Philip P. Wiener. New York: Scribner, 1953.

Lenski, R. C. H. *The Interpretation of II Corinthians*. Minneapolis: Fortress, 1948.

Lewis, C. S. *The Problem of Pain*. New York: Macmillan, 1962.

———. *The Screwtape Letters*. New York: HarperCollins, 2001.

Lewis, Theodore J. "CT 13.33–34 and Ezekiel 32: Lion-Dragon Myths." *Journal of the American Oriental Society* 116 (1996) 28–47.

Lewy, C. "Is the Notion of Disembodied Existence Self-Contradictory?" *Proceedings of the Aristotelian Society* 43 (1942–43) 59–78.

Licona, Michael R. *The Resurrection of Jesus: A New Historiographical Approach*. Downers Grove, IL: InterVarsity, 2010.

Lipton, Peter. *Inference to the Best Explanation*. London: Routledge, 1991.

Lobert, Annie. Interview in "Does Satan Exist?" *ABC Nightline*, 2009. https://www.youtube.com/watch?v=Vg3-pwIPoX4.

Locke, John. *A Discourse of Miracles*. In *The Works of John Locke*, 8:256–65. 9th ed. London: C. and J. Rivington et al., 1794.

———. *An Essay Concerning Human Understanding*. In *Philosophical Works: An Essay Concerning Human Understanding*, edited by James Augustus St. John. Vol. 2. London: Bell, 1877.

Lockwood, D. N. J., and A. J. C. Reid. "The Diagnosis of Leprosy is Delayed in the United Kingdom." *QJM* 94 (2001) 207–12.

Loose, Jonathan J., Angus Menuge, and J. P. Moreland, eds. *The Blackwell Companion to Substance Dualism*. Oxford: Blackwell, 2017.

Loreno, Darcie. "Ghost Attacks Photographer in PA House 'Haunted' with Demons, Spirits." *Fox43*, July 26, 2014. http://fox43.com/2014/07/25/ghost-attacks-in-hanover-haunted-house/#axzz38baFhcRq>.

Loschen, E. L. "Psychiatry and Religion: A Variable History." *Journal of Religion and Health* 13 (1974) 137–41.

Lovejoy, Arthur O. *The Great Chain of Being: A Study of the History of an Idea*. Cambridge, MA: Harvard University Press, 2001.

Lowe, E. J. *An Introduction to the Philosophy of Mind*. Cambridge: Cambridge University Press, 2000.

Lund, David H. *The Conscious Self: The Immaterial Center of Subjective States*. Amherst, MA: Humanity, 2005.

———. *Death and Consciousness*. Jefferson, NC: McFarland, 1985.

———. *Persons, Souls and Death: A Philosophical Investigation of an Afterlife*. Jefferson, NC: McFarland, 2009.

Lycan, William G. "Giving Dualism Its Due." *Australasian Journal of Philosophy* 87 (2009) 551–63.

———. "Qualitative Experience in Machines." In *The Digital Phoenix: How Computers are Changing Philosophy*, edited by Terrell Ward Bynum and James H. Moor, 171–92. Oxford: Blackwell, 1998.

Lys, Daniel. "The Israelite Soul According to the LXX." *Vetus Testamentum* 16 (1966) 181–228.

Mackay, Robert William. *The Tübingen School and Its Antecedents: A Review of the History and Present Condition of Modern Theology*. London: Williams and Norgate, 1863.

Madell, Geoffrey. "The Road to Substance Dualism." In *The Metaphysics of Consciousness*, edited by Pierfrancesco Basile, Julian Kiverstein, and Pauline Phemister, 45–60. Cambridge: Cambridge University Press, 2010.

Magiorkinis, Emmanouil, Kalliopi Sidiropoulou, and Aristidis Diamantis. "Hallmarks in the History of Epilepsy: Epilepsy in Antiquity." *Epilepsy and Behavior* 17 (2010) 103–8.

Malebranche, Nicolas. *De la Recherche de la Vérité*. Edited and translated by T. M. Lennon and P. J. Olscamp. Columbus: Ohio State University Press, 1980.

Mann, Christopher Stephen. *Mark: A New Translation with Introduction and Commentary*. Anchor Bible 27. New York: Doubleday, 1986.

Marmadoro, Anna. "Is Being One Only One? The Uniqueness of Platonic Forms." *Apeiron* 41 (2008) 211–27.

Martyr, Justin. *The First Apology*. In *The First and Second Apologies*, edited and translated by Leslie William Barnard, 23–72. Mahwah, NJ: Paulist, 1997.

———. *The Second Apology*. In *The Apostolic Fathers with Justin Martyr and Irenaeus*, edited and translated by Alexander Roberts, James Donaldson, and Arthur Cleveland Coxe, 188–93. The Ante-Nicene Fathers 1. New York: Scribner's, 1903.

Marx, Alfred. "La chute de 'Lucifer' (Esaïe 14,12–15; Luc 10,18): Préhistoire d'un mythe." *Revue d'histoire et de philosophie religieuses* 80 (2000) 171–85.

Mascall, E. L. *Christian Theology and Natural Science: Some Questions on their Relations*. New York: Ronald, 1956.

Mason, Perry C. "The Devil and St. Anselm." *International Journal for Philosophy of Religion* 9 (1978) 1–15.

Matera, Frank J. *II Corinthians: A Commentary*. Louisville: Westminster John Knox, 2003.

McCann, Hugh J. *Creation and the Sovereignty of God*. Bloomington: Indiana University Press, 2012.

McColly, Grant. "Paradise Lost." *The Harvard Theological Review* 32 (1939) 181–236.

McCraw, Benjamin W. "Reformed Demonology?" In *Philosophical Approaches to the Devil*, edited by Robert Arp and Benjamin McCraw, 145–56. Routledge Studies in the Philosophy of Religion. New York: Routledge, 2016.

McDonald, Lee Martin. "2 Corinthians." In *The Bible Knowledge Background Commentary: Acts-Philemon*, edited by Craig A. Evans, Isobel A. H. Combes, and Daniel M. Gurtner, 375–458. Colorado Springs: David C. Cook, 2004.

McGinn, Bernard. *Antichrist: Two Thousand Years of the Human Fascination with Evil*. New York: Columbia University Press, 1999.

McGrew, Lydia. *Hidden in Plain View: Undesigned Coincidences in the Gospels and Acts*. Chillicothe, OH: DeWard, 2017.

McGrew, Timothy. "Miracles." *The Stanford Encyclopedia of Philosophy*. Edited by Edward N. Zalta. 2016. https://plato.stanford.edu/archives/win2016/entries/miracles/.

McGrew, Timothy, and Lydia McGrew. "The Argument from Miracles: A Cumulative Case for the Resurrection of Jesus of Nazareth." In *The Blackwell Companion to Natural Theology*, edited by William Lane Craig and J. P. Moreland, 593–662. Oxford: Wiley-Blackwell, 2009.

McNamara, Paul. "A Theist's Nightmare." In *Philosophical Approaches to the Devil*, edited by Robert Arp and Benjamin McCraw, 119–33. Routledge Studies in the Philosophy of Religion. London: Routledge, 2016.

Meier, Samuel. "Signs and Wonders." In *Dictionary of the Old Testament Pentateuch*, edited by T. Desmond Alexander and David Baker, 755–62. Downers Grove, IL: InterVarsity, 2003.

Merricks, Trenton. "The Resurrection of the Body." In *The Oxford Handbook of Philosophical Theology*, edited by Thomas P. Flint and Michael C. Rea, 476–90. New York: Oxford University Press, 2009.

———. "There Are No Criteria of Identity Over Time." *Noûs* 32 (1998) 106–24.

Meier, John. *A Marginal Jew*. Vol. 2, *Mentor, Message, and Miracles*. New York: Doubleday, 1994.

Meyers, Edward P. "Angel." In *Eerdmans Dictionary of the Bible*, edited by David Noel Freedman, 63–64. Grand Rapids: Eerdmans, 2000.

Midelfort, H. C. Erik. *Exorcism and Enlightenment: Johann Joseph Gassner and the Demons of Eighteenth-Century Germany*. New Haven: Yale University Press, 2005.

Midgley, Mary. *Science as Salvation*. London: Routledge, 1992.

Mihai, Adrian. "Soul's Aitherial Abode According to the Poteidaia Epitaph and the Presocratic Philosophers." *Numen: International Review for the History of Religions* 57 (2010) 552–82.

Milgrom, J. *Leviticus 1-16: A New Translation with Introduction and Commentary*. AB 3. New York: Doubleday, 1991.

Milton, John. *Paradise Lost*. In *Milton's Paradise Lost and Paradise Regained*, edited by J. Edmonston, 1–385. T. Nelson and Sons, 1854.

———. *Paradise Regained*. In *Milton's Paradise Lost and Paradise Regained*, edited by J. Edmonston, 387–408. T. Nelson and Sons, 1854.

Mitchell, Piers. "Retrospective Diagnosis and the Use of Historical Texts for Investigating Disease in the Past." *International Journal of Paleopathology* 1 (2011) 81–88.

Montgomery, John Warwick, ed. *Demon Possession: Papers Presented at the University of Notre Dame*. Irvine, CA: NRP, 2015.

———. *Principalities and Powers*. Minneapolis: Bethany, 1973.

Moreland, J. P. "If You Can't Reduce, You Must Eliminate: Why Kim's Version of Physicalism Isn't Close Enough." *Philosophia Christi* 7 (2005) 463–73.

Moreland, J. P., and Gary Habermas. *Beyond Death: Exploring the Evidence for Immortality*. Wheaton, IL: Crossway, 1998.

Moreland, J. P., and Scott Rae. *Body and Soul: Human Nature and the Crisis in Ethics*. Downers Grove, IL: InterVarsity, 2000.

Morey, Robert. *Satan's Devices: Breaking Free from the Schemes of the Enemy*. Eugene, OR: Harvest, 1993.

Mowinckel, Sigmund. "לחש." In *Hebrew and Semitic Studies Presented to Godfrey Rolles Driver Driver in Celebration of His Seventieth Birthday, 20 August 1962*, edited by D. Winton Thomas and W. D. McHardy, 95–103. Oxford: Clarendon, 1963.

Murison, Ross G. "The Serpent in the Old Testament." *The American Journal of Semitic Languages and Literatures* 21 (1905) 115–30.

Murphy, Francesca Aran. *1 Samuel*. Brazos Theological Commentary on the Bible. Grand Rapids: Baker, 2010.

Murphy, Nancey. *Bodies and Souls, or Spirited Bodies?* New York: Cambridge University Press, 2006.

Murray, Michael. *Nature Red in Tooth and Claw*. New York: Oxford University Press, 2008.

Bibliography

Nagel, Thomas. *Mind and Cosmos: Why the Materialist Neo-Darwinian Conception of Nature Is Almost Certainly False*. New York: Oxford University Press, 2012.

———. *The View from Nowhere*. New York: Oxford University Press, 1986.

Newman, John Henry. "Victory of Good over Evil." In *Sermon Notes of John Henry Cardinal Newman, 1849–4878*, edited by Fathers of the Birmingham Oratory, 221–22. London: Longmans and Green, 1913.

Newman, Robert C. "The Ancient Exegesis of Genesis 6:2, 4." *Grace Theological Journal* 5 (1984) 13–36.

Noegel, Scott B. "Moses and Magic: Notes on the Book of Exodus." *Journal of the Ancient Near Eastern Society* 24 (1996) 45–59.

Nordell, P. A. "The Old Testament Doctrine of the Spirit of God." *The Old Testament Student* 4 (1885) 433–44.

Nozick, Robert. *Philosophical Explanations*. Cambridge, MA: Harvard University Press, 1981.

O'Connor, Timothy. "Causality, Mind, and Free Will." *Nous-Supplement: Philosophical Perspectives* 14 (2000) 105–17.

O'Daly, Gerard. *Augustine's Philosophy of Mind*. Berkeley: University of California Press, 1987.

Olbert, Charles M., and Gary J. Gala. "Supervenience and Psychiatry: Are Mental Disorders Brain Disorders?" *Journal of Theoretical and Philosophical Psychology* 35 (2015) 203–19.

Olshausen, Hermann. *Biblical Commentary on the New Testament*. Translated by John Henry Augustus Ebrard and Augustus Wiesinger. 6 vols. New York: Sheldon, 1866.

Olyan, Saul M. *A Thousand Thousands Served Him: Exegesis and the Naming of Angels in Ancient Judaism*. Tübingen: J. C. B. Mohr, 1993.

O'Mathúna, Dónal P. "Divination, Magic." In *Dictionary of the Old Testament Pentateuch*, edited by T. Desmond Alexander and David Baker, 193–97. Downers Grove, IL: InterVarsity, 2003.

Origen. *Against Celsus*. Edited by Alexander Roberts, James Donaldson, and Arthur Cleveland Coxe. The Ante-Nicene Fathers 4. New York: Scribner's, 1886.

———. *De Principiis*. Edited by Alexander Roberts, James Donaldson, and Arthur Cleveland Coxe. The Ante-Nicene Fathers 4. New York: Scribner's, 1886.

Oropeza, B. J. *99 Answers to Questions about Angels, Demons and Spiritual Warfare*. Downers Grove, IL: InterVarsity, 1997.

Pagels, Elaine. *The Origin of Satan: How Christians Demonized Jews, Pagans, and Heretics*. New York: Vintage, 1995.

Paige, Terence. "Who Believes in 'Spirit'? Πνεῦμα in Pagan Usage and Implications for the Gentile Christian Mission." *The Harvard Theological Review* 95 (2002) 417–36.

Paley, William. *The Clergyman's Companion in Visiting the Sick*. In *The Works of William Paley, D.D.* Philadelphia: J. J. Woodward, 1836.

———. *Horae Paulinae, or the Truth of the Scripture History of St Paul, Evinced by a Comparison of the Epistles which Bear his Name with the Acts of the Apostles, and with one Another*. 10th ed. London: Rivington et al., 1819.

———. *View of the Evidences of Christianity in Three Parts*. Edited by T. R. Birks. London: The Religious Tract Society, 1848.

Pannenberg, Wolfhart. *Systematic Theology*. Vol. 2. Translated by Geoffrey M. Bromiley. Grand Rapids: Eerdmans, 1994.

Papineau, David. *Theory and Meaning*. Oxford: Clarendon, 1979.

Bibliography

Parkin, David. "Wafting on the Wind: Smell and the Cycle of Spirit and Matter." *The Journal of the Royal Anthropological Institute* 13 (2007) S39–S53.

Parsons, Keith. "The Universe Is Probable; The Resurrection Is Not." In *Does God Exist? The Craig-Flew Debate*, edited by Stan W. Wallace, 115–30. London: Routledge, 2003.

Partridge, Christopher. "Alien Demonology: The Christian Roots of the Malevolent Extraterrestrial in UFO Religions and Abduction Spiritualities." *Religion* 34 (2004) 163–89.

———. *The Re-Enchantment of the West*. Vol. 2. London: T. & T. Clark, 2005.

Partridge, Christopher, and Eric Christianson. "Introduction." In *The Lure of the Dark Side: Satan and Western Demonology in Popular Culture*, edited by Christopher Partridge and Eric Christianson, 1–23. London: Routledge, 2014.

Pascal, Blaise. *Lettres Provinciales*. Translated by A. J. Krailsheimer. Harmondsworth: Penguin, 1967.

Patrides, C. A. "The Salvation of Satan." *Journal of the History of Ideas* 28 (1967) 467–78.

Paulsen, David. "Early Christian Belief in a Corporeal Deity: Origen and Augustine as Reluctant Witnesses." *The Harvard Theological Review* 83 (1990) 105–16.

Paulus, Heinrich. *Das Leben Jesu als Grundlage einer reinen Geschichte des Urchristentums*. 2 vols. Heidelberg: C. F. Winter, 1828.

Pawl, Timothy, and Kevin Timpe. "Heavenly Freedom: A Reply to Cowan." *Faith and Philosophy* 30 (2013) 188–97.

———. "Incompatibilism, Sin, and Free Will in Heaven." *Faith and Philosophy* 26 (2009) 398–419.

Peirce, C. S. "Pragmatism as the Logic of Abduction." In *The Essential Peirce: Selected Philosophical Writings*, edited by the Peirce Edition Project, 2:226–41. Bloomington: Indiana University Press, 1998.

Penelhum, Terence. *Religion and Rationality: An Introduction to the Philosophy of Religion*. New York: Random House, 1971.

Perry, John. *Knowledge, Possibility, and Consciousness*. Cambridge, MA: MIT Press, 2003.

Phillips, John. *Exploring 2 Corinthians: An Expository Commentary*. Grand Rapids: Kregel, 2002.

Philo. *On the Creation of the Cosmos According to Moses*. Translated by David T. Runia. Leiden: Brill, 2001.

Plantinga, Alvin. *God, Freedom, and Evil*. Grand Rapids: Eerdmans, 1974.

———. "Is Belief in God Properly Basic?" *Noûs* 15 (1981) 41–52.

———. *The Nature of Necessity*. New York: Oxford University Press, 1974.

———. "Supralapsarianism, or 'O Felix Culpa.'" In *Christian Faith and the Problem of Evil*, edited by Peter van Inwagen, 1–25. Grand Rapids: Eerdmans, 2004.

———. *Warranted Christian Belief*. New York: Oxford University Press, 2000.

Plato. *Laws*. In *Plato: Complete Works*, edited by John M. Cooper, 1318–616. Translated by Trevor J. Saunders. Indianapolis: Hackett, 1997.

———. *Meno*. In *Plato: Complete Works*, edited by John M. Cooper, 870–97. Translated by G. M. A. Grube. Indianapolis: Hackett, 1997.

———. *Phaedo*. In *Plato: Complete Works*, edited by John M. Cooper, 49–100. Translated by G. M. A. Grube. Indianapolis: Hackett, 1997.

———. *The Republic*. In *Plato: Complete Works*, edited by John M. Cooper, 971–1223. Translated by G. M. A. Grube and C. D. C. Reeve. Indianapolis: Hackett, 1997.

———. *Symposium*. In *Plato: Complete Works*, edited by John M. Cooper, 457–505. Translated by Alexander Nehemas and Paul Woodruff. Indianapolis: Hackett, 1997.

———. *Thaetetus*. In *Plato: Complete Works*, edited by John M. Cooper, 157–234. Translated by M. J. Levett. Indianapolis: Hackett, 1997.

———. *Timaeus*. In *Plato: Complete Works*, edited by John M. Cooper, 1224–91. Translated by Donald J. Zeyl. Indianapolis: Hackett, 1997.

Plutarch. *A Discourse Concerning Socrates's Daemon*. In *Plutarch's Morals*, translated by William W. Goodwin, 2:378–423. Boston: Little and Brown, 1874.

———. *Of Isis and Osiris*. In *Plutarch's Lives and Writing: Essays and Miscellanies*, translated by William W. Goodwin, 4:65–139. Boston: Little and Brown, 1909.

Power, William L. "Ontological Arguments for Satan and Other Sorts of Evil Beings." *Dialogue* 31 (1992) 667–76.

Prince, Derek. *They Shall Expel Demons: What You Need to Know about Demons—Your Invisible Enemies*. Grand Rapids: Chosen, 1998.

Pseudo-Dionysius. *On the Divine Names*. In *Dionysius the Areopagite on the Divine Names and the Mystical Theology*. Translated by Clarence E. Rolt. New York: Cosimo, 2007.

Quine, W. V. O. "Naturalism; or, Living within One's Means." *Dialectica* 49 (1995) 251–61.

———. *The Pursuit of Truth*. Cambridge, MA: Harvard University Press, 1992.

Radcliffe, Matthew, and Daniel D. Hutto. "Introduction." In *Folk Psychology Re-Assessed*, edited by Matthew Radcliffe and Daniel D. Hutto, 1–24. Dordrecht: Springer, 2007.

Richman, Robert J. "The Ontological Proof of the Devil." *Philosophical Studies* 9 (1958) 63–64.

———. "A Serious Look at the Ontological Argument." *Ratio* 18 (1976) 85–89.

Ricoeur, Paul. *The Symbolism of Evil*. New York: Harper & Row, 1967.

Rist, John. *Plotinus: The Road to Reality*. Cambridge: Cambridge University Press, 1967.

Ronning, John L. "The Curse of the Serpent (Genesis 3:15) in Biblical Theology and Hermeneutics." PhD diss., Westminster Theological Seminary, 1997.

Rooker, Mark. "Theophany." In *Dictionary of the Old Testament Pentateuch*, edited by T. Desmond Alexander and David W. Baker, 859–64. Downers Grove, IL: InterVarsity, 2003.

Rosenberg, Alex. *The Atheist's Guide to Reality: Enjoying Life without Illusions*. New York: Norton, 2011.

Rousseau, David. "Understanding Spiritual Awareness in Terms of Anomalous Information Access." *The Open Information Science Journal* 3 (2011) 40–53.

Routledge, Robin. "'My Spirit' in Genesis 6:1-4." *Journal of Pentecostal Theology* 20 (2011) 232–51.

Russell, Jeffrey Burton. *The Devil: Perceptions of Evil from Antiquity to Primitive Christianity*. Ithaca: Cornell University, 1977.

———. *Mephistopheles: The Devil in the Modern World*. Ithaca: Cornell University Press, 1986.

———. *The Prince of Darkness: Radical Evil and the Power of Good in History*. Ithaca: Cornell University Press, 1988.

———. *Satan: The Early Christian Tradition*. Ithaca: Cornell University Press, 1981.

Ryle, Gilbert. *The Concept of Mind*. London: Hutchinson, 1949.

Sandywell, Barry. *Presocratic Reflexivity: The Construction of Philosophical Discourse c. 600-450 BC*. Logological Investigations 3. New York: Routledge, 1996.

Schaeffer, Francis. *Genesis in Space and Time*. Downers Grove, IL: InterVarsity, 1972.

Schellenberg, J. L. *The Hiddenness Argument: Philosophy's New Challenge to Belief in God*. Oxford: Oxford University Press, 2015.

Bibliography

Schemm, Peter R., Jr. "The Agents of God: Angels." In *A Theology for the Church*, edited by Daniel L. Akin, 293–330. Nashville: B&H, 2007.

Schiavo, Luigi. "The Temptation of Jesus: The Eschatological Battle and The New Ethic of the First Followers of Jesus in Q." *Journal for the Study of the New Testament* 25 (2002) 141–64.

Schlagel, Richard H. *Contextual Realism: A Metaphysical Framework for Modern Science*. New York: Paragon, 1986.

———. *The Vanquished Gods: Science, Religion, and the Nature of Belief*. Amherst: Prometheus, 2001.

Schleiermacher, Friedrich. *The Christian Faith*. Edited by Paul T. Nimmo. Translated by H. R. Mackintosh. London: Bloomsbury, 2016.

Schoemaker, William Ross. "The Use of 'Ruah' in the Old Testament and of 'Pneuma' in the New Testament." PhD diss., the University of Chicago, 1903.

Schweitzer, Albert. *The Quest of the Historical Jesus: A Critical Study of Its Progress from Reimarus to Wrede*. Translated by W. Montgomery. London: Adam and Charles Black, 1910.

Scot, Reginald. *The Discoverie of Witchcraft*. Edited by Brinsley Nicholson. London: Elliot Stock, 1886.

Scott, Walter. *The Existence of Evil Spirits Proved; and their Agency, Particularly in Relation to the Human Race, Explained and Illustrated*. London: Jackson and Walford, 1843.

Scotus, John Duns. *Ordinatio*. In *John Duns Scotus: Selected Writings on Ethics*, edited and translated by Thomas Williams. Oxford: Oxford University Press, 2017.

Sklar, Jay. *Leviticus*. Downers Grove, IL: InterVarsity, 2014.

Sluhovsky, Moshe. *Believe Not Every Spirit: Possession, Mysticism, and Discernment in Early Modern Catholicism*. Chicago: The University of Chicago Press, 2007.

Smart, J. J. C. "Sensations and Brain Processes." *Philosophical Review* 68 (1959) 141–56.

Smith, Steven G. "Daimon Thinking and the Question of Spiritual Power." *The Heythrop Journal* 55 (2014) 173–87.

Spinoza, Baruch. "On Devils." In *Spinoza's Short Treatise on God, Man, and His Well-Being*, edited by A. Wolf, 143. London: Adam and Charles Black, 1910.

Stanford, Peter. *The Devil: A Biography*. London: Heinemann, 1996.

Stein, D. J., et al. "What is a Mental/Psychiatric Disorder? From DSM-IV to DSM-V." *Psychological Medicine* 40 (2010) 1759–65.

Stein, Robert H. *Luke*. Nashville, TN: B&H, 1992.

Steinmann, Andrew E. "Cherubim." In *Dictionary of the Old Testament Pentateuch*, edited by T. Desmond Alexander and David W. Baker, 112–13. Downers Grove, IL: InterVarsity, 2003.

Storms, C. Samuel. *Tough Topics: Biblical Answers to 25 Challenging Questions*. Wheaton, IL: Crossway, 2013.

Strauss, David Friedrich. *The Life of Jesus: Critically Examined*. Translated by George Eliot. London: Sonnenchein, 1892.

Strawson, Galen. *Mental Reality*. Cambridge, MA: MIT Press, 1994.

Strawson, P. F. *Individuals*. London: Routledge, 1964.

Strickland, Lloyd. *Leibniz and the Two Sophies: The Philosophical Correspondence*. Toronto: CRRS, 2011.

Sudduth, Michael. *A Philosophical Critique of Empirical Arguments for Postmortem Survival*. Basingstoke: Palgrave, 2015.

Bibliography

Swinburne, Richard. *The Christian God*. Oxford: Oxford University Press, 1994.

———. *The Evolution of the Soul*. Revised ed. Oxford: Oxford University Press, 1997.

———. *The Existence of God*. 2nd ed. Oxford: Oxford University Press, 2013.

———. *Mind, Brain, and Free Will*. Oxford: Oxford University Press, 2013.

———. "Personal Identity." *Proceedings of the Aristotelian Society* 74 (1973–74) 232–40.

———. *The Resurrection of God Incarnate*. Oxford: Oxford University Press, 2003.

Szasz, Thomas S. "The Myth of Mental Illness." In *Perspectives in Abnormal Behavior*, edited by Richard J. Morris, 4–11. New York: Pergamon, 1974.

Taliaferro, Charles. "A Modal Argument for Dualism." *Southern Journal of Philosophy* 24 (1986) 95–108.

Tate, Marvin E. "Satan in the Old Testament." *Review and Expositor* 89 (1992) 461–74.

Tatian. *Address of Tatian to the Greeks*. In *Tatian, Theophilus, and the Clementine Recognitions*, edited by Alexander Roberts and James Donaldson, 1–45. Translated by B. P. Prattenrcus Dods and Thomas Smith. Ante-Nicene Christian Library 3. Edinburgh: T. & T. Clark, 1867.

Tertullian. *De Anima*. Translated by J. M. Meulenhoff. Amsterdam: Apologetics, 1947.

———. *Apology*. In *The Sacred Writings of Tertullian*, translated by Peter Holmes and Sidney Thewall, 1:13–70. Altenmünster: Jazzybee, 2017.

Thijsson, Hans. "Condemnation of 1277." *Stanford Encyclopedia of Philosophy*. http://plato.stanford.edu/entries/condemnation/.

Thomas, Emily. "The Spatial Location of God and Casper the Friendly Ghost." *Think* 8 (2009) 53–61.

Thuswaldner, Gregor, and Daniel Russ, eds. *The Hermeneutics of Hell: Visions and Representations of the Devil in World Literature*. New York: Palgrave, 2017.

Tillich, Paul. *Systematic Theology*. Vol. 1. Chicago: University of Chicago Press, 1951.

Travis, Stephen H. "Psychology." In *Dictionary of the Later New Testament*, edited by Ralph P. Martin and Peter H. Davids, 984–88. Downers Grove, IL: InterVarsity, 1997.

Trethowan, Dom I. *An Essay in Christian Philosophy*. London: Longmans and Green, 1954.

Twelftree, Graham H. "Demon, Devil, Satan." In *Dictionary of Jesus and the Gospels*, edited by Joel B. Green, Scot McKnight, and I. Howard Marshall, 163–72. Downers Grove, IL: InterVarsity, 1992.

———. *In the Name of Jesus: Exorcism among Early Christians*. Grand Rapids: Baker Academic, 2007.

———. *Jesus the Exorcist: A Contribution to the Study of the Historical Jesus*. Eugene: Wipf & Stock, 2010.

———. "Temptation of Jesus." In *Dictionary of Jesus and the Gospels*, edited by Joel B. Green, Scot McKnight, and I. Howard Marshall, 821–27. Downers Grove, IL: InterVarsity, 1992.

Unger, Merrill F. *Biblical Demonology: A Study of Spiritual Forces at Work Today*. Grand Rapids: Kregel, 1994.

"Urticaria." In *Black's Medical Dictionary*, edited by Harvey Marcovitch, 694. 43rd ed. London: Bloomsbury, 2017.

Van Inwagen, Peter. *Material Beings*. Ithaca: Cornell University Press, 1990.

———. "A Materialist Ontology of the Human Person." In *Persons: Human and Divine*, edited by Peter van Inwagen and Dean Zimmerman, 199–215. New York: Oxford University Press, 2007.

Bibliography

Vázquez, Charlie. "Interview with a Demonologist." *The Huffington Post*, October 10, 2015. http://www.huffingtonpost.com/charlie-vazquez/interview-with-a-demonolo_b_8221570.html.

Walton, John H. *The Lost World of Adam and Eve: Genesis 2–3 and the Human Origins Debate*. Downers Grove, IL: IVP Academic, 2015.

Walton, John H., Victor H. Matthews, and Mark W. Chavalas. *The IVP Bible Background Commentary: Old Testament*. Downers Grove, IL: InterVarsity, 2000.

———. *Job: The NIV Application Commentary*. Grand Rapids: Zondervan, 2012.

Waters, Kenneth. "Matthew 27:52–53 as Apocalyptic Apostrophe: Temporal-Spatial Collapse in the Gospel of Matthew." *Journal of Biblical Literature* 122 (2003) 494–502.

Watt, W. Montgomery. *Muhammad: Prophet and Statesman*. Oxford: Oxford University Press, 1961.

Weber, D. A., and C. R. Reynolds. "Clinical Perspectives on Neurobiological Effects of Psychological Trauma." *Neuropsychology Review* 14 (2004) 115–29.

Wedi, Bettina. "Urticaria." *Journal der Deutschen Dermatologischen Gesellschaft* 6 (2008) 306–17.

Wiebe, Phillip H. "Finite Spirits as Theoretical Entities." *Religious Studies* 40 (2004) 341–50.

———. *God and Other Spirits: Intimations of Transcendence in Christian Experience*. New York: Oxford University Press, 2004.

Wierenga, Edward. *The Nature of God: An Inquiry Into Divine Attributes*. Ithaca: Cornell University Press, 1989.

Williams, Daniel Day. *God's Grace and Man's Hope*. New York: Harper, 1949.

Williams, Peter S. *The Case for Angels*. London: Paternoster, 2002.

———. "In Defence of Angelology." Unpublished, 2014.

Wilson, Edward O. *Consilience: The Unity of Knowledge*. New York: Vintage, 1999.

Wilson, J. V. Kinnier. "Leprosy in Ancient Mesopotamia." *Revue d'Assyriologie et d'archéologie orientale* 60 (1966) 47–58.

Wippel, John. "Norman Kretzmann on Aquinas's Attribution of Will and of Freedom to Create to God." *Religious Studies* 39 (2003) 287–98.

Witmer, Amanda. *Jesus, the Galilean Exorcist: His Exorcisms in Social and Political Context*. London: Bloomsbury, 2012.

Wood, William. "Anselm of Canterbury on the Fall of the Devil: The Hard Problem, the Harder Problem, and a New Formal Model of the First Sin." *Religious Studies* 52 (2016) 223–45.

Wray, T. J., and Gregory Mobley. *The Birth of Satan: Tracing the Devil's Biblical Roots*. New York: Palgrave, 2005.

Wright, N. T. *The Resurrection of the Son of God*. Minneapolis: Fortress, 2003.

YouGov. "Do You Personally Believe in the Existence of the Devil or Not?" September 12-13, 2013. http://cdn.yougov.com/cumulus_uploads/document/vhyn6fdnkp/tabs_exorcism_0912132013%20%281%29.pdf.

———. "18% of Brits Believe in Possession by the Devil." 2013. https://yougov.co.uk/news/2013/09/27/18-brits-believe-possession-devil-and-half-america/.

Youngblood, Ronald F. "Fallen Star: The Evolution of Lucifer." *Bible Review-Washington* 14 (1998) 22–31.

Youngson, Robert M. "Kyphosis." In *Collins Dictionary of Medicine*. 4th ed. London: HarperCollins, 2005. https://search.credoreference.com/content/entry/collinsmed/kyphosis/0.

Author and Name Index

Adler, Mortimer J., 61–63, 64, 65, 71, 109, 127–28, 168, 183, 250, 273
Africanus, Julius, 231
Alden, Robert L., 26
Allestree, Richard, 87
Almond, Philip C., 39, 72
Alston, William P., 112–14, 120
Anexagoras, 40
Anaximander, 40
Anaximines, 40, 171
Anselm, 18, 27, 30, 74–77, 79, 98, 100–1
Aquinas, Thomas, 6, 18, 30, 53, 55, 56–57, 61, 64, 65, 70, 74–75, 83, 87, 103, 105, 106, 108, 132, 161, 187, 213–14, 218, 248–49, 266, 273
Aristotle, 41, 71, 102–3, 105, 108–9, 154, 187, 265
Armstrong, David A., 155–56
Arnold, Clinton E., 252
Athenagoras, 50, 227
Audi, Robert, 258
Augustine, 6, 14, 18, 30, 35, 52–56, 57, 64, 70, 74, 87, 104, 106, 152, 173, 177, 189–90, 212, 225, 231, 259–61, 273, 278

Bacon, Francis, 58–59
Baergen, Ralph, 124, 258
Bailey, Andrew, 188
Bailey, Michael D., 53
Baker, Lynne Rudder, 166
Bamberger, Bernard J., 27, 39, 73, 83, 84
Barber, Theodore Xenophone, 262
Barnard, Leslie William, 50
Barnett, Paul, 246
Bauckham, Richard, 19, 21, 195
Beckwith, Francis J., 262
Bekker, Balthasar, 86
Belleville, Linda L., 245
Benoit, Pierre, 239
Betty, L. Stafford, 95, 280
Birney, Leroy, 230–31
Blomberg, Craig L., 136, 146

Blount, Brian K., 19, 32, 208
Blunt, John James, 135–36
Boa, Kenneth D., 87
Bonaventure, 55–56, 64–65, 151, 161
Boring, M. Eugene, 133
Boureau, Alain, 53
Bourget, David, 86
Bowman, Robert M., Jr., 87
Boyd, Gregory A., 70, 79, 227, 233, 264, 278
Braude, Stephen E., 125, 159, 197–98, 203
Broadus, John Albert, 241
Brown, Christopher M., 74
Brown, Raymond E., 231, 235, 241, 252
Bryant, Richard A., 261
Bultmann, Rudolf, 140
Burkill, T. A., 138
Burnet, Josh, 40, 171

Caldwell, William, 245
Calverley, David Smith, 261
Campbell, Keith, 155
Campbell, Lynne, 71
Carr, David, 225
Cartwright, Nancy, 124, 258
Cavin, Robert Greg, 128
Chalmers, David J., 86, 163
Charles, J. Daryl, 19
Chilton, Bruce, 134
Christianson, Eric, 2
Chrysippus, 43, 44
Churchland, Paul and Patricia, 92, 191
Cicero, 151
Clarke, Adam, 226
Clarke, Samuel, 61, 215
Coder, S. Maxwell, 19
Coleridge, Samuel Taylor, 39
Collins, John J., 32
Collins, Raymond F., 133
Conybeare, F.C., 43
Cooper, John W., 169
Cooper, Rachel, 95
Copan, Paul, 213

Author and Name Index

Copleston, Frederick, 41, 162
Corcoran, Kevin, 166, 173
Cowan, Steven B., 74
Cox, Jennifer K., 253
Craig, William Lane, 88, 108, 118, 128, 173, 213
Crockett, William V., 154
Cunningham, Andrew, 235
Cupitt, Don, 81, 88, 90
Cyril of Jerusalem, 170

Davis, John Jefferson, 165
Dawkins, Richard, 89–90
De La Torre, Miguel, 39, 41, 69, 81, 82
Delitzsch, Franz, 35, 225
Descartes, René, 70
Dickason, C. Fred, 17, 18, 20, 128, 170, 183, 223, 257, 263
Diogenes of Apollonia, 40
Dunn, James D. G., 139–40, 168

Eccles, John, 157
Empedocles, 151, 187
Epicurus, 152
Euripides, 44
Evangelatou, Maria, 235
Evans, Gillian R., 57, 260
Evans, Hilary, 281

Farris, Joshua R., 157
Ferguson, Everett, 41, 42, 44, 47, 50, 168
Feser, Edward, 103, 161, 265
Feyerabend, Paul, 120
Fishman, Yonatan, 212
Fitzmyer, Joseph A., 231, 235, 241, 252
Fleetwood, William, 86, 214–15, 218, 251
Flew, Antony, 125, 191
Forsyth, Neil, 22, 39, 82
Foster, John, 157, 159–60, 189, 265
Fowl, Stephen E., 167
Friedkin, William, 122
Fudge, Edward, 154

Gala, Gary J., 95
Gale, Richard, 159
Gallagher, Richard, 122
Garland, David E., 245
Garson, Justin, 95
Gellman, Jerome, 262
Gilson, Étienne, 55
Goetz, Stewart, 157, 169
Goodman, Felicitas D., 116, 186
Graham, George, 94
Guiley, Rosemary, 4
Gundry, Robert H., 246

Habel, Norman C., 23, 233, 236
Habermas, Gary, 130, 169
Haight, David, 99–100
Haight, Marjorie, 99
Harris, Murray J., 247
Harrison, Roland Kenneth, 224, 233
Hasker, William, 157, 266
Hawking, Stephen, 89
Heiser, Michael S., 30, 35, 37, 105, 226, 229, 232
Henderson, James, 89
Herbert, Nick, 205
Hernández, Albert, 39, 41, 69, 81–82
Hesiod, 21, 42
Hick, John, 104
Hitchens, Christopher, 84, 88
Hoadly, Benjamin, 215, 218
Hobbes, Thomas, 7, 59, 60, 64–65, 152–55, 171
Hodge, Alexander, 145
Hodge, Charles, 246
Hoehner, Harold W, 167
Hoffman, Joshua, 164
Hopkin, Charles Edward, 53, 83
Horn, Luke, 188
Houran, James, 269
Hume, David, 60, 132, 144, 188

Insel, T., 95
Ivanovska, Inta, 54–55, 212, 260

Jacobs, Nathan A., 161–64, 172
Jehle, David, 188
Johnson, David Kyle, 84, 89, 120–22, 124
Johnson, Luke Timothy, 253
Joines, Karen R., 225
Jones, Scott C., 33–34
Josephus, Flavius, 34, 136, 226, 249
Joshi, Purushottam, 89, 92
Justin Martyr, 20, 50–51, 64, 70, 227, 273

Kaiser, Walter, Jr., 230–31
Kalisch, M. M., 226
Kandel, E. R., 95
Kant, Immanuel, 117, 261
Kay, William K., 116
Keck, David, 53, 55–56, 161, 207
Keener, Craig S., 18, 32, 116, 195, 267, 284
Kelly, Henry Ansgar, 4, 14, 23, 26, 32–33, 36, 39, 54, 78, 86
Kelly, Stewart E., 70, 278
Kihlstrom, John F., 242
Kim, Jaegwon, 155–56, 183, 187–89, 201
Koch, Kurt E., 116, 170, 257
Kreeft, Peter, 61–63, 64–65, 170, 273
Kretzmann, Norman, 105
Kuhn, Thomas, 120, 124, 258

Author and Name Index

Lactantius, 50, 64
Lane, William L., 252
Lange, Rense, 269
Langton, Edward, 134
Larmer, Robert, 92
Latourette, Kenneth Scott, 52
Law, Stephen, 97, 102
Leibniz, G. W., 106, 196
Lenski, R. C. H., 247
Lewis, C. S., 5, 61, 67, 70, 78, 278
Lewis, Theodore J., 33–34
Lewy, C., 155
Licona, Michael, 130
Lipton, Peter, 110
Lobert, Annie, 114
Locke, John, 59–60, 64–65, 86, 159, 271
Loose, Jonathan J., 157
Loschen, E. L., 92
Lovejoy, Arthur, 106
Lowe, E. J., 188
Lund, David H., 125, 157, 159, 163, 281
Lycan, William G., 156, 160
Lys, Daniel, 171

Mackay, Robert William, 217
Madell, Geoffrey, 188
Malebranche, Nicolas, 61
Mallard, David, 261
Marmadoro, Anna, 154
Mascall, E. L., 70, 278
Mason, Perry C., 100–101
Matera, Frank J., 167
McCann, Hugh J., 109
McColly, Grant, 245
McCraw, Benjamin W., 114, 117, 257
McDonald, Lee Martin, 246
McGinn, Bernard, 249
McGrew, Lydia, 128, 135
McGrew, Timothy, 128, 132
McNamara, Paul, 97–98, 126
Meier, John, 138–39
Meier, Samuel, 136, 249–50
Menuge, Angus, 157
Merricks, Trenton, 159, 166
Meyers, Edward P., 183
Michel, Anneliese, 115–16, 186
Midelfort, H. C. Erik, 58
Midgley, Mary, 89
Milton, John, 2, 28, 60, 239
Mitchell, Piers, 235
Mlodinow, Leonard, 89
Mobley, Gregory, 23, 39
Montgomery, John Warwick, 95, 245
Moreland, J. P., 157, 169, 179, 188–89, 265
Morey, Robert, 27–28, 245

Murison, Ross G., 33, 249
Murphy, Nancey, 166
Murphy, Roland E., 231, 235, 241, 252
Murray, Michael, 70, 104, 199, 278

Nagel, Thomas, 156
Newman, John Henry, 61
Newman, Robert C., 227
Noegel, Scott B., 251
Nordell, P. A., 171
Nozick, Robert, 159

O'Connor, Timothy, 189
O'Daly, Gerard, 57, 190
O'Mathúna, Dónal P., 249
Olbert, Charles M., 95
Olshausen, Hermann, 145
Olyan, Saul M., 16
Origen, 3, 22, 28, 37, 40, 51, 54, 64, 74, 87, 149, 170, 273
Oropeza, B. J., 17, 175–76

Pagels, Elaine, 23, 39, 41, 84, 225
Paige, Terence, 171
Paley, William, 61, 135
Pannenberg, Wolfhart, 128
Papineau, David, 124, 258
Parkin, David, 171
Parrish, Stephen E., 262
Parry, Robin, 116
Parsons, Keith, 128
Partridge, Christopher, 2, 268, 281
Pascal, Blaise, 61
Patrides, C. A., 15
Paulsen, David, 172
Paulus, Heinrich, 145
Pawl, Timothy, 74
Peirce, C. S., 211
Penelhum, Terence, 70, 278
Perry, John, 157
Phillips, John, 245–46
Philo, 225
Plantinga, Alvin, 2, 13, 70, 112–14, 117–18, 162, 241
Plato, 3, 42–43, 44, 51, 71, 101, 105, 171, 192, 247
Plutarch, 42, 44
Popper, Karl, 157
Power, William L., 99
Prince, Derek, 257, 268
Pseudo-Dionysius, 6, 16, 55–56, 62, 64, 70, 107, 273

Quine, W. V. O., 157

Author and Name Index

Rasmussen, Joshua, 188
Richman, Robert J., 99
Ronning, John L., 34
Rosenberg, Alex, 89
Rosenkrantz, Gary, 164
Rousseau, David, 157
Routledge, Robin, 227
Russ, Daniel, 39
Russell, Jeffrey Burton, 13, 18, 26, 39, 49, 51, 57–58, 60, 70–71, 281
Ryle, Gilbert, 158

Sandywell, Barry, 40
Schaeffer, Francis, 35, 225
Schellenberg, J. L., 80
Schemm, Peter R., Jr., 245
Schiavo, Luigi, 240
Schlagel, Richard H., 125
Schleiermacher, Friedrich, 27, 72–73, 78–79
Schoemaker, William Ross, 171–72
Schweitzer, Albert, 145
Scot, Reginald, 85–86
Scott, Walter, 26, 249
Scotus, John Duns, 162
Sklar, Jay, 45
Sluhovsky, Moshe, 170
Smart, J. J. C., 157
Smith, Steven G., 60
Socrates, 42, 43
Spinoza, Baruch, 72, 132
Stanford, Peter, 39
Stein, D. J., 95
Stein, Robert H., 18
Steinmann, Andrew E., 16
Storms, C. Samuel, 223, 233, 263
Strauss, David Friedrich, 41, 58, 145–46
Strawson, Galen, 155
Strawson, P. F., 163
Strickland, Lloyd, 106
Sudduth, Michael, 125

Swinburne, Richard, 111, 128, 157, 159–60, 162, 183–84
Szasz, Thomas S., 93

Taliaferro, Charles, 157, 169
Tate, Marvin E., 28, 224
Tatian (the Assyrian), 50–51, 64–65
Tertullian, 28, 37, 50–51, 64, 74, 151, 195, 273
Thomas, Emily, 164
Thuswaldner, Gregor, 39
Tillich, Paul, 41
Timpe, Kevin, 74
Travis, Stephen H., 168
Trethowan, Dom I., 70, 278
Twelftree, Graham H., 25, 134, 137–38, 141–42, 146, 240, 243

Unger, Merrill F., 17, 42, 45, 58, 87, 127–28, 170, 174, 191, 233, 239, 244–45, 248, 263, 267–68

Van Inwagen, Peter, 166, 255
Voltaire, 60, 144

Walton, John H., 23, 36, 195, 226, 233, 236, 249, 282
Waters, Kenneth, 239
Wiebe, Phillip H., 62–63, 64–65, 111, 119, 122, 124–25
Wierenga, Edward, 234
Williams, Daniel Day, 225
Williams, Peter S., 62–63, 64, 65, 273
Wilson, Edward O., 89
Wilson, J. V. Kinnier, 235
Wippel, John, 105
Witmer, Amanda, 133–35, 137, 138–44
Wood, William, 75, 76
Wray, T. J., 23, 39
Wright, N. T., 130

Xenocrates, 43–44

Youngblood, Ronald F., 24

Subject Index

adiabolism, 71, 97
aeviternitas, 55
ancestral spirits, 195
"angel of light," 8, 35, 245–48
"angel of the Lord," 175
angelology, 1, 14–17, 53, 55–56, 61–62, 161, 207
angelophany, 175. *See also* "angel of the Lord" *and* theophany
angels (fallen). *See* demonology: angels (fallen)
animal suffering, 70, 278. *See also* theodicy
anthropological dualism, 155–57, 166, 168–69, 181, 186, 264–67
Antichrist, 58, 249
Apollonius of Tyana, 146
apophatic, 62
apparitions, 35, 41, 51, 59, 124, 184, 195, 208, 214, 224, 226, 268–69, 281
aseity (of God), 5, 254
Asmodeus, 47
atheism, 88
atheist, 84, 89
Azazel, 45, 266–67

Babylon, 36, 46, 48, 179
Babylon, King of, 25–28
Balaam, 175, 207–9
Beelzebul, 6, 24, 129, 141–43, 241
"bent double," 200, 243–45
Big Bang, the, 103, 173

Capernaum demoniac, 132–34, 136–39. *See also* exorcisms *and* possessions (demonic)
Cartesian dualism, 157, 264–65
cherubim, 16, 18, 27–28
cognitive science, 89, 93, 279
compatibilism, 74, 86
consciousness, 158
conservativism, principle of, 121
conversion disorder, 140, 243
cosmic dualism, 166, 168–169
credulity, principle of, 111
criterialism, 159

daimon, 4, 17, 41–42, 50, 64, 171, 255, 273
demoniac, 132, 134
demonology
   "aerial" ontology, 40–41, 50–51, 55–56, 64, 151, 153, 171, 173, 177, 256, 273
   angels (fallen), 17–21, 28, 31, 33, 38, 46, 48, 50, 53, 61, 76–79, 227–32, 238
   anti-realism, 7, 61, 65, 69–96, 97, 98, 121, 126, 127, 273
   cognitive interaction, 7, 8, 168, 184, 185–97, 199–202, 206, 210–12, 218–19, 223, 233, 237, 241, 243, 252, 260, 262–63, 274–75, 276, 279–80
   diabolical harassments, 114–15, 117–23
   diabolical invasions, 115–123, 126. *See also* exorcisms *and* possessions (demonic)
   dualism as precedent for, 264–67
   in the Bible, 17–21
   psychodynamic immaterialism, 275–77
   psychokinesis, 7, 8, 184, 185, 197–201, 202–4, 206–7, 209–12, 213–214, 216, 218–19, 223–24, 226–27, 232, 238, 241, 243, 245, 249, 250–53, 258, 262–70, 274, 282
   pure immaterialism, 6, 7, 56, 59, 64, 151, 152, 160, 165, 166, 173, 176–78, 180–82, 225–26, 233, 238, 254, 256–57, 259, 261–62, 269, 273–75, 284
   realism, 5, 7, 38–40, 69–71, 73, 80, 82, 84–85, 88–91, 95–96, 97–148, 151, 257, 273, 275, 277, 279, 285
   seductive vs. coercive, 185
devil-of-the-gaps argument, the, 88–96, 121
diabolical experiences. *See* demonology: diabolical harassments *and* demonology: diabolical invasions
diabolical miracles, 217, 267–268
diabology, 7, 13, 49, 71, 97, 103–4, 126. *See also* demonology.
Diagnostic and Statistical Manual of Mental Disorders (DSM), 93–94, 140, 242
Dissociative Identity Disorder, 93–94, 190, 280

Subject Index

divine council, 16, 22–23, 80
Dominican, 3, 56, 61–62
donkey. *See* Balaam

elephantiasis. *See* leprosy
eliminative materialism, 92
emergent dualism, 266
Enoch (Pseudepigrapha), 19–20, 33, 45–47, 50, 167, 227–29
epilepsy, 93, 115–16, 139–40
essentialism, 101
"evil god," 102
exorcisms, 8, 18, 48, 88, 93, 116, 121–22, 132–48, 225, 240, 244–45, 280. *See also* demonology: diabolical invasions *and* possessions (demonic)
extraterrestrials, 123

fallen angels. *See* demonology: angels (fallen)
"familiar spirit," 170
folk psychology, 92, 191
Franciscan, 55–56, 151, 197
functional neurological symptom disorder. *See* conversion disorder

Gabriel, 16, 31, 161–63, 190
Gehenna, 21. *See also* hell (doctrine of)
Gerasene (Gadarene) demoniac, 79, 134–37, 145. *See also* exorcisms *and* possessions (demonic)
ghosts, 89, 144, 153–54, 183
god of this world, 36–37
Great Chain of Being, 55, 105–9, 168

Hades, 21, 163–65. *See also* hell (doctrine of)
haecceitas, 162
hallucinations. *See* psycho-projection
hauntings, 123, 210
heaven, 5, 18, 20, 23–28, 32, 42, 61, 105, 165, 167, 194, 213, 216, 232–34, 240
"heavenly places," 167, 173, 224
hell (doctrine of), 21, 78, 154–55
homoion-homoioi, 187
hylomorphism, 55–56, 65, 151, 161, 204, 265–67

idealism, 144, 258
incompatibilism, 74, 83, 86, 87, 96
intermediary beings, 41, 45, 54, 55, 110, 146, 158, 167–68, 189
Islam, 52, 84
Jesus, 4, 7, 8, 15, 18–19, 21, 23–24, 26, 29, 32, 35, 41, 46, 48–49, 58, 69, 79–81, 88, 123, 127–148, 164, 172, 175, 196–97, 213, 216–18, 221, 225, 237–41, 243–45, 248–50, 252–53, 279

Jubilees (Pseudepigrapha), 20, 46–47, 227, 229, 231
Judaism, 24, 28, 33
Judas, 24, 48, 164, 196

Kalām Cosmological Argument, the, 108
kyphosis, 244–45

leprosy, 214, 235
levitation, 63, 279
Lucifer, 6, 18, 24, 25–27, 28, 39

Manichaeism, 166, 212, 214
"material spirit," 51–52, 54, 178, 204. *See also* demonology: "aerial" ontology
materialism, 59, 152, 157, 159, 166, 180
mental disorder(s), 1, 89–90, 92–95, 116, 242, 279. *See also* mental illness
mental illness, 93, 122
Michael the Archangel, 16, 24, 194
miracles, 2, 51, 58, 85, 86, 119, 127–28, 130–32, 147, 184, 202, 207, 209, 212, 214–18, 248–51. *See also* diabolical miracles
"moonstruck," 140. *See also* epilepsy
Moorean shift, 85
Muhammad, 52
Multiple Personality Disorder, 93

natural diabology. *See* diabology
Nebridius, 190
necromancy, 193
Nephilim, 47, 227–28, 230–32. *See also* "sons of God"

Occam's Razor, 31, 63, 209, 219
occulture, 268
omnibenevolence (of God), 5, 104
omnipotence (of God), 73, 99, 100, 183, 203, 204
omniscience (of God), 5, 17, 73, 76, 79, 99–100, 131, 183, 203–4, 262
open theism, 79
Ouija board, 121, 124

pairing problem, 155, 204–5
Pan, 45
paranormal activity, 89–91, 123–25, 257–62, 281
phantasm, 153, 259–261
philosophy of demonology, 13, 15, 17, 19, 21, 23, 25, 27, 29, 31, 33, 35, 37, 240, 277, 281–84
philosophy of mind, 157, 191, 204, 254
philosophy of religion, 3, 4, 69, 97, 101, 128, 277
plenitude, principle of, 106, 108–10, 125, 146
pneumatology, 1, 44, 173
poltergeist(s), 124, 183, 217, 267-69

Subject Index

possessions (demonic), 2, 82, 89, 95, 279–81. *See also* demonology: diabolical invasions *and* exorcisms
    vs. mental disorders, 92–95
possible worlds, 101, 110
"Prince of Persia," 162, 163
"Prince of Tyre," 27–28
properly basic beliefs, 111
psychiatry, 1, 89, 92, 95, 275, 279–80
psychodynamic immaterialism. *See* demonology: psychodynamic immaterialism
psychokinesis. *See* demonology: psychokinesis
psychology, 1, 88–89, 94–95, 140, 191, 242, 275, 279
psycho-projection, 261, 268–69, 281
pure immaterialism. *See* demonology: pure immaterialism

Ransom Theory of Atonement (Christus Victor), 69
rationalism, 144
"Reformed Demonology," 114, 117–18, 257
religious experience, 111, 114, 117, 119, 126
res cogitans, 179, 185

"Sammael," 37
"Satan," 21–25
satyr, 45
scala naturae. *See* Great Chain of Being
schizophrenia, 93, 115
Scholasticism, 53, 55–57
seizures, 139–40
sensus diaboli, 117–18
sensus divinitatis, 112, 117–18
seraphim, 16
serpent, 8, 16, 21, 26, 32, 33–36, 57, 224–27, 228, 238, 249, 282–83
serpent-dragon, 34, 36

"signs and wonders," 213, 248–51
sola Scriptura, 228
"sons of God," 18, 22, 23, 46, 50, 227–33, 238
spiritual warfare, 2, 283–84
subjectness, 159–60
substance dualism. *See* anthropological dualism
superstition, 2, 41, 58, 248, 267–69, 279, 284
Syrophoenician woman's daughter, the, 137–39. *See also* exorcisms *and* possessions (demonic)

Tartarus, 20–21, 229
telepathy, 190–91, 193
temptation of Jesus, 8, 24, 48, 69, 238–40. *See also* demonology: diabolical harassments
theism, 5, 13, 71, 88, 98, 102, 105, 118, 123, 126, 183, 209
theodicy, 70, 278
theophany, 175. *See also* "angel of the Lord" *and* angelophany
Thomistic dualism, 204, 265–66
transmutation, 247, 260

UFOs, 89, 281
unclean spirit, 132–34, 137–39, 170
undesigned coincidence(s), 135–36, 143
uniformity, principle of, 196
universals, 161, 205–6
urticaria, 236–37, 279–80

warfare theodicy. *See* theodicy
Watchers, 19, 227
witches, 83, 85–86
"witch craze," 4, 83, 249

Zohar of Kabbalah, 228
Zoroastrianism, 31, 101

www.ingramcontent.com/pod-product-compliance
Lightning Source LLC
Chambersburg PA
CBHW060508300426
44112CB00017B/2583